Shojo Beat

S•A
Special A

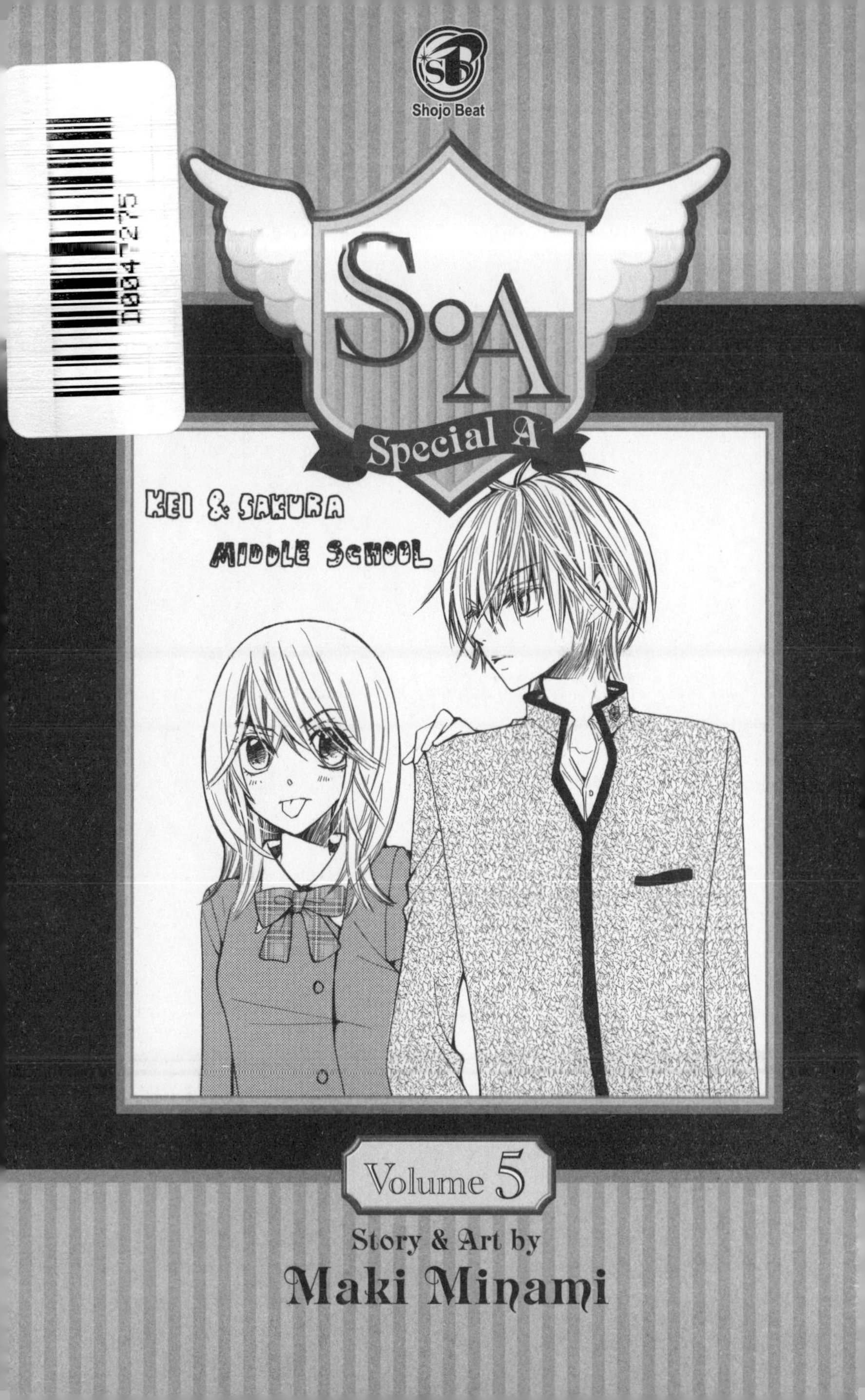
KEI & SAKURA
MIDDLE SCHOOL

Volume 5

Story & Art by
Maki Minami

STORY

★At the tender age of 6, carpenter's daughter Hikari Hanazono suffered her first loss to the wealthy Kei Takishima in a wrestling match. Now the hardworking Hikari has followed Kei to the most elite school for the rich just to beat him! I call this story "Overthrow Takishima! Rise Above Perpetual Second Place!!" It's the story of Hikari's sweat, tears and passion, with a little bit of love thrown in!

★Hikari was helping set Sakura up with Kei...until she realized her own feelings. Then Sakura fell for Jun!

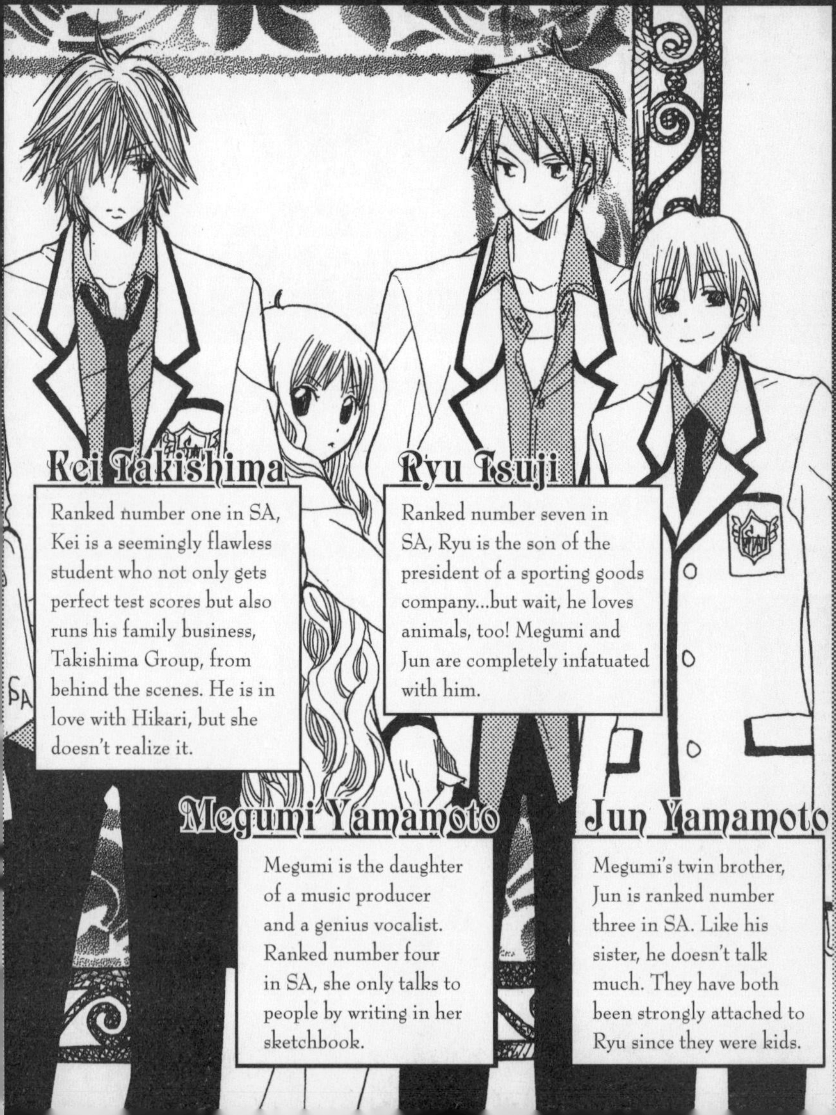
Kei Takishima
Ranked number one in SA, Kei is a seemingly flawless student who not only gets perfect test scores but also runs his family business, Takishima Group, from behind the scenes. He is in love with Hikari, but she doesn't realize it.
Ryu Tsuji
Ranked number seven in SA, Ryu is the son of the president of a sporting goods company...but wait, he loves animals, too! Megumi and Jun are completely infatuated with him.
Megumi Yamamoto
Megumi is the daughter of a music producer and a genius vocalist. Ranked number four in SA, she only talks to people by writing in her sketchbook.
Jun Yamamoto
Megumi's twin brother, Jun is ranked number three in SA. Like his sister, he doesn't talk much. They have both been strongly attached to Ryu since they were kids.

S·A CHARACTERS

Hikari goes to an elite school called Hakusenkan High School. This school divides each grade level into groups A through F, according to the students' test scores. Group A includes only the top seven students in each class. Then the top seven students from all grades' A groups are put into a group called Special A, which is considered much higher than all others. Known as SA, they are "the elite among the elite."

What is "Special A"?

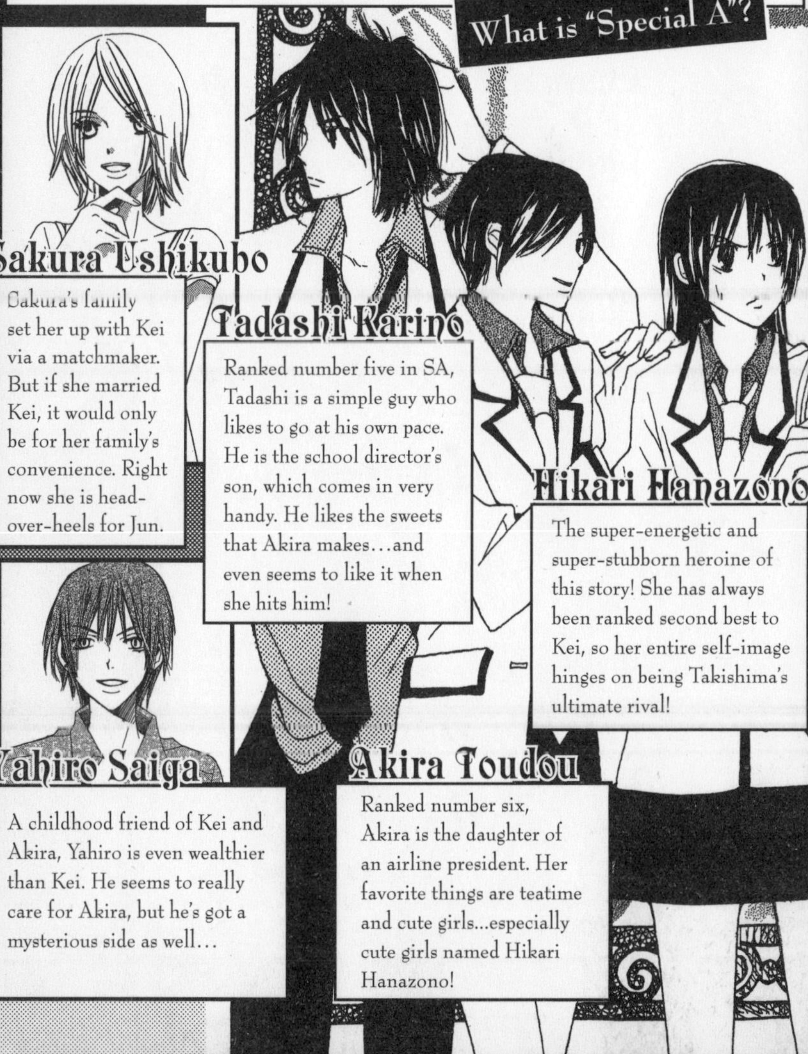

Sakura Ushikubo

Sakura's family set her up with Kei via a matchmaker. But if she married Kei, it would only be for her family's convenience. Right now she is head-over-heels for Jun.

Tadashi Karino

Ranked number five in SA, Tadashi is a simple guy who likes to go at his own pace. He is the school director's son, which comes in very handy. He likes the sweets that Akira makes…and even seems to like it when she hits him!

Hikari Hanazono

The super-energetic and super-stubborn heroine of this story! She has always been ranked second best to Kei, so her entire self-image hinges on being Takishima's ultimate rival!

Yahiro Saiga

A childhood friend of Kei and Akira, Yahiro is even wealthier than Kei. He seems to really care for Akira, but he's got a mysterious side as well…

Akira Toudou

Ranked number six, Akira is the daughter of an airline president. Her favorite things are teatime and cute girls...especially cute girls named Hikari Hanazono!

Contents

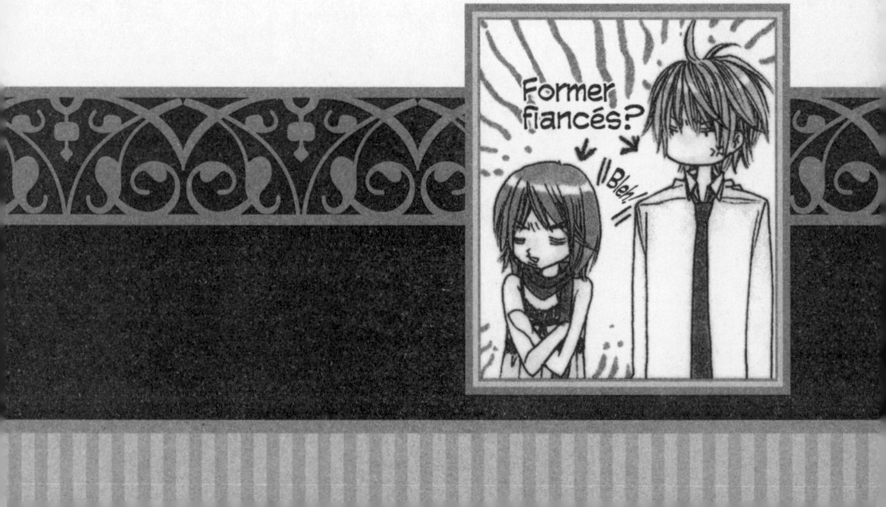

Former fiancés?
Bleh!

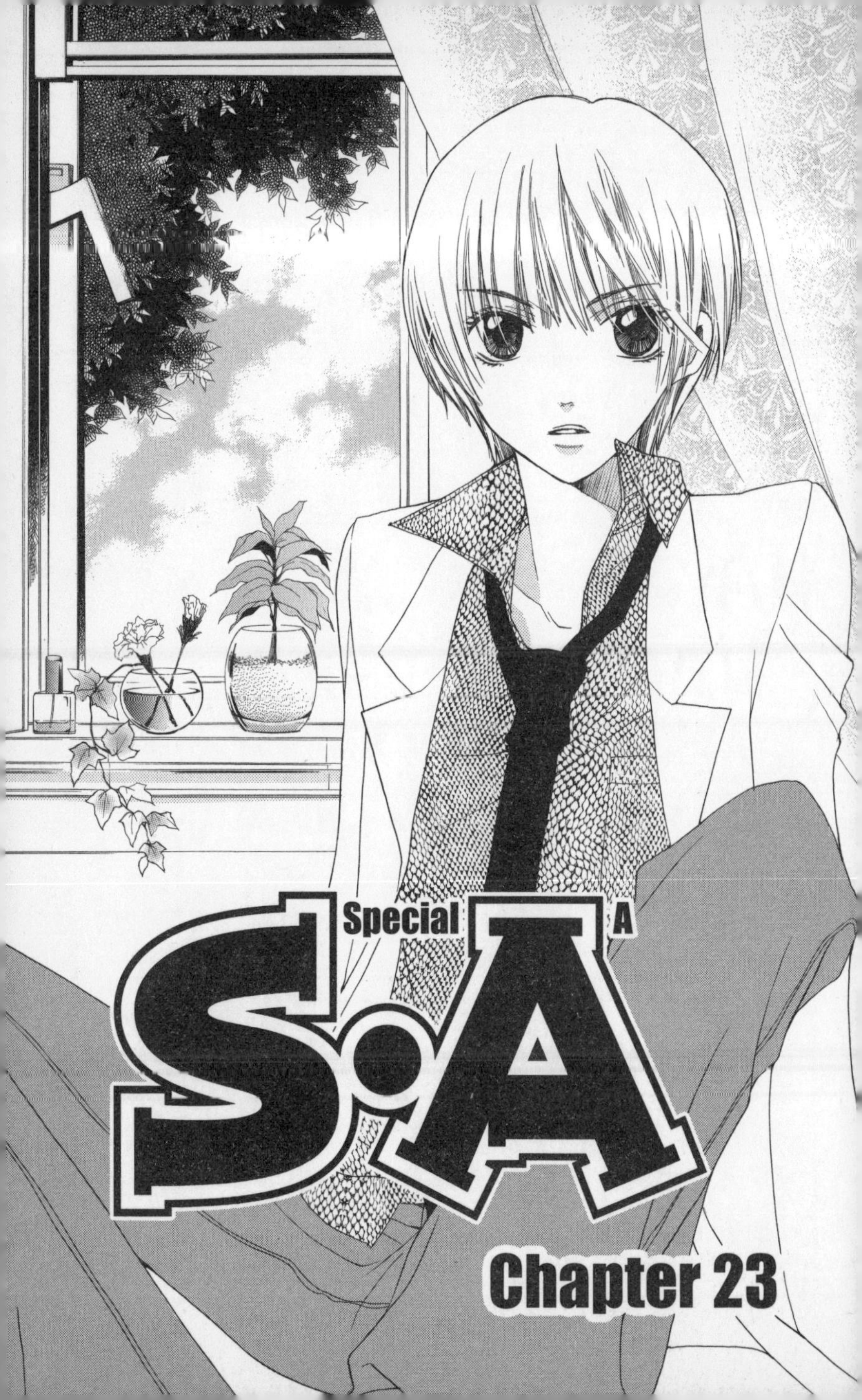
Special A
S.A
Chapter 23

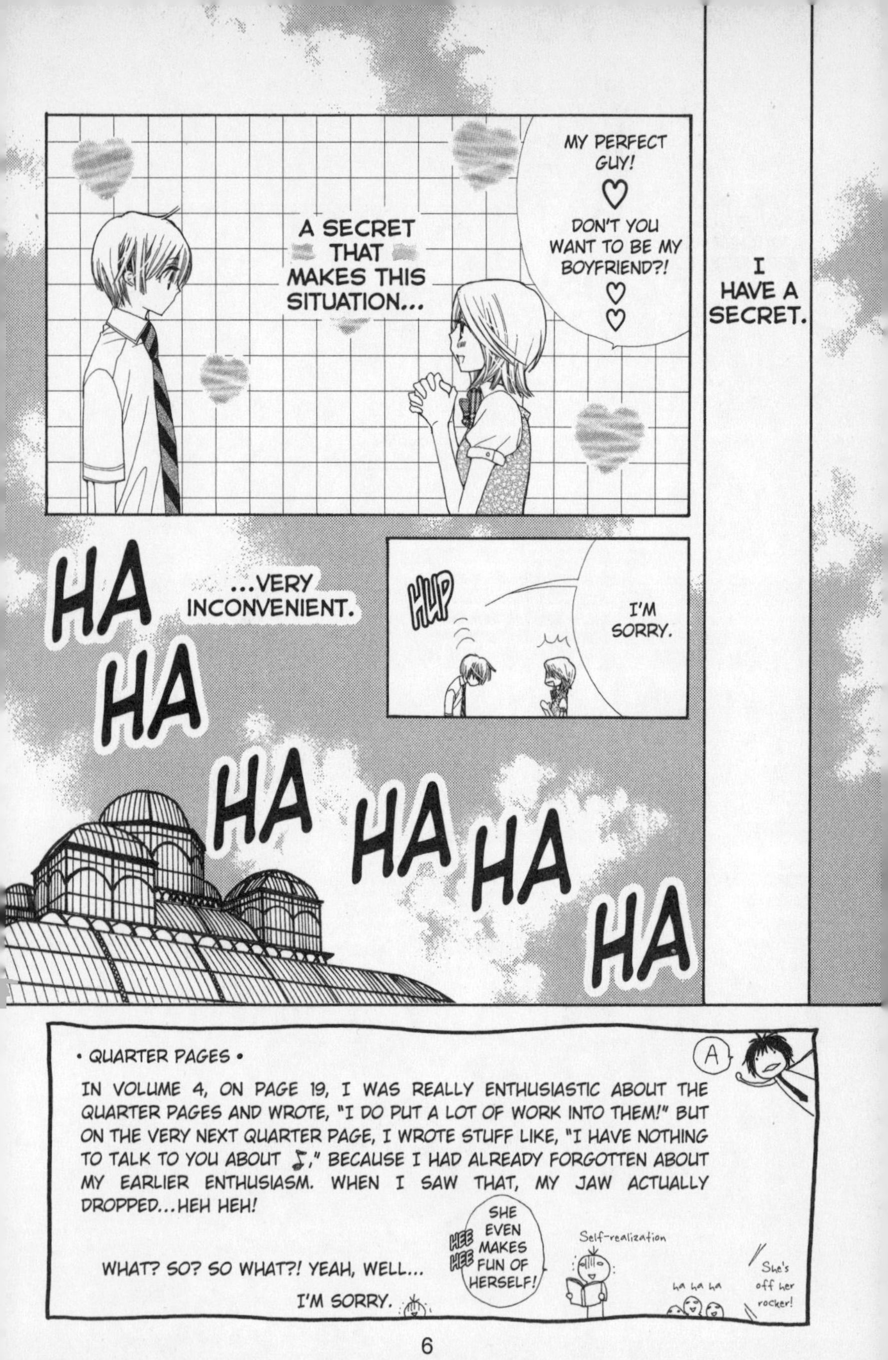
I HAVE A SECRET.
MY PERFECT GUY! ♡ DON'T YOU WANT TO BE MY BOYFRIEND?! ♡ ♡
A SECRET THAT MAKES THIS SITUATION...
I'M SORRY.
HUP
...VERY INCONVENIENT.
HA HA HA HA HA HA

• QUARTER PAGES •

IN VOLUME 4, ON PAGE 19, I WAS REALLY ENTHUSIASTIC ABOUT THE QUARTER PAGES AND WROTE, "I DO PUT A LOT OF WORK INTO THEM!" BUT ON THE VERY NEXT QUARTER PAGE, I WROTE STUFF LIKE, "I HAVE NOTHING TO TALK TO YOU ABOUT ♪," BECAUSE I HAD ALREADY FORGOTTEN ABOUT MY EARLIER ENTHUSIASM. WHEN I SAW THAT, MY JAW ACTUALLY DROPPED...HEH HEH!

WHAT? SO? SO WHAT?! YEAH, WELL...

I'M SORRY.

HEE HEE

SHE EVEN MAKES FUN OF HERSELF!

Self-realization

ha ha ha

She's off her rocker!

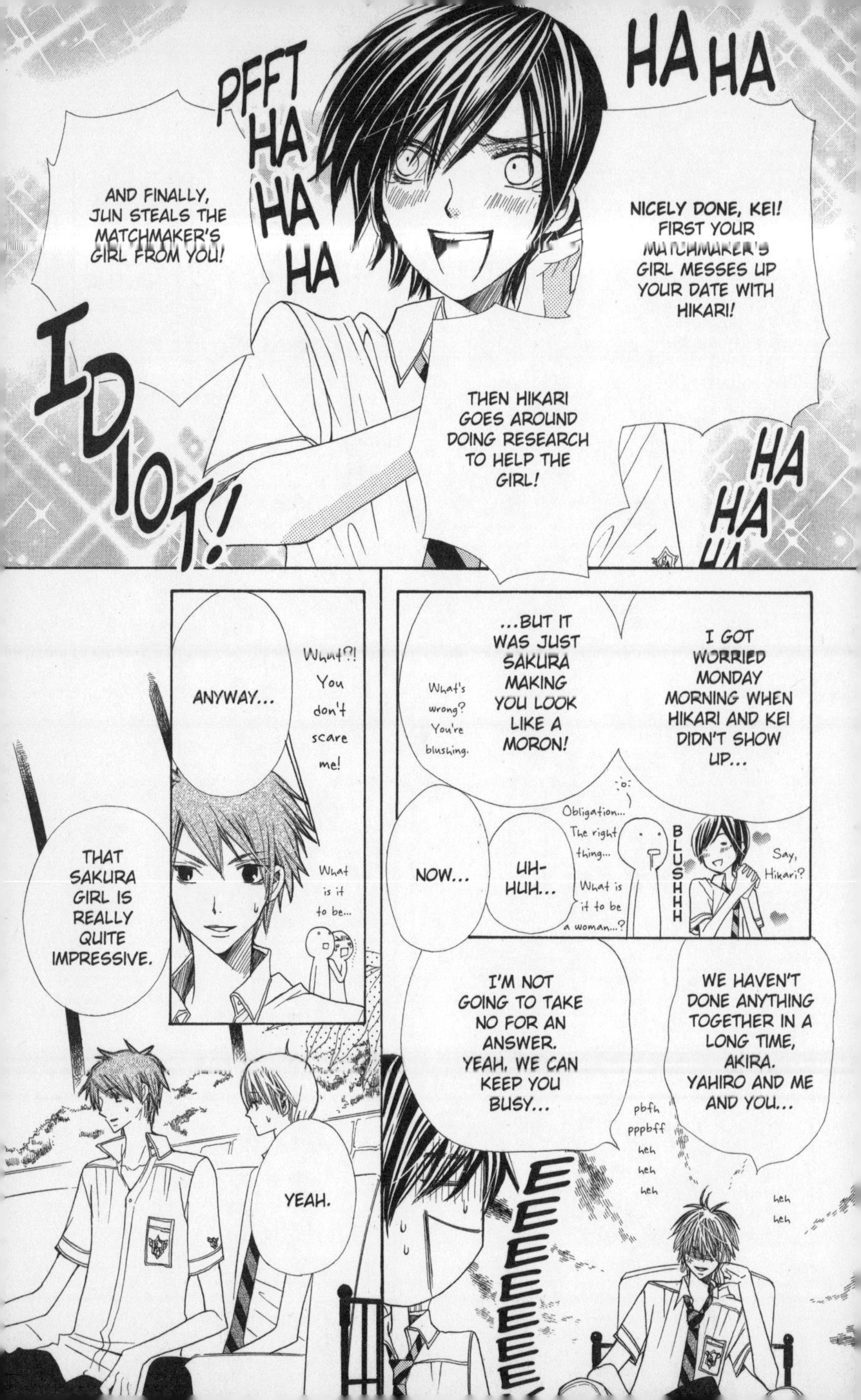
HA HA
NICELY DONE, KEI! FIRST YOUR MATCHMAKER'S GIRL MESSES UP YOUR DATE WITH HIKARI!
PFFT HA HA HA HA
THEN HIKARI GOES AROUND DOING RESEARCH TO HELP THE GIRL!
AND FINALLY, JUN STEALS THE MATCHMAKER'S GIRL FROM YOU!
HA HA
IDIOT!
I GOT WORRIED MONDAY MORNING WHEN HIKARI AND KEI DIDN'T SHOW UP...
...BUT IT WAS JUST SAKURA MAKING YOU LOOK LIKE A MORON!
What's wrong? You're blushing.
Say, Hikari?
BLUSHHH
Obligation... The right thing... What is it to be a woman...?
UH-HUH...
NOW...
WE HAVEN'T DONE ANYTHING TOGETHER IN A LONG TIME, AKIRA. YAHIRO AND ME AND YOU...
I'M NOT GOING TO TAKE NO FOR AN ANSWER. YEAH, WE CAN KEEP YOU BUSY...
pbfh pppbff heh heh heh
heh heh
EEEEEEEE
What?! You don't scare me!
ANYWAY...
What is it to be...
THAT SAKURA GIRL IS REALLY QUITE IMPRESSIVE.
YEAH.

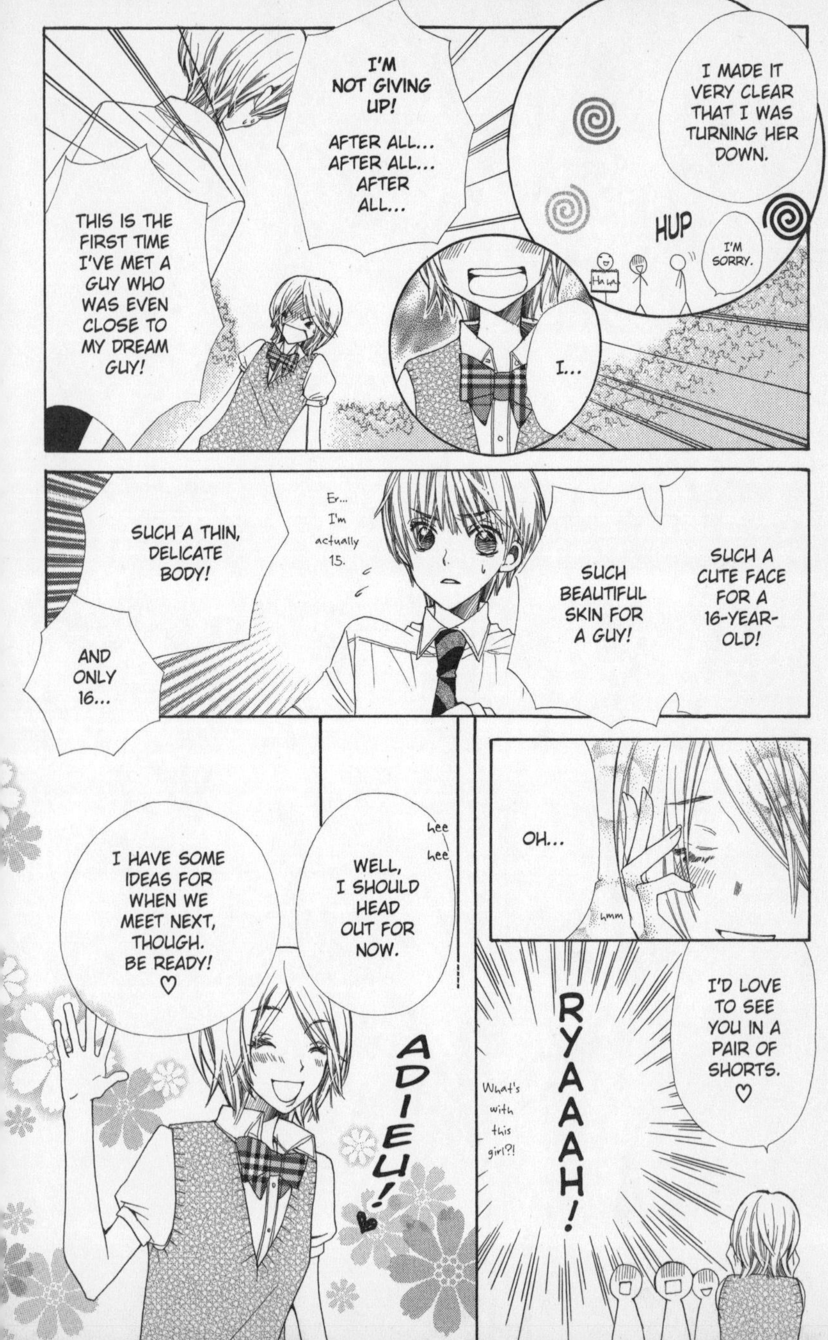
I MADE IT VERY CLEAR THAT I WAS TURNING HER DOWN.
I'M SORRY.
HUP
Ha ha
I...
I'M NOT GIVING UP!
AFTER ALL... AFTER ALL... AFTER ALL...
THIS IS THE FIRST TIME I'VE MET A GUY WHO WAS EVEN CLOSE TO MY DREAM GUY!
SUCH A CUTE FACE FOR A 16-YEAR-OLD!
SUCH BEAUTIFUL SKIN FOR A GUY!
Er... I'm actually 15.
SUCH A THIN, DELICATE BODY!
AND ONLY 16...
OH...
hmm
I'D LOVE TO SEE YOU IN A PAIR OF SHORTS. ♡
RYAAAH!
What's with this girl?!
hee hee
WELL, I SHOULD HEAD OUT FOR NOW.
I HAVE SOME IDEAS FOR WHEN WE MEET NEXT, THOUGH. BE READY! ♡
ADIEU! ♥

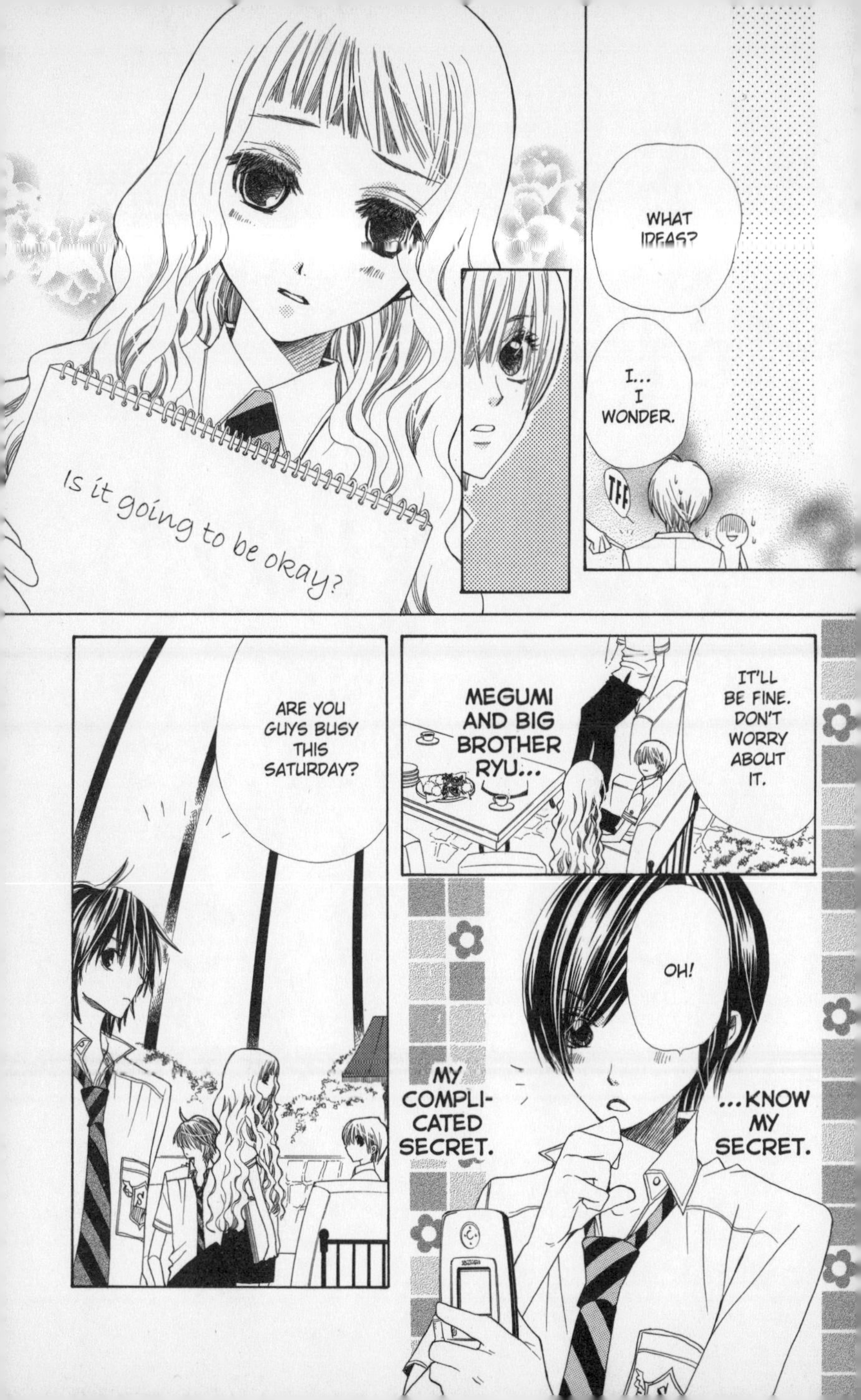
WHAT IDEAS?
I... I WONDER.
Is it going to be okay?
IT'LL BE FINE. DON'T WORRY ABOUT IT.
MEGUMI AND BIG BROTHER RYU...
OH!
...KNOW MY SECRET.
MY COMPLICATED SECRET.
ARE YOU GUYS BUSY THIS SATURDAY?

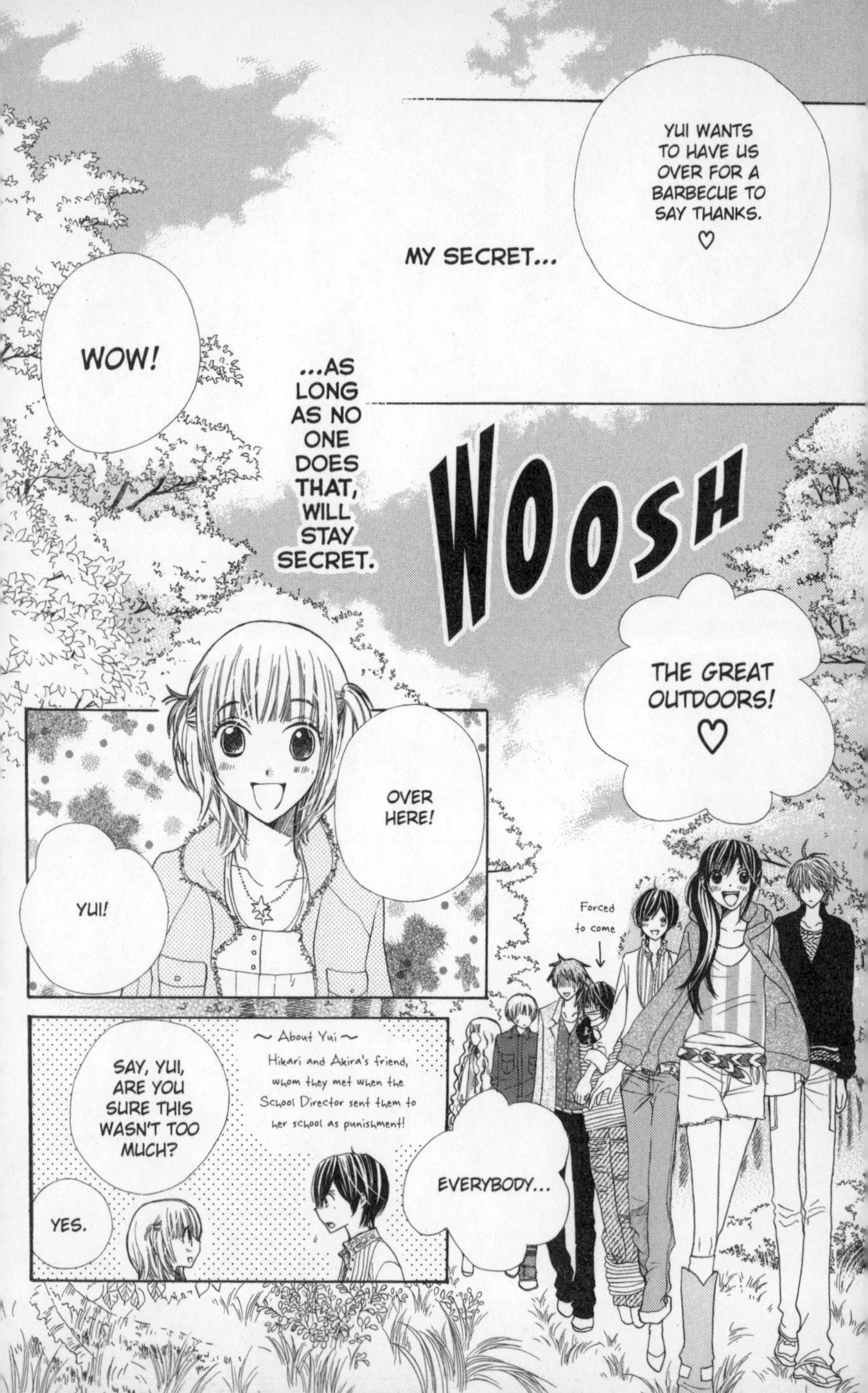
YUI WANTS TO HAVE US OVER FOR A BARBECUE TO SAY THANKS. ♡
MY SECRET...
WOW!
...AS LONG AS NO ONE DOES THAT, WILL STAY SECRET.
WOOSH
THE GREAT OUTDOORS! ♡
OVER HERE!
YUI!
Forced to come
EVERYBODY...
~ About Yui ~ Hikari and Akira's friend, whom they met when the School Director sent them to her school as punishment!
SAY, YUI, ARE YOU SURE THIS WASN'T TOO MUCH?
YES.

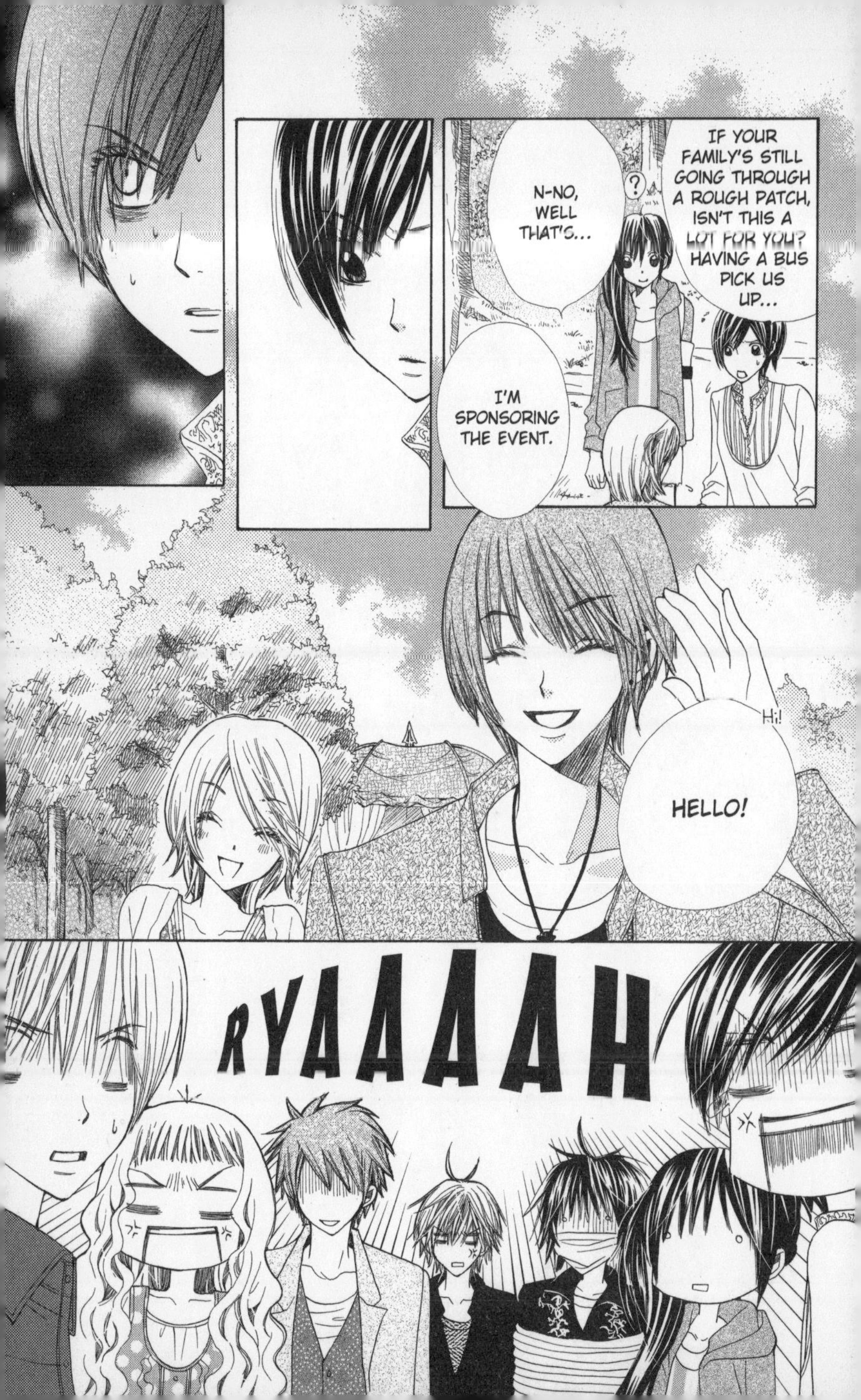
IF YOUR FAMILY'S STILL GOING THROUGH A ROUGH PATCH, ISN'T THIS A LOT FOR YOU? HAVING A BUS PICK US UP...
?
N-NO, WELL THAT'S...
I'M SPONSORING THE EVENT.
Hi!
HELLO!
RYAAAAH

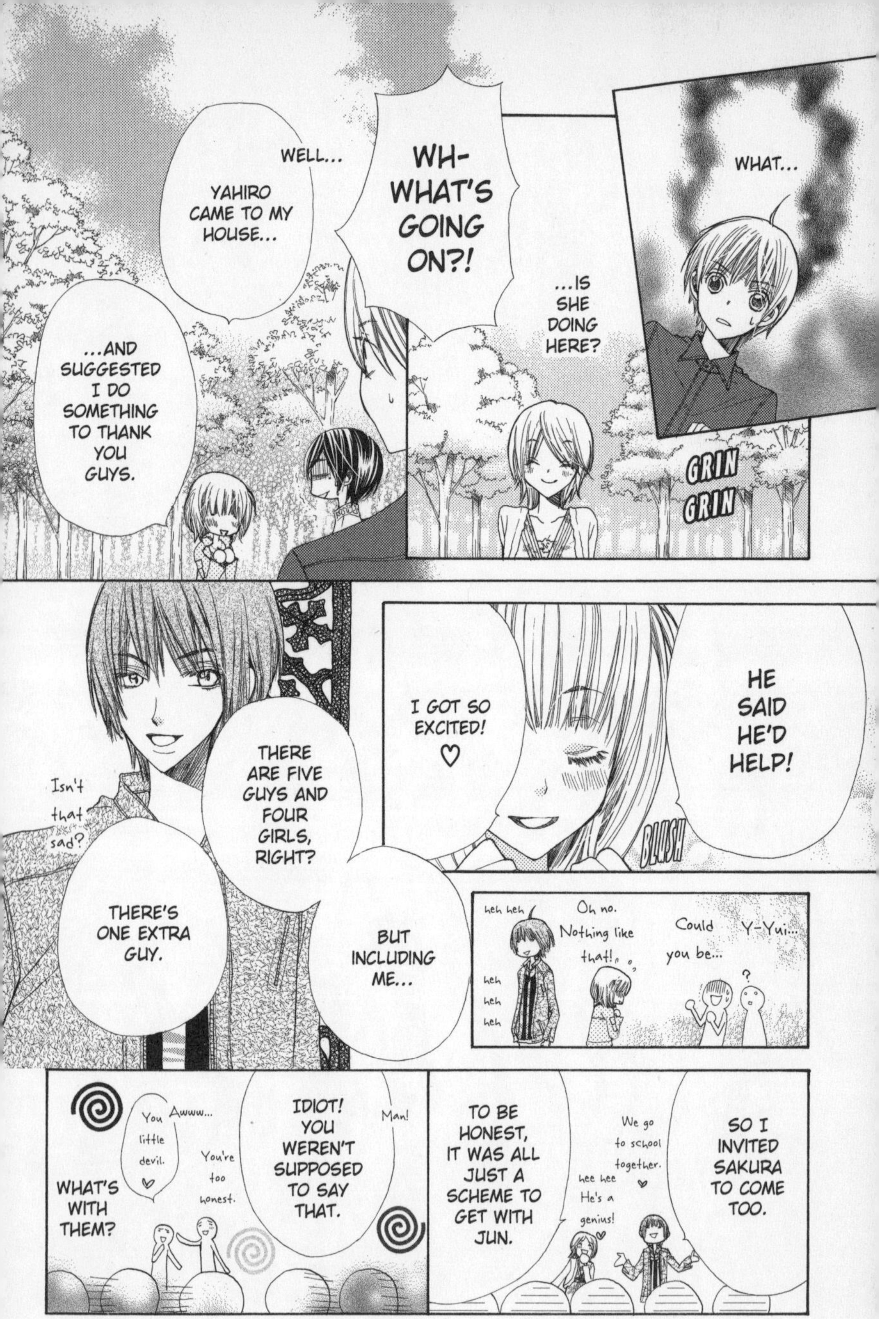
WHAT...
...IS SHE DOING HERE?
GRIN GRIN
WH- WHAT'S GOING ON?!
WELL...
YAHIRO CAME TO MY HOUSE...
...AND SUGGESTED I DO SOMETHING TO THANK YOU GUYS.
HE SAID HE'D HELP!
I GOT SO EXCITED! ♡
BLUSH
Y-Yui...
Could you be...
Oh no. Nothing like that!
heh heh
heh heh heh
THERE ARE FIVE GUYS AND FOUR GIRLS, RIGHT?
BUT INCLUDING ME...
THERE'S ONE EXTRA GUY.
Isn't that sad?
SO I INVITED SAKURA TO COME TOO.
We go to school together. ♡
hee hee He's a genius!
TO BE HONEST, IT WAS ALL JUST A SCHEME TO GET WITH JUN.
Man!
IDIOT! YOU WEREN'T SUPPOSED TO SAY THAT.
You're too honest.
Awww...
You little devil. ♡
WHAT'S WITH THEM?

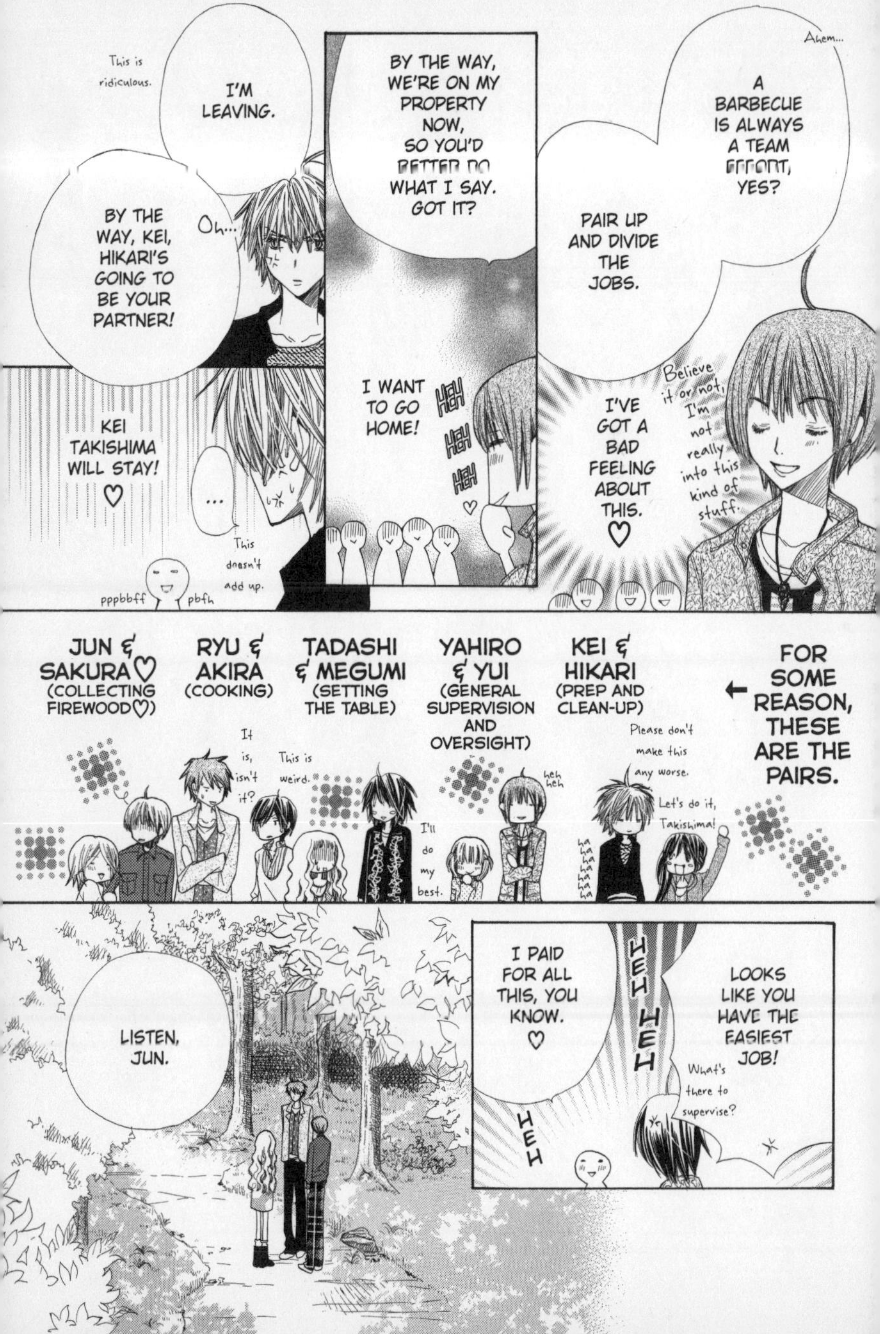
Ahem...
A BARBECUE IS ALWAYS A TEAM EFFORT, YES?
PAIR UP AND DIVIDE THE JOBS.
Believe it or not, I'm not really into this kind of stuff.
I'VE GOT A BAD FEELING ABOUT THIS. ♡
BY THE WAY, WE'RE ON MY PROPERTY NOW, SO YOU'D BETTER DO WHAT I SAY. GOT IT?
HAH HAH HAH ♡
I WANT TO GO HOME!
This is ridiculous.
I'M LEAVING.
Oh...
BY THE WAY, KEI, HIKARI'S GOING TO BE YOUR PARTNER!
KEI TAKISHIMA WILL STAY! ♡
...
This doesn't add up.
pppbbff pbfh
FOR SOME REASON, THESE ARE THE PAIRS.
KEI & HIKARI (PREP AND CLEAN-UP)
YAHIRO & YUI (GENERAL SUPERVISION AND OVERSIGHT)
TADASHI & MEGUMI (SETTING THE TABLE)
RYU & AKIRA (COOKING)
JUN & SAKURA♡ (COLLECTING FIREWOOD♡)
Please don't make this any worse.
Let's do it, Takishima!
ha ha ha ha ha ha ha
heh heh
I'll do my best.
This is weird.
It is, isn't it?
LOOKS LIKE YOU HAVE THE EASIEST JOB!
What's there to supervise?
HEH HEH HEH
I PAID FOR ALL THIS, YOU KNOW. ♡
LISTEN, JUN.

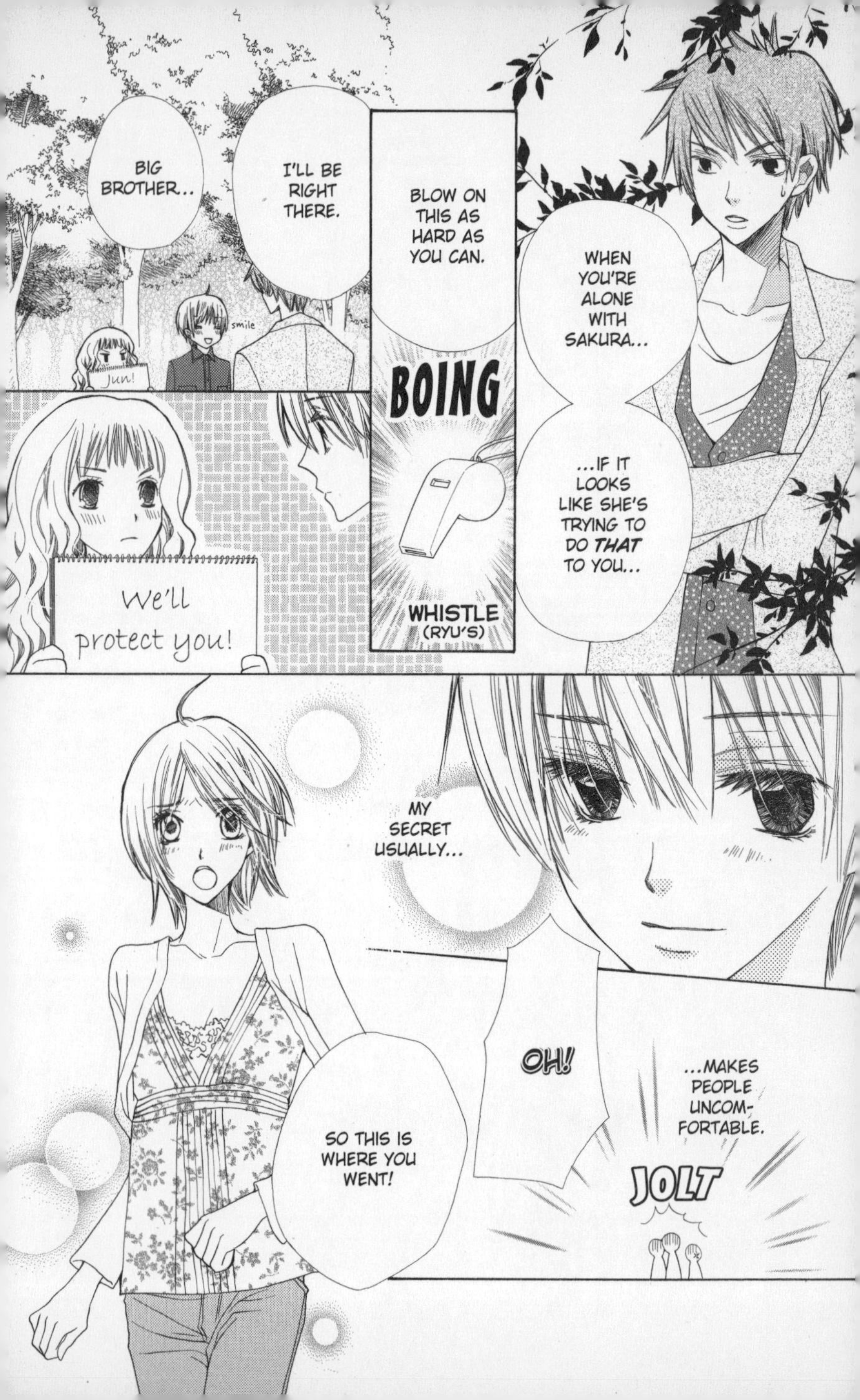
WHEN YOU'RE ALONE WITH SAKURA...
...IF IT LOOKS LIKE SHE'S TRYING TO DO *THAT* TO YOU...
BLOW ON THIS AS HARD AS YOU CAN.
BOING
WHISTLE (RYU'S)
I'LL BE RIGHT THERE.
BIG BROTHER...
smile
Jun!
We'll protect you!
MY SECRET USUALLY...
...MAKES PEOPLE UNCOM-FORTABLE.
OH!
JOLT
SO THIS IS WHERE YOU WENT!

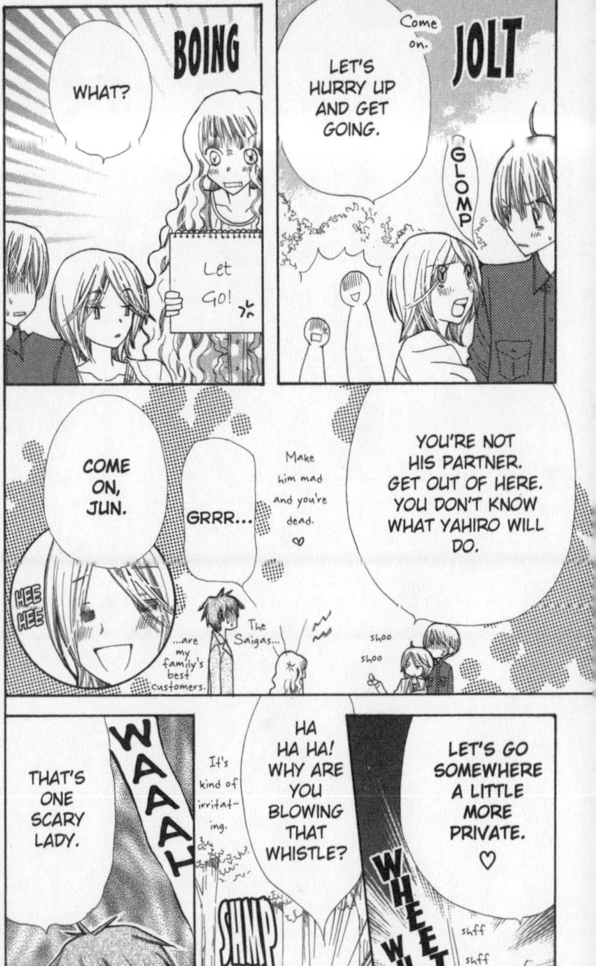
Come on.
LET'S HURRY UP AND GET GOING.
JOLT
GLOMP
BOING
WHAT?
Let Go!
YOU'RE NOT HIS PARTNER. GET OUT OF HERE. YOU DON'T KNOW WHAT YAHIRO WILL DO.
Make him mad and you're dead. ♡
shoo shoo
GRRR...
The Saigas...
...are my family's best customers.
COME ON, JUN.
HEE HEE
LET'S GO SOMEWHERE A LITTLE MORE PRIVATE. ♡
WHEET WHEET WHEEET
shff shff shff shff shff shff
HA HA HA! WHY ARE YOU BLOWING THAT WHISTLE?
It's kind of irritating.
SHMP
!!!
WAAAH
THAT'S ONE SCARY LADY.

1

•GREETINGS•

HELLO & HOW ARE YOU?

I'M MAKI MINAMI. WE'RE ALREADY ON THE FIFTH VOLUME! IT'S GOING SO FAST!

THERE'S NO LETTING UP NOW, AND IT'S ALL THANKS TO YOU!

hup hup

I CAN'T BELIEVE THE SERIES HAS LASTED THIS LONG.

REALLY...

It's a miracle!!

WELL, IF YOU LIKE IT SO FAR.. PLEASE STICK WITH US UNTIL THE END!

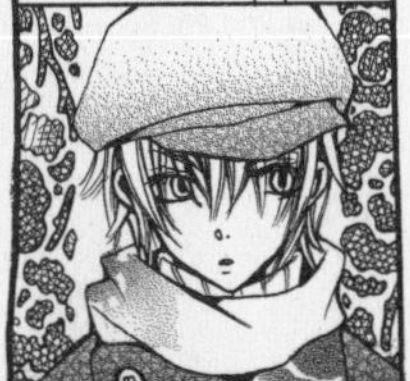

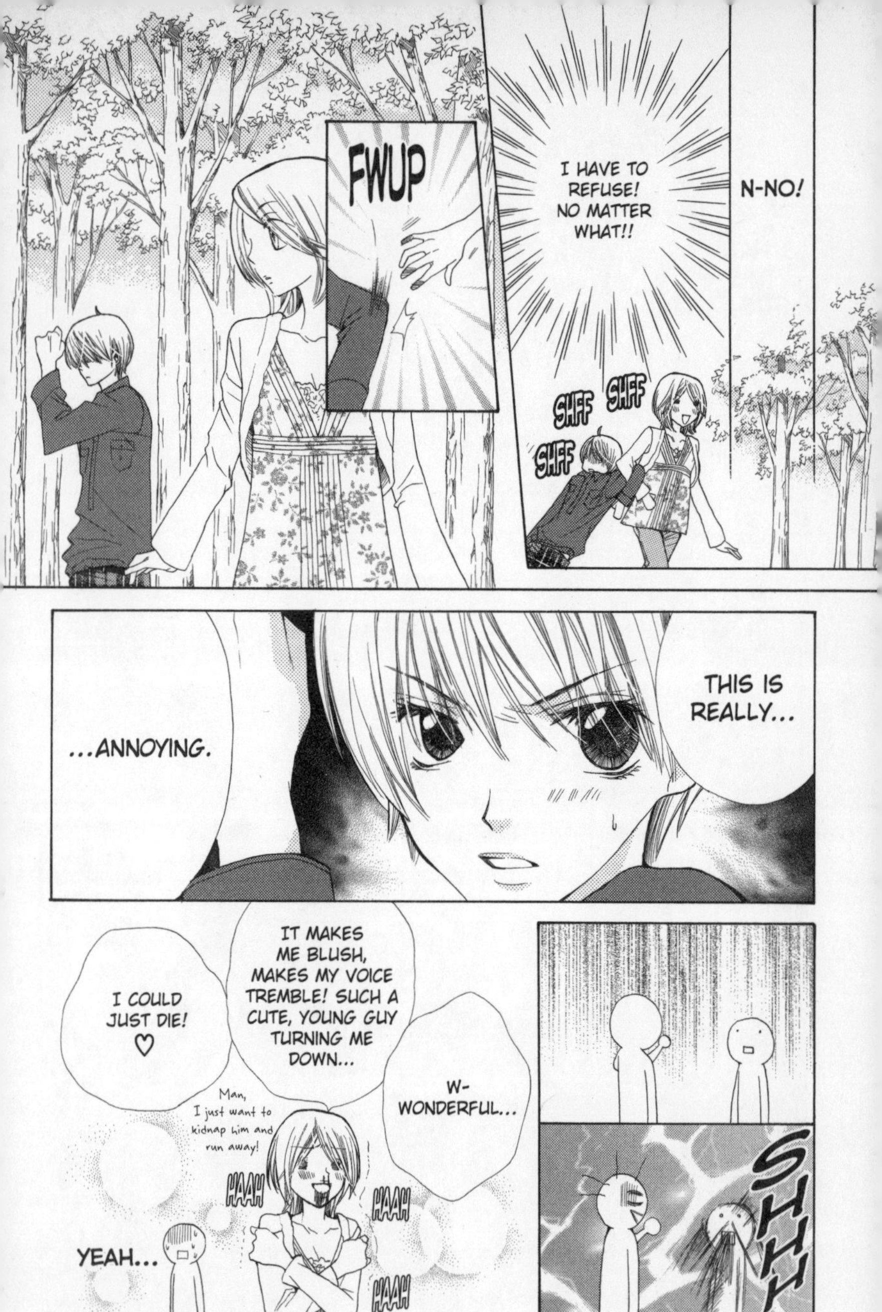
N-NO!
I HAVE TO REFUSE! NO MATTER WHAT!!
SHFF SHFF
SHFF
FWUP
THIS IS REALLY...
...ANNOYING.
SHHH
W- WONDERFUL...
IT MAKES ME BLUSH, MAKES MY VOICE TREMBLE! SUCH A CUTE, YOUNG GUY TURNING ME DOWN...
I COULD JUST DIE! ♡
Man, I just want to kidnap him and run away!
HAAH
HAAH
HAAH
YEAH...

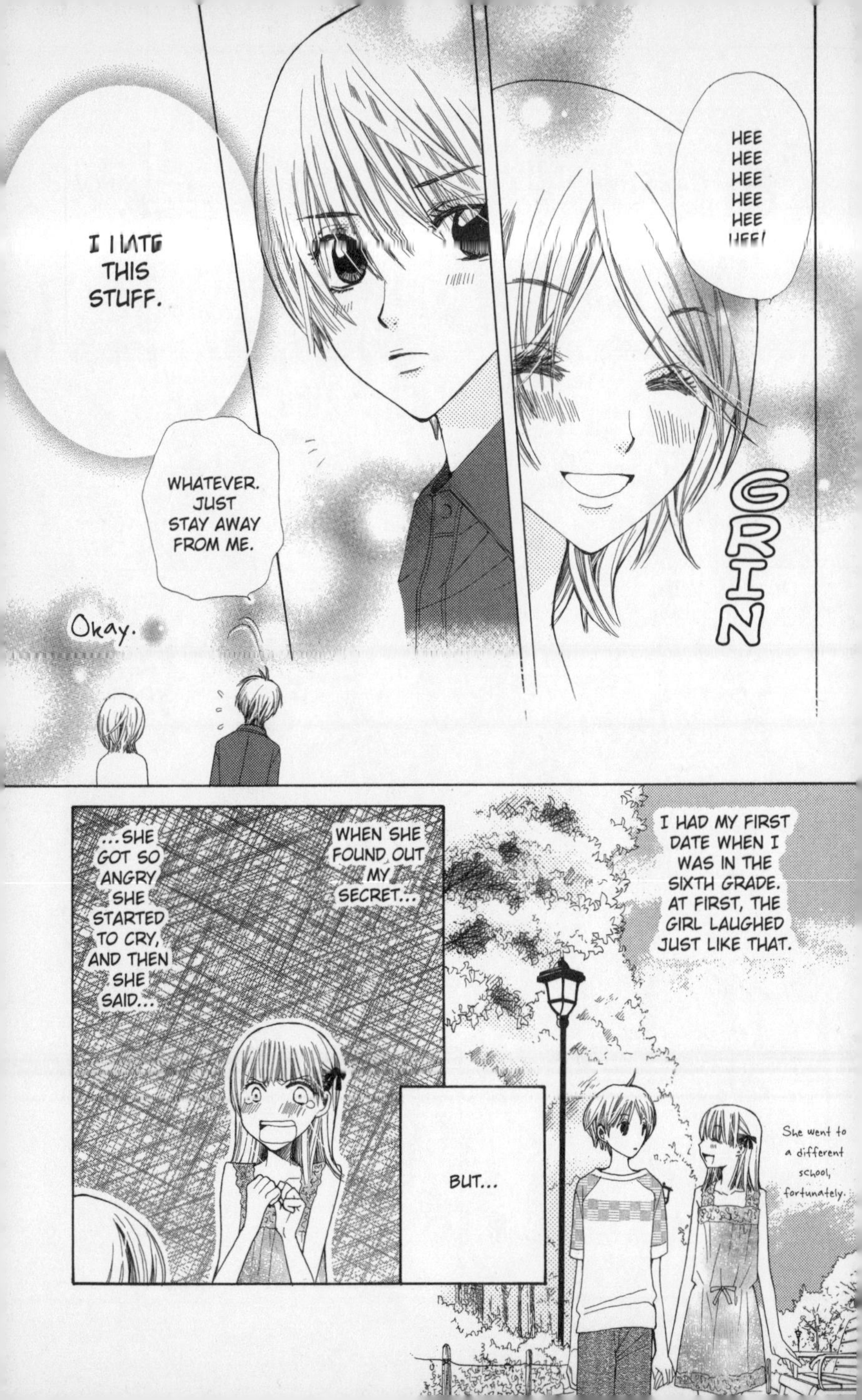
HEE HEE HEE HEE HEE HEE!
GRIN
I HATE THIS STUFF.
WHATEVER. JUST STAY AWAY FROM ME.
Okay.
I HAD MY FIRST DATE WHEN I WAS IN THE SIXTH GRADE. AT FIRST, THE GIRL LAUGHED JUST LIKE THAT.
She went to a different school, fortunately.
BUT...
WHEN SHE FOUND OUT MY SECRET...
...SHE GOT SO ANGRY SHE STARTED TO CRY, AND THEN SHE SAID...

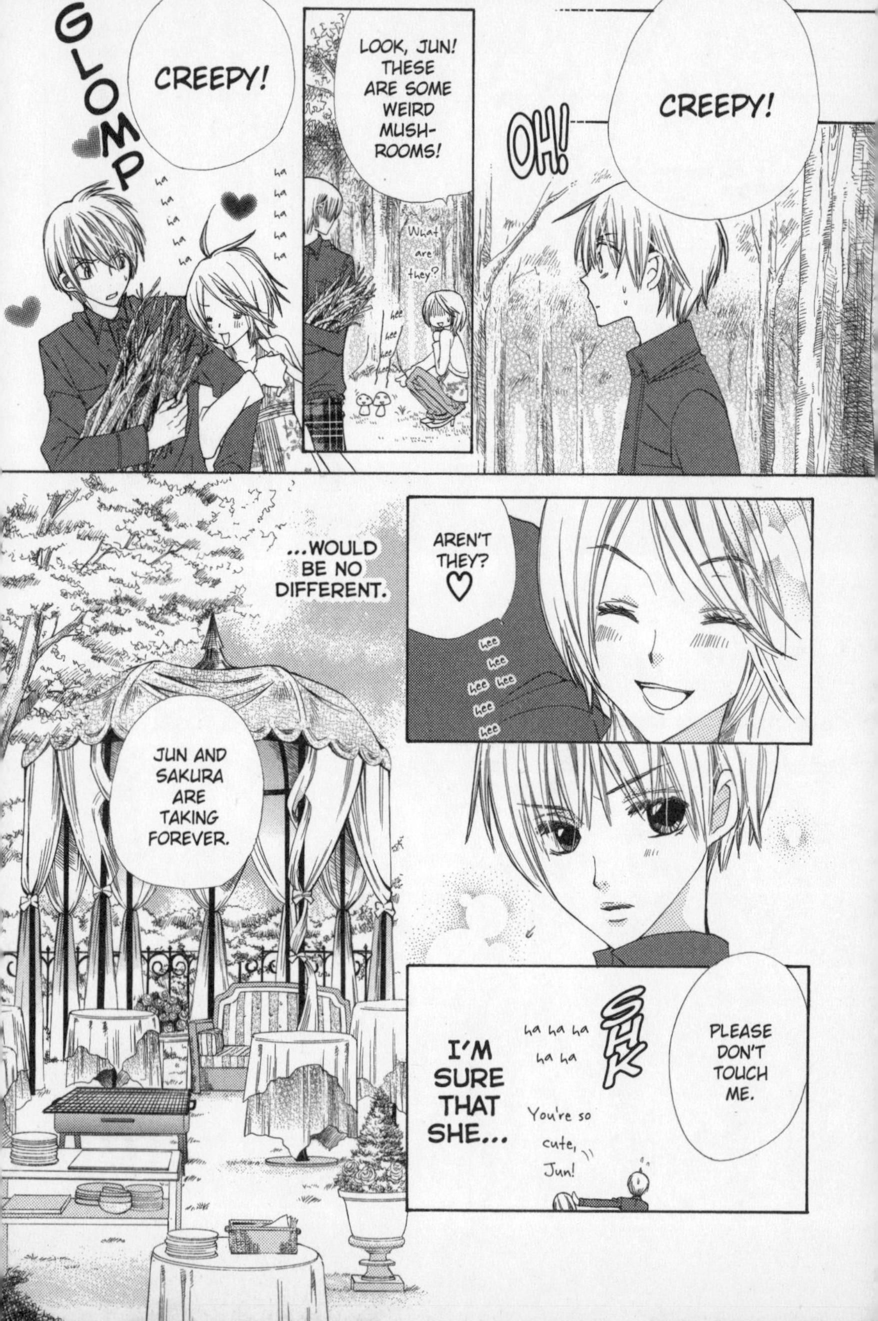
CREEPY!
OH!
LOOK, JUN! THESE ARE SOME WEIRD MUSH-ROOMS!
What are they?
hee hee hee hee
CREEPY!
GLOMP
ha ha ha ha ha
ha ha ha ha ha
AREN'T THEY? ♡
hee hee hee hee hee hee
PLEASE DON'T TOUCH ME.
SHK
ha ha ha ha ha
You're so cute, Jun!
I'M SURE THAT SHE...
...WOULD BE NO DIFFERENT.
JUN AND SAKURA ARE TAKING FOREVER.

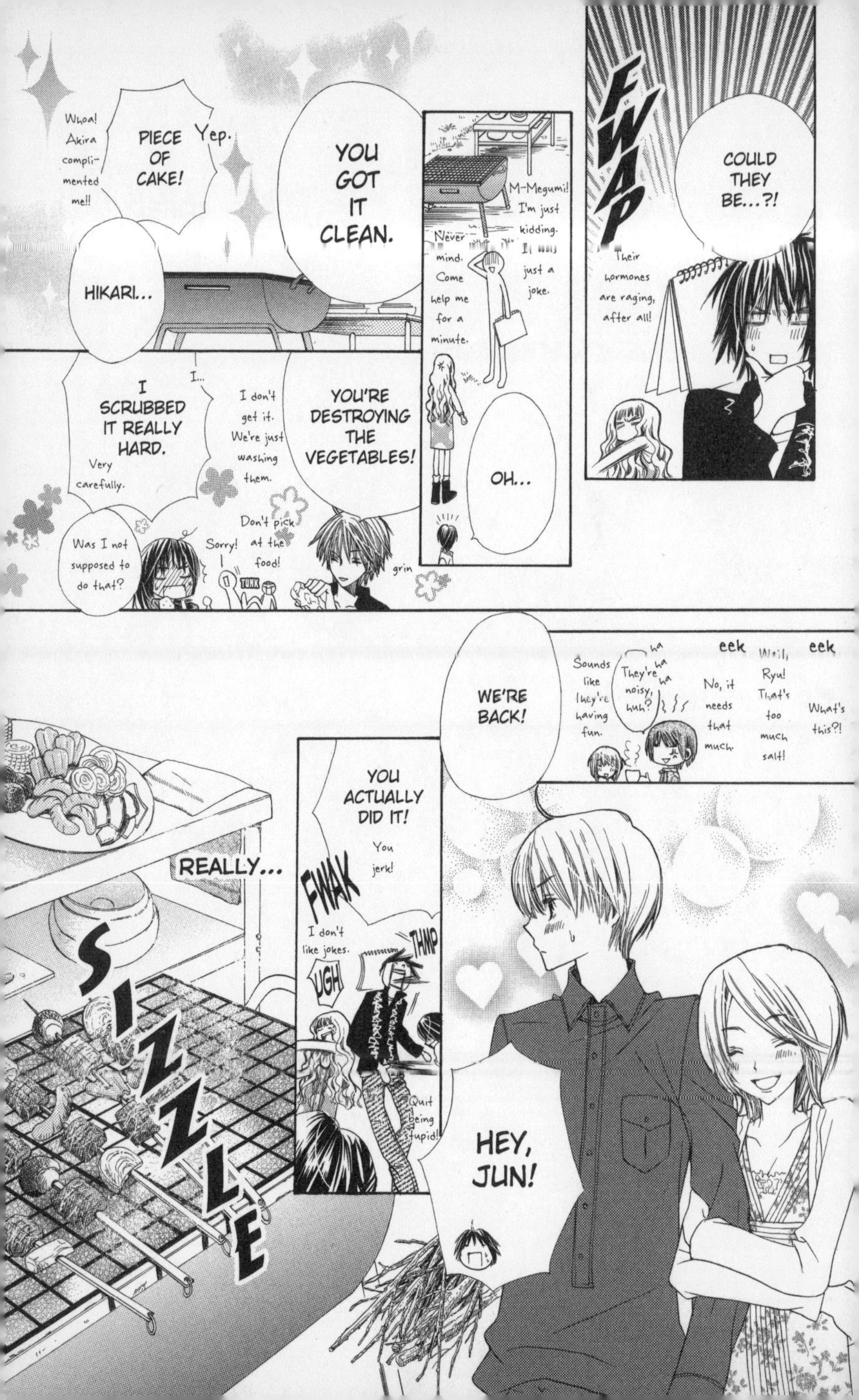
FWAP
COULD THEY BE...?!
Their hormones are raging, after all!
M-Megumi! I'm just kidding.
just a joke.
Never mind. Come help me for a minute.
OH...
YOU GOT IT CLEAN.
Yep.
PIECE OF CAKE!
Whoa! Akira complimented me!!
HIKARI...
YOU'RE DESTROYING THE VEGETABLES!
I don't get it. We're just washing them.
I...
I SCRUBBED IT REALLY HARD.
Very carefully.
Don't pick at the food!
grin
Sorry!
TUNK
Was I not supposed to do that?
eek
What's this?!
eek
Well, Ryu! That's too much salt!
No, it needs that much.
ha ha ha
They're noisy, huh?
Sounds like they're having fun.
WE'RE BACK!
HEY, JUN!
YOU ACTUALLY DID IT!
You jerk!
FWAK
I don't like jokes.
THMP
UGH
Quit being stupid!
REALLY...
SIZZLE

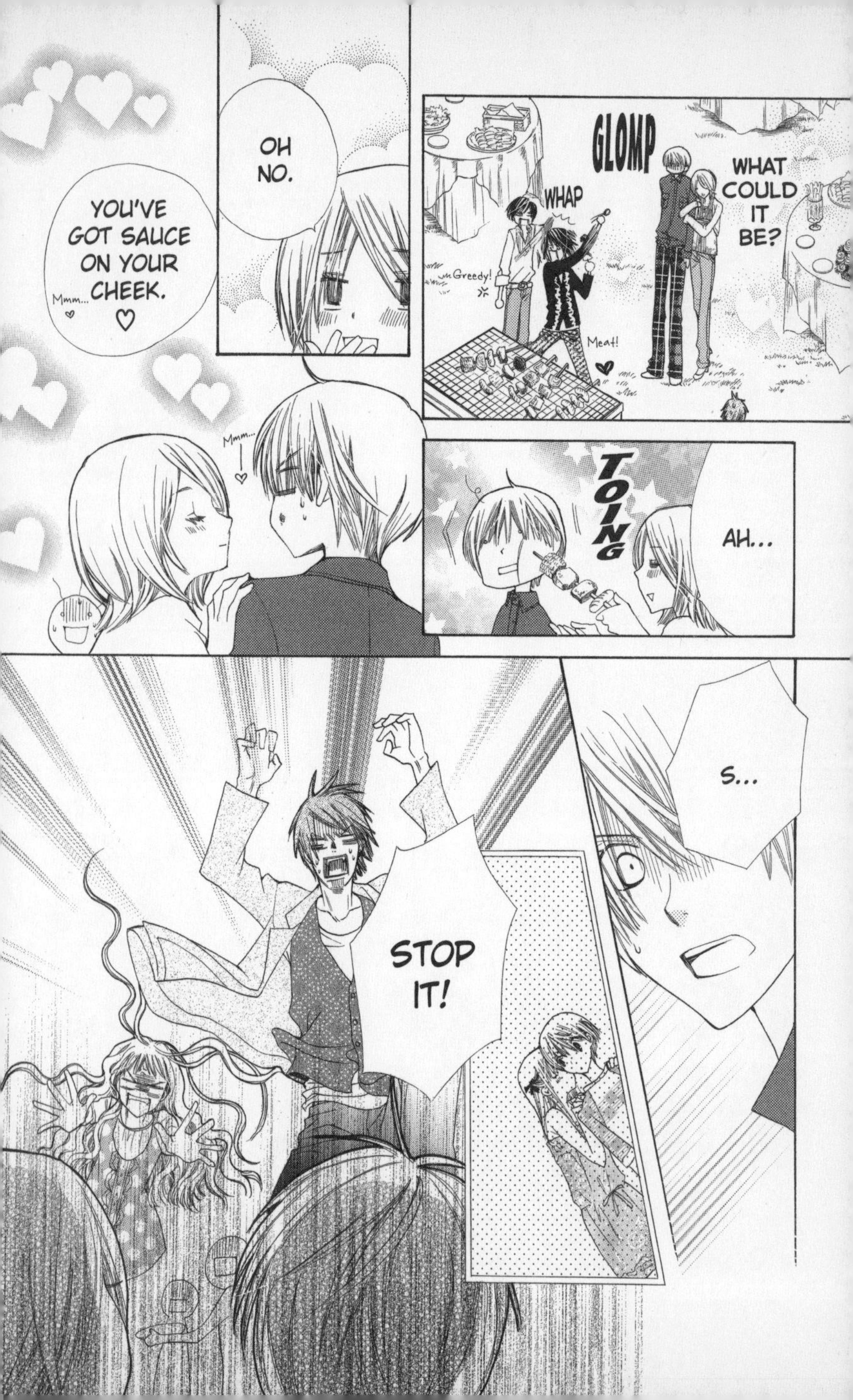
WHAT COULD IT BE?
GLOMP
WHAP
Greedy!
Meat!
AH...
TOING
OH NO.
YOU'VE GOT SAUCE ON YOUR CHEEK.
Mmm...
Mmm...
S...
STOP IT!

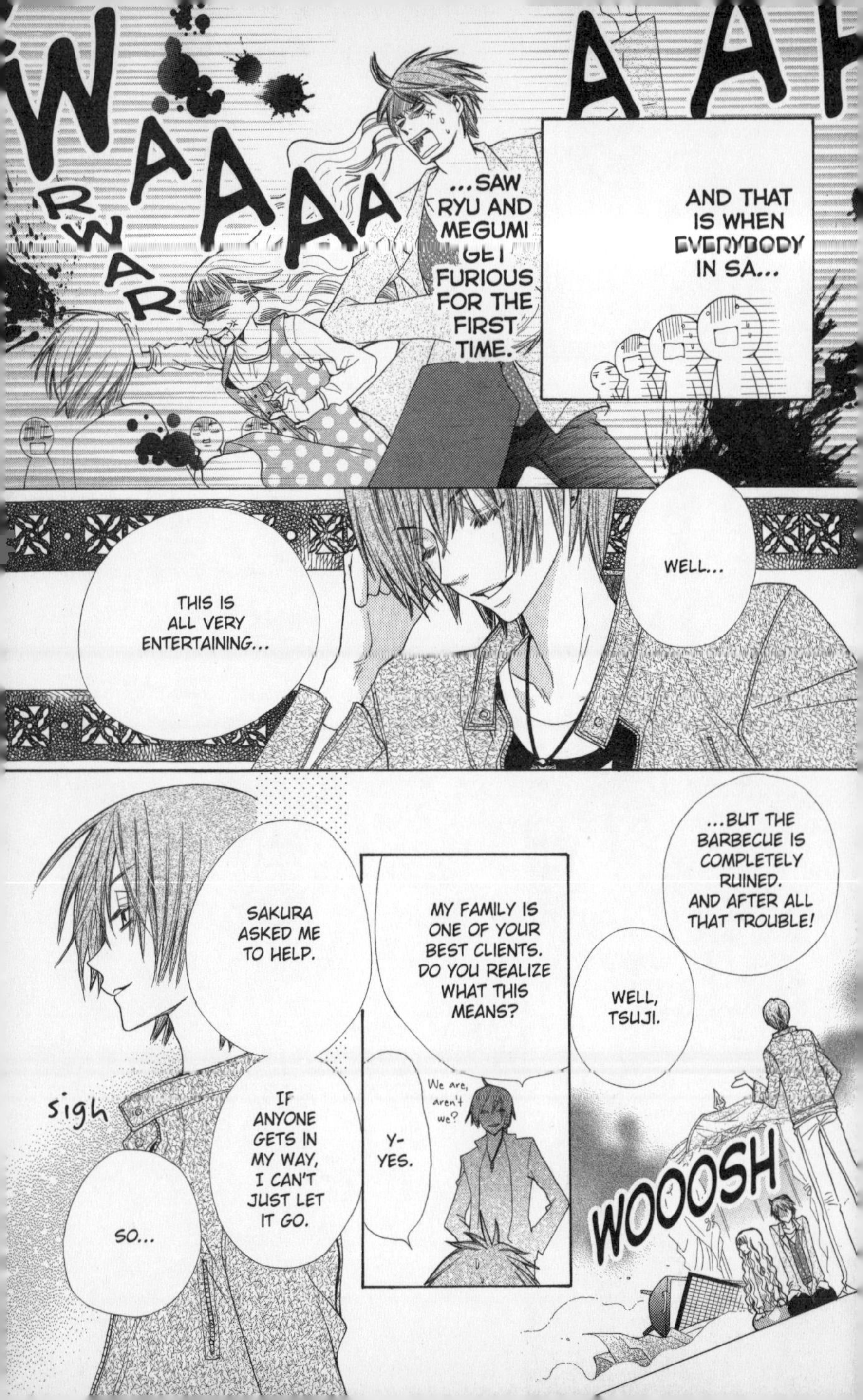
AND THAT IS WHEN EVERYBODY IN SA...
...SAW RYU AND MEGUMI GET FURIOUS FOR THE FIRST TIME.
WAAAAAAH
RWAR
WELL...
THIS IS ALL VERY ENTERTAINING...
...BUT THE BARBECUE IS COMPLETELY RUINED. AND AFTER ALL THAT TROUBLE!
WOOOSH
WELL, TSUJI.
MY FAMILY IS ONE OF YOUR BEST CLIENTS. DO YOU REALIZE WHAT THIS MEANS?
We are, aren't we?
Y-YES.
SAKURA ASKED ME TO HELP.
IF ANYONE GETS IN MY WAY, I CAN'T JUST LET IT GO.
sigh
SO...

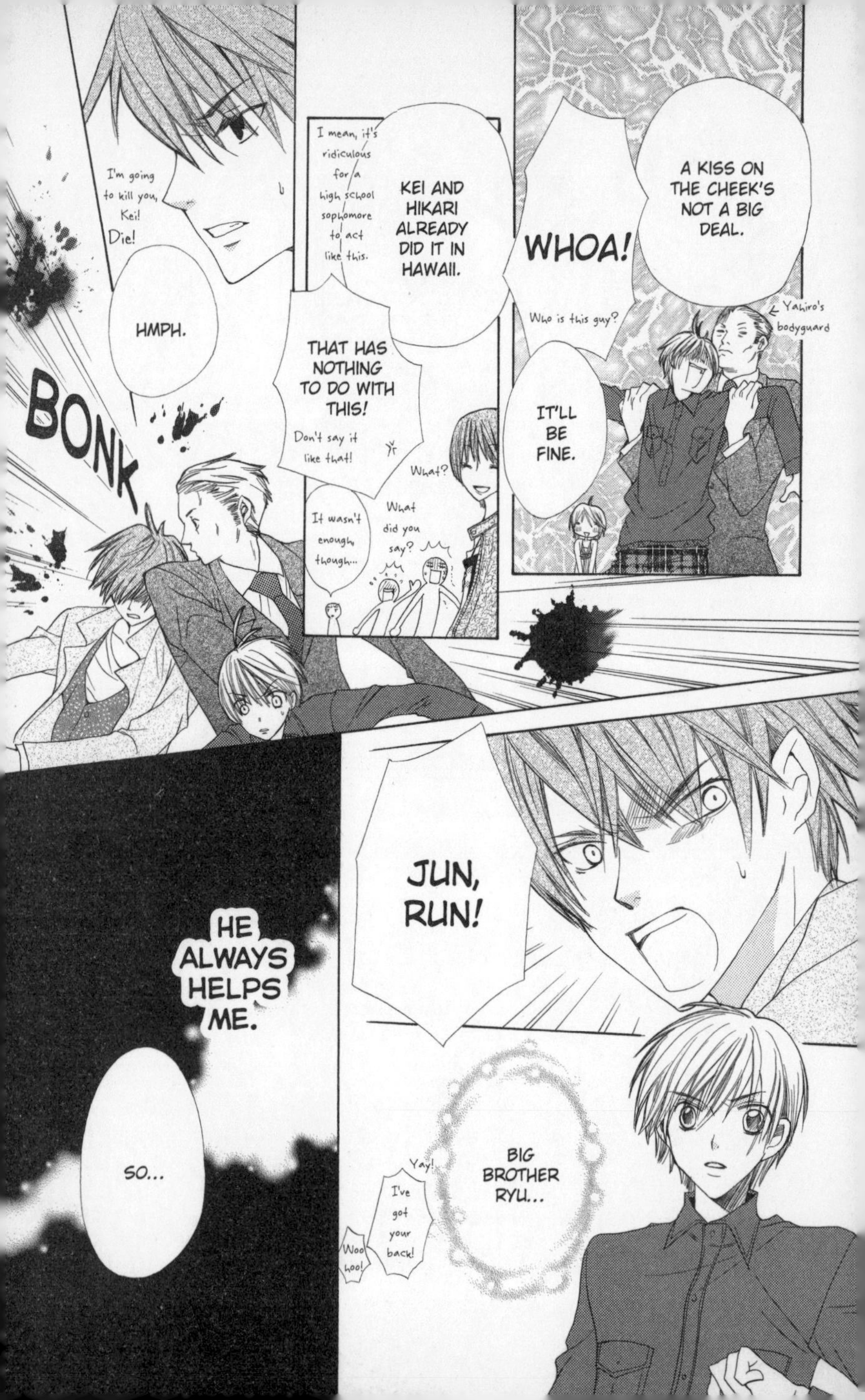
A KISS ON THE CHEEK'S NOT A BIG DEAL.
WHOA!
Who is this guy?
Yahiro's bodyguard
IT'LL BE FINE.
KEI AND HIKARI ALREADY DID IT IN HAWAII.
I mean, it's ridiculous for a high school sophomore to act like this.
THAT HAS NOTHING TO DO WITH THIS!
Don't say it like that!
What?
What did you say?
It wasn't enough, though...
I'm going to kill you, Kei! Die!
HMPH.
BONK
JUN, RUN!
BIG BROTHER RYU...
Yay!
I've got your back!
Woo hoo!
HE ALWAYS HELPS ME.
SO...

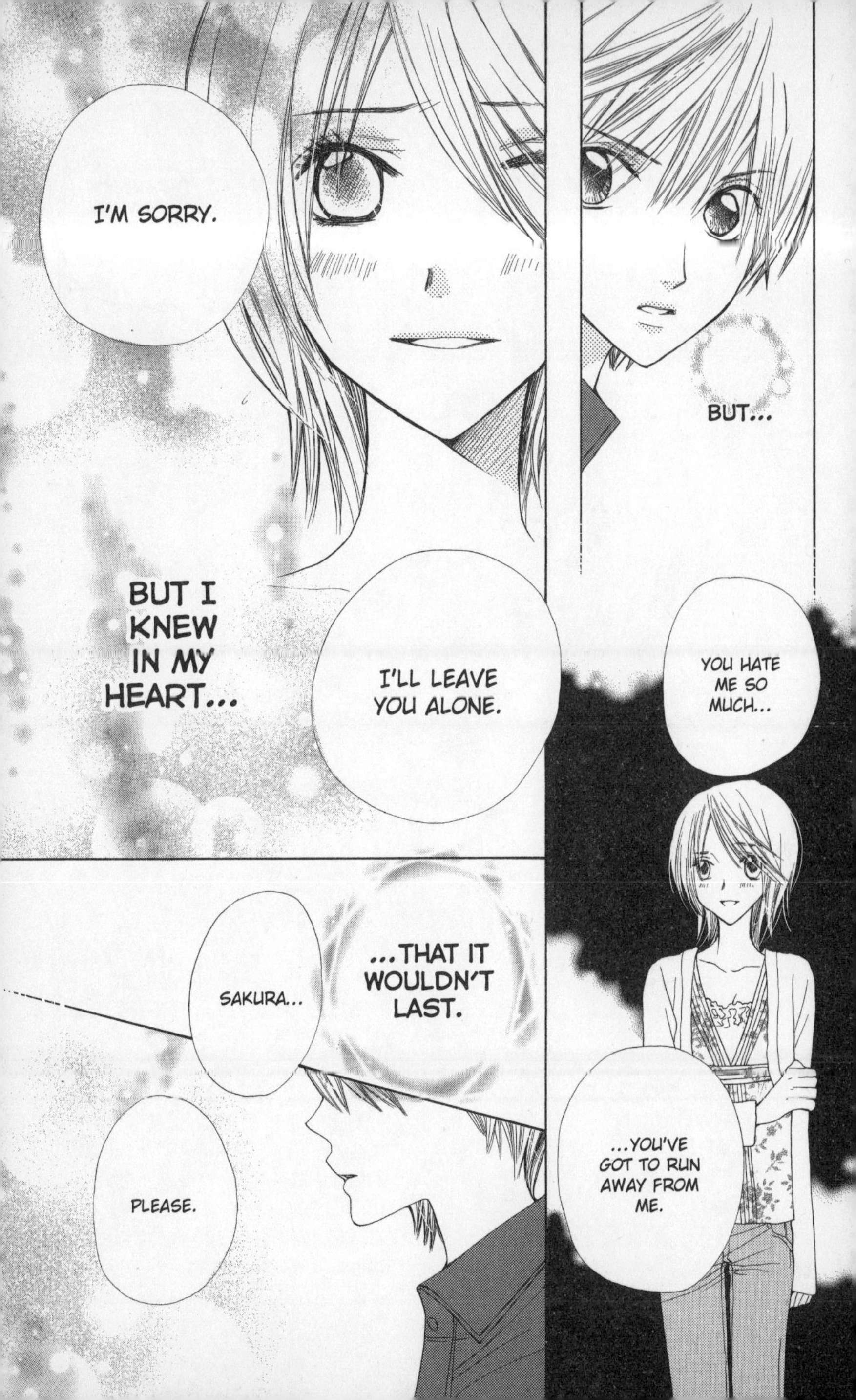
BUT...
YOU HATE ME SO MUCH...
...YOU'VE GOT TO RUN AWAY FROM ME.
I'M SORRY.
I'LL LEAVE YOU ALONE.
BUT I KNEW IN MY HEART...
...THAT IT WOULDN'T LAST.
SAKURA...
PLEASE.

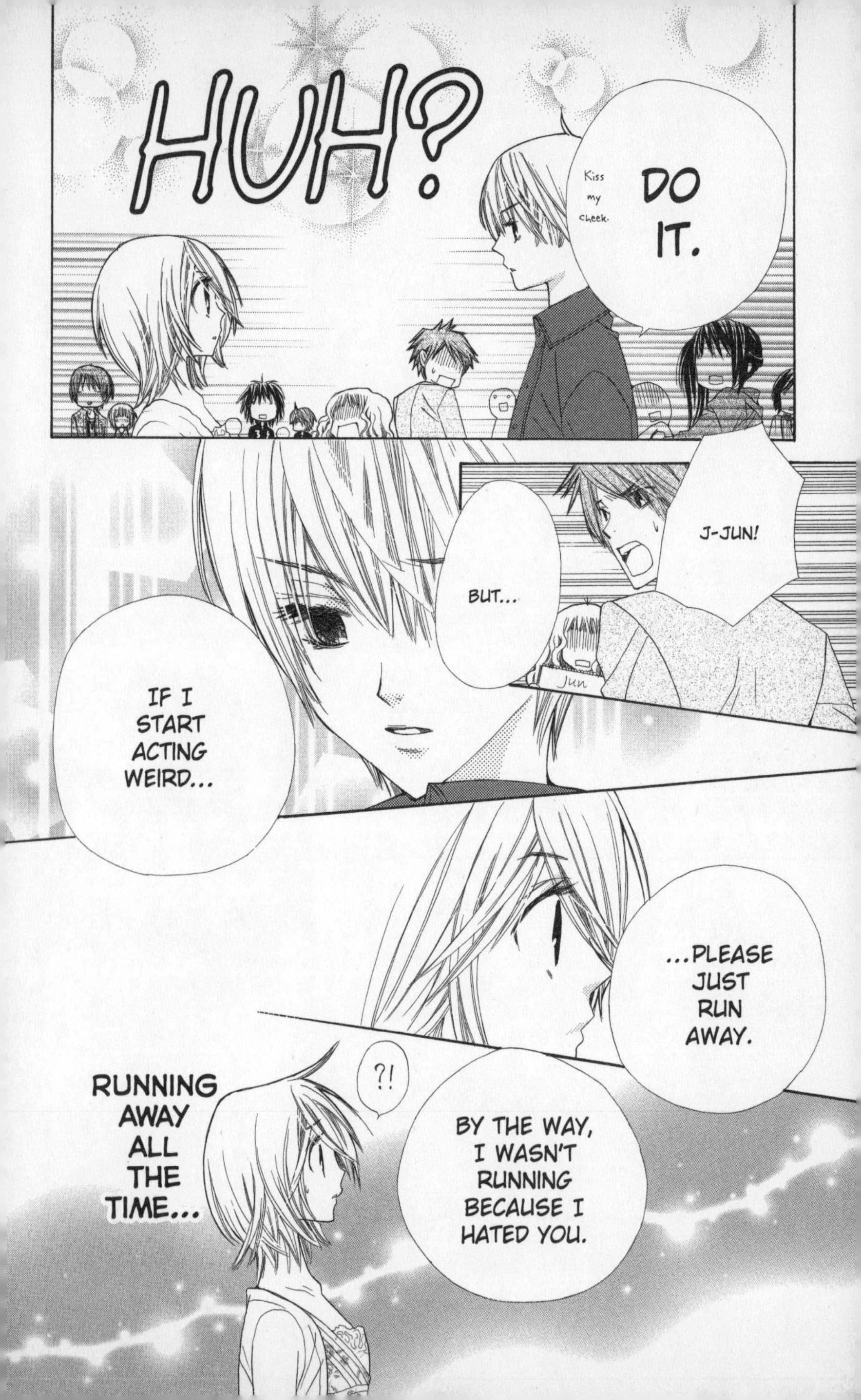
DO IT.
Kiss my cheek.
HUH?
J-JUN!
BUT...
Jun
IF I START ACTING WEIRD...
...PLEASE JUST RUN AWAY.
?!
BY THE WAY, I WASN'T RUNNING BECAUSE I HATED YOU.
RUNNING AWAY ALL THE TIME...

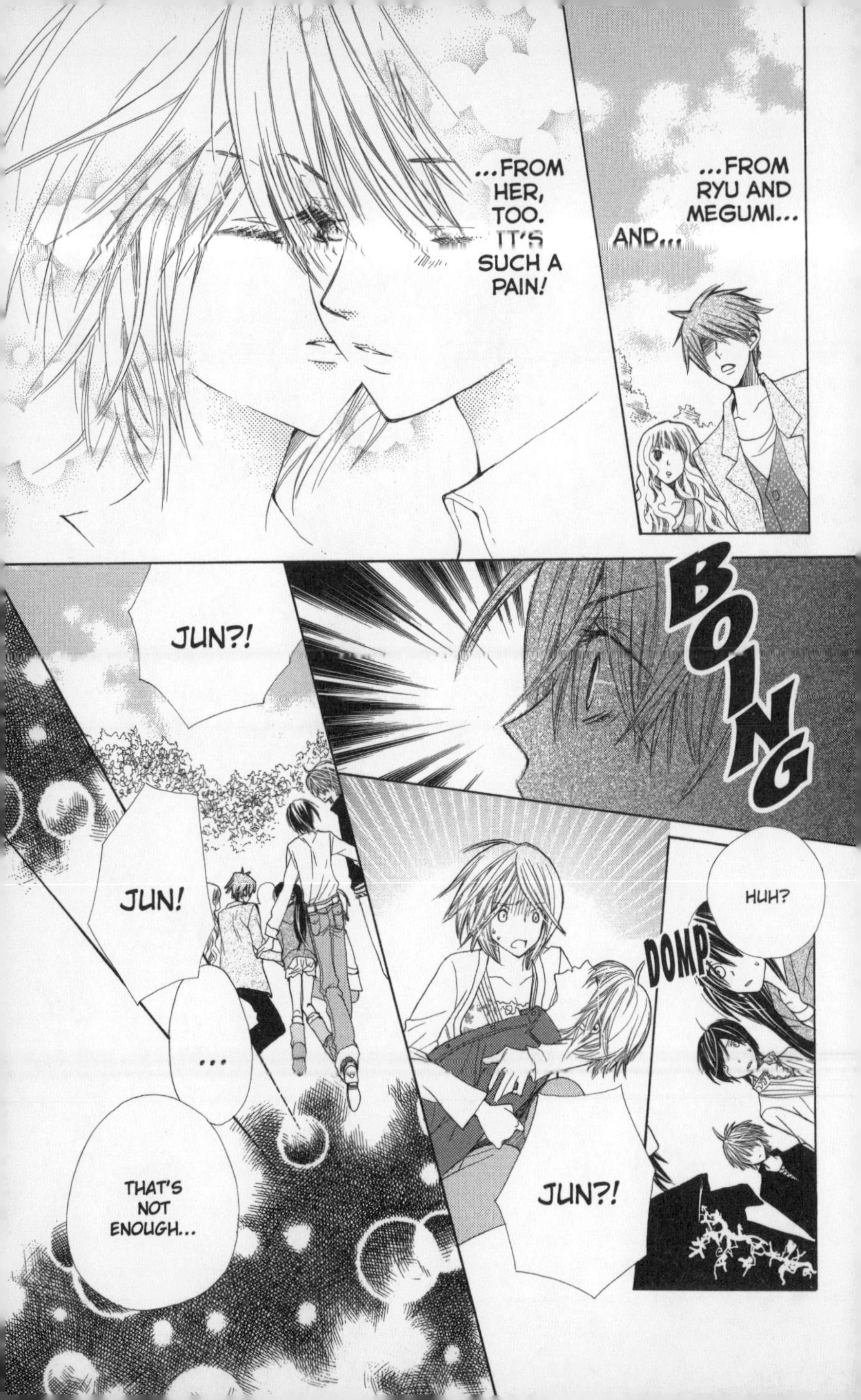
...FROM RYU AND MEGUMI...
AND...
...FROM HER, TOO. IT'S SUCH A PAIN!
BOING
HUH?
DOMP
JUN?!
JUN?!
JUN!
...
THAT'S NOT ENOUGH...

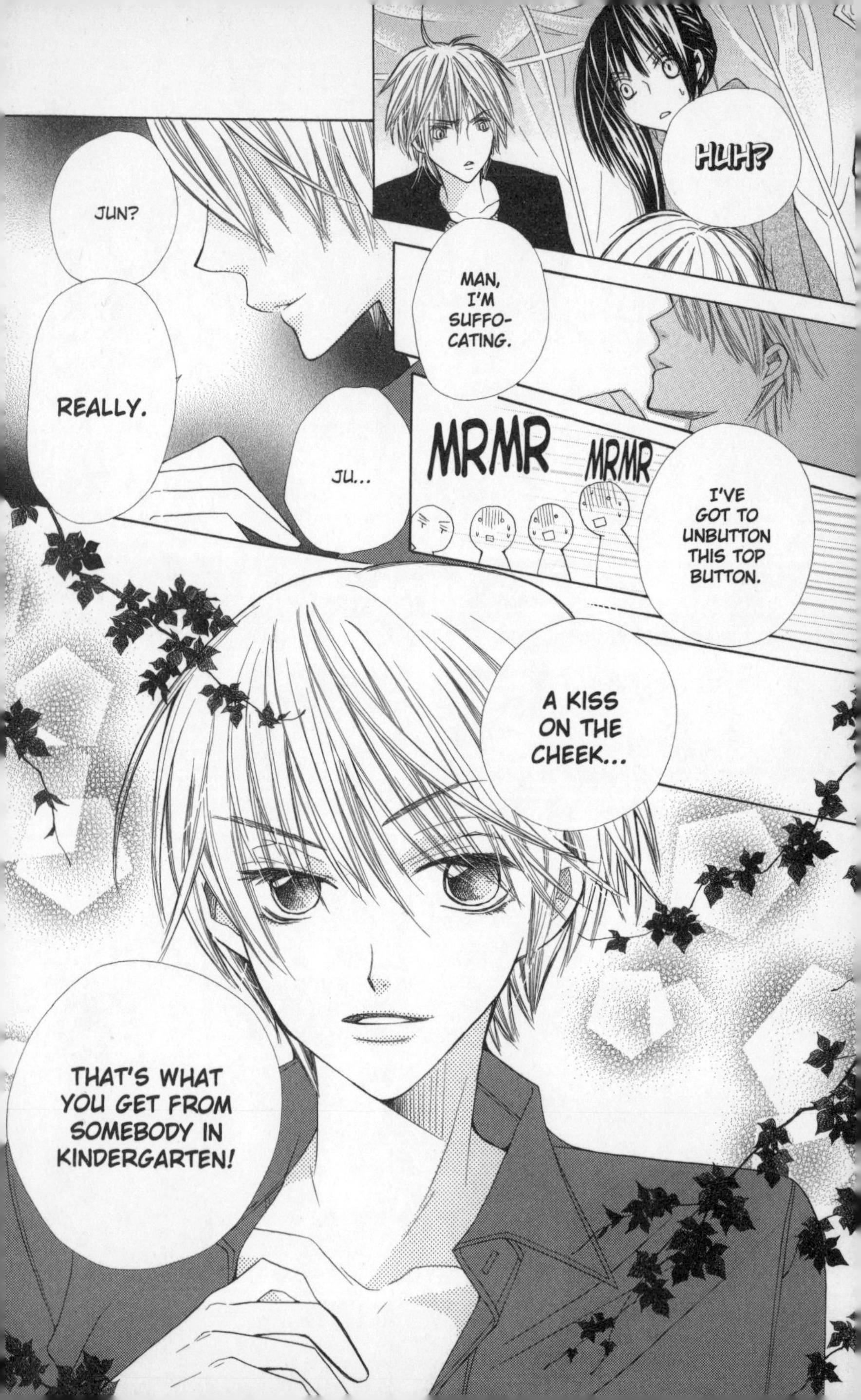
HUH?
MAN, I'M SUFFO-CATING.
MRMR
MRMR
I'VE GOT TO UNBUTTON THIS TOP BUTTON.
JUN?
REALLY.
JU...
A KISS ON THE CHEEK...
THAT'S WHAT YOU GET FROM SOMEBODY IN KINDERGARTEN!

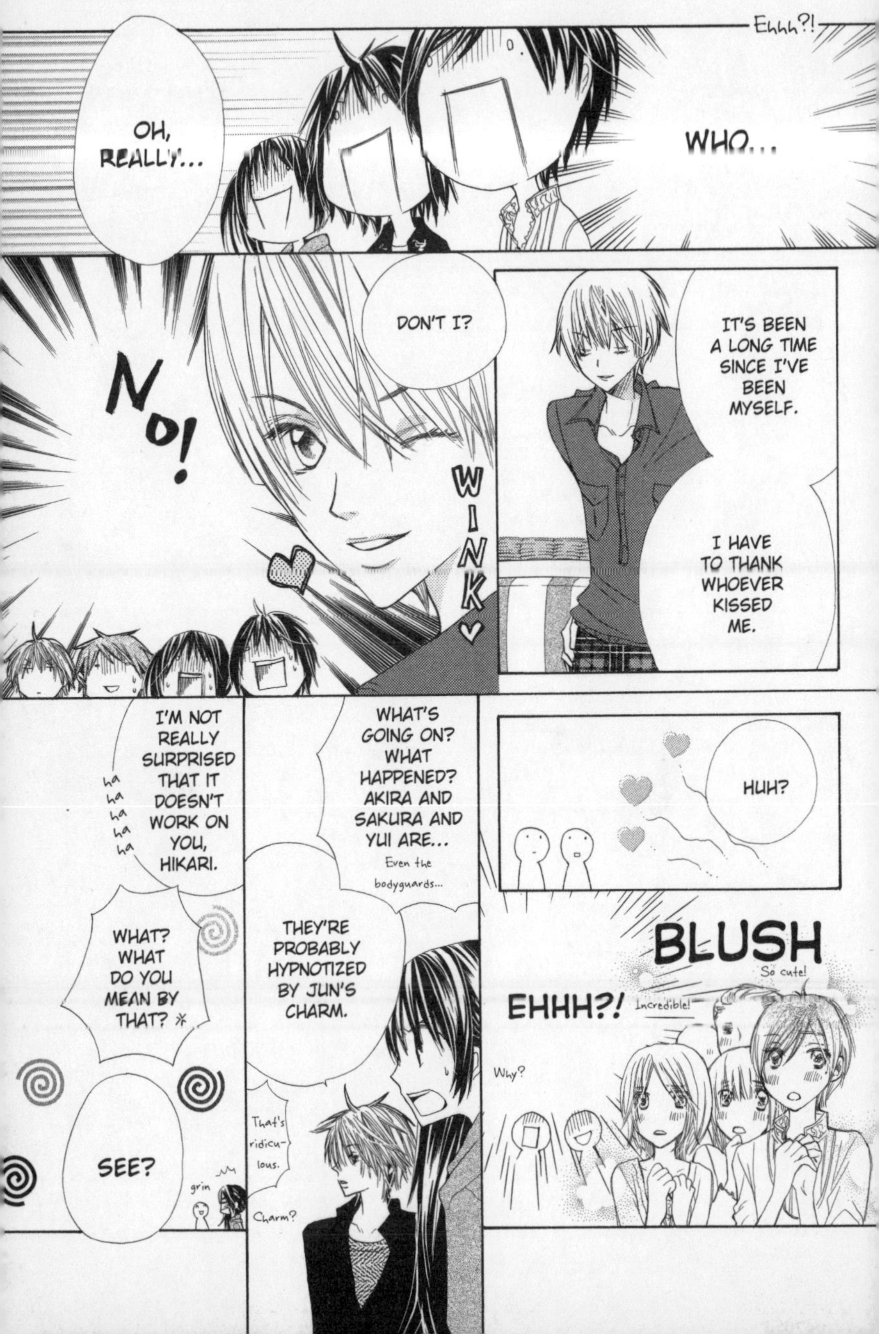
Ehhh?!
WHO...
OH, REALLY...
IT'S BEEN A LONG TIME SINCE I'VE BEEN MYSELF.
I HAVE TO THANK WHOEVER KISSED ME.
DON'T I?
WINK
NO!
HUH?
BLUSH
So cute!
EHHH?!
Incredible!
Why?
WHAT'S GOING ON? WHAT HAPPENED? AKIRA AND SAKURA AND YUI ARE...
Even the bodyguards...
THEY'RE PROBABLY HYPNOTIZED BY JUN'S CHARM.
That's ridiculous.
Charm?
I'M NOT REALLY SURPRISED THAT IT DOESN'T WORK ON YOU, HIKARI.
ha ha ha ha ha
WHAT? WHAT DO YOU MEAN BY THAT?
SEE?
grin

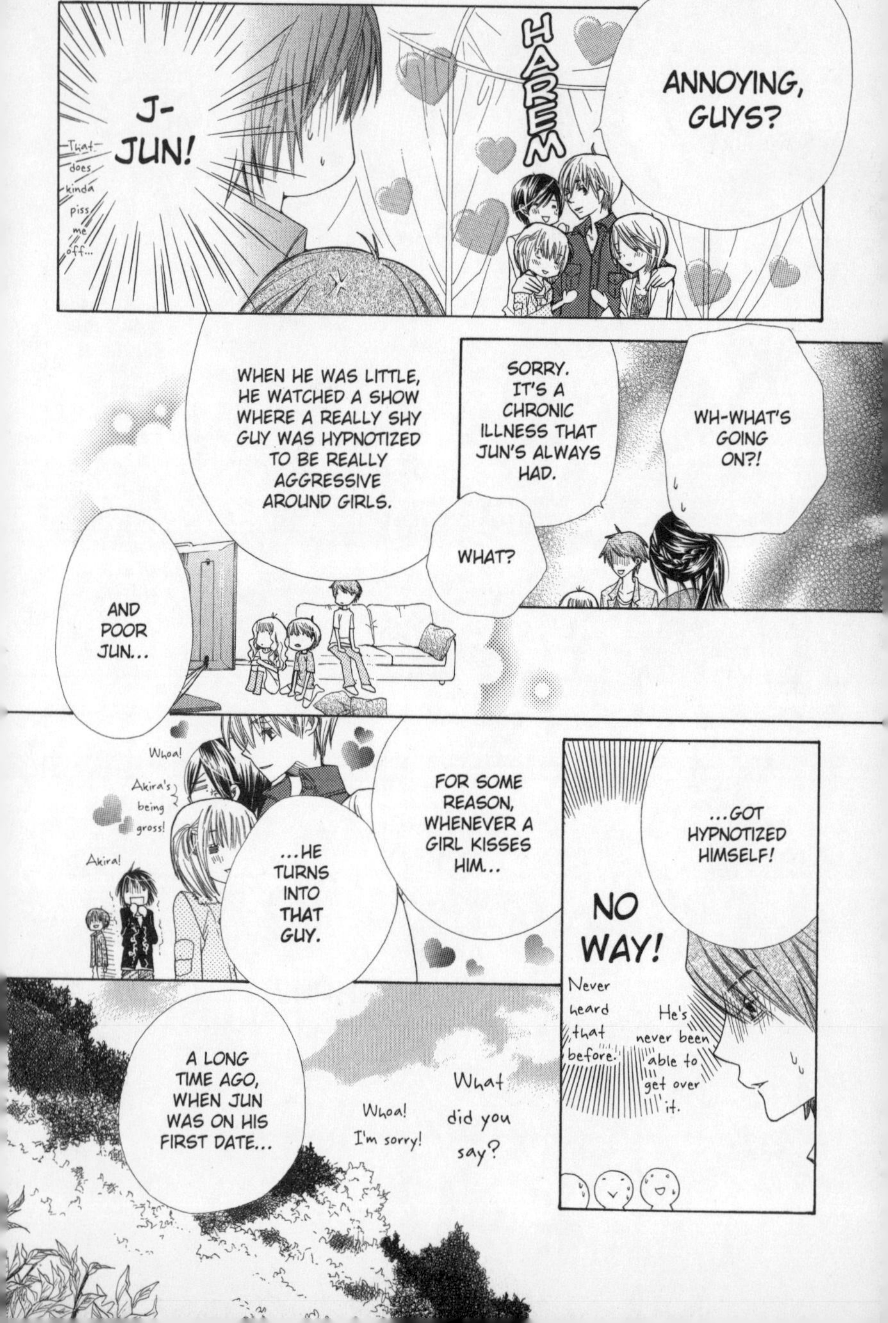
ANNOYING, GUYS?
HAREM
J-JUN!
That does kinda piss me off...
WH-WHAT'S GOING ON?!
SORRY. IT'S A CHRONIC ILLNESS THAT JUN'S ALWAYS HAD.
WHAT?
WHEN HE WAS LITTLE, HE WATCHED A SHOW WHERE A REALLY SHY GUY WAS HYPNOTIZED TO BE REALLY AGGRESSIVE AROUND GIRLS.
AND POOR JUN...
...GOT HYPNOTIZED HIMSELF!
NO WAY!
He's never been able to get over it.
Never heard that before.
FOR SOME REASON, WHENEVER A GIRL KISSES HIM...
...HE TURNS INTO THAT GUY.
Whoa!
Akira's being gross!
Akira!
A LONG TIME AGO, WHEN JUN WAS ON HIS FIRST DATE...
What did you say?
Whoa! I'm sorry!

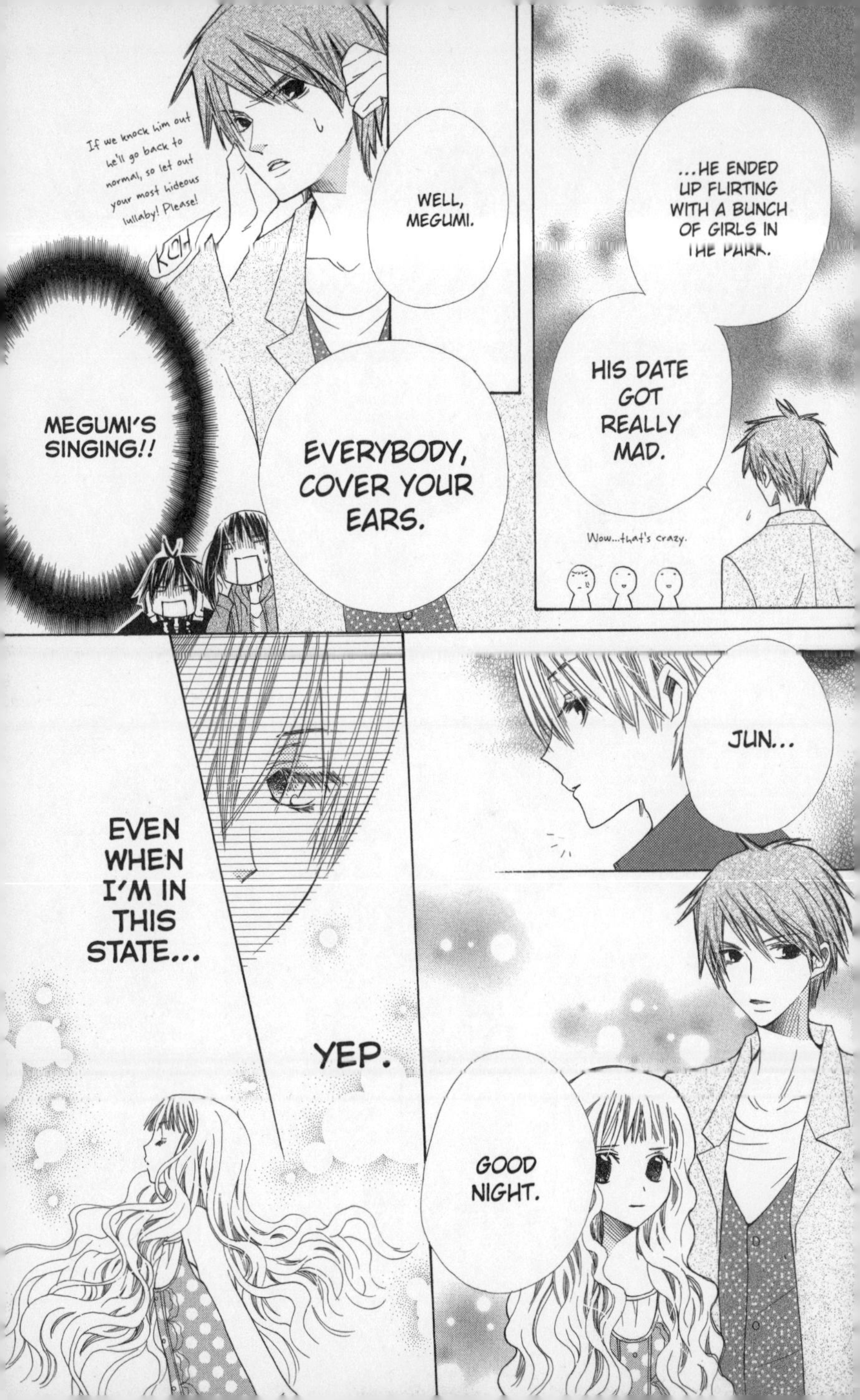
...HE ENDED UP FLIRTING WITH A BUNCH OF GIRLS IN THE PARK.
HIS DATE GOT REALLY MAD.
Wow...that's crazy.
WELL, MEGUMI.
If we knock him out he'll go back to normal, so let out your most hideous lullaby! Please!
KCH
EVERYBODY, COVER YOUR EARS.
MEGUMI'S SINGING!!
JUN...
GOOD NIGHT.
EVEN WHEN I'M IN THIS STATE...
YEP.

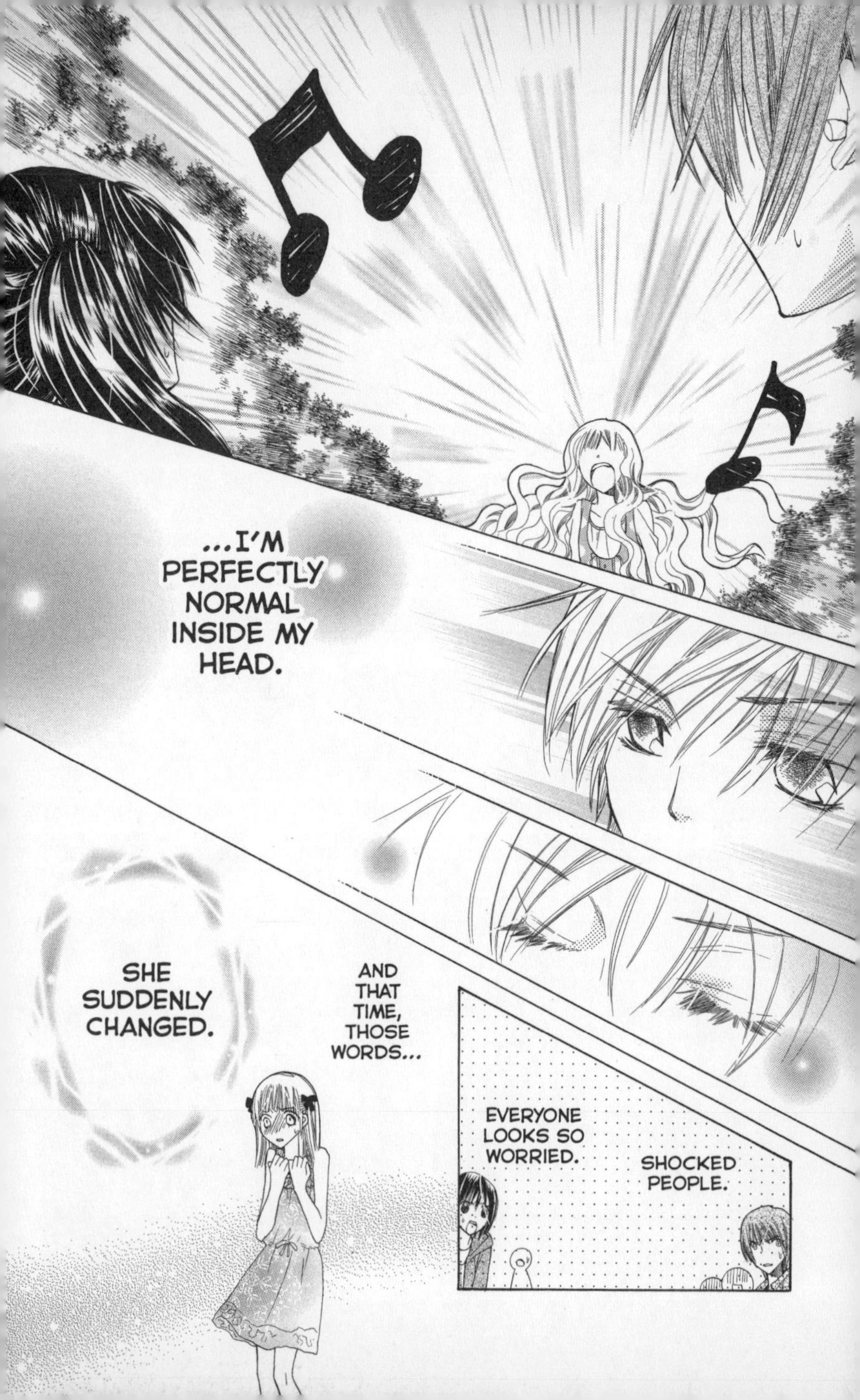
...I'M PERFECTLY NORMAL INSIDE MY HEAD.
SHOCKED PEOPLE.
EVERYONE LOOKS SO WORRIED.
AND THAT TIME, THOSE WORDS...
SHE SUDDENLY CHANGED.

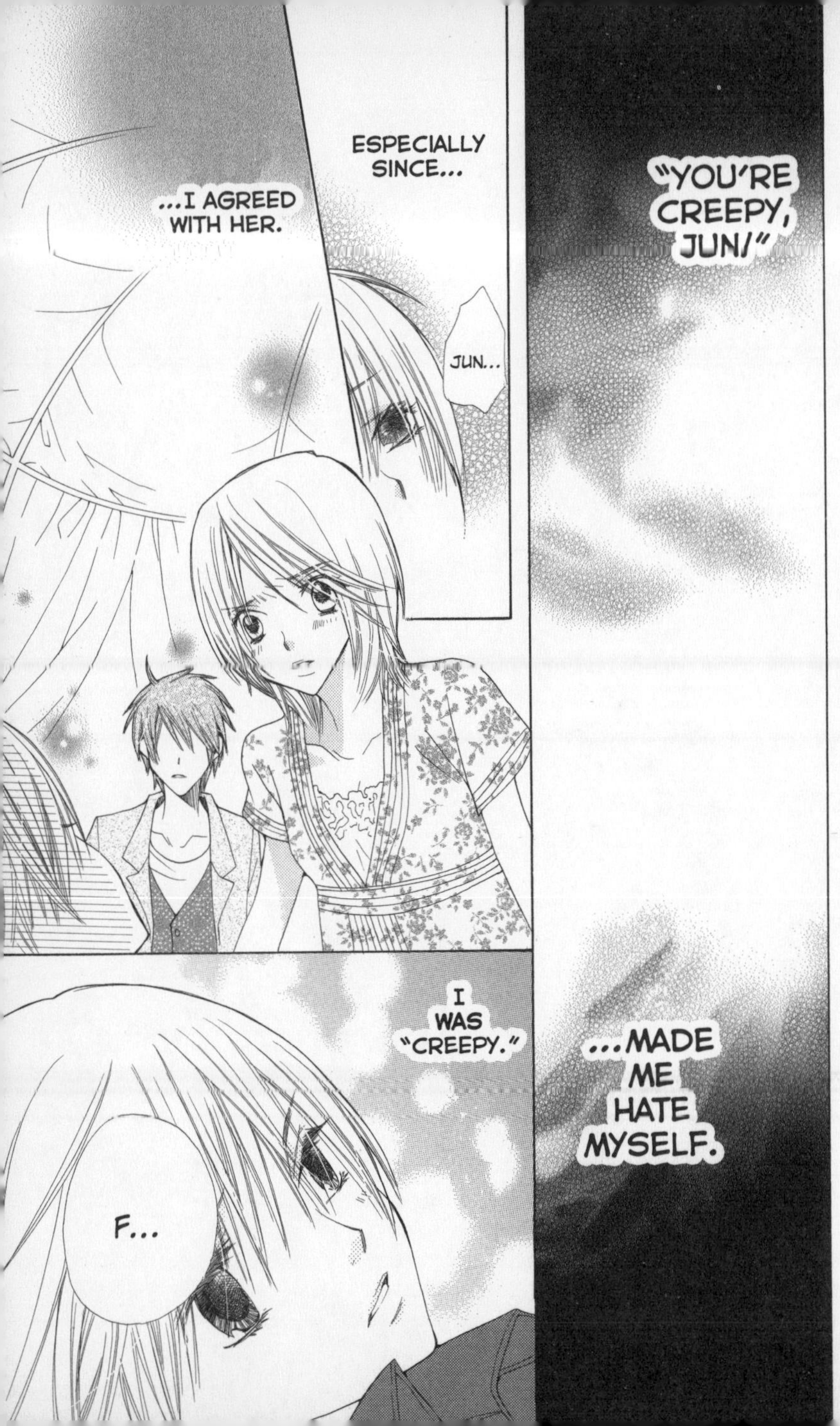
"YOU'RE CREEPY, JUN!"
...MADE ME HATE MYSELF.
ESPECIALLY SINCE...
JUN...
...I AGREED WITH HER.
I WAS "CREEPY."
F...

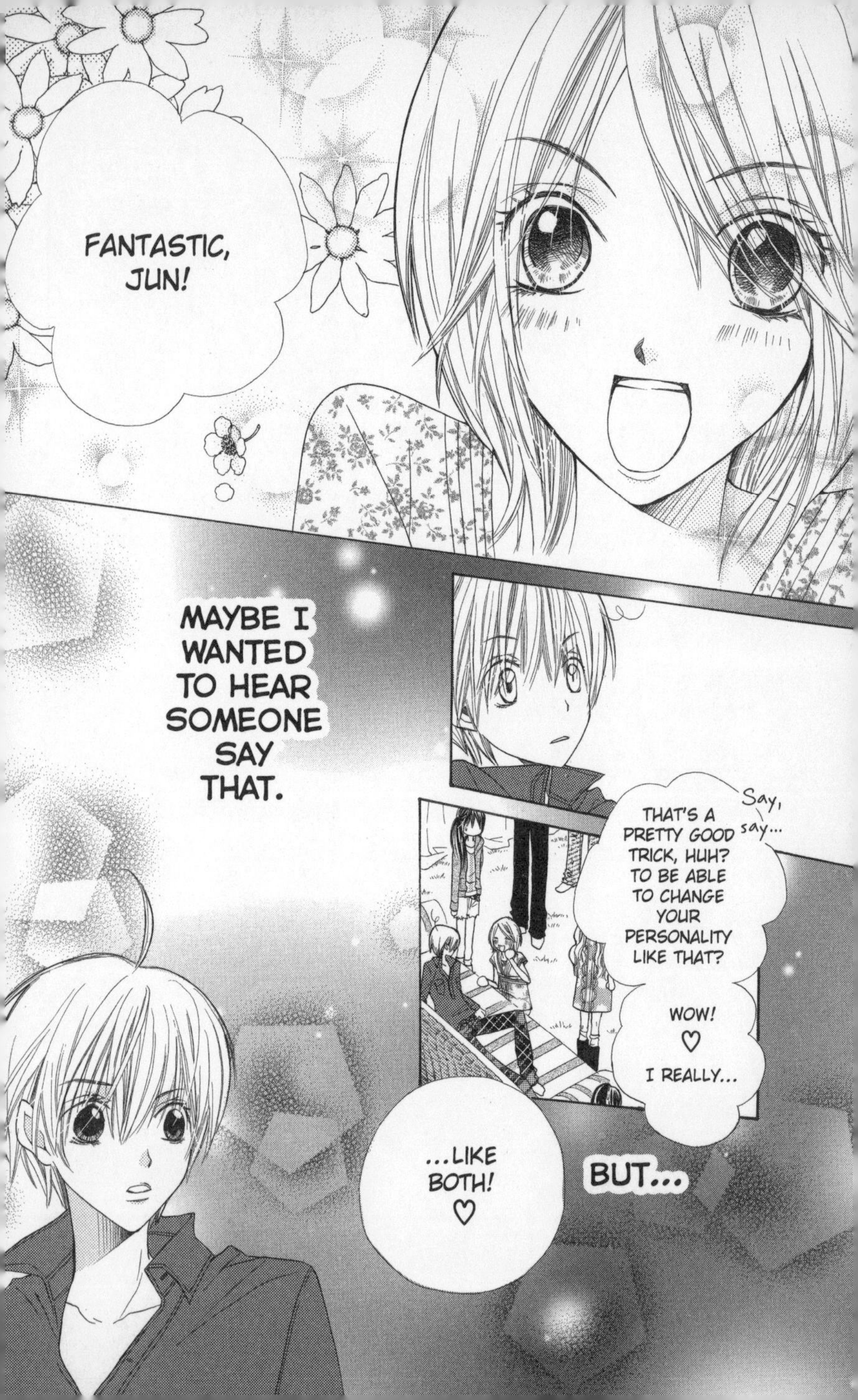
FANTASTIC, JUN!
Say, say...
THAT'S A PRETTY GOOD TRICK, HUH? TO BE ABLE TO CHANGE YOUR PERSONALITY LIKE THAT?
WOW! ♡ I REALLY...
...LIKE BOTH! ♡
BUT...
MAYBE I WANTED TO HEAR SOMEONE SAY THAT.

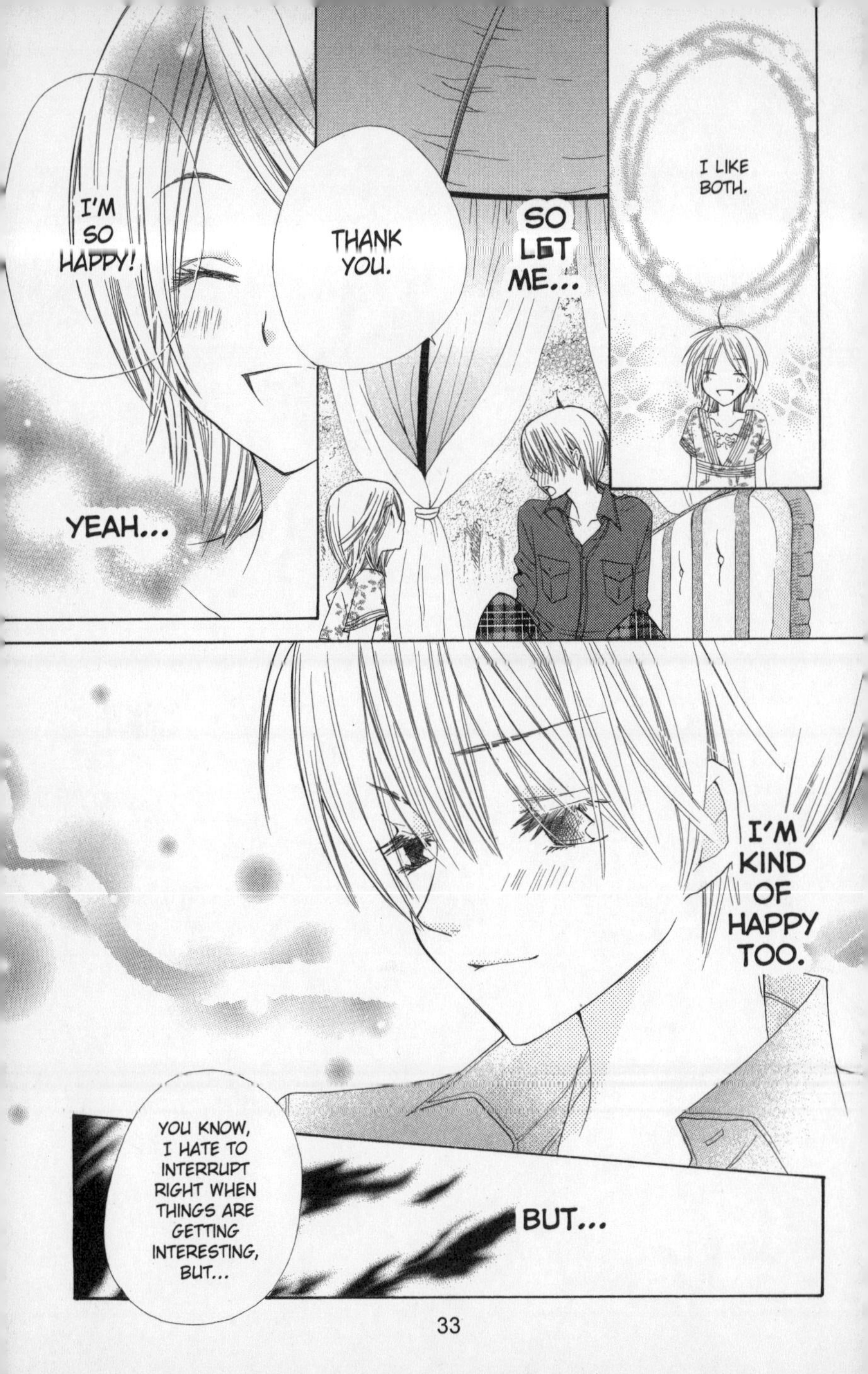
I LIKE BOTH.
SO LET ME...
THANK YOU.
I'M SO HAPPY!
YEAH...
I'M KIND OF HAPPY TOO.
BUT...
YOU KNOW, I HATE TO INTERRUPT RIGHT WHEN THINGS ARE GETTING INTERESTING, BUT...

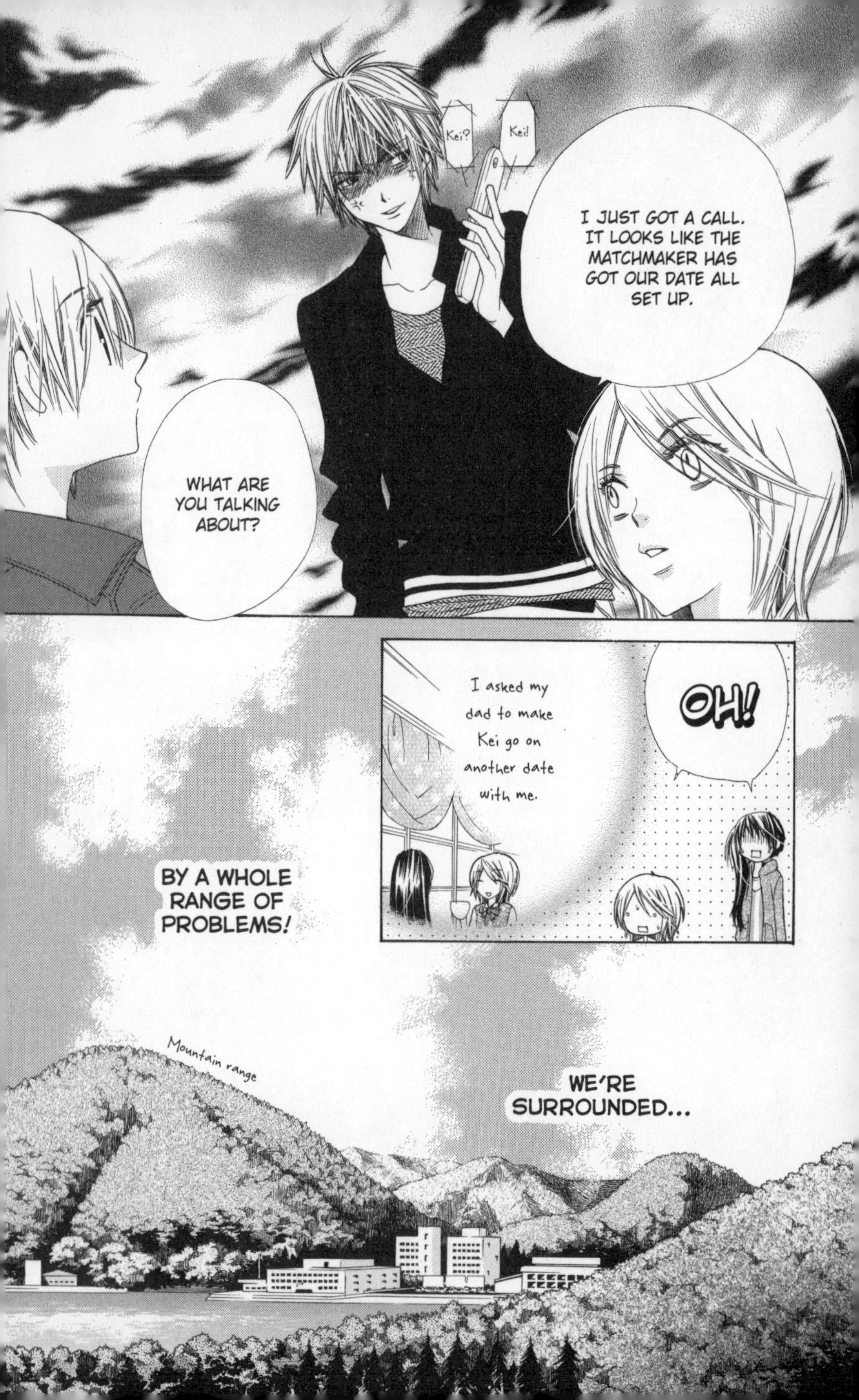
Kei!
Kei?
I JUST GOT A CALL. IT LOOKS LIKE THE MATCHMAKER HAS GOT OUR DATE ALL SET UP.
WHAT ARE YOU TALKING ABOUT?
OH!
I asked my dad to make Kei go on another date with me.
WE'RE SURROUNDED...
BY A WHOLE RANGE OF PROBLEMS!
Mountain range

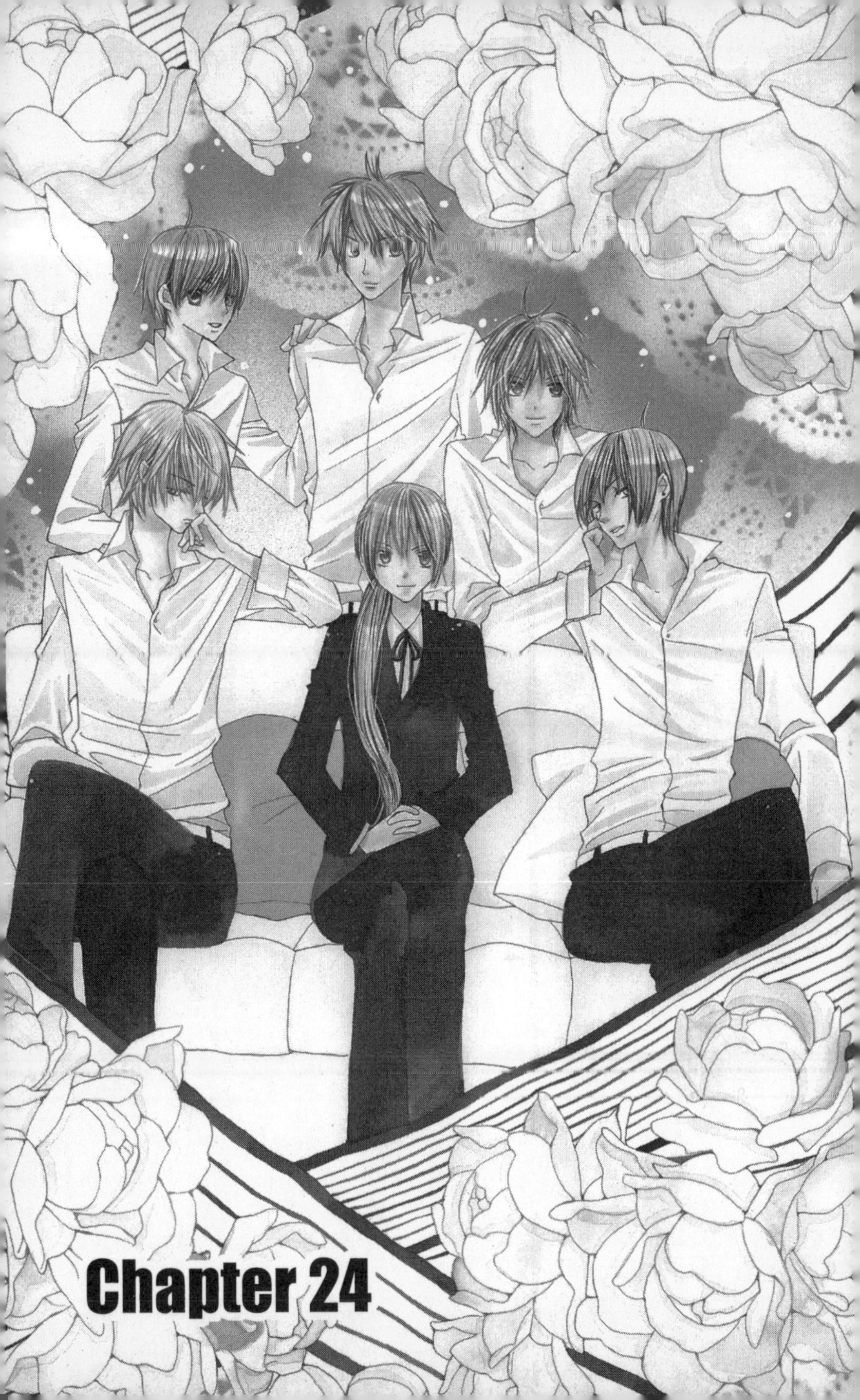
Chapter 24

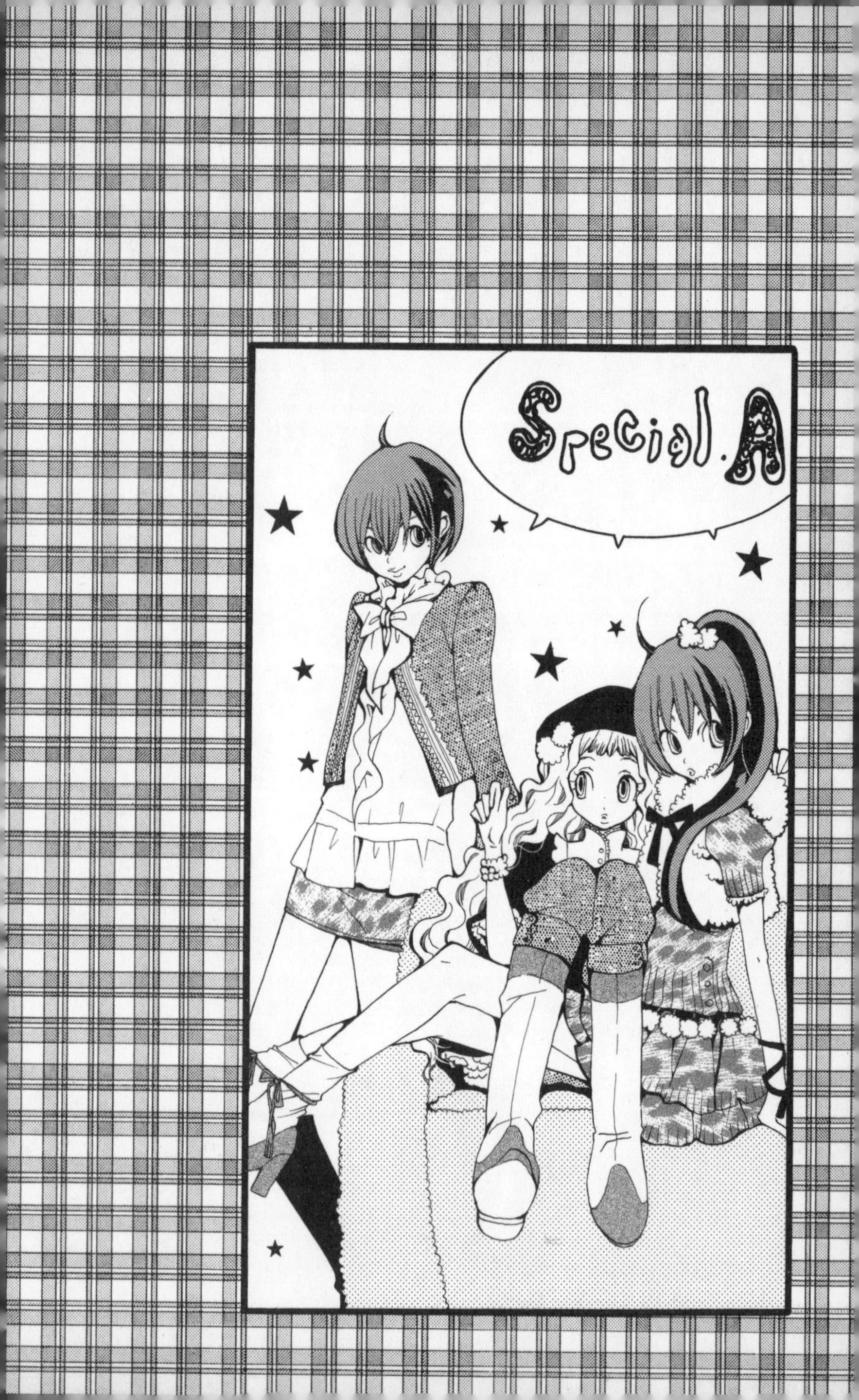
Special.A

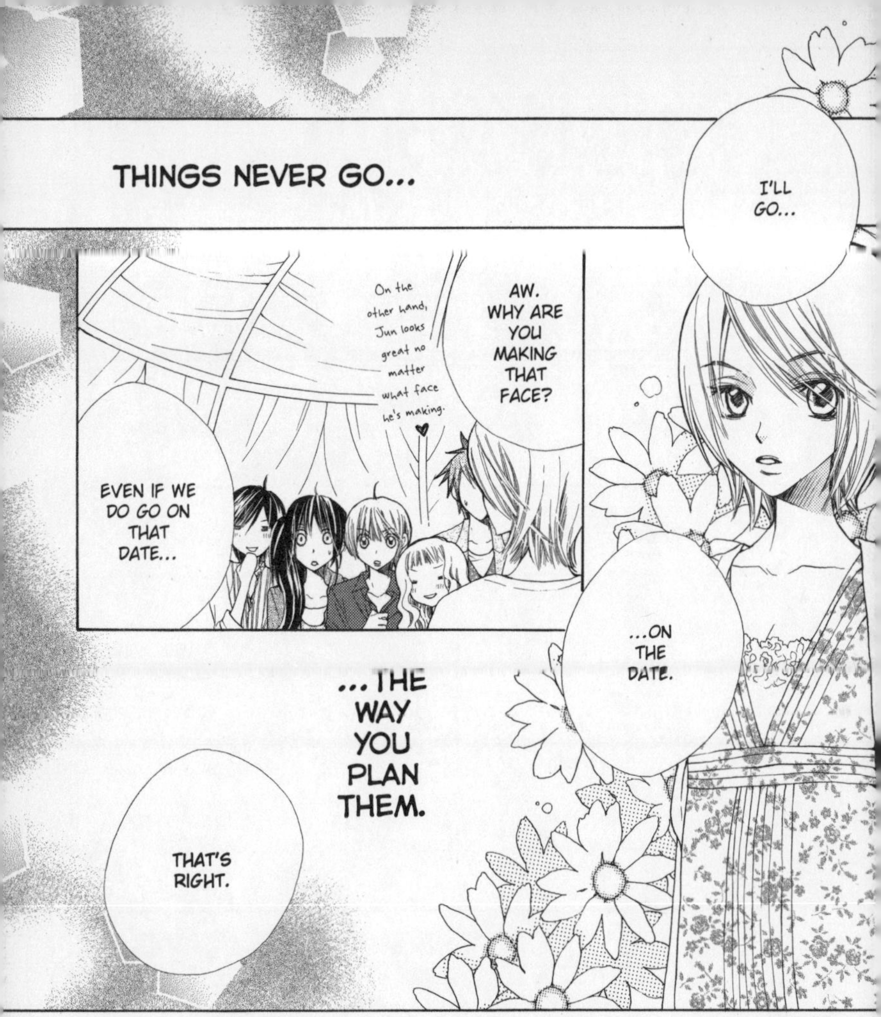
I'LL GO...
THINGS NEVER GO...
...ON THE DATE.
AW. WHY ARE YOU MAKING THAT FACE?
On the other hand, Jun looks great no matter what face he's making.
EVEN IF WE DO GO ON THAT DATE...
...THE WAY YOU PLAN THEM.
THAT'S RIGHT.

•BOOK SIGNINGS ①•

ON AUGUST 21, AT FUJI'S BUNENDO BOOKSTORE'S COMIC SQUARE, WE HELD A BOOK SIGNING. AND IT'S ALL THANKS TO YOU, AND A LOT OF OTHER PEOPLE! WHEN I FIRST HEARD I WAS SLATED TO DO A BOOK SIGNING, I WAS REALLY WORRIED. I MEAN, AN AUTOGRAPH SESSION...YOU KNOW?!! I'M GOING TO HAVE TO DO AT LEAST FIVE GOOD DEEDS A DAY OR I'M DOOMED!! HAAH HAAH HAAH HAAH HAAH HAAH

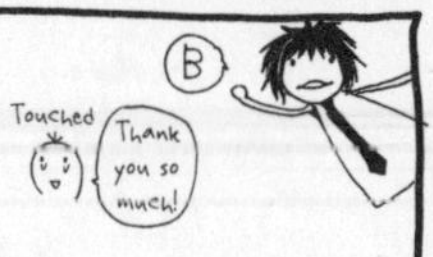
B
Touched
Thank you so much!

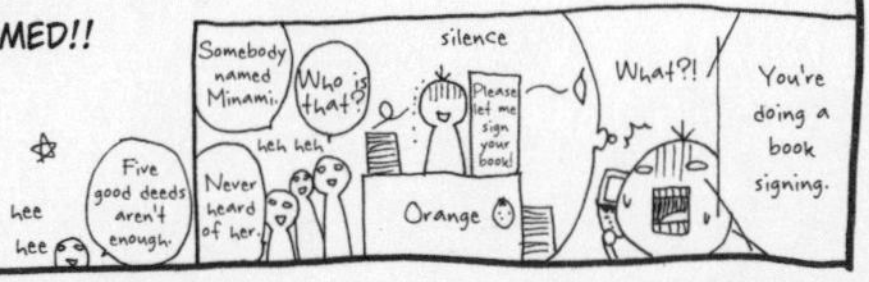
You're doing a book signing.
What?!
silence
Somebody named Minami.
Who is that?
Please let me sign your book!
Orange
heh heh
Never heard of her.
Five good deeds aren't enough.
hee hee

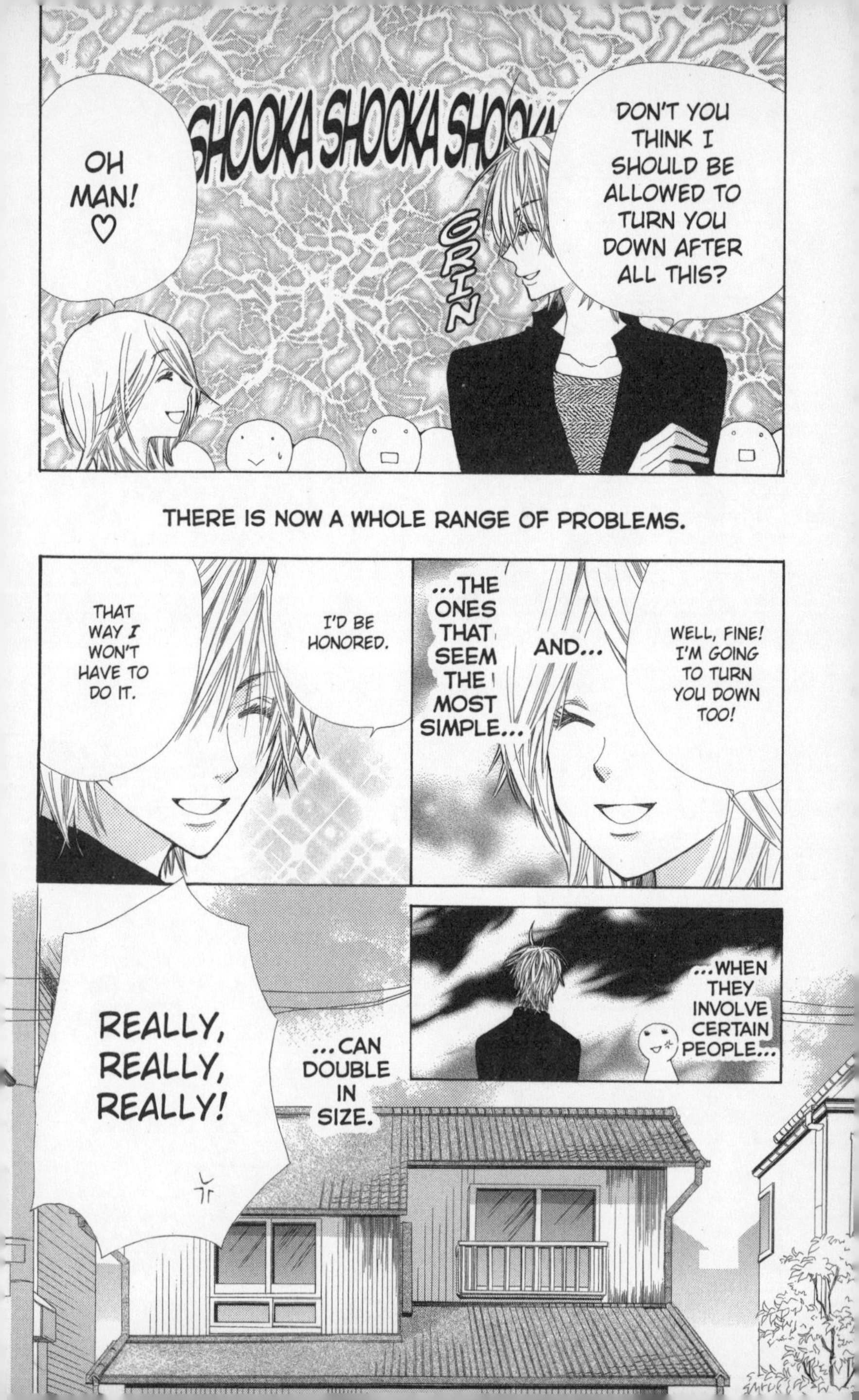
DON'T YOU THINK I SHOULD BE ALLOWED TO TURN YOU DOWN AFTER ALL THIS?
GRIN
SHOOKA SHOOKA
OH MAN! ♡
THERE IS NOW A WHOLE RANGE OF PROBLEMS.
WELL, FINE! I'M GOING TO TURN YOU DOWN TOO!
AND...
...THE ONES THAT SEEM THE MOST SIMPLE...
I'D BE HONORED.
THAT WAY I WON'T HAVE TO DO IT.
...WHEN THEY INVOLVE CERTAIN PEOPLE...
...CAN DOUBLE IN SIZE.
REALLY, REALLY, REALLY!

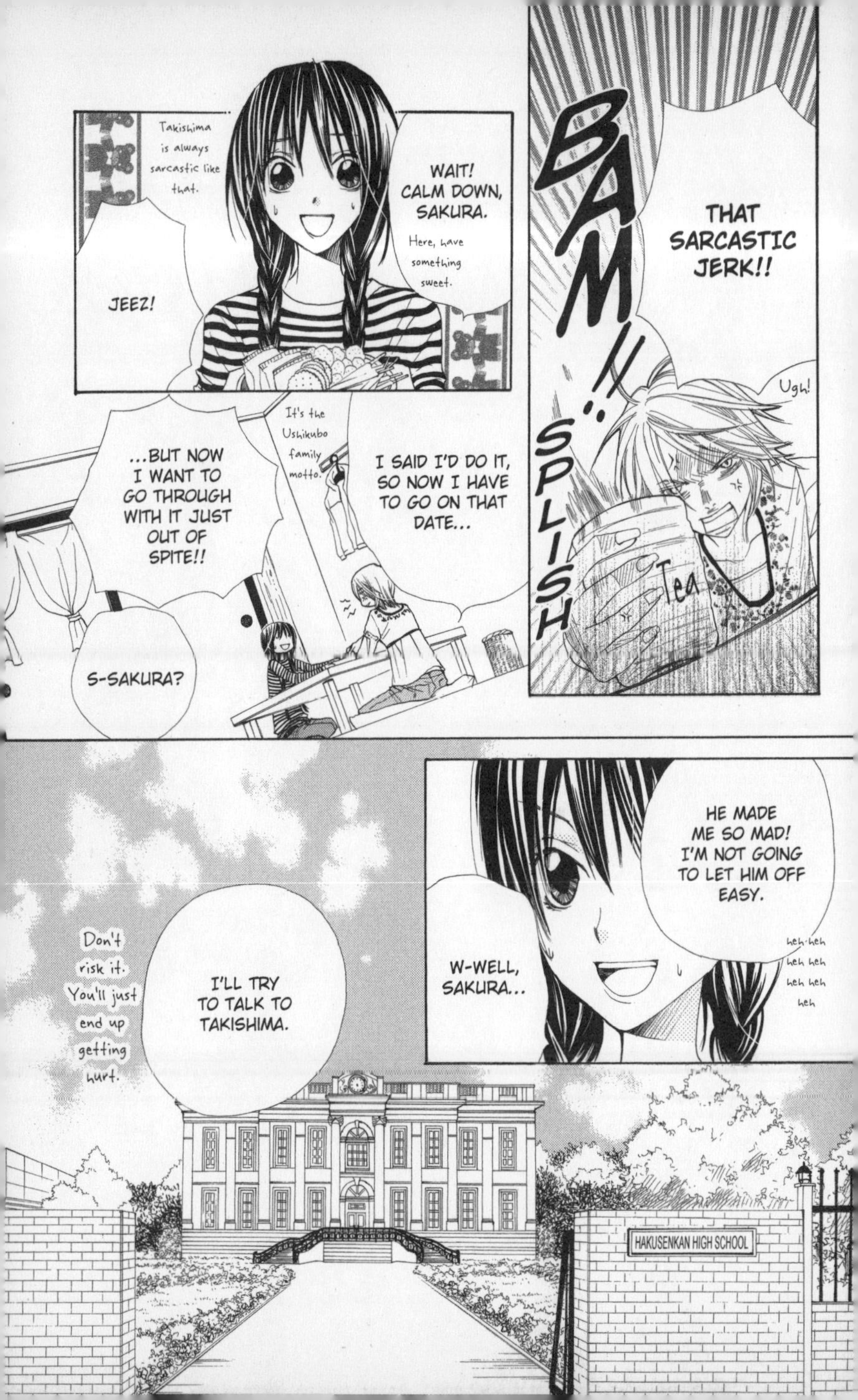
BAM!!
THAT SARCASTIC JERK!!
Ugh!
SPLISH
Tea
WAIT! CALM DOWN, SAKURA.
Here, have something sweet.
Takishima is always sarcastic like that.
JEEZ!
I SAID I'D DO IT, SO NOW I HAVE TO GO ON THAT DATE...
It's the Ushikubo family motto.
...BUT NOW I WANT TO GO THROUGH WITH IT JUST OUT OF SPITE!!
S-SAKURA?
HE MADE ME SO MAD! I'M NOT GOING TO LET HIM OFF EASY.
heh heh heh heh heh heh heh
W-WELL, SAKURA...
I'LL TRY TO TALK TO TAKISHIMA.
Don't risk it. You'll just end up getting hurt.
HAKUSENKAN HIGH SCHOOL

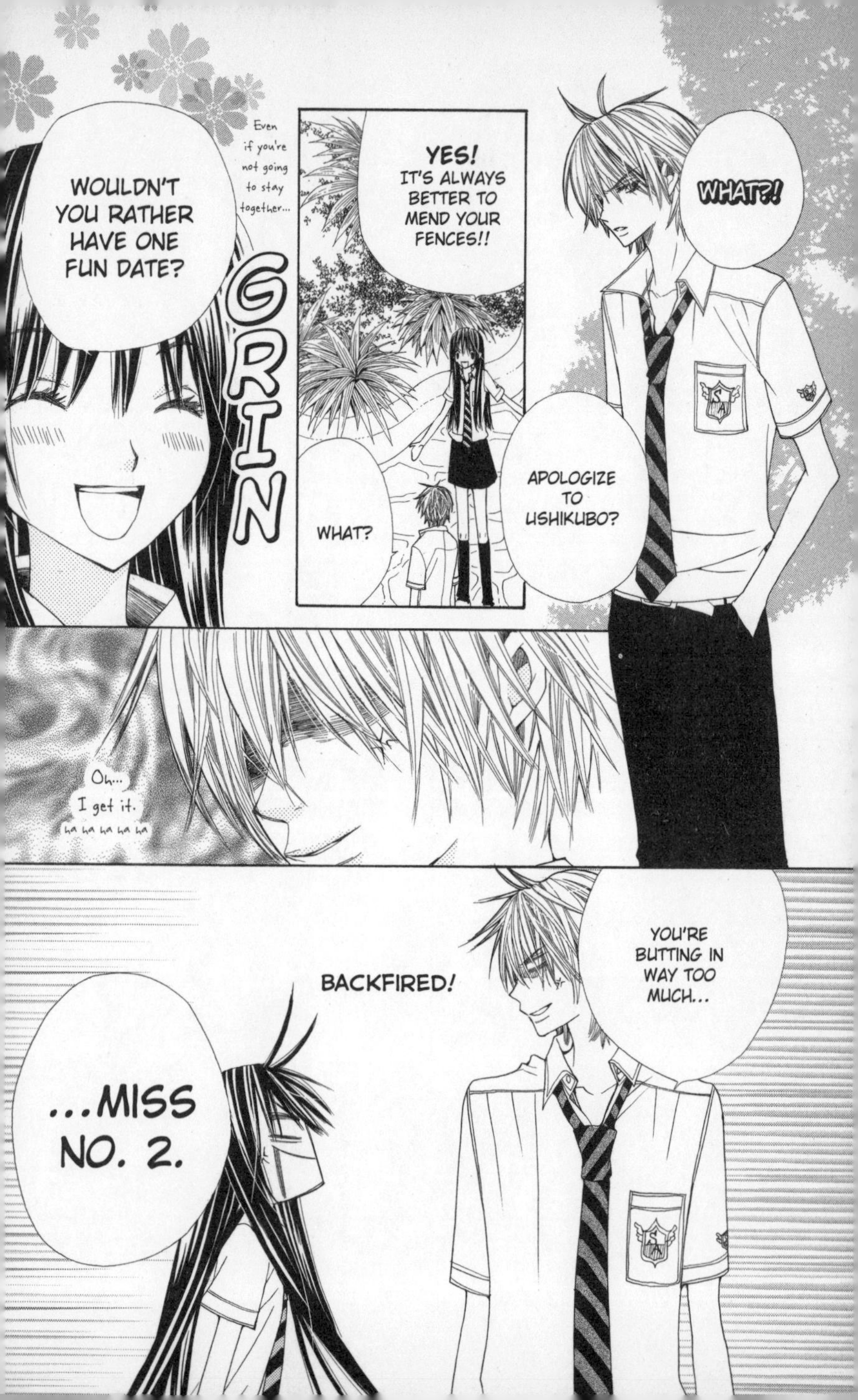
WHAT?!
APOLOGIZE TO USHIKUBO?
YES! IT'S ALWAYS BETTER TO MEND YOUR FENCES!!
WHAT?
Even if you're not going to stay together...
WOULDN'T YOU RATHER HAVE ONE FUN DATE?
GRIN
Oh... I get it.
ha ha ha ha ha
YOU'RE BUTTING IN WAY TOO MUCH...
BACKFIRED!
...MISS NO. 2.

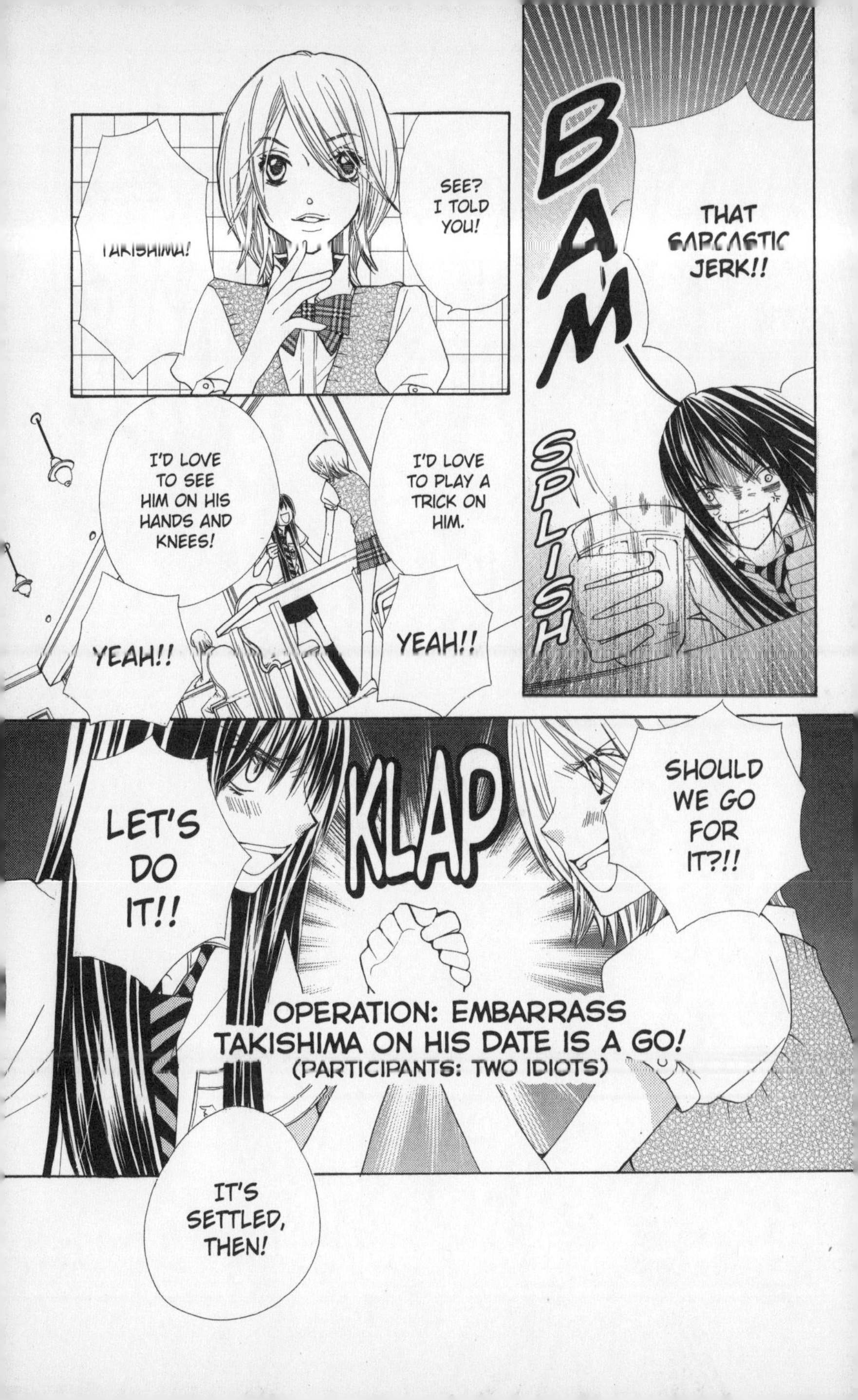
BAM
THAT SARCASTIC JERK!!
SPLISH
SEE? I TOLD YOU!
TAKISHIMA!
I'D LOVE TO PLAY A TRICK ON HIM.
I'D LOVE TO SEE HIM ON HIS HANDS AND KNEES!
YEAH!!
YEAH!!
SHOULD WE GO FOR IT?!!
KLAP
LET'S DO IT!!
OPERATION: EMBARRASS TAKISHIMA ON HIS DATE IS A GO!
(PARTICIPANTS: TWO IDIOTS)
IT'S SETTLED, THEN!

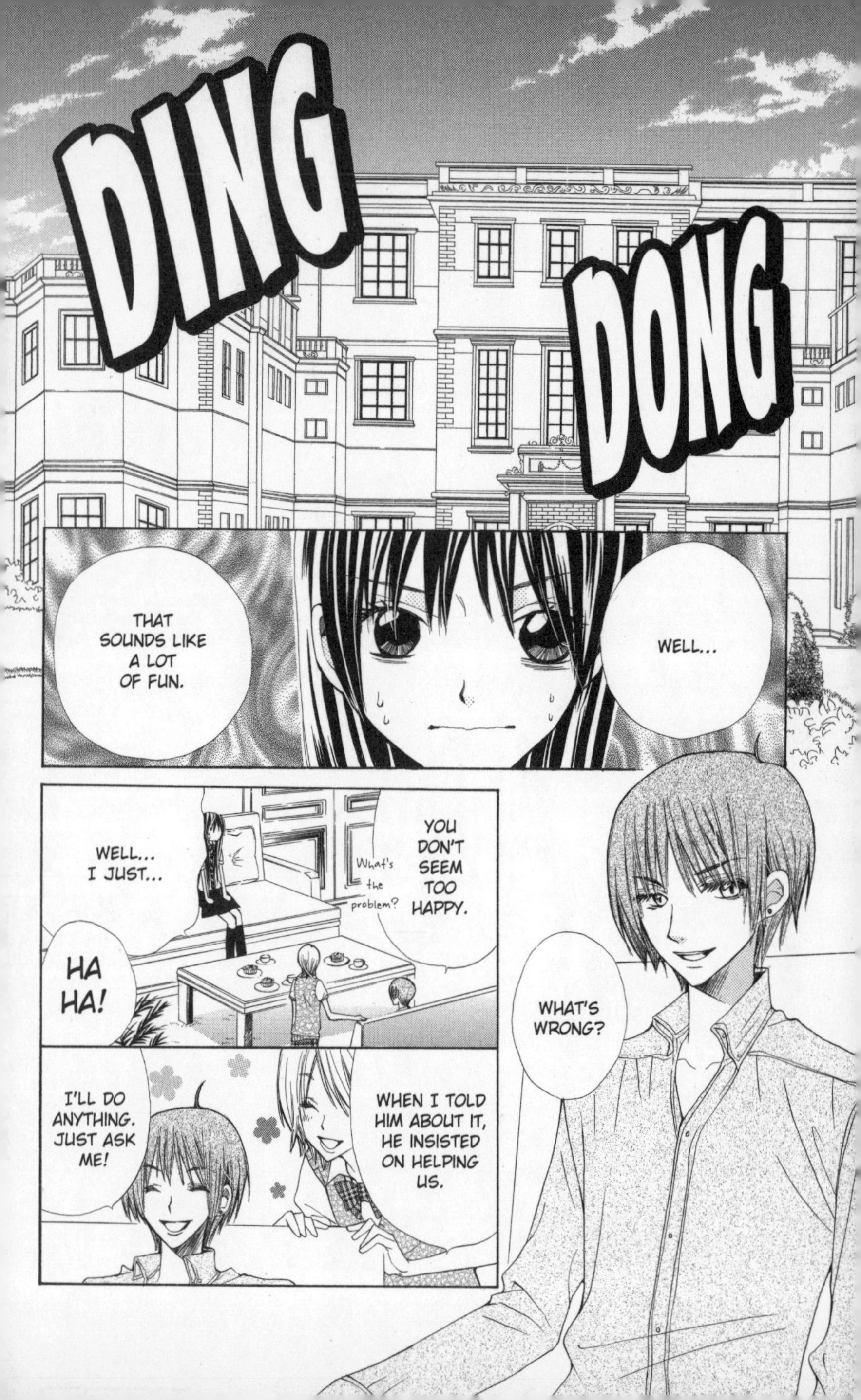
DING
DONG
WELL...
THAT SOUNDS LIKE A LOT OF FUN.
WHAT'S WRONG?
YOU DON'T SEEM TOO HAPPY.
What's the problem?
WELL... I JUST...
HA HA!
WHEN I TOLD HIM ABOUT IT, HE INSISTED ON HELPING US.
I'LL DO ANYTHING. JUST ASK ME!

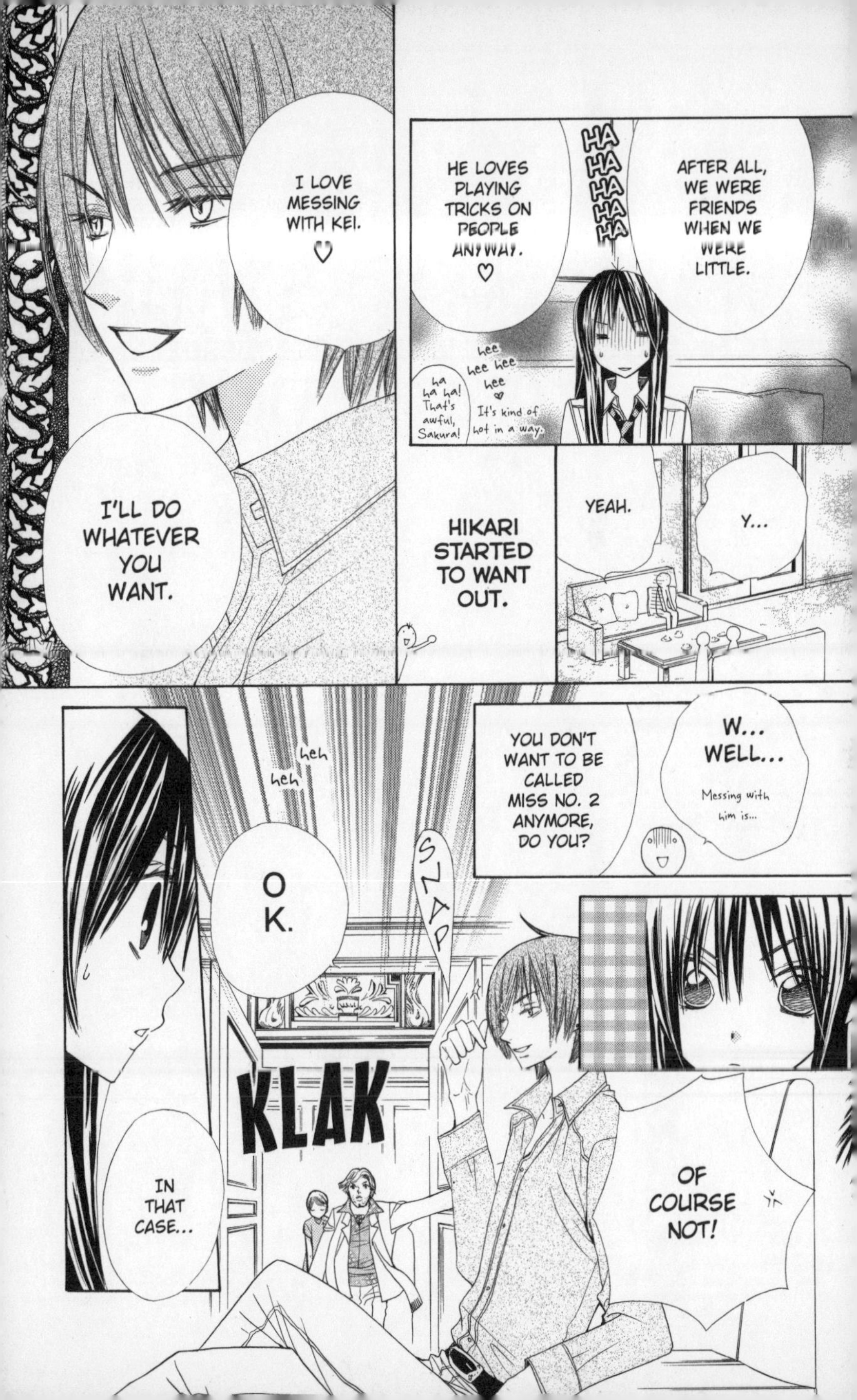
AFTER ALL, WE WERE FRIENDS WHEN WE WERE LITTLE.
HA HA HA HA HA
HE LOVES PLAYING TRICKS ON PEOPLE ANYWAY. ♡
hee hee hee hee ♡
It's kind of hot in a way.
ha ha ha! That's awful, Sakura!
Y...
YEAH.
HIKARI STARTED TO WANT OUT.
I LOVE MESSING WITH KEI. ♡
I'LL DO WHATEVER YOU WANT.
W... WELL...
Messing with him is...
YOU DON'T WANT TO BE CALLED MISS NO. 2 ANYMORE, DO YOU?
OF COURSE NOT!
SNAP
heh heh
OK.
KLAK
IN THAT CASE...

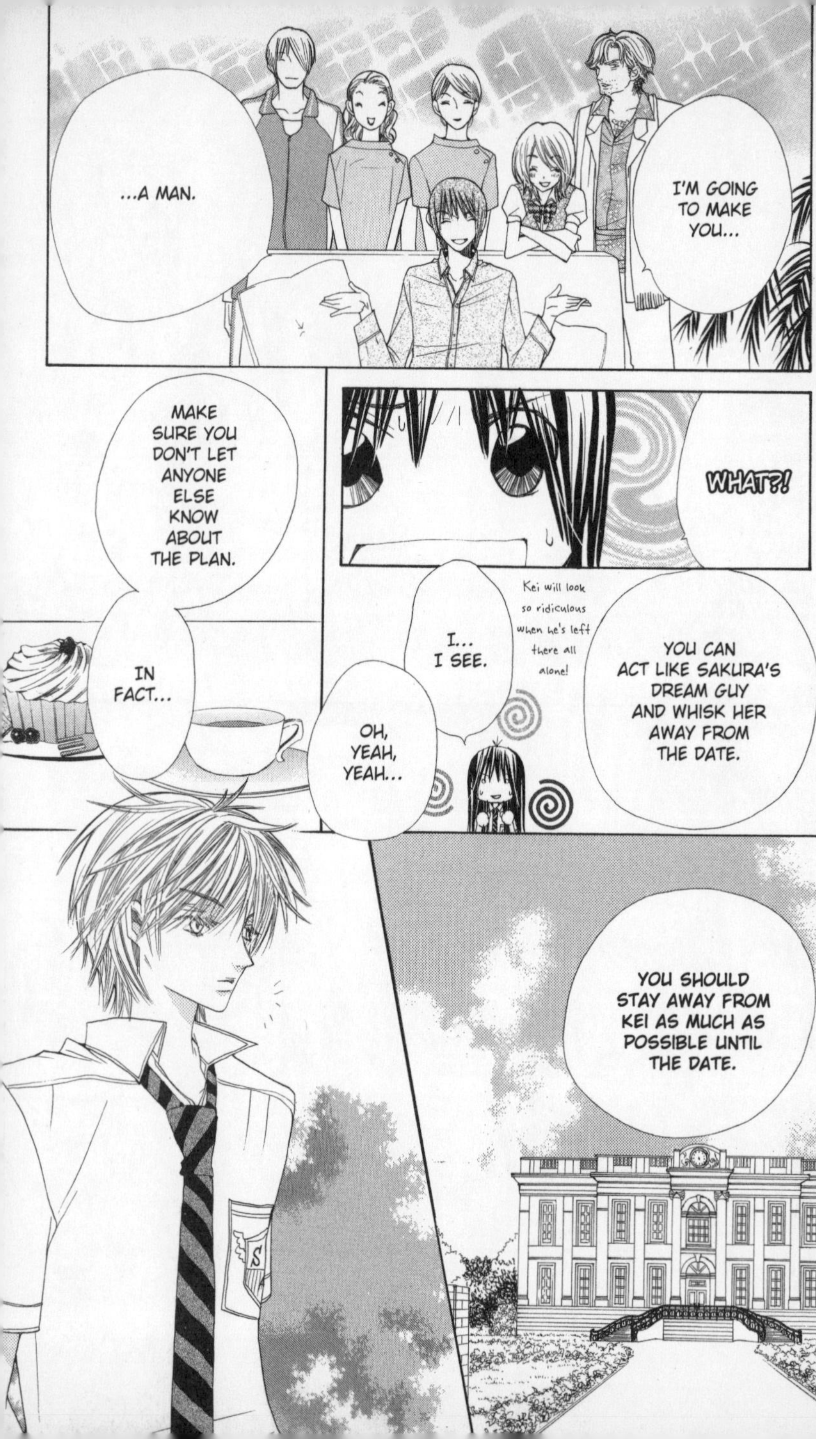

I'M GOING TO MAKE YOU...
...A MAN.
WHAT?!
YOU CAN ACT LIKE SAKURA'S DREAM GUY AND WHISK HER AWAY FROM THE DATE.
I... I SEE.
Kei will look so ridiculous when he's left there all alone!
OH, YEAH, YEAH...
MAKE SURE YOU DON'T LET ANYONE ELSE KNOW ABOUT THE PLAN.
IN FACT...
YOU SHOULD STAY AWAY FROM KEI AS MUCH AS POSSIBLE UNTIL THE DATE.

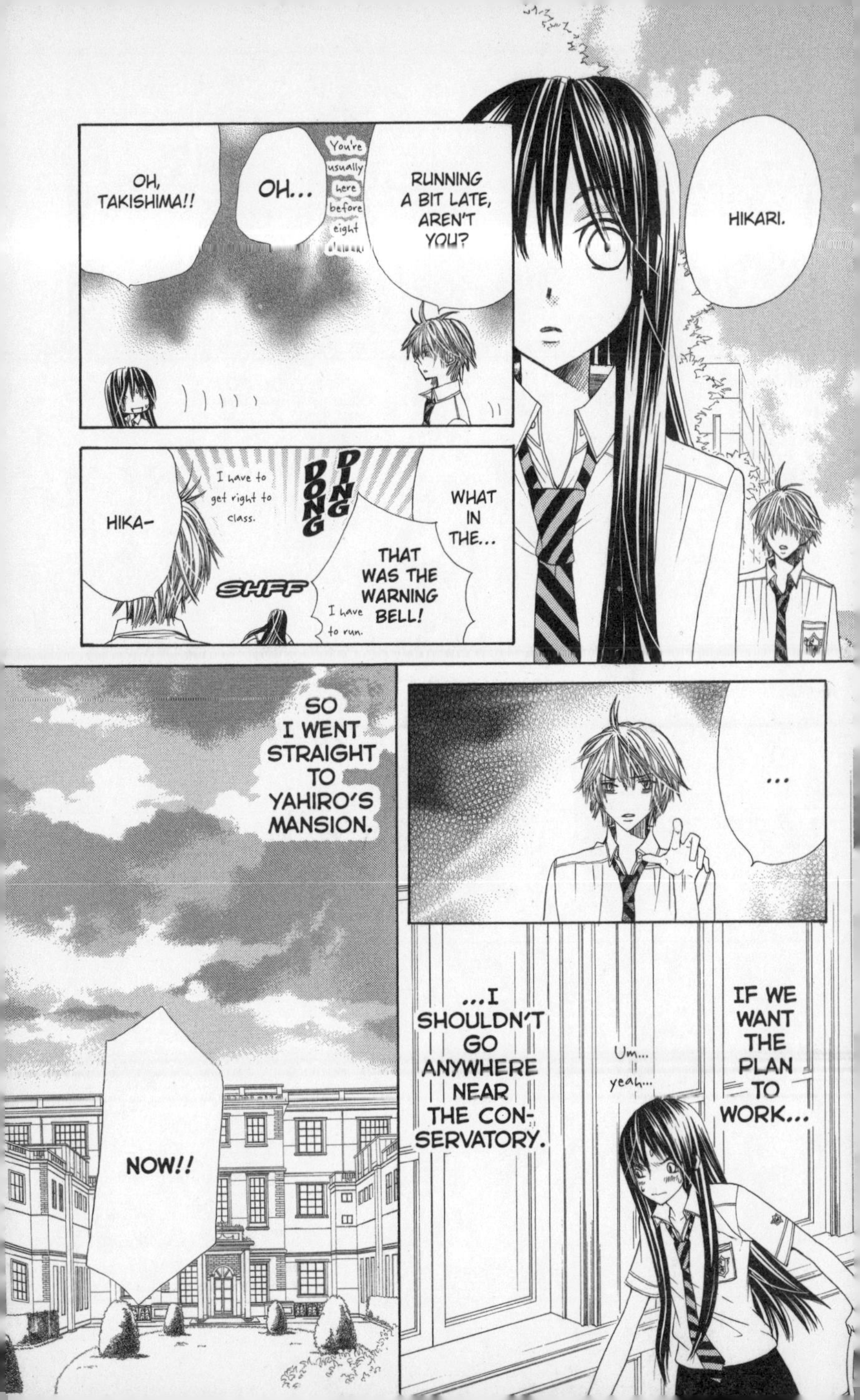
HIKARI.
RUNNING A BIT LATE, AREN'T YOU?
You're usually here before eight
OH...
OH, TAKISHIMA!!
WHAT IN THE...
DING DONG
THAT WAS THE WARNING BELL!
I have to run.
SHFF
I have to get right to class.
HIKA-
...
IF WE WANT THE PLAN TO WORK...
Um... yeah...
...I SHOULDN'T GO ANYWHERE NEAR THE CON-SERVATORY.
SO I WENT STRAIGHT TO YAHIRO'S MANSION.
NOW!!

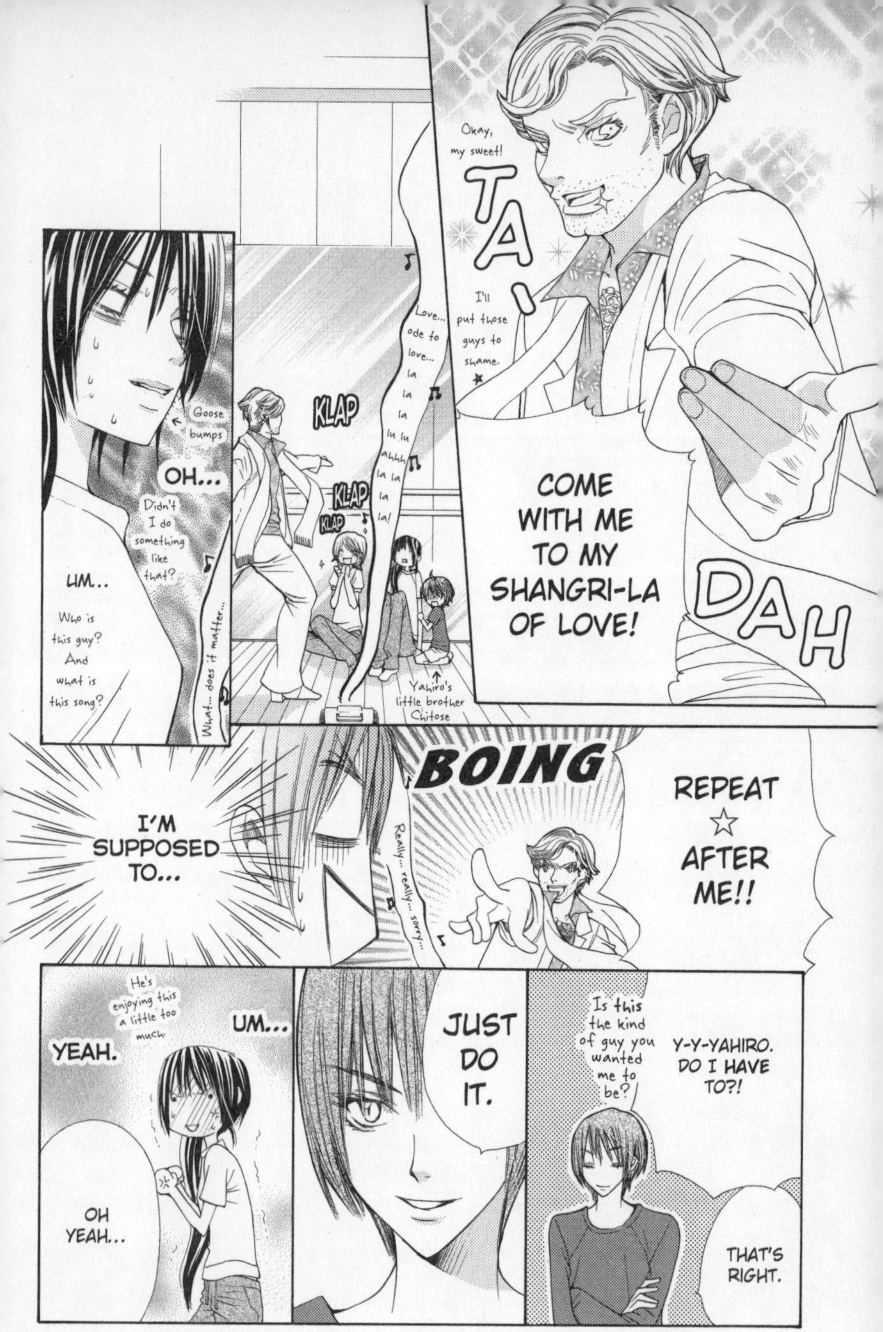

Okay, my sweet!
TA-DAH
I'll put those guys to shame.
COME WITH ME TO MY SHANGRI-LA OF LOVE!
Love... ode to love... la la la lu lu ahhh la la la la!
KLAP
KLAP
KLAP
Yahiro's little brother Chitose
Goose bumps
OH...
Didn't I do something like that?
UM...
Who is this guy? And what is this song?
What... does it matter...
REPEAT ☆ AFTER ME!!
BOING
Really... really... sorry...
I'M SUPPOSED TO...
Y-Y-YAHIRO. DO I HAVE TO?!
Is this the kind of guy you wanted me to be?
THAT'S RIGHT.
JUST DO IT.
UM...
He's enjoying this a little too much
YEAH.
OH YEAH...

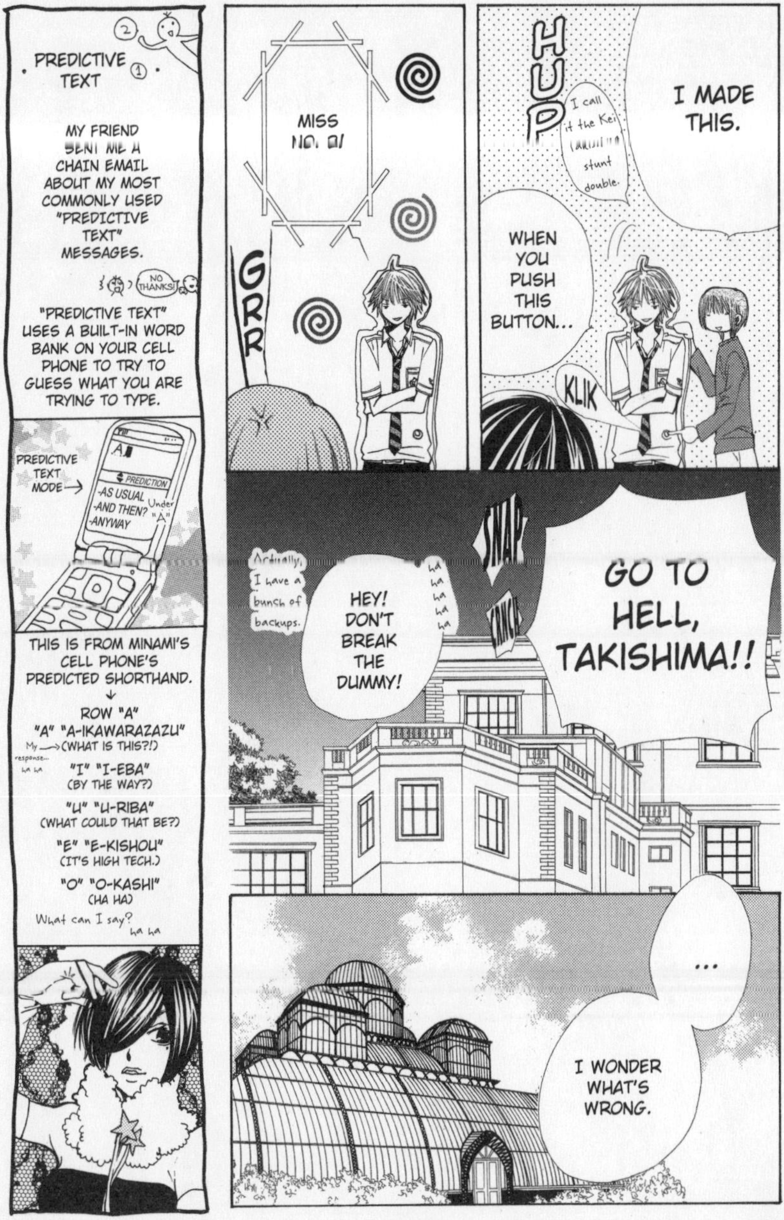

I MADE THIS.
HUP
I call it the Kei
stunt double.
WHEN YOU PUSH THIS BUTTON...
KLIK
MISS
GRR
SNAP
CRNCH
GO TO HELL, TAKISHIMA!!
ha ha ha ha ha
HEY! DON'T BREAK THE DUMMY!
Actually, I have a bunch of backups.
...
I WONDER WHAT'S WRONG.
PREDICTIVE TEXT
MY FRIEND SENT ME A CHAIN EMAIL ABOUT MY MOST COMMONLY USED "PREDICTIVE TEXT" MESSAGES.
NO THANKS!
"PREDICTIVE TEXT" USES A BUILT-IN WORD BANK ON YOUR CELL PHONE TO TRY TO GUESS WHAT YOU ARE TRYING TO TYPE.
PREDICTIVE TEXT MODE
A
PREDICTION
-AS USUAL
-AND THEN?
-ANYWAY
Under "A"
THIS IS FROM MINAMI'S CELL PHONE'S PREDICTED SHORTHAND.
ROW "A"
"A" "A-IKAWARAZAZU"
My response... ha ha
(WHAT IS THIS?!)
"I" "I-EBA"
(BY THE WAY?)
"U" "U-RIBA"
(WHAT COULD THAT BE?)
"E" "E-KISHOU"
(IT'S HIGH TECH.)
"O" "O-KASHI"
(HA HA)
What can I say? ha ha

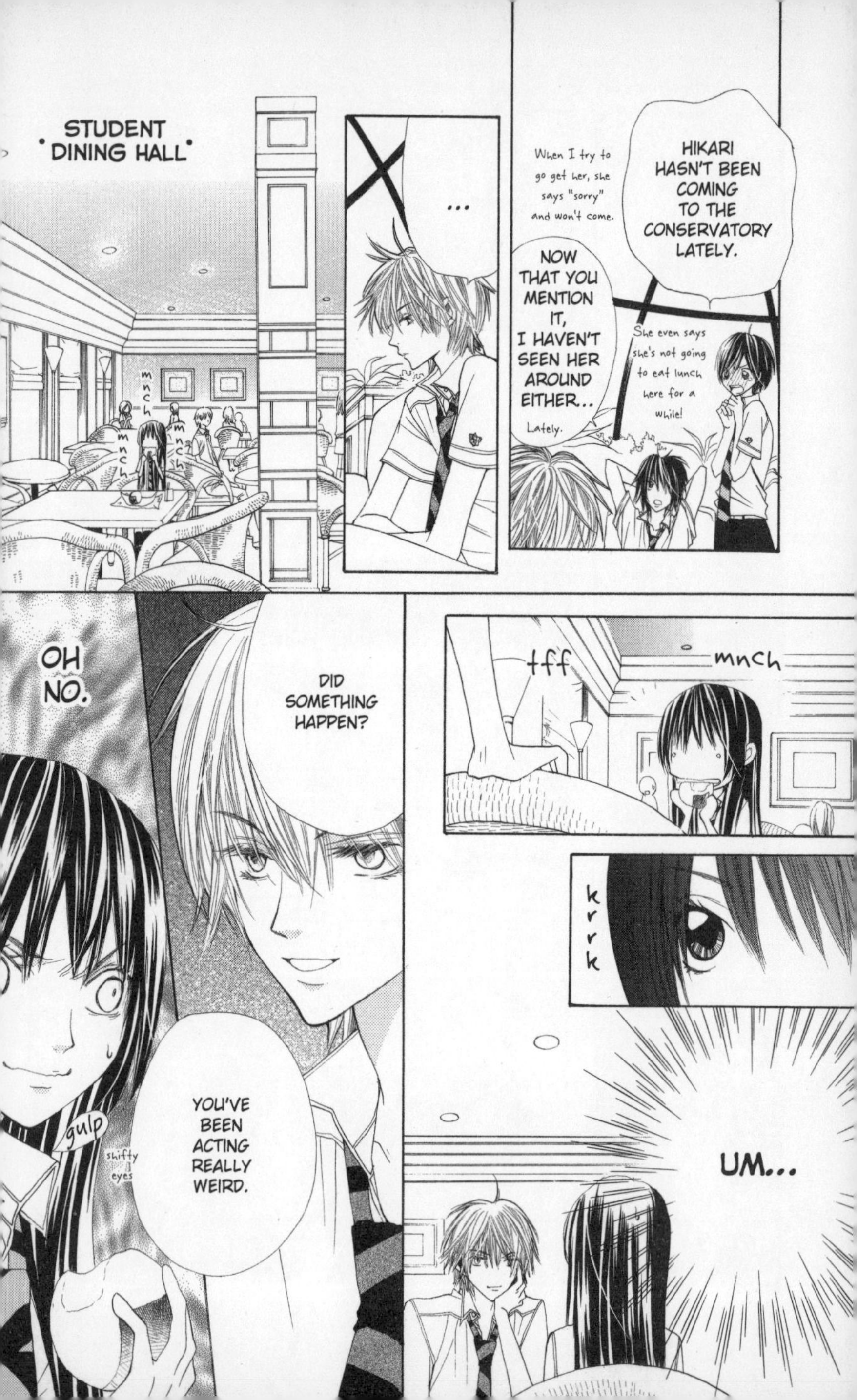
HIKARI HASN'T BEEN COMING TO THE CONSERVATORY LATELY.
When I try to go get her, she says "sorry" and won't come.
She even says she's not going to eat lunch here for a while!
NOW THAT YOU MENTION IT, I HAVEN'T SEEN HER AROUND EITHER...
Lately.
...
STUDENT DINING HALL
mnch
mnch
mnch
mnch
tff
krrk
UM...
DID SOMETHING HAPPEN?
YOU'VE BEEN ACTING REALLY WEIRD.
OH NO.
gulp
shifty eyes

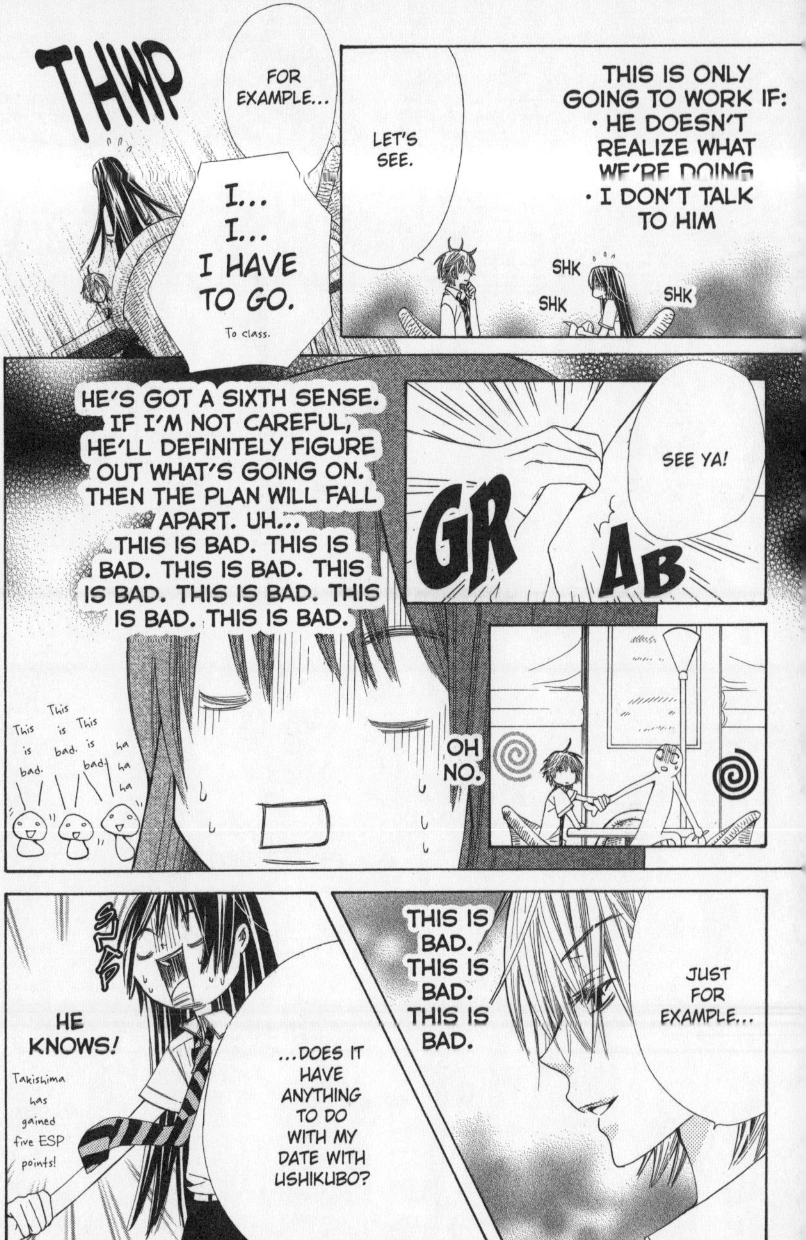
THIS IS ONLY GOING TO WORK IF:
· HE DOESN'T REALIZE WHAT WE'RE DOING
· I DON'T TALK TO HIM
LET'S SEE.
FOR EXAMPLE...
SHK
SHK
SHK
THWP
I... I... I HAVE TO GO.
To class.
SEE YA!
GR AB
OH NO.
HE'S GOT A SIXTH SENSE. IF I'M NOT CAREFUL, HE'LL DEFINITELY FIGURE OUT WHAT'S GOING ON. THEN THE PLAN WILL FALL APART. UH... THIS IS BAD. THIS IS BAD. THIS IS BAD. THIS IS BAD. THIS IS BAD. THIS IS BAD. THIS IS BAD.
This is bad.
This is bad.
This is bad.
ha ha ha
JUST FOR EXAMPLE...
THIS IS BAD. THIS IS BAD. THIS IS BAD.
...DOES IT HAVE ANYTHING TO DO WITH MY DATE WITH USHIKUBO?
HE KNOWS!
Takishima has gained five ESP points!

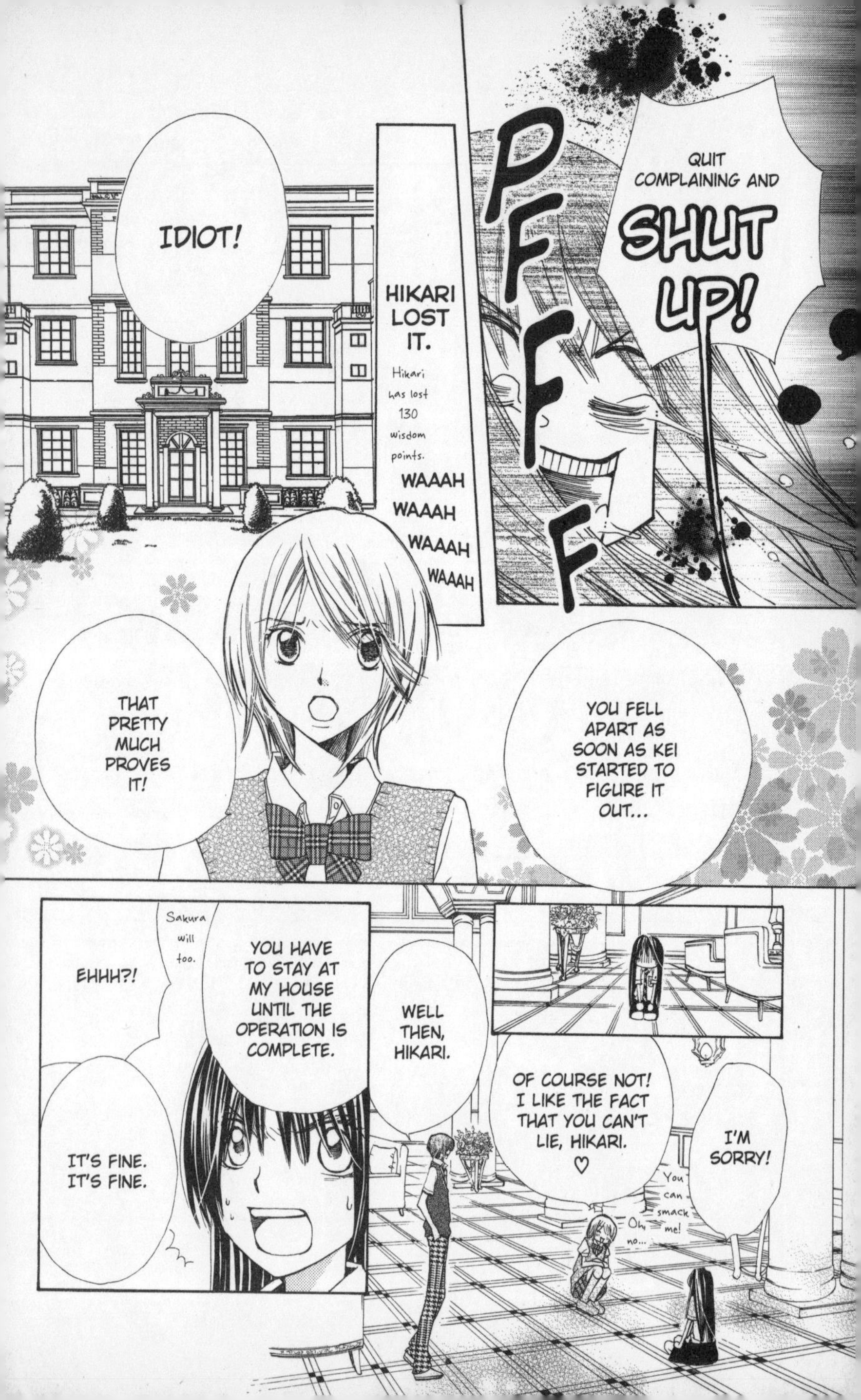
QUIT COMPLAINING AND SHUT UP!
PFFF
HIKARI LOST IT.
Hikari has lost 130 wisdom points.
WAAAH WAAAH WAAAH WAAAH
IDIOT!
YOU FELL APART AS SOON AS KEI STARTED TO FIGURE IT OUT...
THAT PRETTY MUCH PROVES IT!
I'M SORRY!
You can smack me!
Oh no...
OF COURSE NOT! I LIKE THE FACT THAT YOU CAN'T LIE, HIKARI. ♡
WELL THEN, HIKARI.
YOU HAVE TO STAY AT MY HOUSE UNTIL THE OPERATION IS COMPLETE.
Sakura will too.
EHHH?!
IT'S FINE. IT'S FINE.

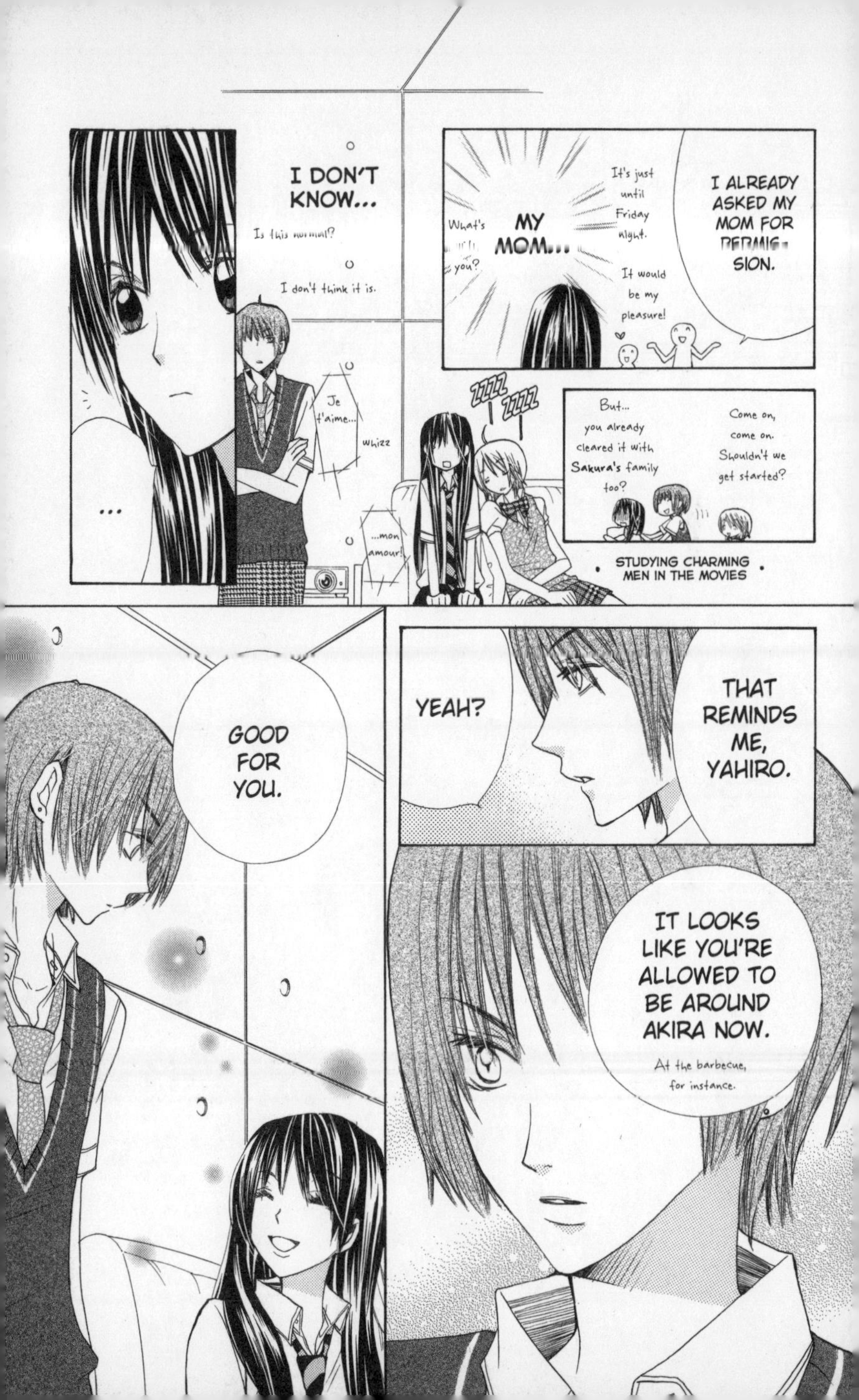

I ALREADY ASKED MY MOM FOR PERMISSION.
It's just until Friday night.
It would be my pleasure!
MY MOM...
What's
you?
Come on, come on. Shouldn't we get started?
But... you already cleared it with Sakura's family too?
STUDYING CHARMING MEN IN THE MOVIES
ZZZZ
ZZZZ
I DON'T KNOW...
Is this normal?
I don't think it is.
Je t'aime...
whizz
...mon amour!
...
THAT REMINDS ME, YAHIRO.
YEAH?
IT LOOKS LIKE YOU'RE ALLOWED TO BE AROUND AKIRA NOW.
At the barbecue, for instance.
GOOD FOR YOU.

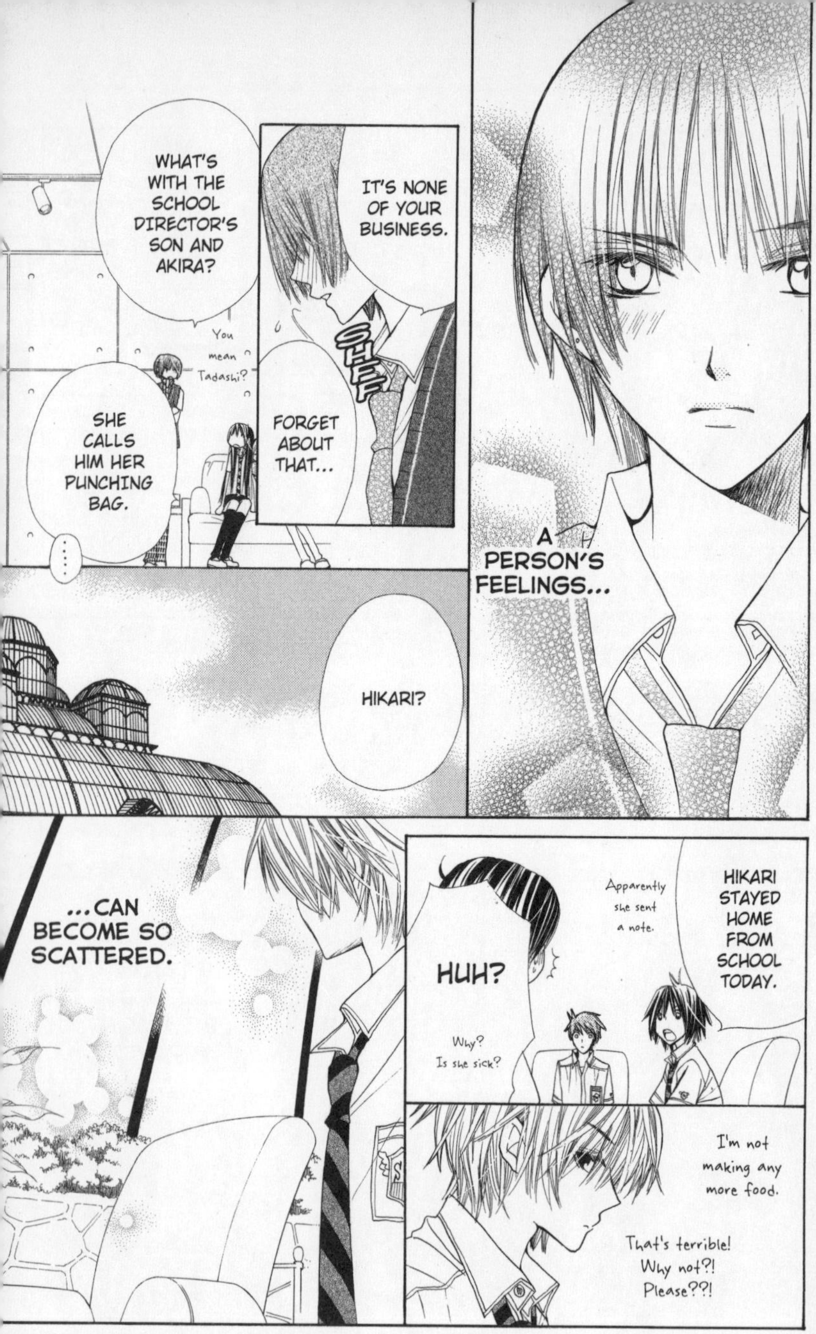
A PERSON'S FEELINGS...
WHAT'S WITH THE SCHOOL DIRECTOR'S SON AND AKIRA?
You mean Tadashi?
SHE CALLS HIM HER PUNCHING BAG.
......
IT'S NONE OF YOUR BUSINESS.
SHFF
FORGET ABOUT THAT...
HIKARI?
HIKARI STAYED HOME FROM SCHOOL TODAY.
Apparently she sent a note.
HUH?
Why? Is she sick?
I'm not making any more food.
That's terrible! Why not?! Please??!
...CAN BECOME SO SCATTERED.

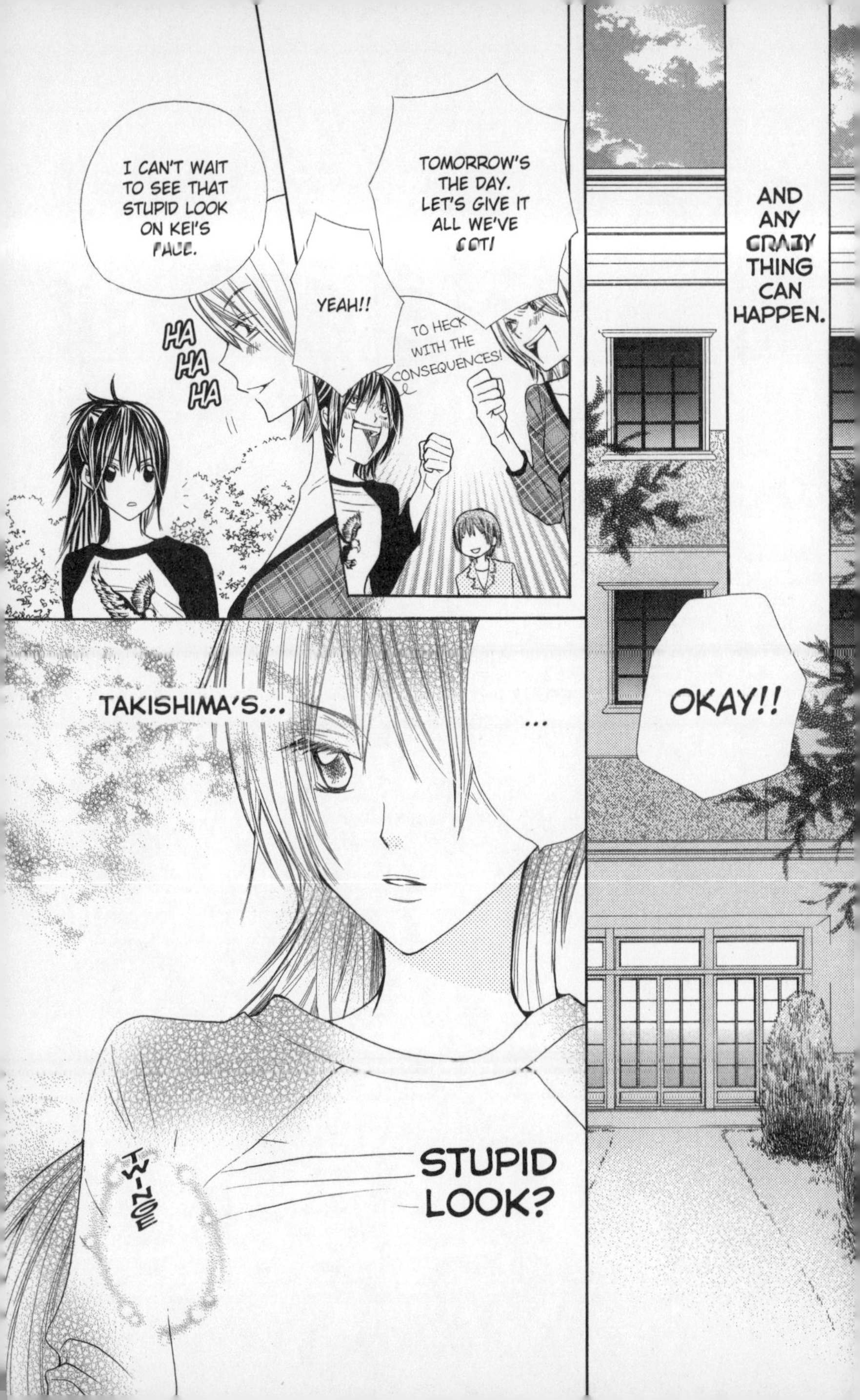

AND ANY CRAZY THING CAN HAPPEN.
OKAY!!
TOMORROW'S THE DAY. LET'S GIVE IT ALL WE'VE GOT!
YEAH!!
TO HECK WITH THE CONSEQUENCES!
I CAN'T WAIT TO SEE THAT STUPID LOOK ON KEI'S FACE.
HA HA HA
...
TAKISHIMA'S...
STUPID LOOK?
TWINGE

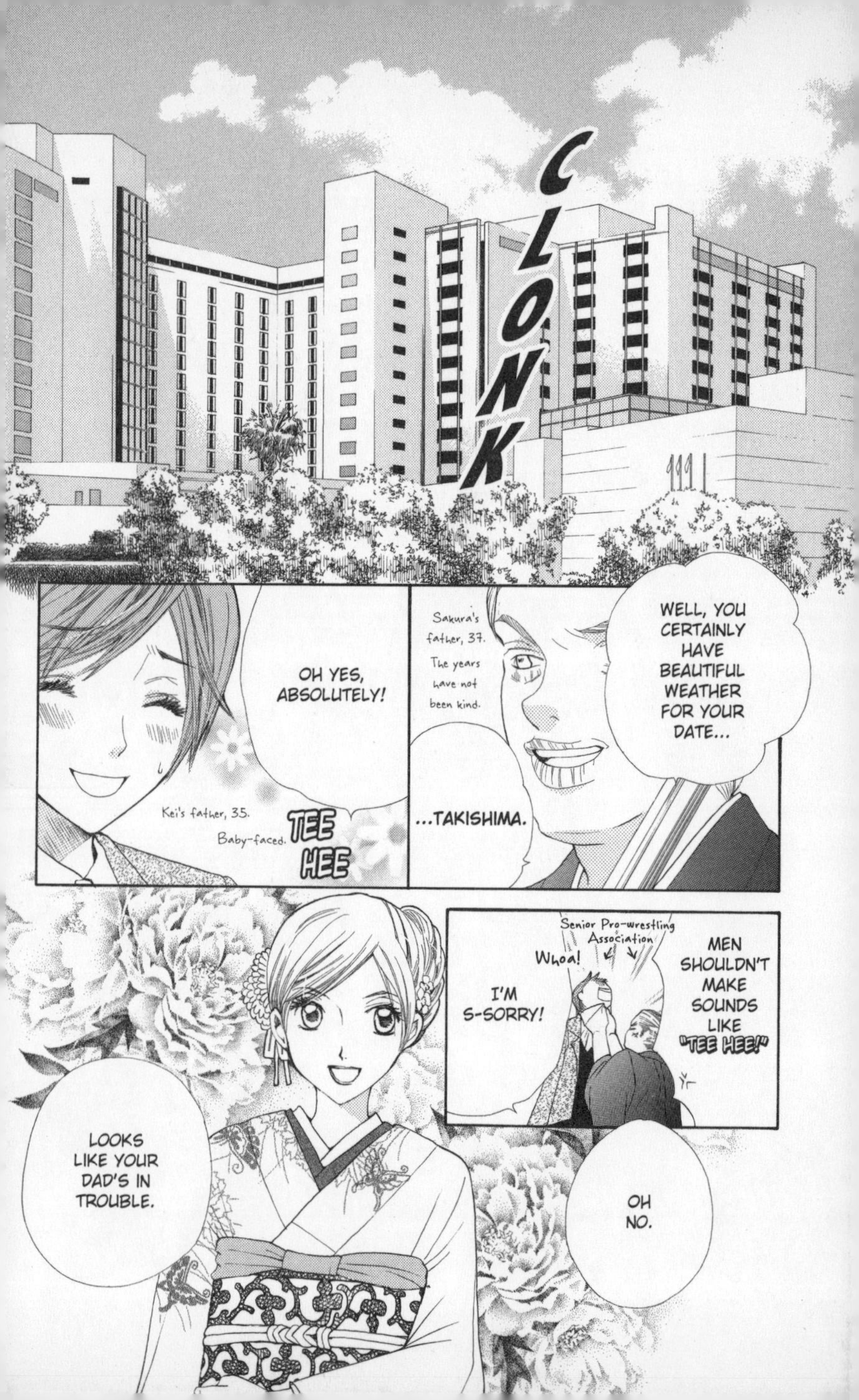
CLONK
Sakura's father, 37. The years have not been kind.
WELL, YOU CERTAINLY HAVE BEAUTIFUL WEATHER FOR YOUR DATE...
...TAKISHIMA.
OH YES, ABSOLUTELY!
TEE HEE
Kei's father, 35. Baby-faced.
MEN SHOULDN'T MAKE SOUNDS LIKE "TEE HEE!"
Senior Pro-wrestling Association
Whoa!
I'M S-SORRY!
LOOKS LIKE YOUR DAD'S IN TROUBLE.
OH NO.

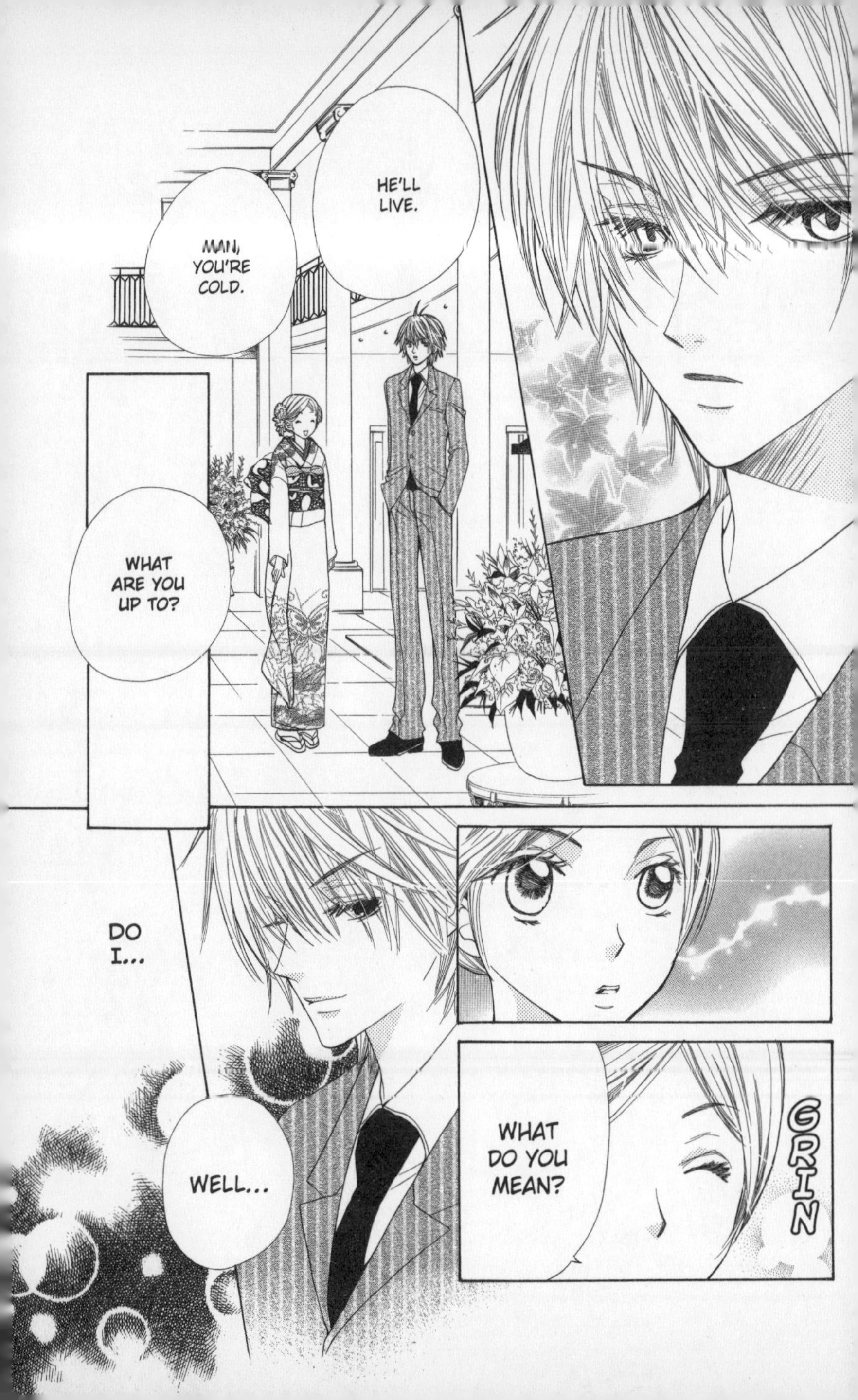
HE'LL LIVE.
MAN, YOU'RE COLD.
WHAT ARE YOU UP TO?
WHAT DO YOU MEAN?
GRIN
DO I...
WELL...

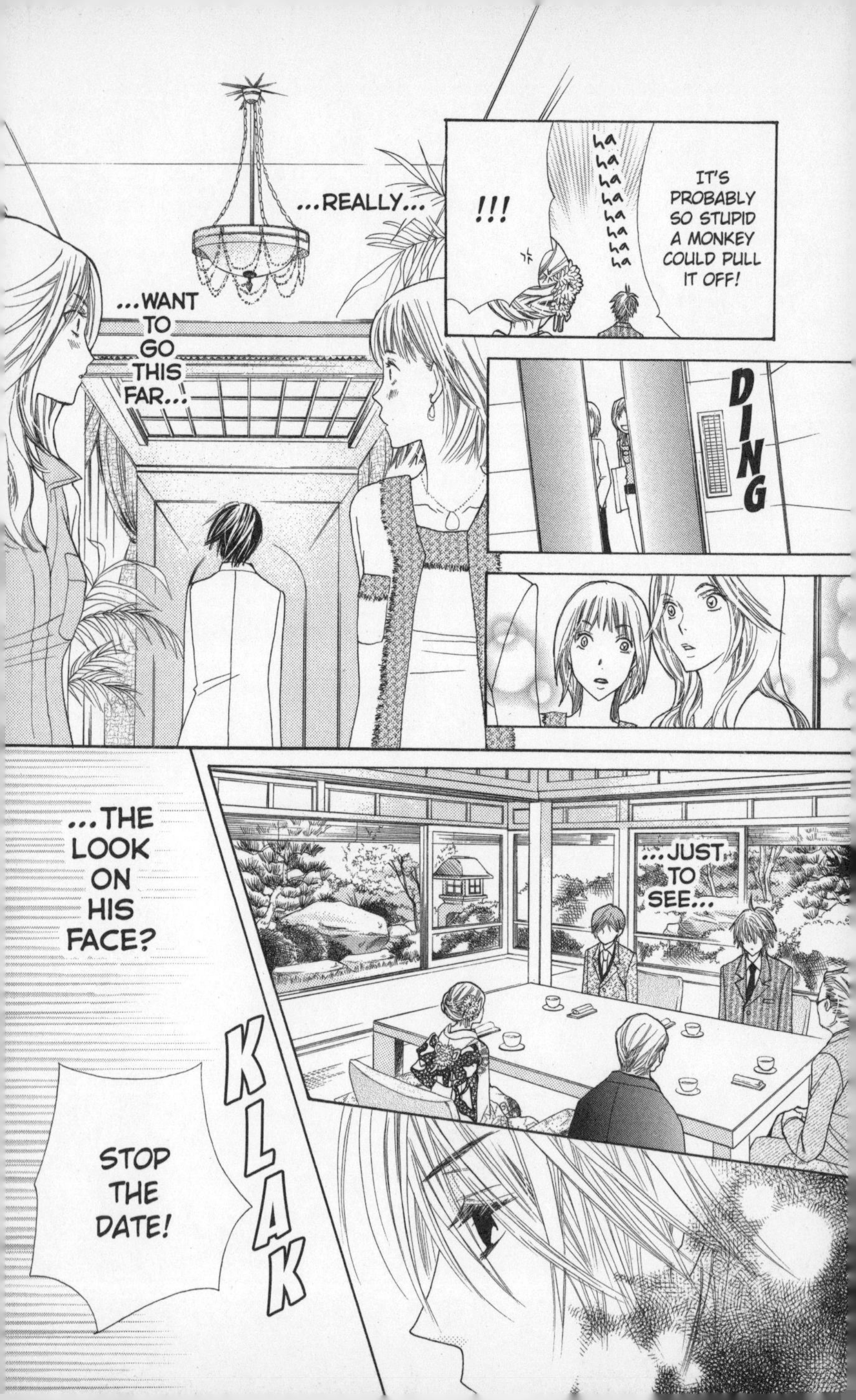
IT'S PROBABLY SO STUPID A MONKEY COULD PULL IT OFF!
ha ha ha ha ha ha ha ha
!!!
DING
...REALLY...
...WANT TO GO THIS FAR...
...JUST TO SEE...
...THE LOOK ON HIS FACE?
KLAK
STOP THE DATE!

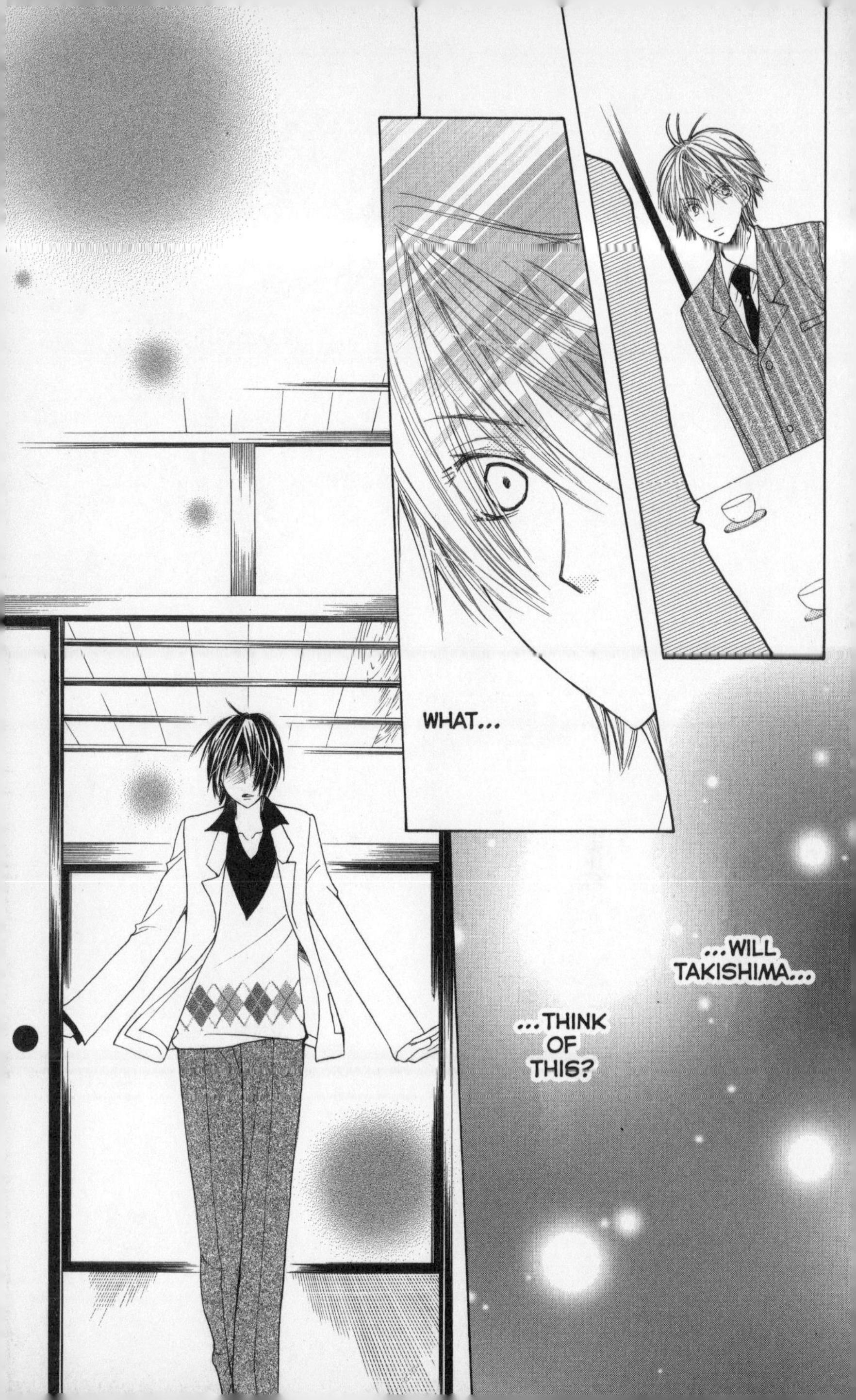
WHAT...
...WILL TAKISHIMA...
...THINK OF THIS?

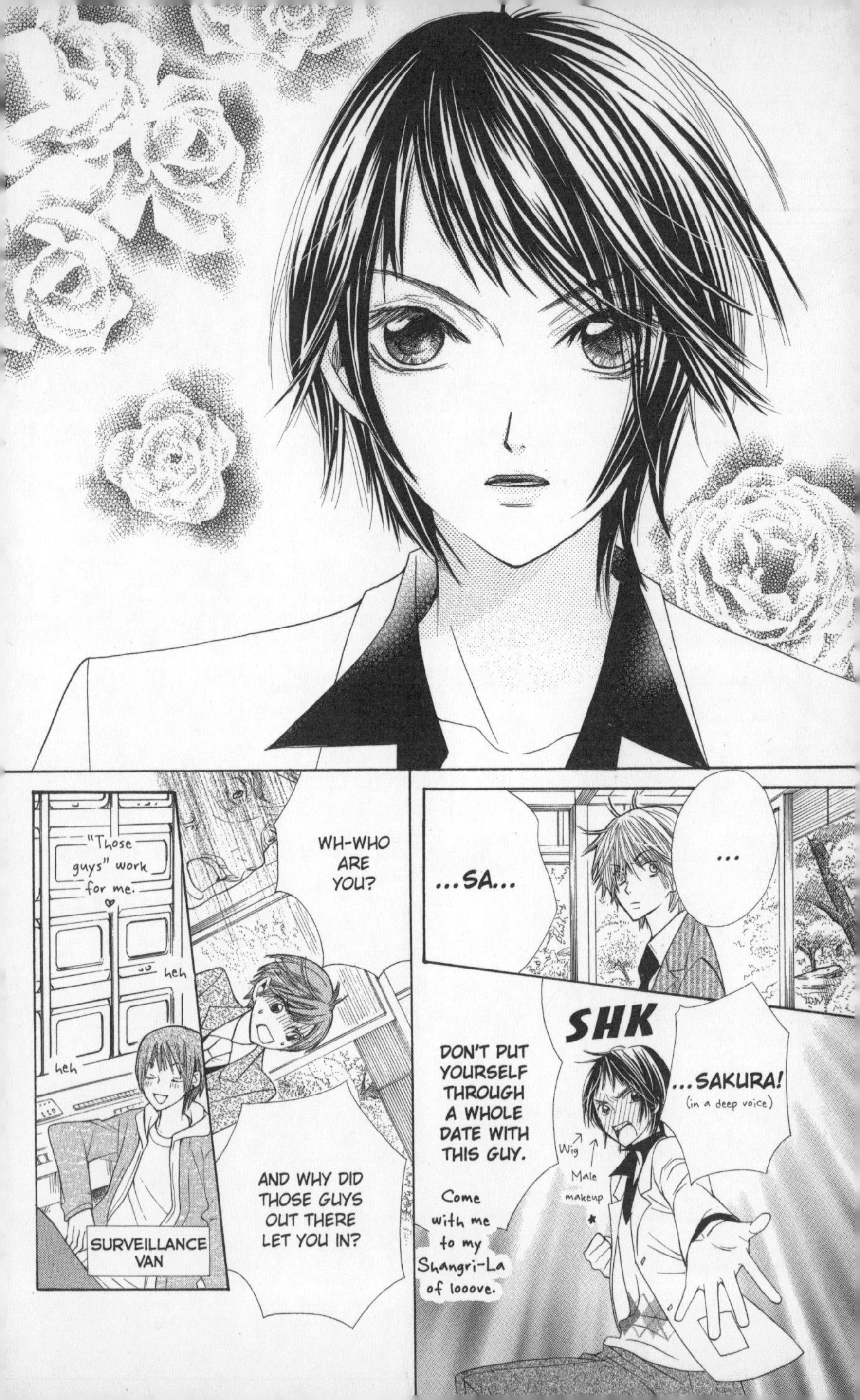
...
...SA...
SHK
...SAKURA!
(in a deep voice)
DON'T PUT YOURSELF THROUGH A WHOLE DATE WITH THIS GUY.
Wig
Male makeup
Come with me to my Shangri-La of looove.
WH-WHO ARE YOU?
"Those guys" work for me.
heh
heh
AND WHY DID THOSE GUYS OUT THERE LET YOU IN?
SURVEILLANCE VAN

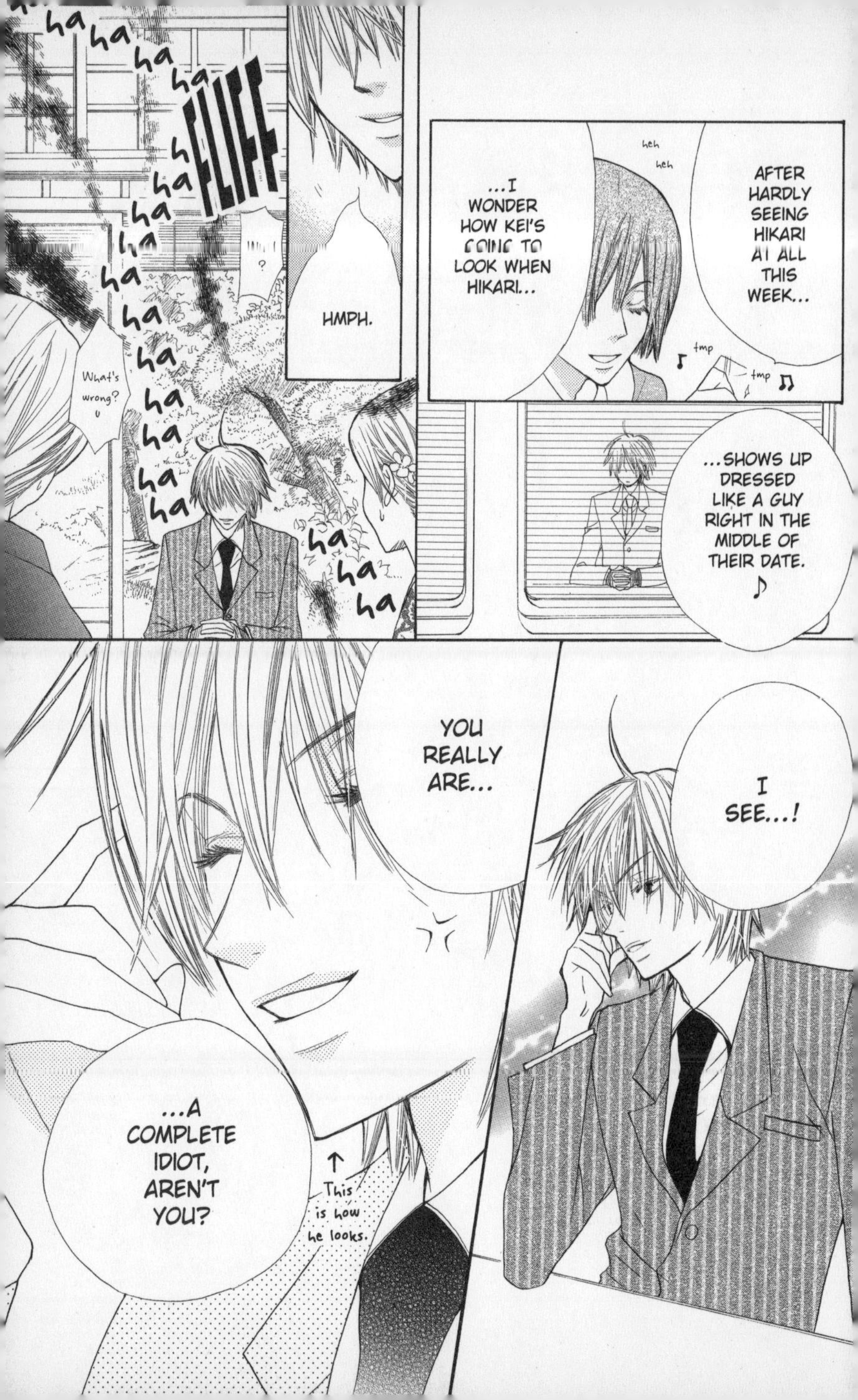
heh
heh
AFTER HARDLY SEEING HIKARI AT ALL THIS WEEK...
...I WONDER HOW KEI'S GOING TO LOOK WHEN HIKARI...
tmp
tmp
...SHOWS UP DRESSED LIKE A GUY RIGHT IN THE MIDDLE OF THEIR DATE.
HMPH.
ha ha ha ha
FLIFF
ha ha ha ha ha ha ha ha ha ha ha
What's wrong?
ha ha ha
I SEE...!
YOU REALLY ARE...
...A COMPLETE IDIOT, AREN'T YOU?
↑ This is how he looks.

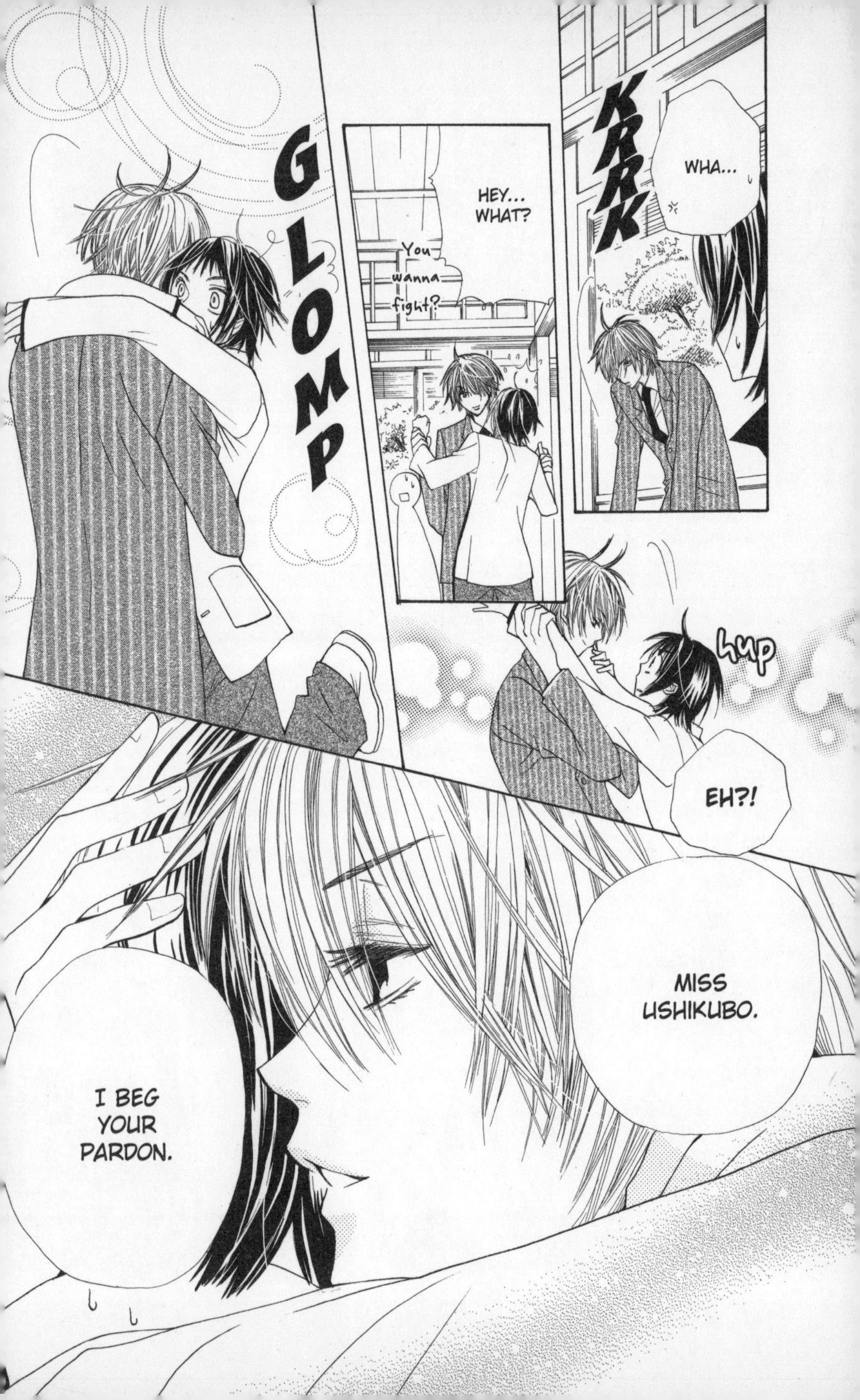
KRRK
WHA...
HEY... WHAT?
You wanna fight?
hup
EH?!
GLOMP
MISS USHIKUBO.
I BEG YOUR PARDON.

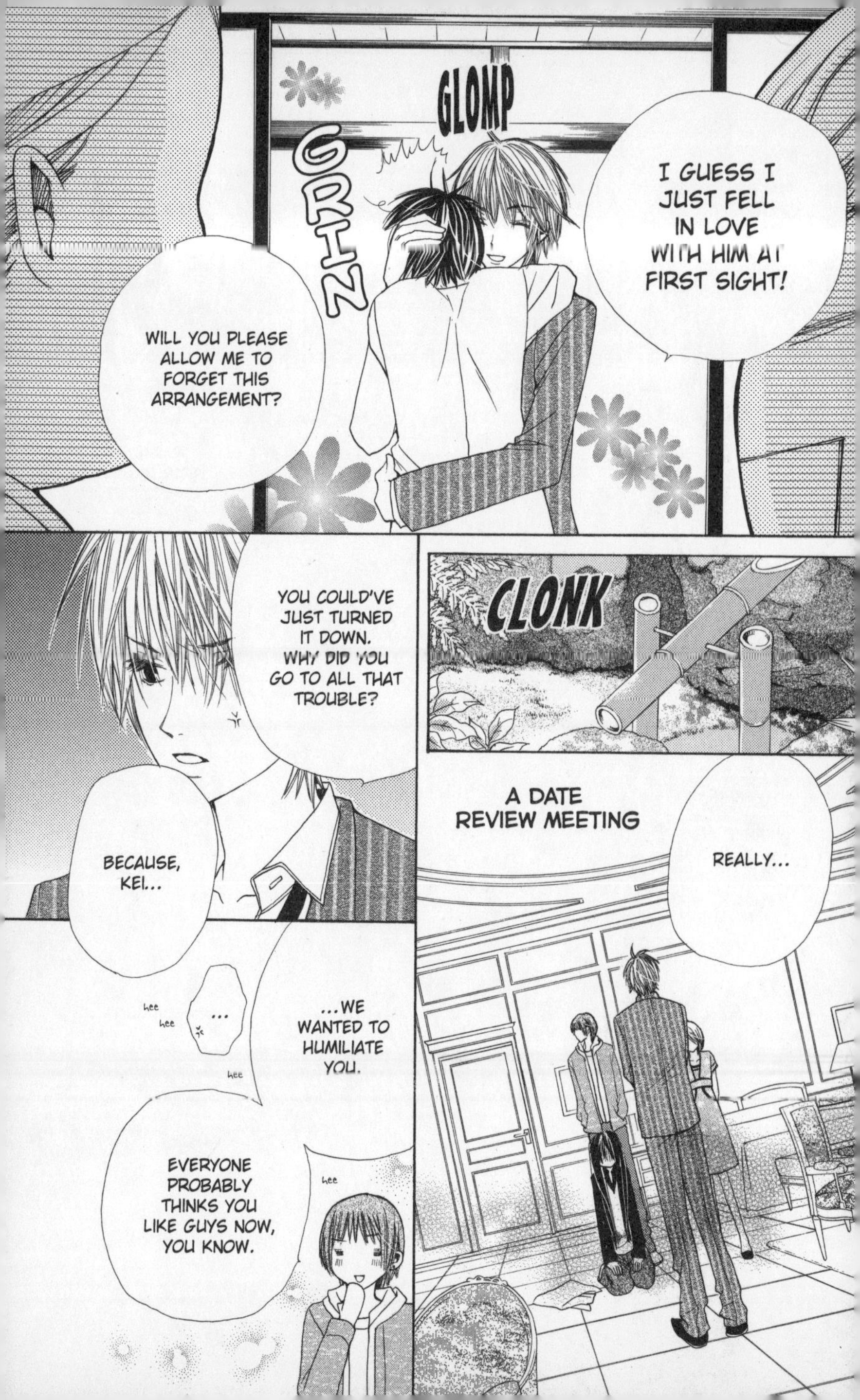
GLOMP
I GUESS I JUST FELL IN LOVE WITH HIM AT FIRST SIGHT!
GRIN
WILL YOU PLEASE ALLOW ME TO FORGET THIS ARRANGEMENT?
CLONK
YOU COULD'VE JUST TURNED IT DOWN. WHY DID YOU GO TO ALL THAT TROUBLE?
BECAUSE, KEI...
A DATE REVIEW MEETING
REALLY...
...WE WANTED TO HUMILIATE YOU.
hee
hee
...
hee
EVERYONE PROBABLY THINKS YOU LIKE GUYS NOW, YOU KNOW.
hee

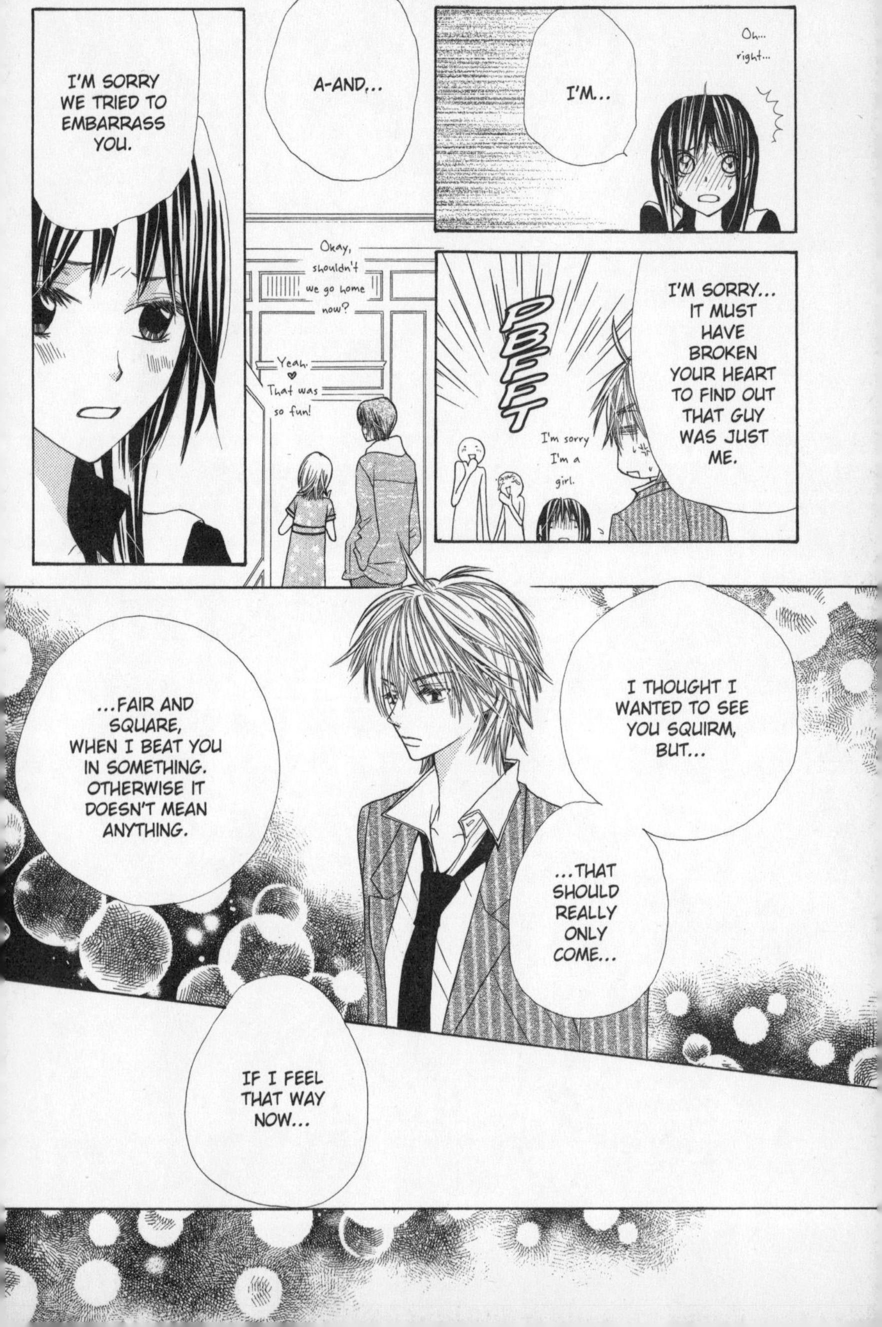
Oh... right...
I'M...
I'M SORRY... IT MUST HAVE BROKEN YOUR HEART TO FIND OUT THAT GUY WAS JUST ME.
PBFFT
I'm sorry I'm a girl.
A-AND,...
I'M SORRY WE TRIED TO EMBARRASS YOU.
Okay, shouldn't we go home now?
Yeah. ♥ That was so fun!
I THOUGHT I WANTED TO SEE YOU SQUIRM, BUT...
...THAT SHOULD REALLY ONLY COME...
...FAIR AND SQUARE, WHEN I BEAT YOU IN SOMETHING. OTHERWISE IT DOESN'T MEAN ANYTHING.
IF I FEEL THAT WAY NOW...

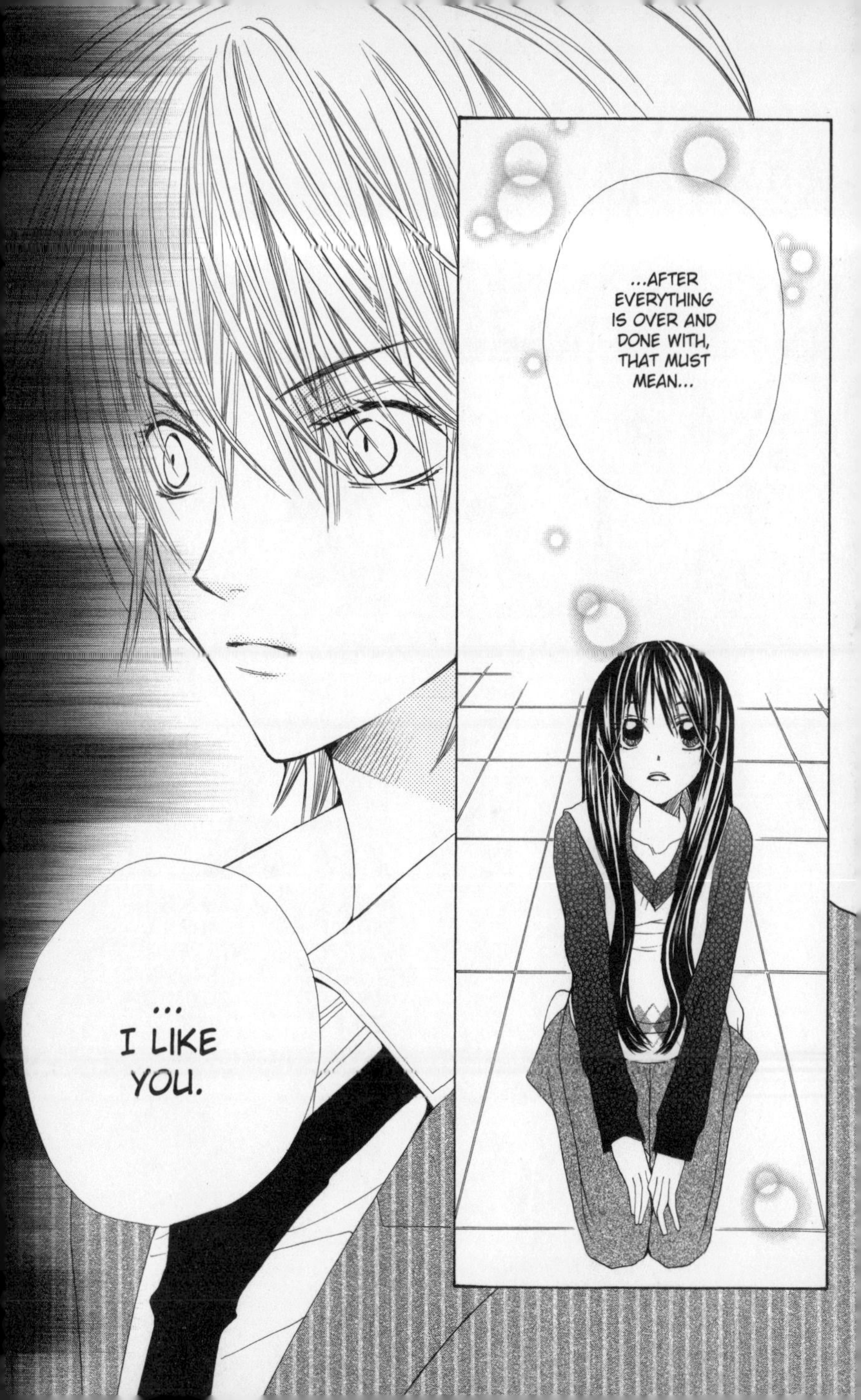
...AFTER EVERYTHING IS OVER AND DONE WITH, THAT MUST MEAN...
... I LIKE YOU.

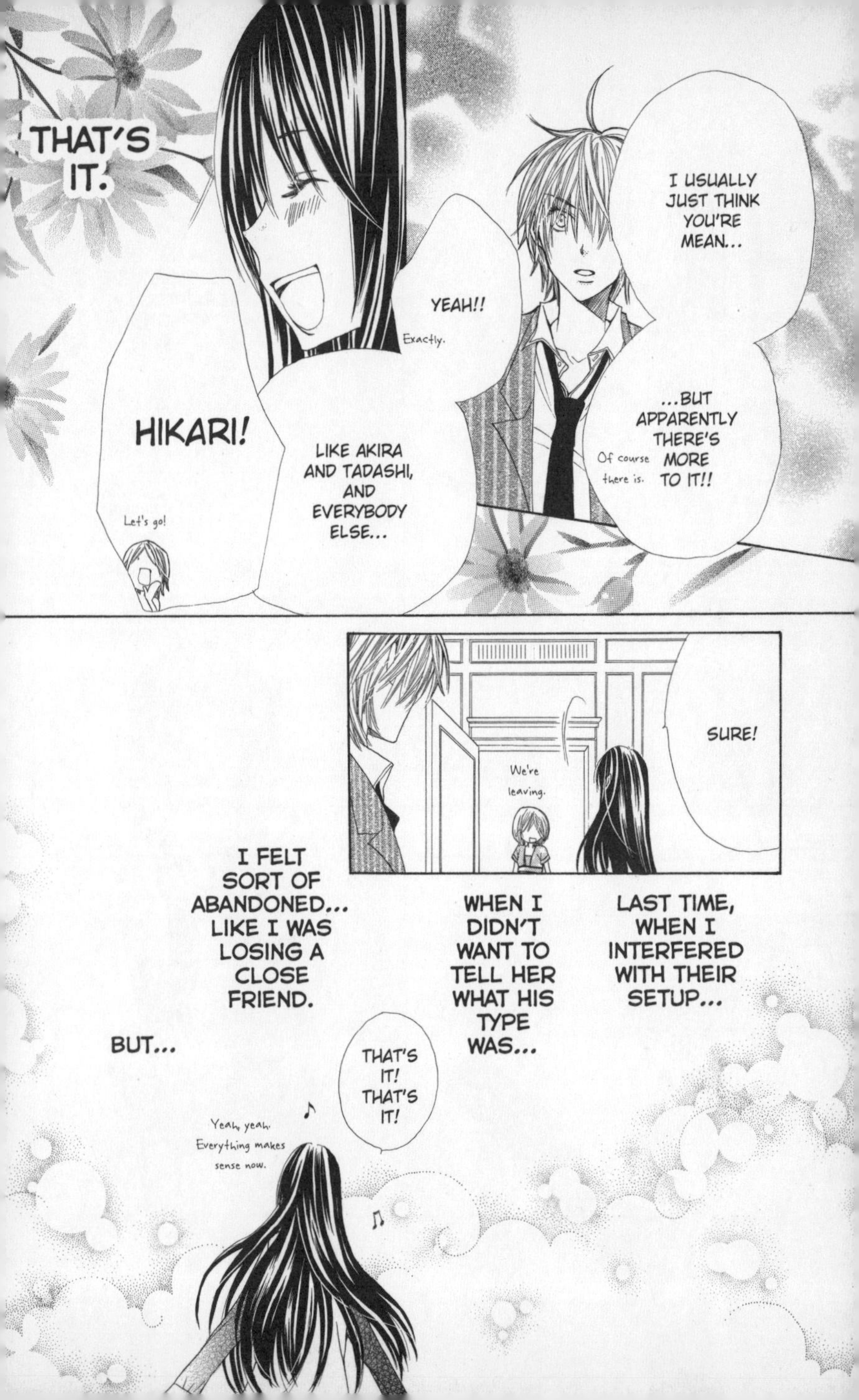
I USUALLY JUST THINK YOU'RE MEAN...
...BUT APPARENTLY THERE'S MORE TO IT!!
Of course there is.
YEAH!!
Exactly.
THAT'S IT.
LIKE AKIRA AND TADASHI, AND EVERYBODY ELSE...
HIKARI!
Let's go!
SURE!
We're leaving.
LAST TIME, WHEN I INTERFERED WITH THEIR SETUP...
WHEN I DIDN'T WANT TO TELL HER WHAT HIS TYPE WAS...
I FELT SORT OF ABANDONED... LIKE I WAS LOSING A CLOSE FRIEND.
BUT...
THAT'S IT! THAT'S IT!
Yeah, yeah. Everything makes sense now.

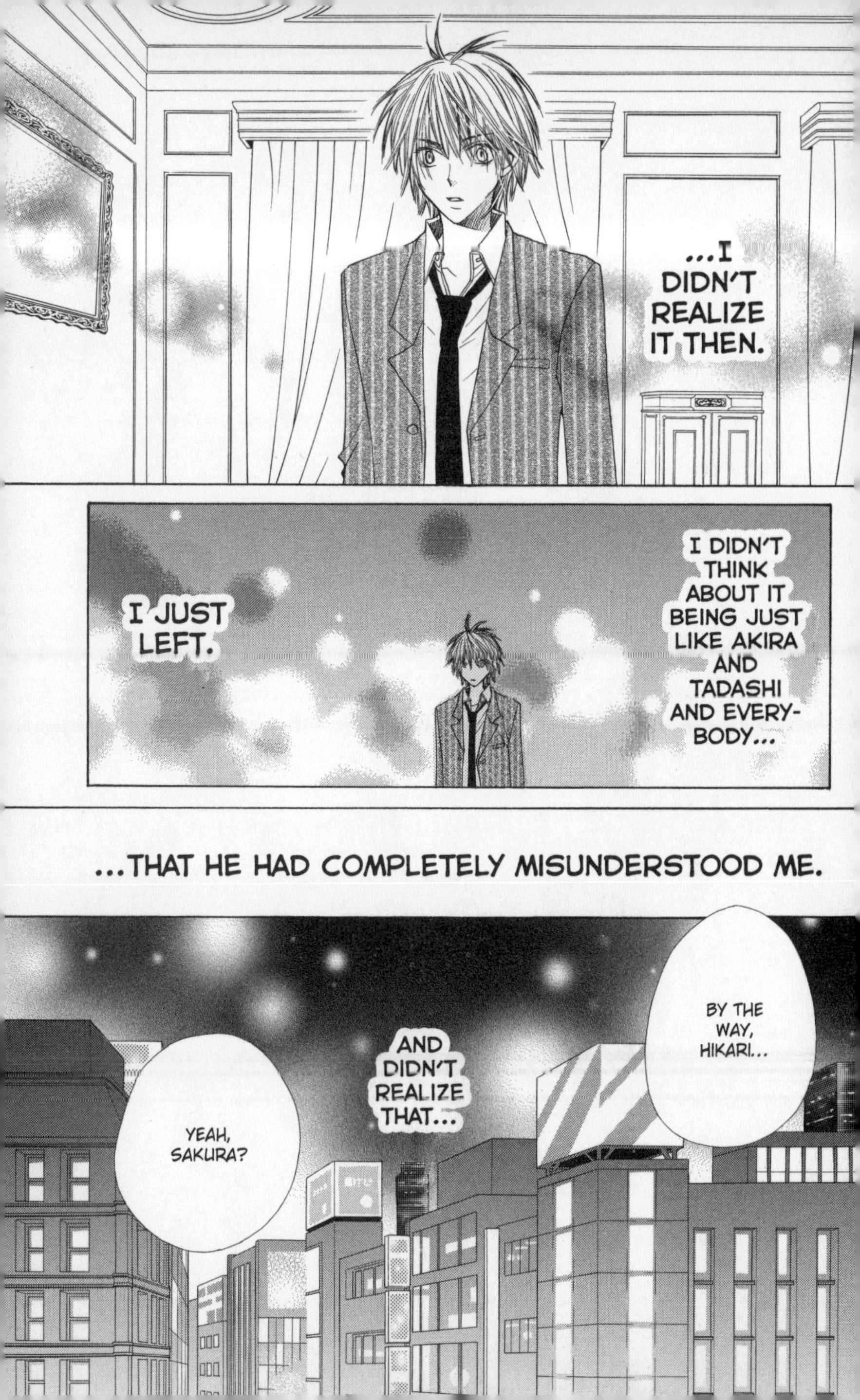
...I DIDN'T REALIZE IT THEN.
I DIDN'T THINK ABOUT IT BEING JUST LIKE AKIRA AND TADASHI AND EVERY-BODY...
I JUST LEFT.
...THAT HE HAD COMPLETELY MISUNDERSTOOD ME.
BY THE WAY, HIKARI...
AND DIDN'T REALIZE THAT...
YEAH, SAKURA?

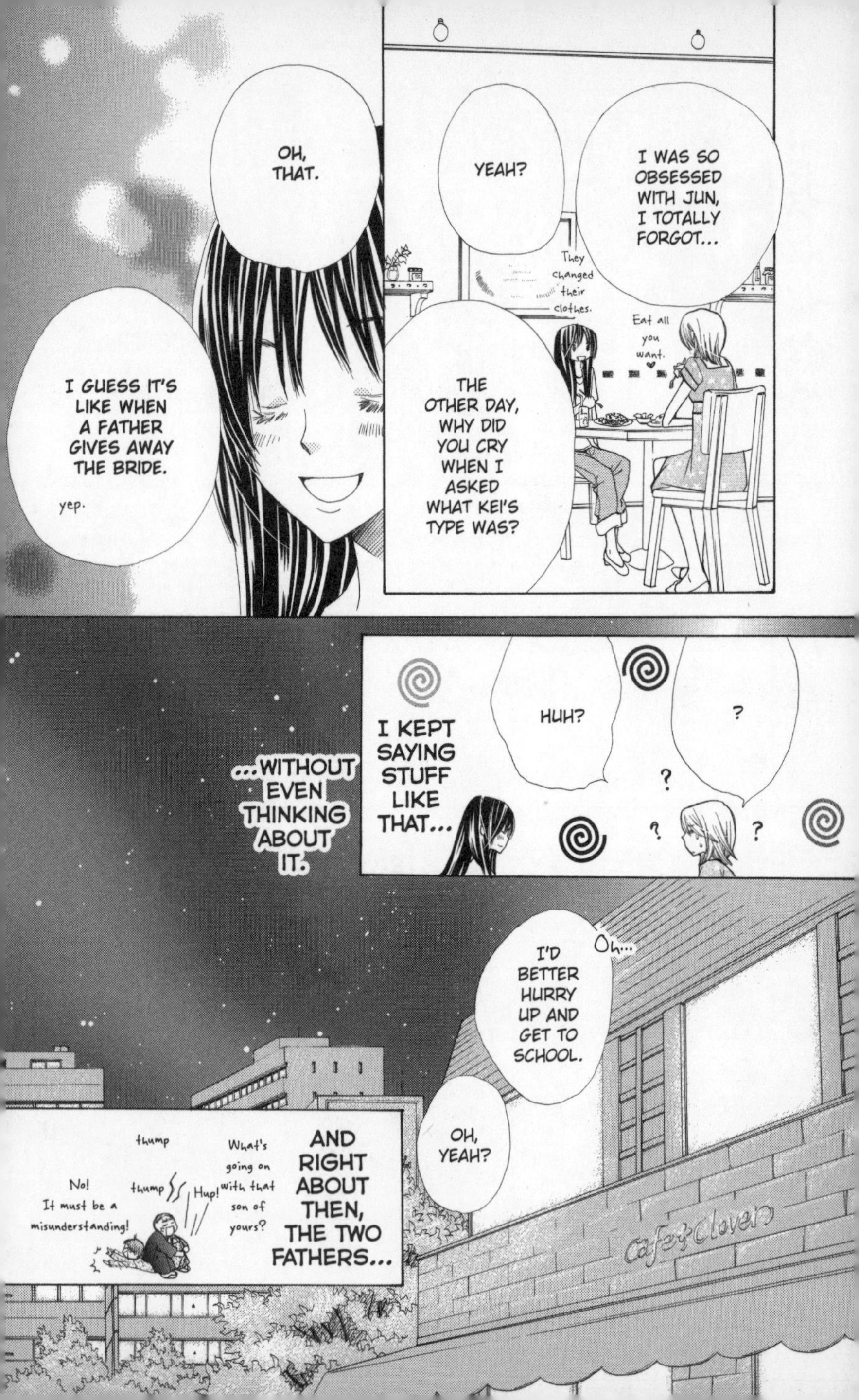

I WAS SO OBSESSED WITH JUN, I TOTALLY FORGOT...
YEAH?
They changed their clothes.
Eat all you want.
THE OTHER DAY, WHY DID YOU CRY WHEN I ASKED WHAT KEI'S TYPE WAS?
OH, THAT.
I GUESS IT'S LIKE WHEN A FATHER GIVES AWAY THE BRIDE.
yep.
?
HUH?
?
?
?
I KEPT SAYING STUFF LIKE THAT...
...WITHOUT EVEN THINKING ABOUT IT.
Oh...
I'D BETTER HURRY UP AND GET TO SCHOOL.
OH, YEAH?
cafe clover
AND RIGHT ABOUT THEN, THE TWO FATHERS...
What's going on with that son of yours?
Hup!
thump
thump
No! It must be a misunderstanding!

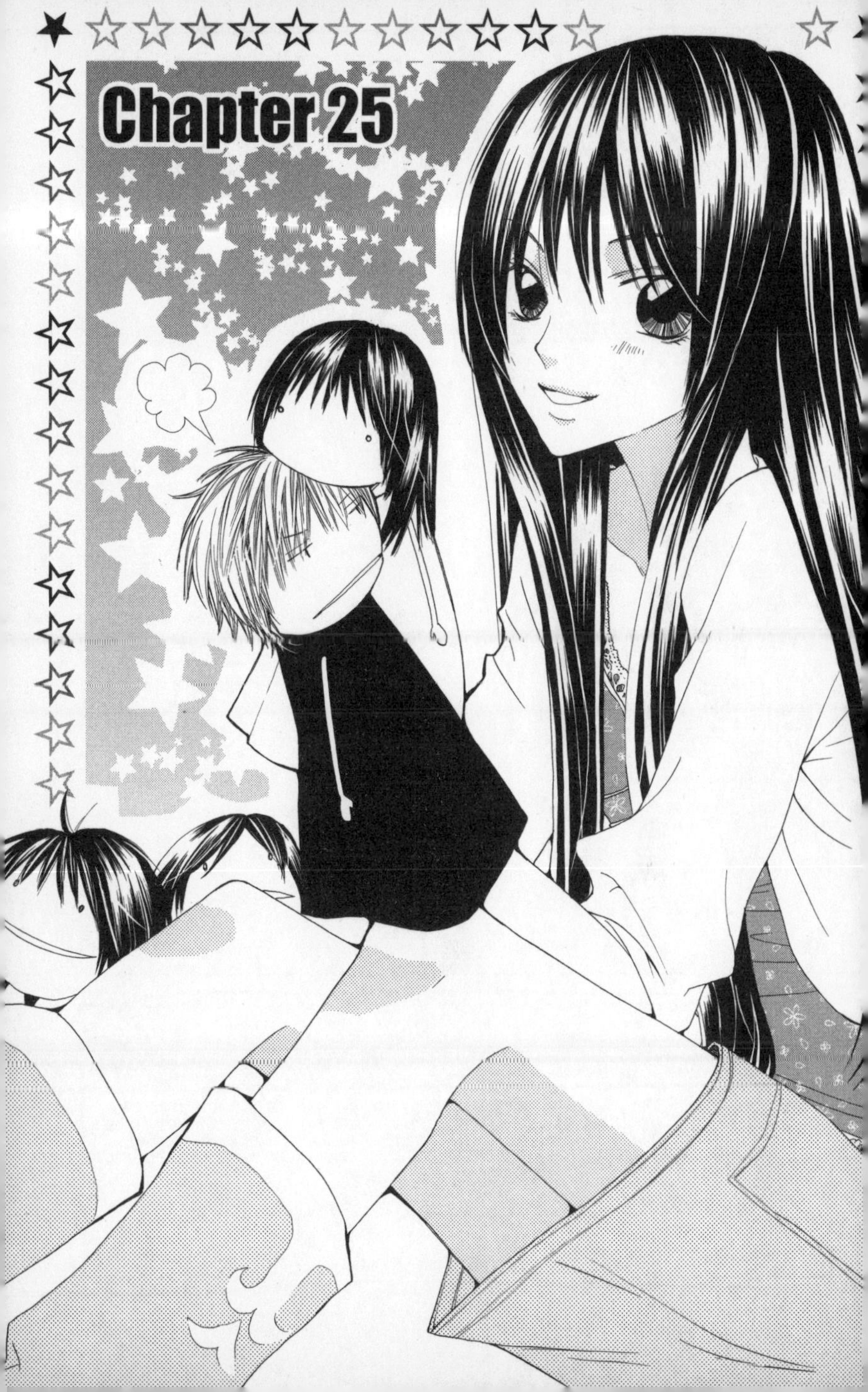
Chapter 25

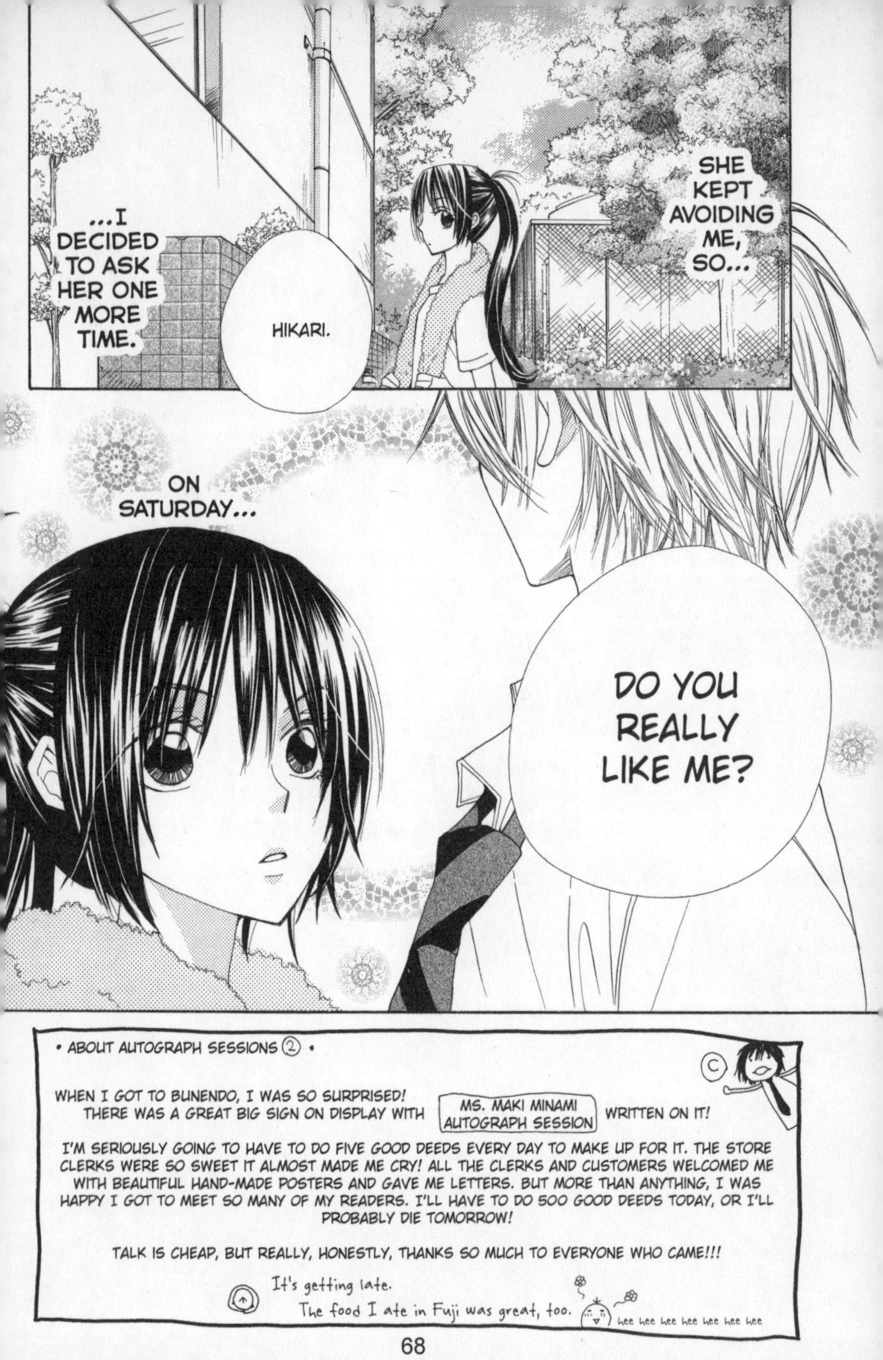
SHE KEPT AVOIDING ME, SO...
...I DECIDED TO ASK HER ONE MORE TIME.
HIKARI.
ON SATURDAY...
DO YOU REALLY LIKE ME?

• ABOUT AUTOGRAPH SESSIONS ② •

WHEN I GOT TO BUNENDO, I WAS SO SURPRISED! THERE WAS A GREAT BIG SIGN ON DISPLAY WITH "MS. MAKI MINAMI AUTOGRAPH SESSION" WRITTEN ON IT!

I'M SERIOUSLY GOING TO HAVE TO DO FIVE GOOD DEEDS EVERY DAY TO MAKE UP FOR IT. THE STORE CLERKS WERE SO SWEET IT ALMOST MADE ME CRY! ALL THE CLERKS AND CUSTOMERS WELCOMED ME WITH BEAUTIFUL HAND-MADE POSTERS AND GAVE ME LETTERS. BUT MORE THAN ANYTHING, I WAS HAPPY I GOT TO MEET SO MANY OF MY READERS. I'LL HAVE TO DO 500 GOOD DEEDS TODAY, OR I'LL PROBABLY DIE TOMORROW!

TALK IS CHEAP, BUT REALLY, HONESTLY, THANKS SO MUCH TO EVERYONE WHO CAME!!!

It's getting late.
The food I ate in Fuji was great, too.
hee hee hee hee hee hee hee

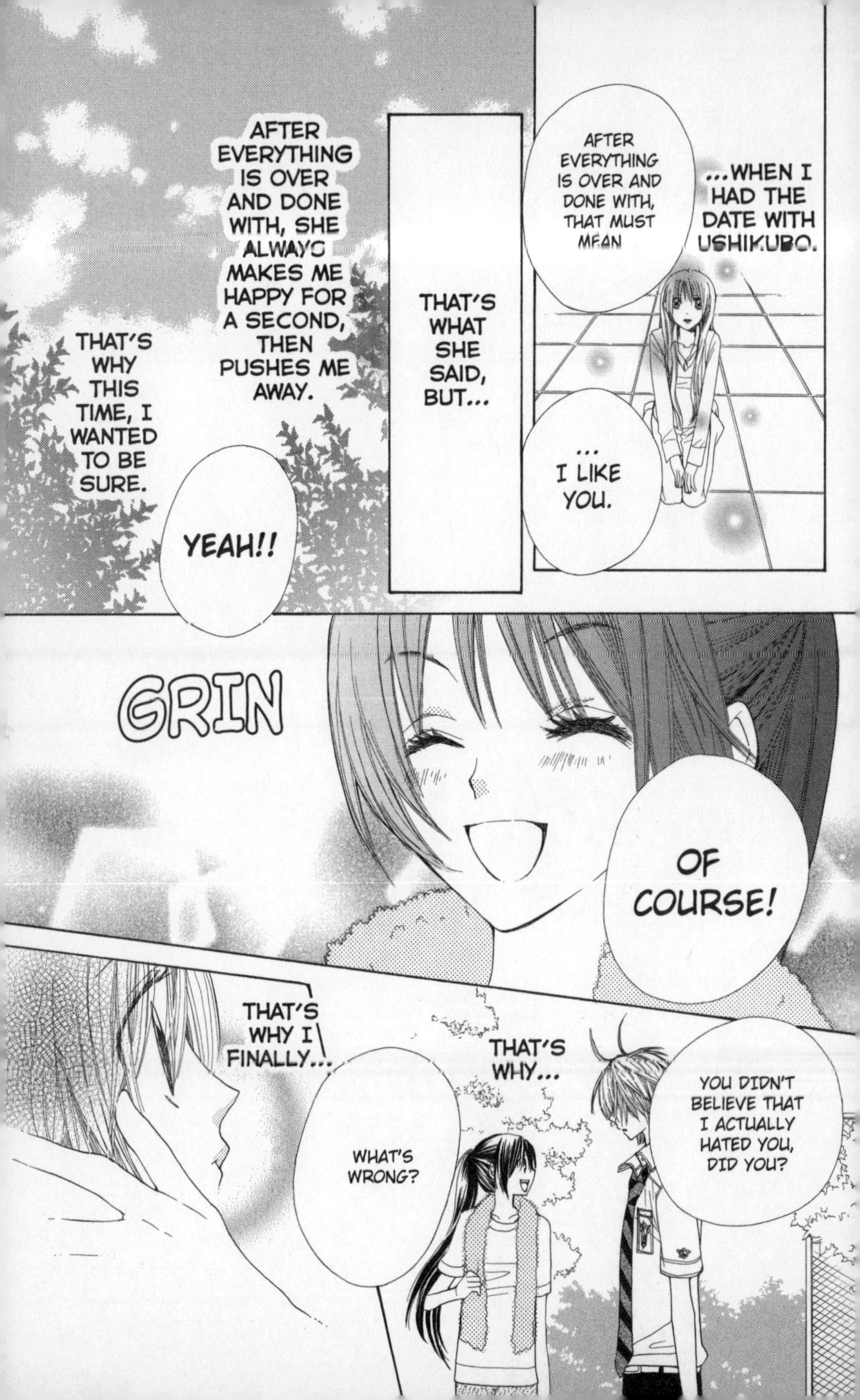
...WHEN I HAD THE DATE WITH USHIKUBO.
AFTER EVERYTHING IS OVER AND DONE WITH, THAT MUST MEAN
... I LIKE YOU.
THAT'S WHAT SHE SAID, BUT...
AFTER EVERYTHING IS OVER AND DONE WITH, SHE ALWAYS MAKES ME HAPPY FOR A SECOND, THEN PUSHES ME AWAY.
THAT'S WHY THIS TIME, I WANTED TO BE SURE.
YEAH!!
OF COURSE!
GRIN
YOU DIDN'T BELIEVE THAT I ACTUALLY HATED YOU, DID YOU?
THAT'S WHY...
WHAT'S WRONG?
THAT'S WHY I FINALLY...

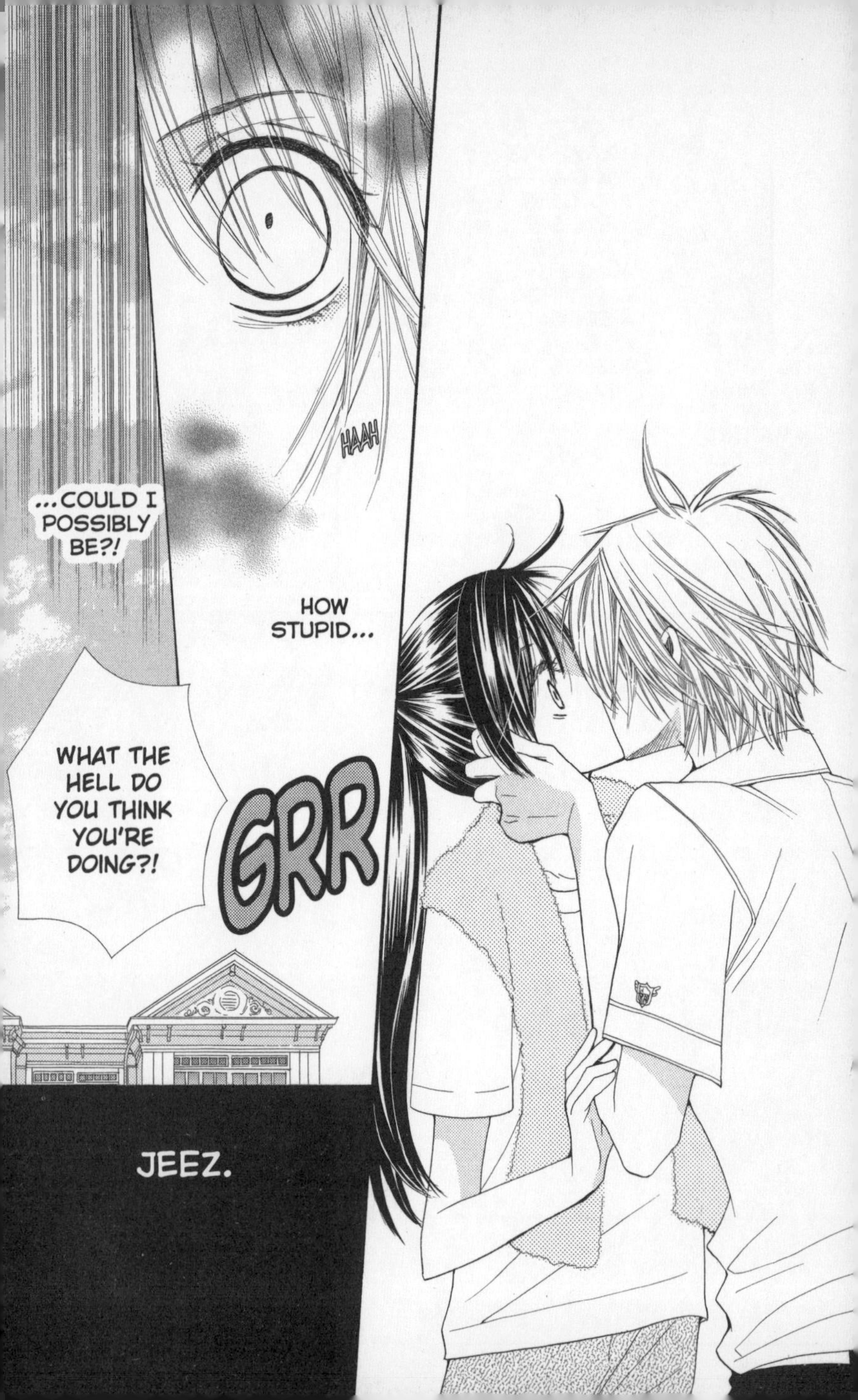

HAAH
...COULD I POSSIBLY BE?!
HOW STUPID...
GRR
WHAT THE HELL DO YOU THINK YOU'RE DOING?!
JEEZ.

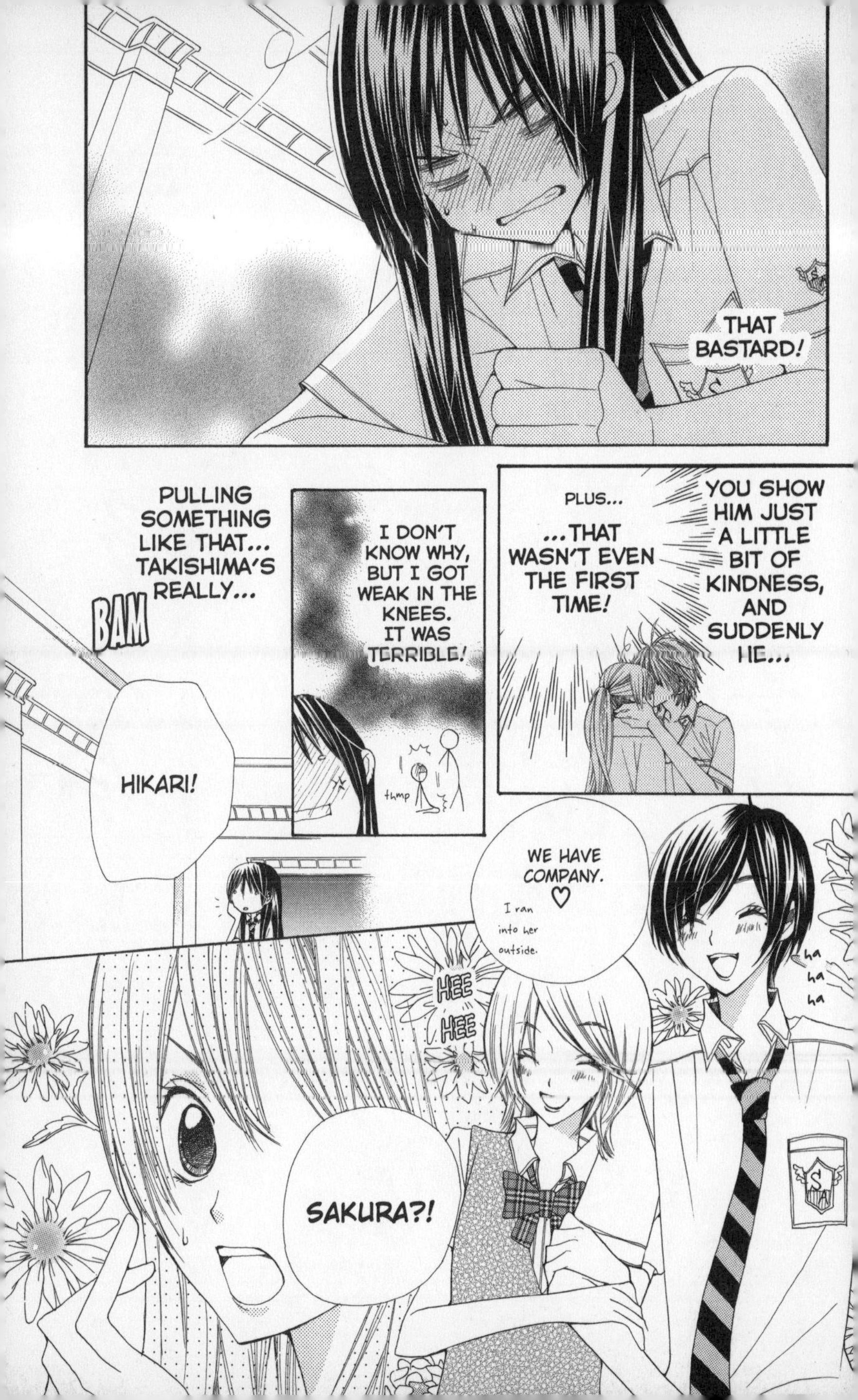
THAT BASTARD!
YOU SHOW HIM JUST A LITTLE BIT OF KINDNESS, AND SUDDENLY HE...
PLUS...
...THAT WASN'T EVEN THE FIRST TIME!
I DON'T KNOW WHY, BUT I GOT WEAK IN THE KNEES. IT WAS TERRIBLE!
thump
PULLING SOMETHING LIKE THAT... TAKISHIMA'S REALLY...
BAM
HIKARI!
WE HAVE COMPANY. ♡
I ran into her outside.
ha ha ha
HEE HEE
SAKURA?!

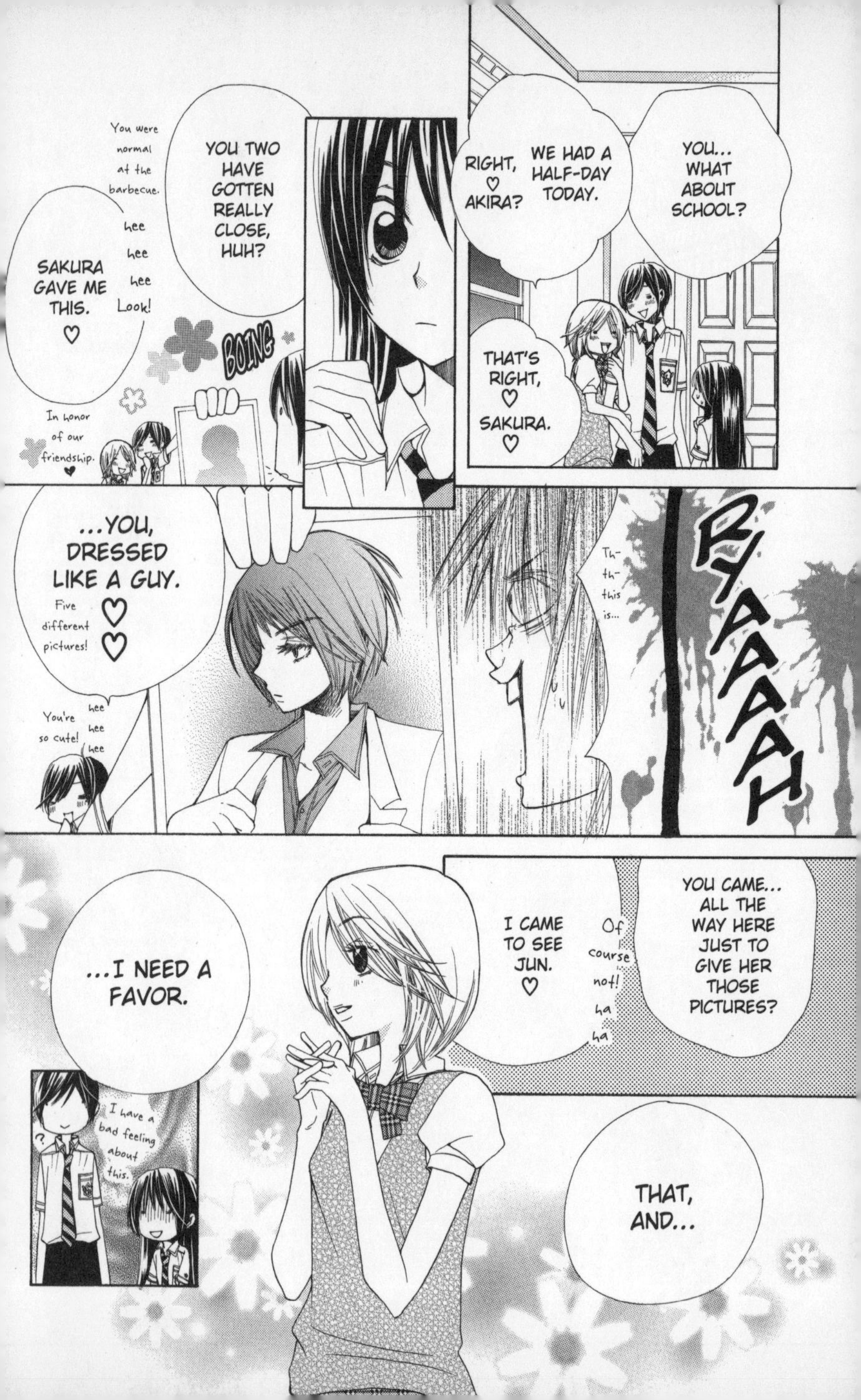

YOU... WHAT ABOUT SCHOOL?
WE HAD A HALF-DAY TODAY.
RIGHT, ♡ AKIRA?
THAT'S RIGHT, ♡ SAKURA. ♡
YOU TWO HAVE GOTTEN REALLY CLOSE, HUH?
You were normal at the barbecue.
hee hee hee Look!
SAKURA GAVE ME THIS. ♡
BOING
In honor of our friendship. ♥
RAAAAH
Th-th-this is...
...YOU, DRESSED LIKE A GUY. ♡ ♡
Five different pictures!
hee hee hee
You're so cute!
YOU CAME... ALL THE WAY HERE JUST TO GIVE HER THOSE PICTURES?
I CAME TO SEE JUN. ♡
Of course not! ha ha
THAT, AND...
...I NEED A FAVOR.
I have a bad feeling about this.

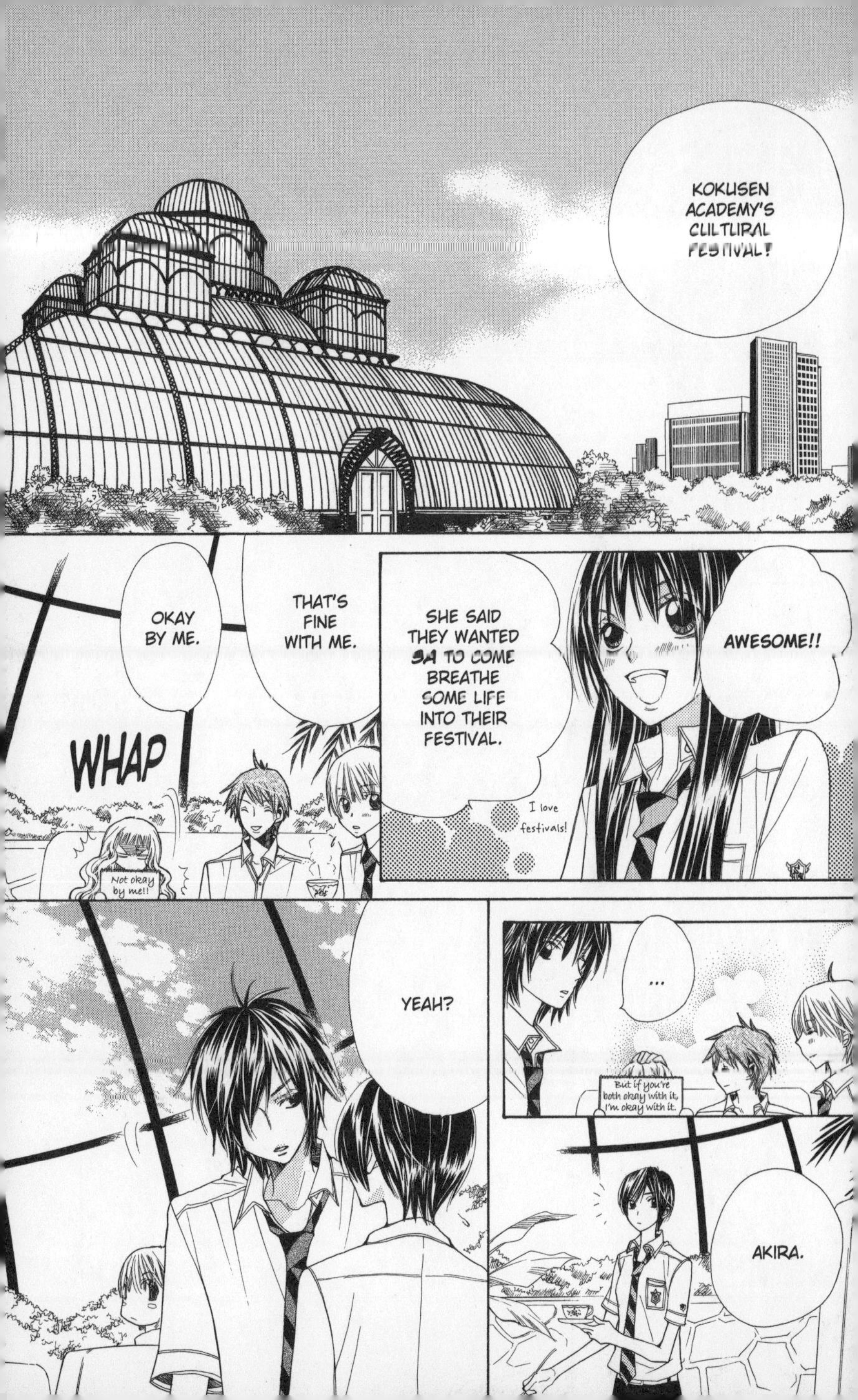
KOKUSEN ACADEMY'S CULTURAL FESTIVAL!
AWESOME!!
SHE SAID THEY WANTED US TO COME BREATHE SOME LIFE INTO THEIR FESTIVAL.
I love festivals!
THAT'S FINE WITH ME.
OKAY BY ME.
WHAP
Not okay by me!!
...
But if you're both okay with it, I'm okay with it.
AKIRA.
YEAH?

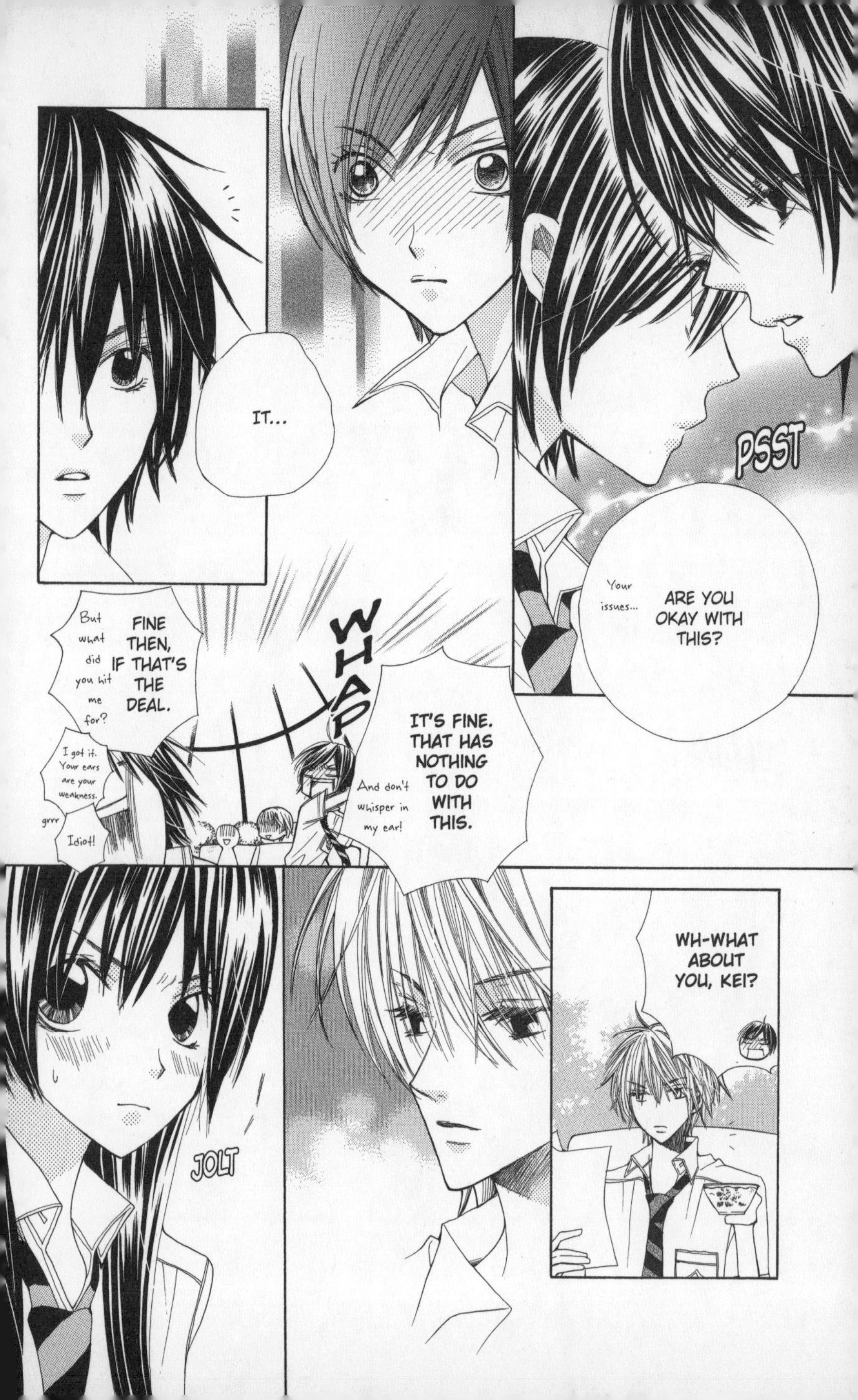
PSST
Your issues... ARE YOU OKAY WITH THIS?
IT...
WHAP
IT'S FINE. THAT HAS NOTHING TO DO WITH THIS.
And don't whisper in my ear!
FINE THEN, IF THAT'S THE DEAL.
But what did you hit me for?
I got it. Your ears are your weakness.
grrr
Idiot!
WH-WHAT ABOUT YOU, KEI?
JOLT

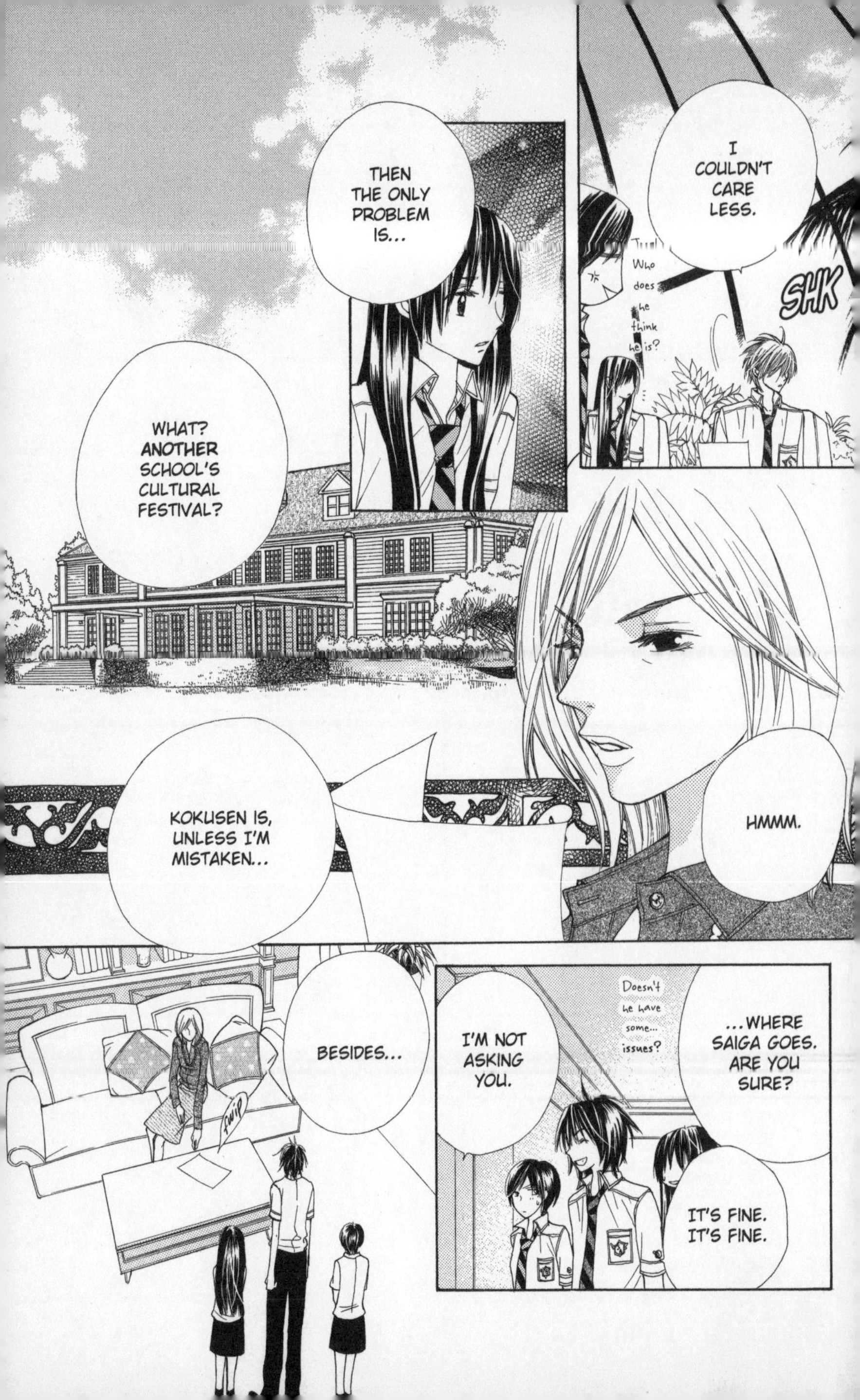
I COULDN'T CARE LESS.
Who does he think he is?
SHK
THEN THE ONLY PROBLEM IS...
WHAT? ANOTHER SCHOOL'S CULTURAL FESTIVAL?
HMMM.
KOKUSEN IS, UNLESS I'M MISTAKEN...
...WHERE SAIGA GOES. ARE YOU SURE?
Doesn't he have some... issues?
I'M NOT ASKING YOU.
IT'S FINE. IT'S FINE.
BESIDES...
fwip

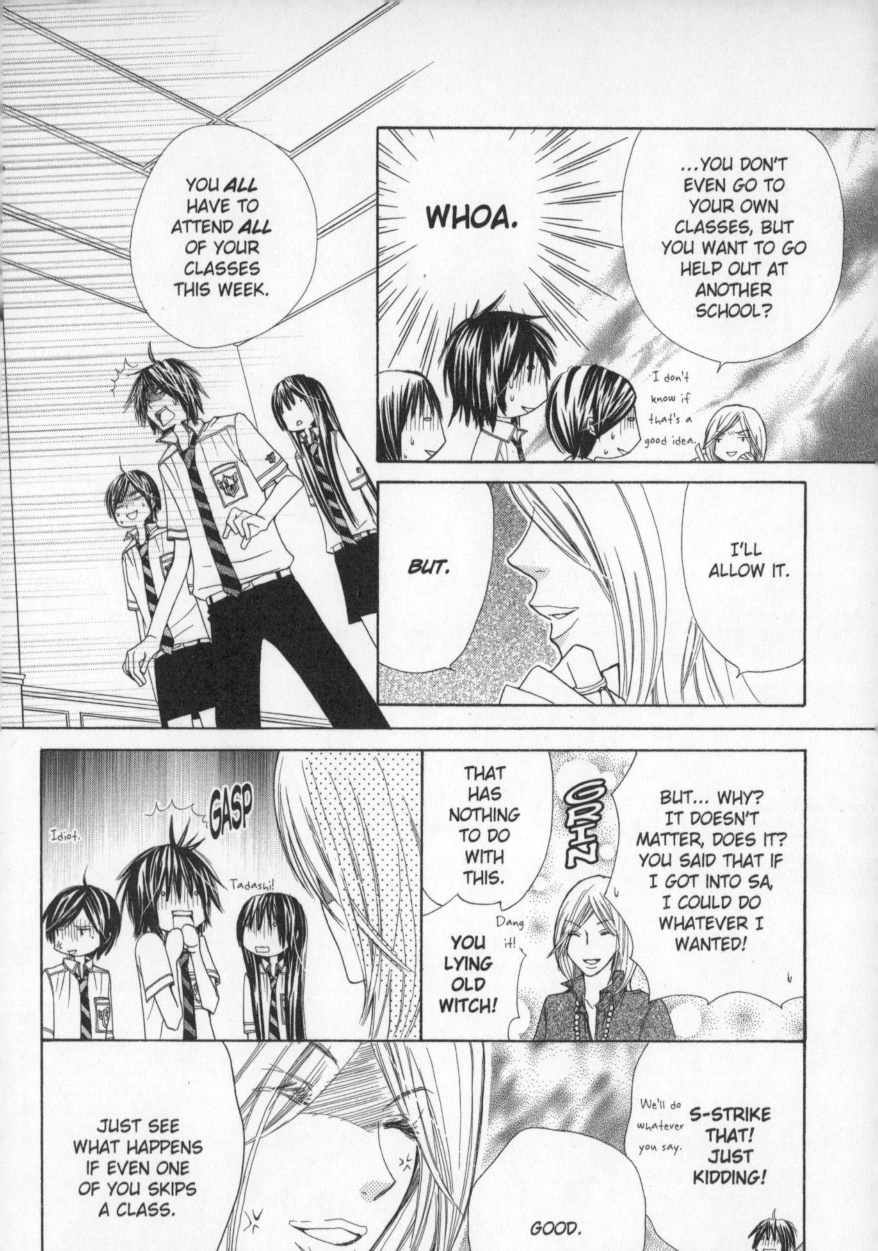
...YOU DON'T EVEN GO TO YOUR OWN CLASSES, BUT YOU WANT TO GO HELP OUT AT ANOTHER SCHOOL?
WHOA.
I don't know if that's a good idea.
I'LL ALLOW IT.
BUT.
YOU ALL HAVE TO ATTEND ALL OF YOUR CLASSES THIS WEEK.
BUT... WHY? IT DOESN'T MATTER, DOES IT? YOU SAID THAT IF I GOT INTO SA, I COULD DO WHATEVER I WANTED!
GRIN
THAT HAS NOTHING TO DO WITH THIS.
Dang it!
YOU LYING OLD WITCH!
GASP
Tadashi!
Idiot.
S-STRIKE THAT! JUST KIDDING!
We'll do whatever you say.
GOOD.
JUST SEE WHAT HAPPENS IF EVEN ONE OF YOU SKIPS A CLASS.

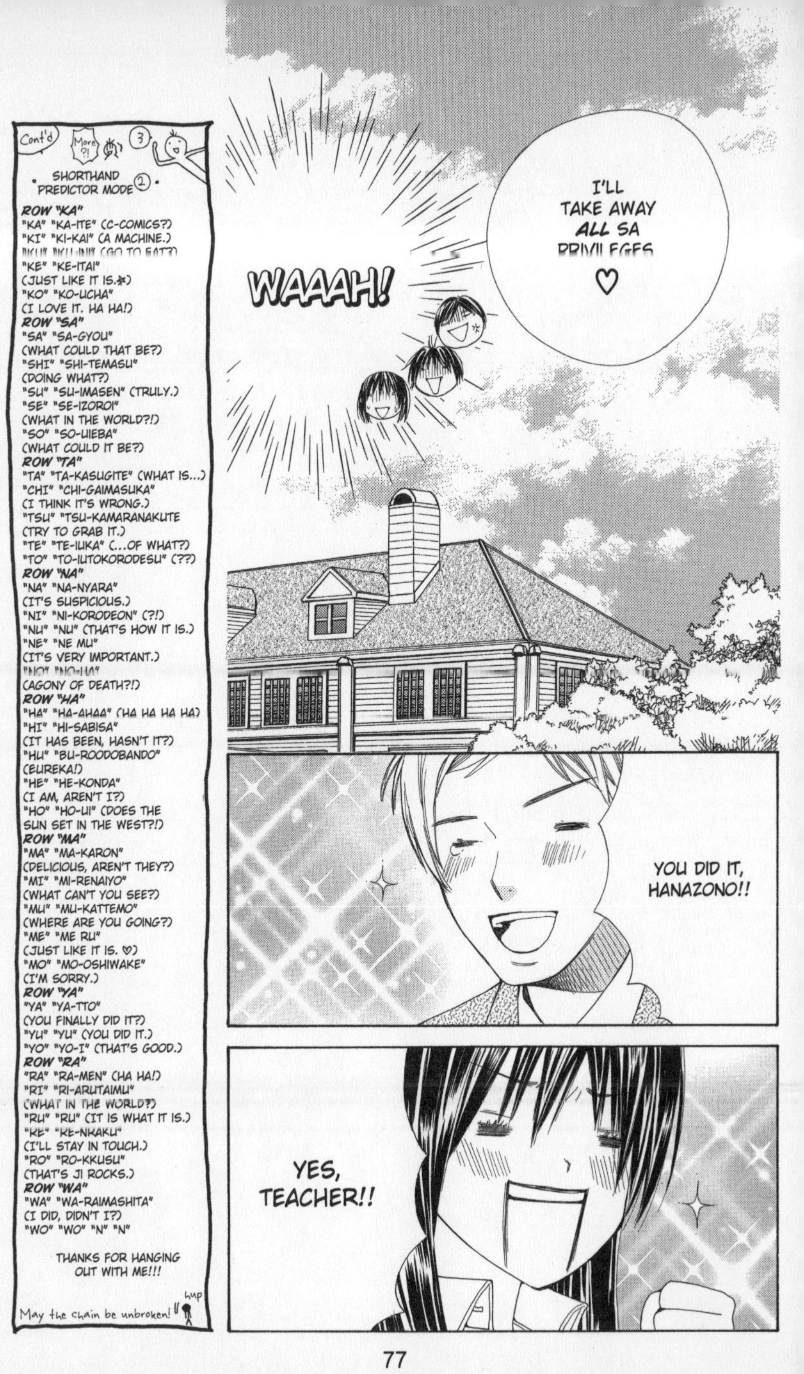
I'LL TAKE AWAY ALL SA PRIVILEGES ♡
WAAAH!
YOU DID IT, HANAZONO!!
YES, TEACHER!!

Cont'd More?! 3

• SHORTHAND PREDICTOR MODE ② •

ROW "KA"
"KA" "KA-ITE" (C-COMICS?)
"KI" "KI-KAI" (A MACHINE.)
"KU" "KU-INI" (GO TO EAT?)
"KE" "KE-ITAI"
(JUST LIKE IT IS.✲)
"KO" "KO-UCHA"
(I LOVE IT. HA HA!)
ROW "SA"
"SA" "SA-GYOU"
(WHAT COULD THAT BE?)
"SHI" "SHI-TEMASU"
(DOING WHAT?)
"SU" "SU-IMASEN" (TRULY.)
"SE" "SE-IZOROI"
(WHAT IN THE WORLD?!)
"SO" "SO-UIEBA"
(WHAT COULD IT BE?)
ROW "TA"
"TA" "TA-KASUGITE" (WHAT IS...)
"CHI" "CHI-GAIMASUKA"
(I THINK IT'S WRONG.)
"TSU" "TSU-KAMARANAKUTE
(TRY TO GRAB IT.)
"TE" "TE-IUKA" (...OF WHAT?)
"TO" "TO-IUTOKORODESU" (??)
ROW "NA"
"NA" "NA-NYARA"
(IT'S SUSPICIOUS.)
"NI" "NI-KORODEON" (?!)
"NU" "NU" (THAT'S HOW IT IS.)
"NE" "NE MU"
(IT'S VERY IMPORTANT.)
"NO" "NO-TA"
(AGONY OF DEATH?!)
ROW "HA"
"HA" "HA-AHAA" (HA HA HA HA)
"HI" "HI-SABISA"
(IT HAS BEEN, HASN'T IT?)
"HU" "BU-ROODOBANDO"
(EUREKA!)
"HE" "HE-KONDA"
(I AM, AREN'T I?)
"HO" "HO-UI" (DOES THE SUN SET IN THE WEST?!)
ROW "MA"
"MA" "MA-KARON"
(DELICIOUS, AREN'T THEY?)
"MI" "MI-RENAIYO"
(WHAT CAN'T YOU SEE?)
"MU" "MU-KATTEMO"
(WHERE ARE YOU GOING?)
"ME" "ME RU"
(JUST LIKE IT IS. ♡)
"MO" "MO-OSHIWAKE"
(I'M SORRY.)
ROW "YA"
"YA" "YA-TTO"
(YOU FINALLY DID IT?)
"YU" "YU" (YOU DID IT.)
"YO" "YO-I" (THAT'S GOOD.)
ROW "RA"
"RA" "RA-MEN" (HA HA!)
"RI" "RI-ARUTAIMU"
(WHAT IN THE WORLD?)
"RU" "RU" (IT IS WHAT IT IS.)
"RE" "RE-NRAKU"
(I'LL STAY IN TOUCH.)
"RO" "RO-KKUSU"
(THAT'S JI ROCKS.)
ROW "WA"
"WA" "WA-RAIMASHITA"
(I DID, DIDN'T I?)
"WO" "WO" "N" "N"

THANKS FOR HANGING OUT WITH ME!!!

May the chain be unbroken!! Lup

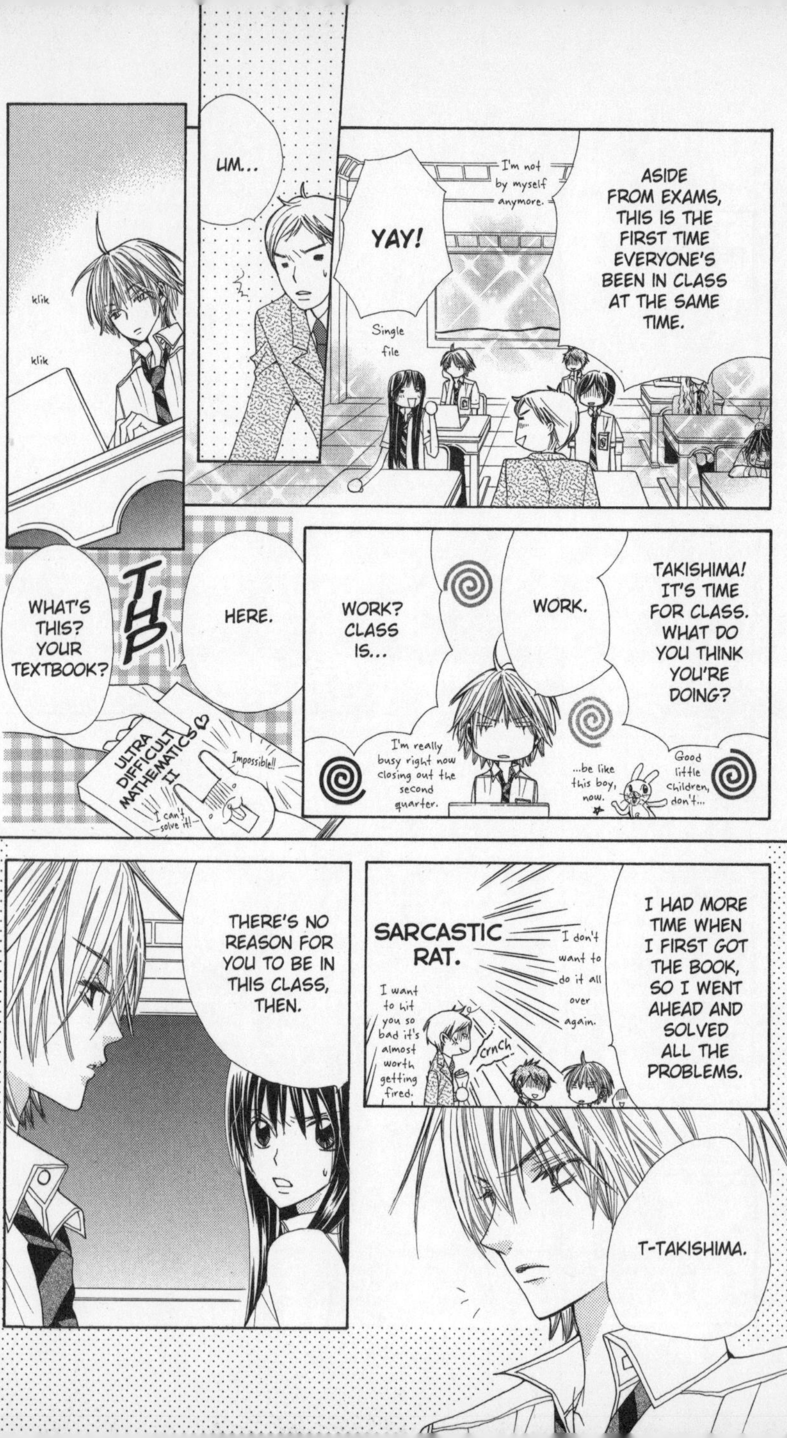
ASIDE FROM EXAMS, THIS IS THE FIRST TIME EVERYONE'S BEEN IN CLASS AT THE SAME TIME.
I'm not by myself anymore.
YAY!
Single file
UM...
klik
klik
TAKISHIMA! IT'S TIME FOR CLASS. WHAT DO YOU THINK YOU'RE DOING?
Good little children, don't...
...be like this boy, now.
WORK.
I'm really busy right now closing out the second quarter.
WORK? CLASS IS...
HERE.
THP
WHAT'S THIS? YOUR TEXTBOOK?
ULTRA DIFFICULT MATHEMATICS II
Impossible!!
I can't solve it!
I HAD MORE TIME WHEN I FIRST GOT THE BOOK, SO I WENT AHEAD AND SOLVED ALL THE PROBLEMS.
I don't want to do it all over again.
SARCASTIC RAT.
I want to hit you so bad it's almost worth getting fired.
crnch
T-TAKISHIMA.
THERE'S NO REASON FOR YOU TO BE IN THIS CLASS, THEN.

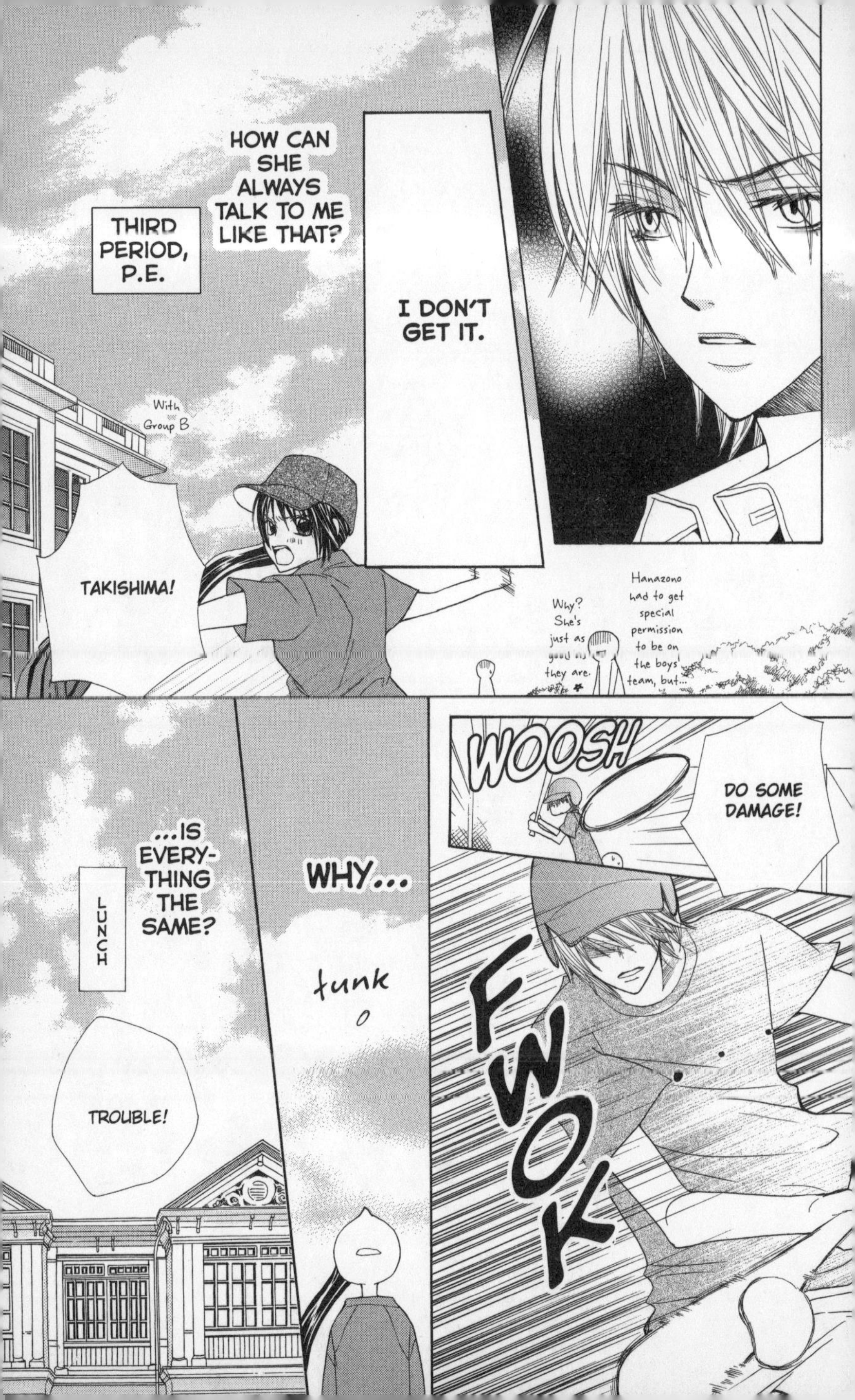
I DON'T GET IT.
HOW CAN SHE ALWAYS TALK TO ME LIKE THAT?
THIRD PERIOD, P.E.
With Group B
TAKISHIMA!
Hanazono had to get special permission to be on the boys team, but...
Why? She's just as good as they are.
WOOSH
DO SOME DAMAGE!
FWOK
WHY...
tunk
...IS EVERY-THING THE SAME?
LUNCH
TROUBLE!

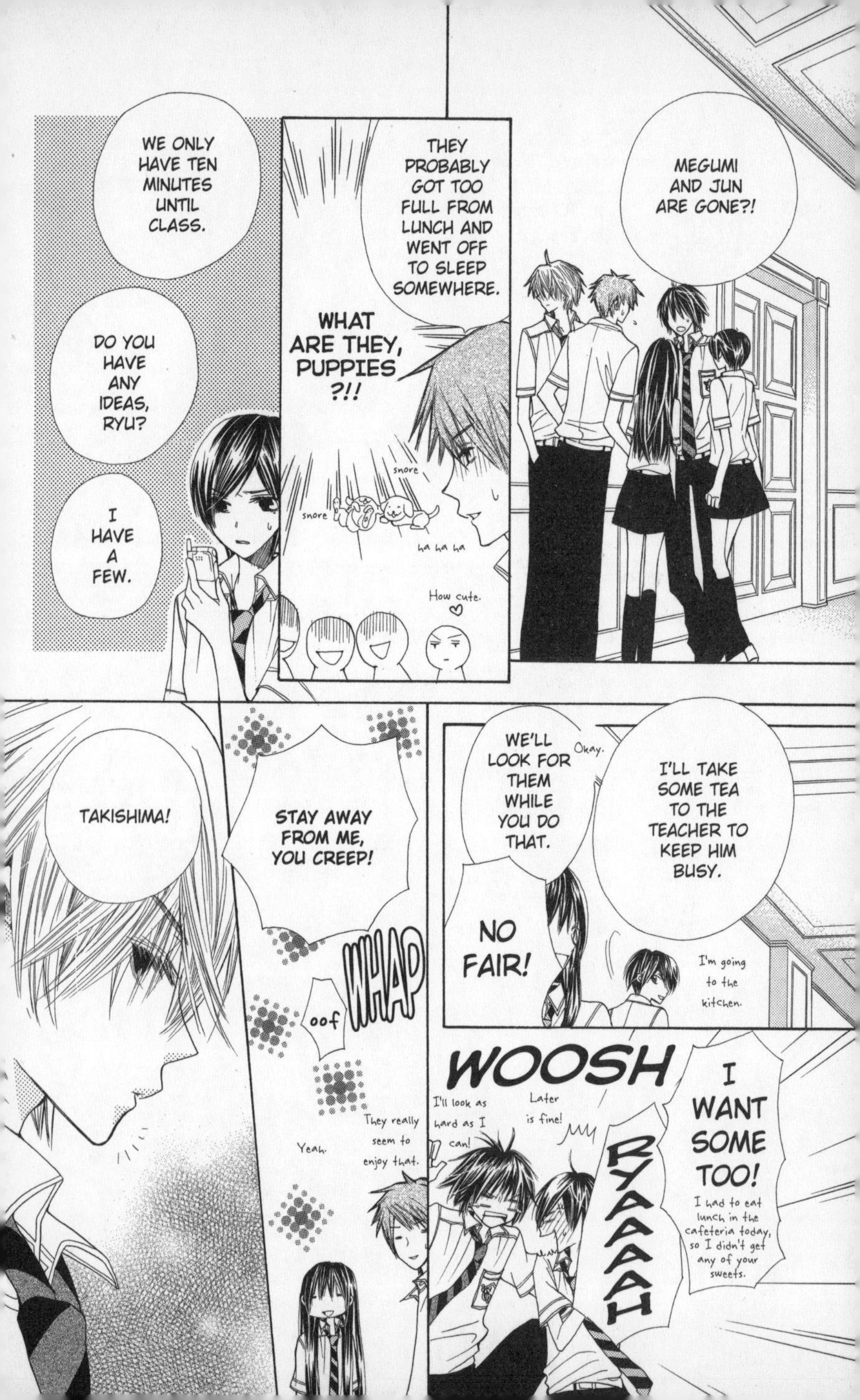
MEGUMI AND JUN ARE GONE?!
THEY PROBABLY GOT TOO FULL FROM LUNCH AND WENT OFF TO SLEEP SOMEWHERE.
WHAT ARE THEY, PUPPIES?!!
snore
snore
ha ha ha
How cute.
WE ONLY HAVE TEN MINUTES UNTIL CLASS.
DO YOU HAVE ANY IDEAS, RYU?
I HAVE A FEW.
I'LL TAKE SOME TEA TO THE TEACHER TO KEEP HIM BUSY.
WE'LL LOOK FOR THEM WHILE YOU DO THAT.
Okay.
NO FAIR!
I'm going to the kitchen.
I WANT SOME TOO!
I had to eat lunch in the cafeteria today, so I didn't get any of your sweets.
WOOSH
Later is fine!
I'll look as hard as I can!
RYAAAAH
STAY AWAY FROM ME, YOU CREEP!
WHAP
oof
They really seem to enjoy that.
Yeah.
TAKISHIMA!

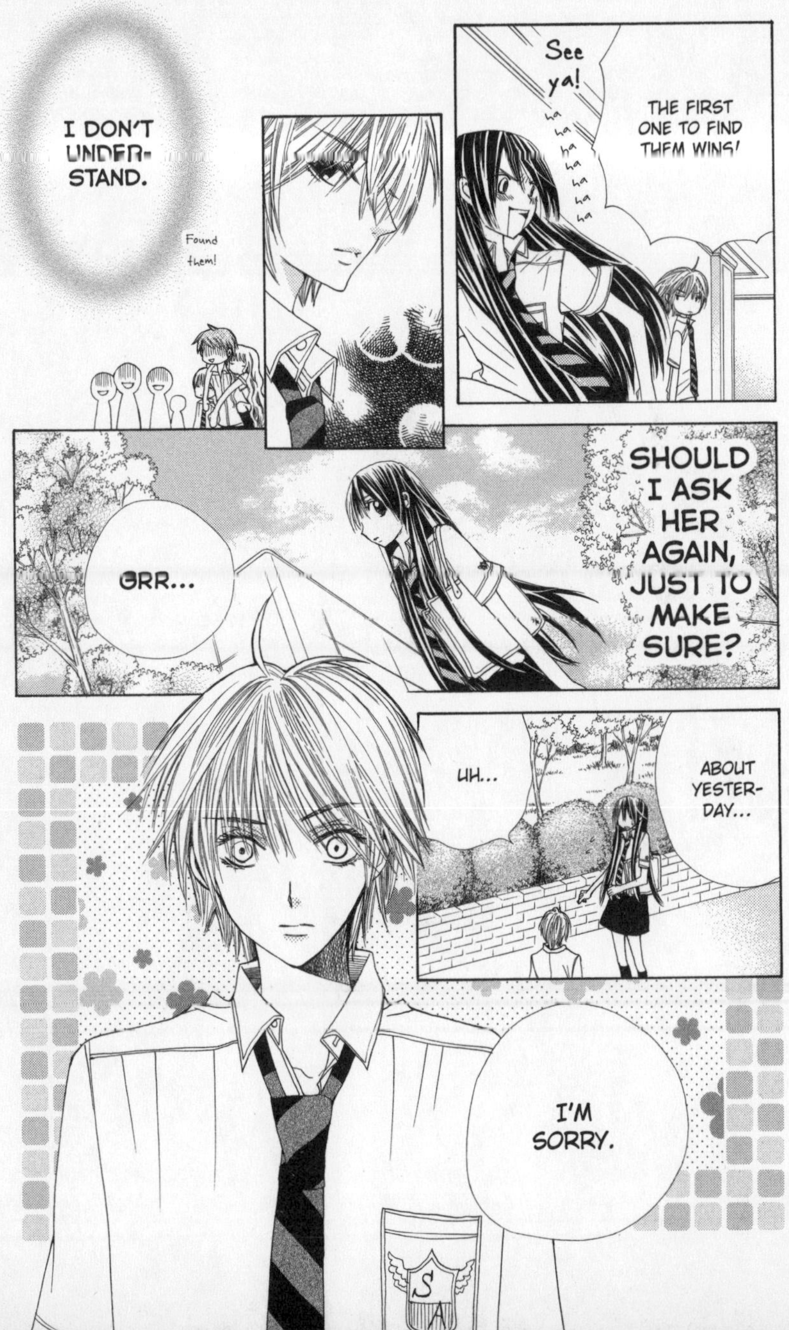
See ya!
ha ha ha ha ha ha ha
THE FIRST ONE TO FIND THEM WINS!
I DON'T UNDER-STAND.
Found them!
SHOULD I ASK HER AGAIN, JUST TO MAKE SURE?
GRR...
ABOUT YESTER-DAY...
UH...
I'M SORRY.

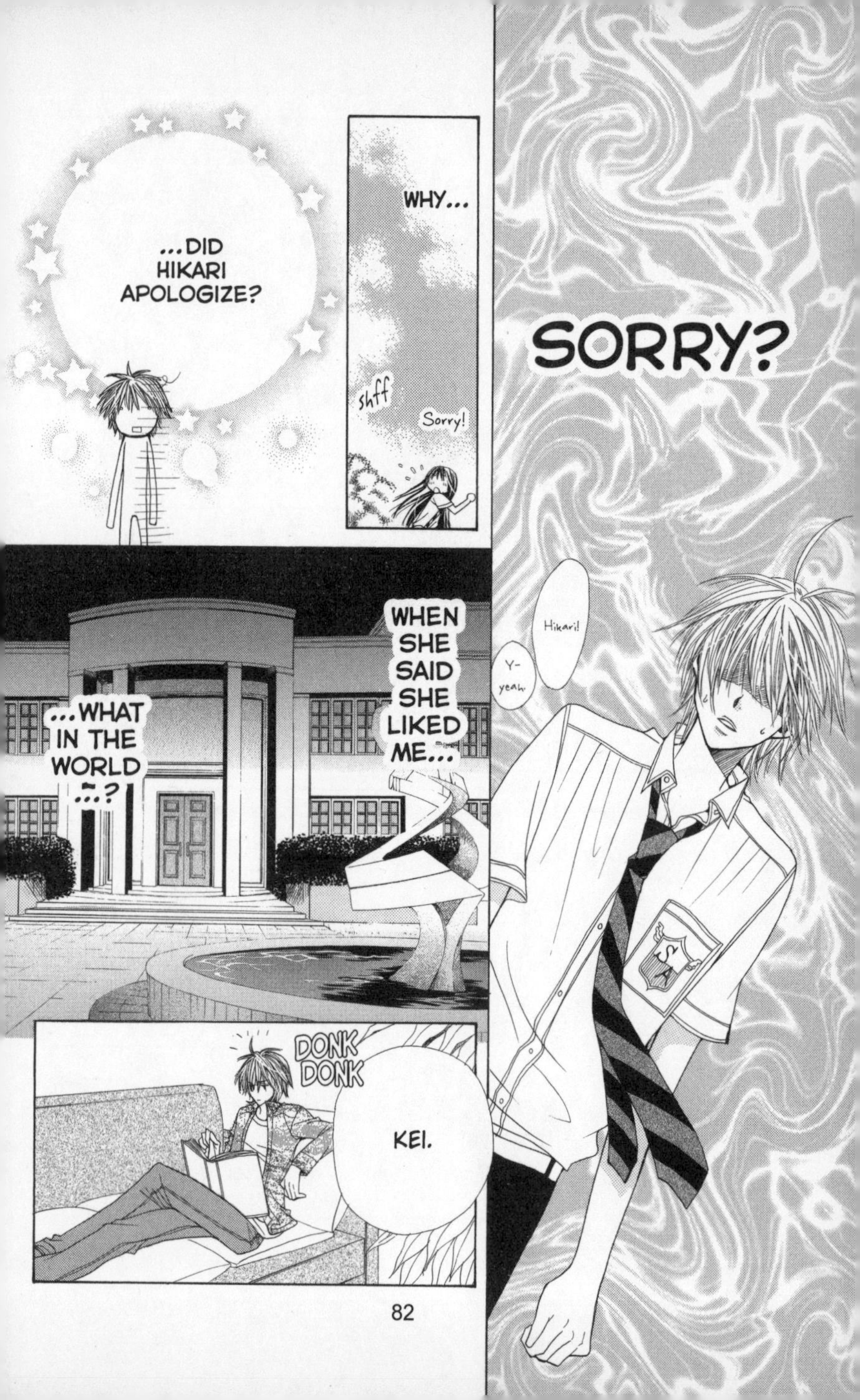
SORRY?
Hikari!
Y-yeah.
WHY...
shff
Sorry!
...DID HIKARI APOLOGIZE?
WHEN SHE SAID SHE LIKED ME...
...WHAT IN THE WORLD...?
DONK DONK
KEI.

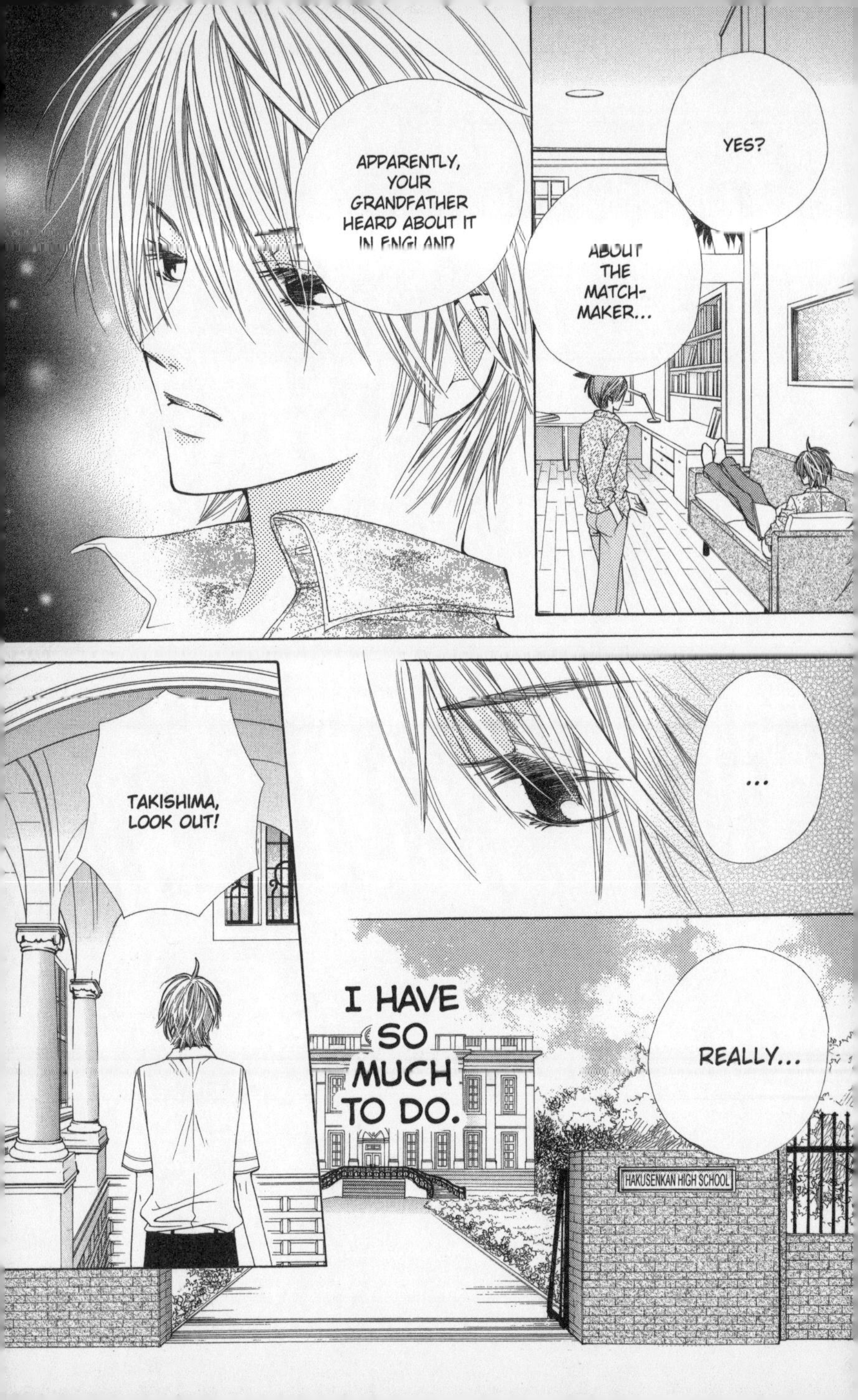
YES?
ABOUT THE MATCH-MAKER...
APPARENTLY, YOUR GRANDFATHER HEARD ABOUT IT IN ENGLAND.
...
REALLY...
I HAVE SO MUCH TO DO.
HAKUSENKAN HIGH SCHOOL
TAKISHIMA, LOOK OUT!

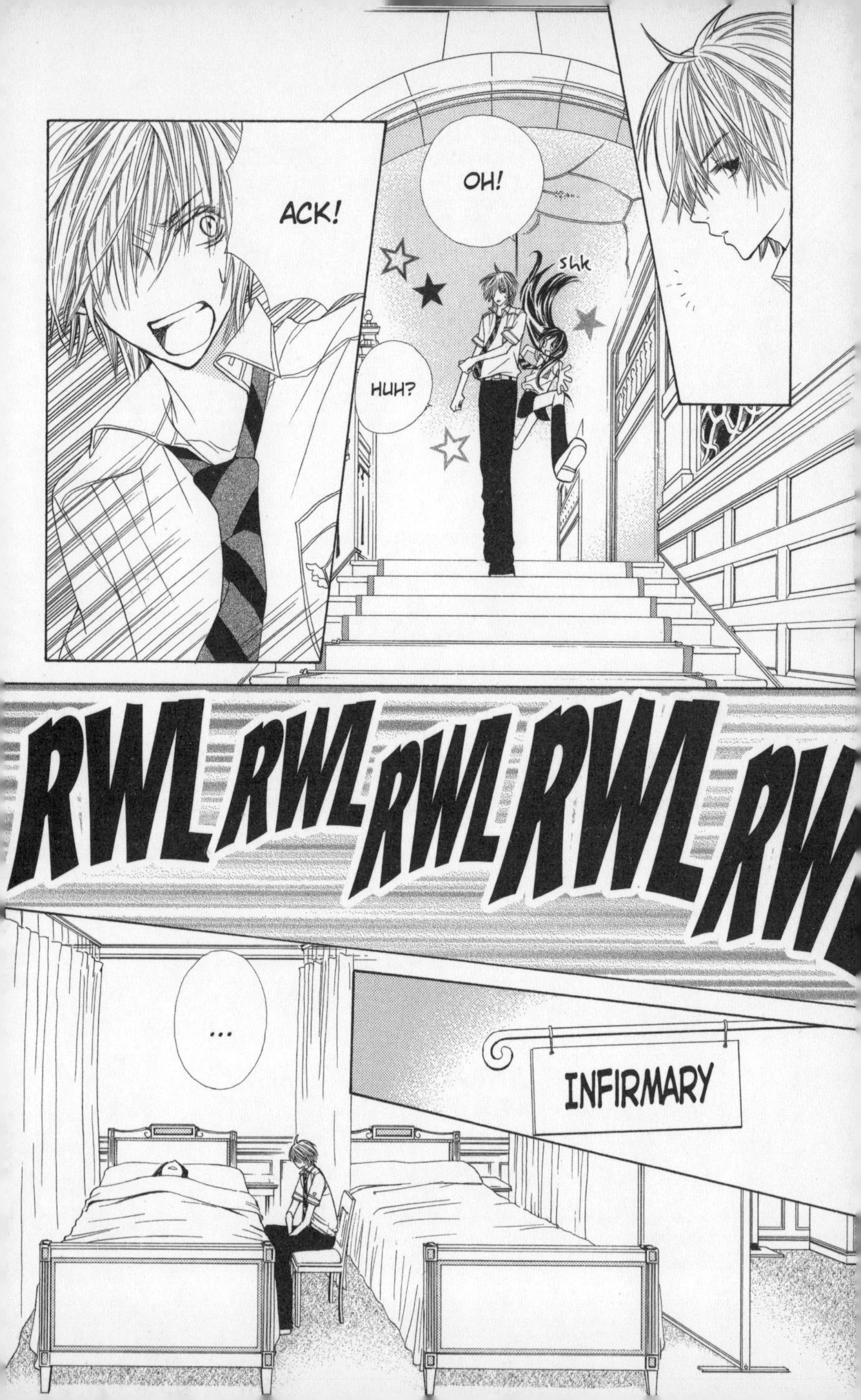

OH!
shk
HUH?
ACK!
RWL RWL RWL RWL RW
INFIRMARY
...

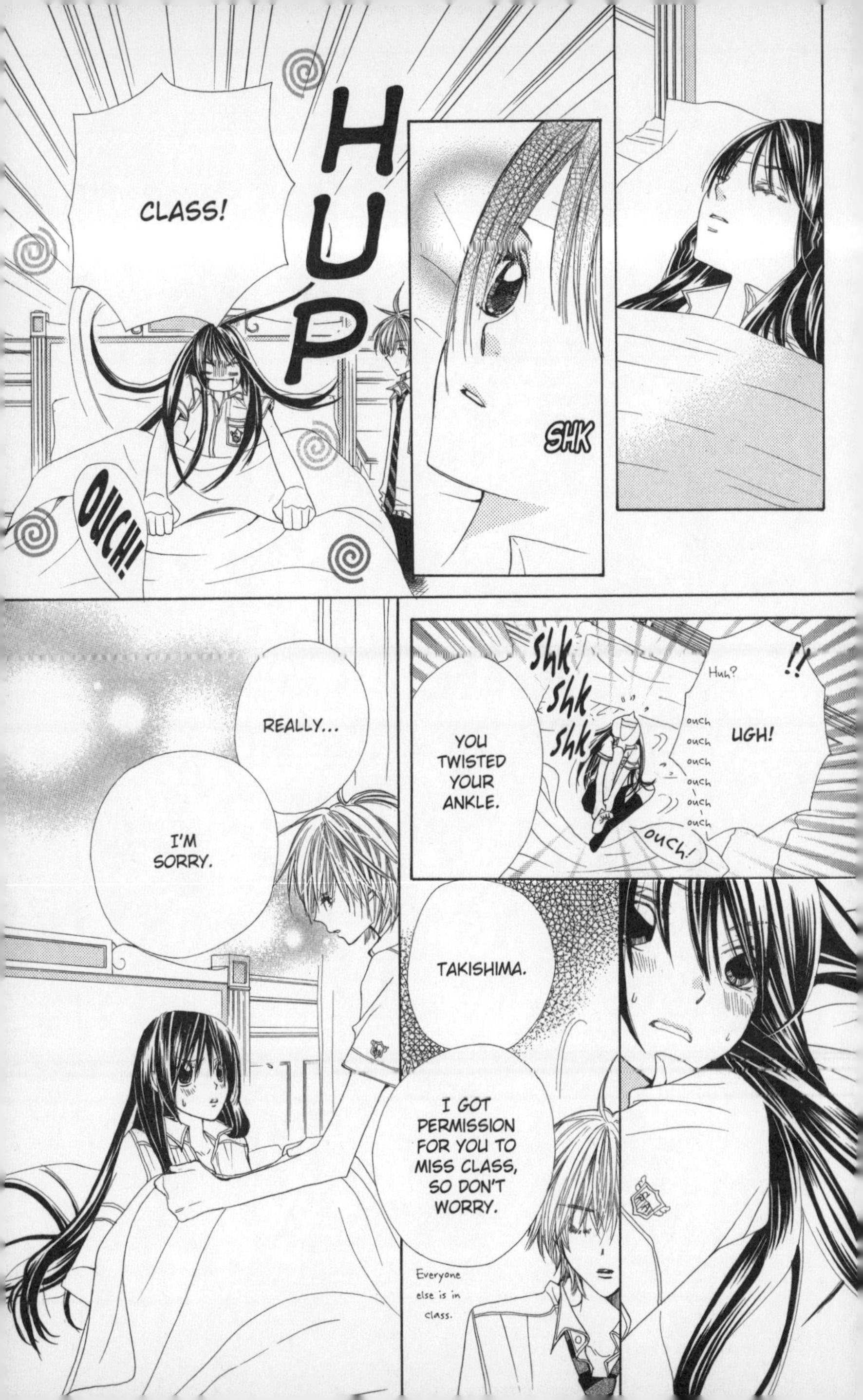
SHK
HUP
CLASS!
OUCH!
!!
Huh?
UGH!
ouch
ouch
ouch
ouch
ouch
ouch
Shk
Shk
Shk
ouch!
YOU TWISTED YOUR ANKLE.
TAKISHIMA.
I GOT PERMISSION FOR YOU TO MISS CLASS, SO DON'T WORRY.
Everyone else is in class.
REALLY...
I'M SORRY.

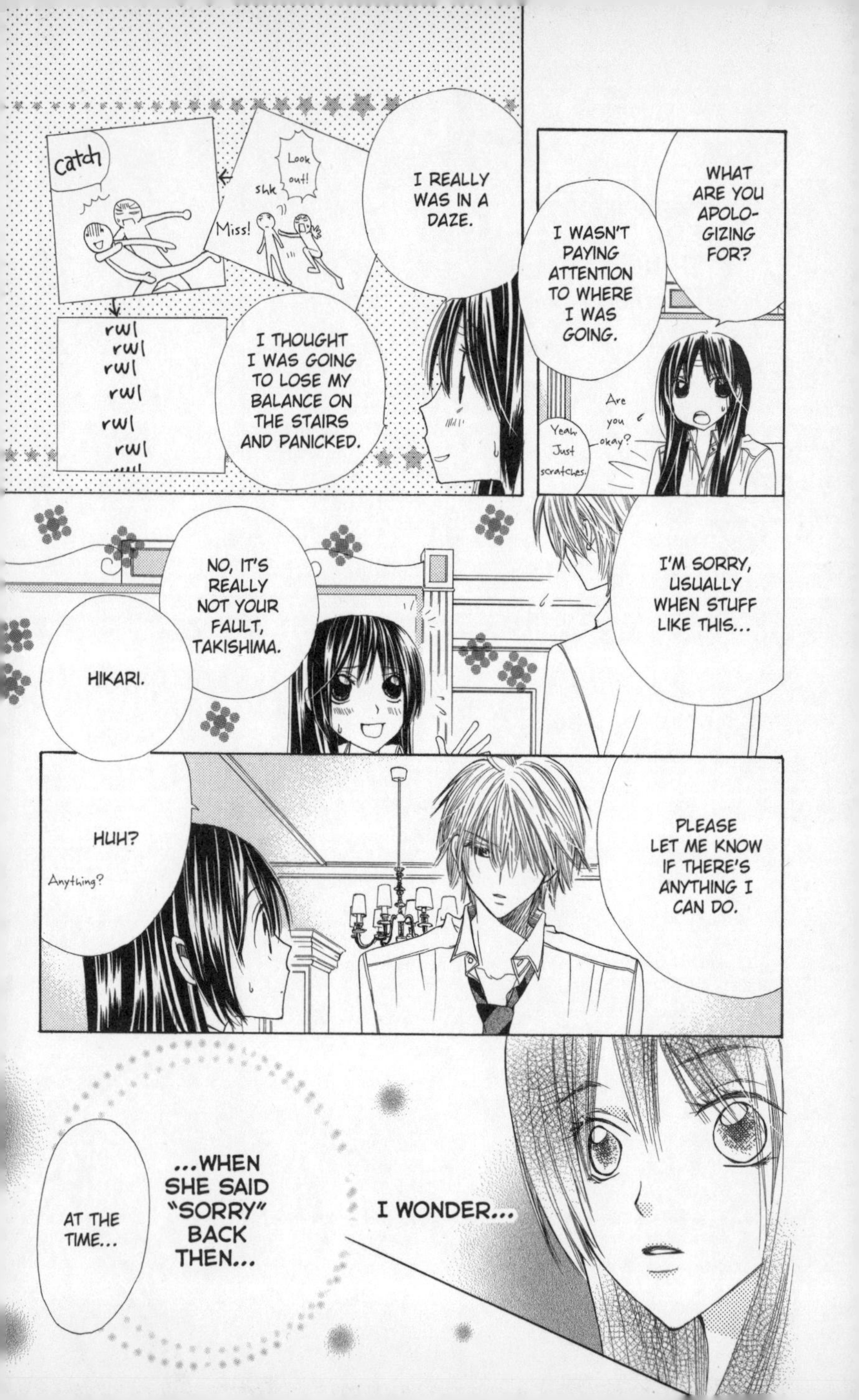
WHAT ARE YOU APOLOGIZING FOR?
I WASN'T PAYING ATTENTION TO WHERE I WAS GOING.
Are you okay?
Yeah. Just scratches.
I REALLY WAS IN A DAZE.
I THOUGHT I WAS GOING TO LOSE MY BALANCE ON THE STAIRS AND PANICKED.
Look out!
shk
Miss!
catch
rwl
rwl
rwl
rwl
rwl
rwl
I'M SORRY, USUALLY WHEN STUFF LIKE THIS...
NO, IT'S REALLY NOT YOUR FAULT, TAKISHIMA.
HIKARI.
PLEASE LET ME KNOW IF THERE'S ANYTHING I CAN DO.
HUH?
Anything?
I WONDER...
...WHEN SHE SAID "SORRY" BACK THEN...
AT THE TIME...

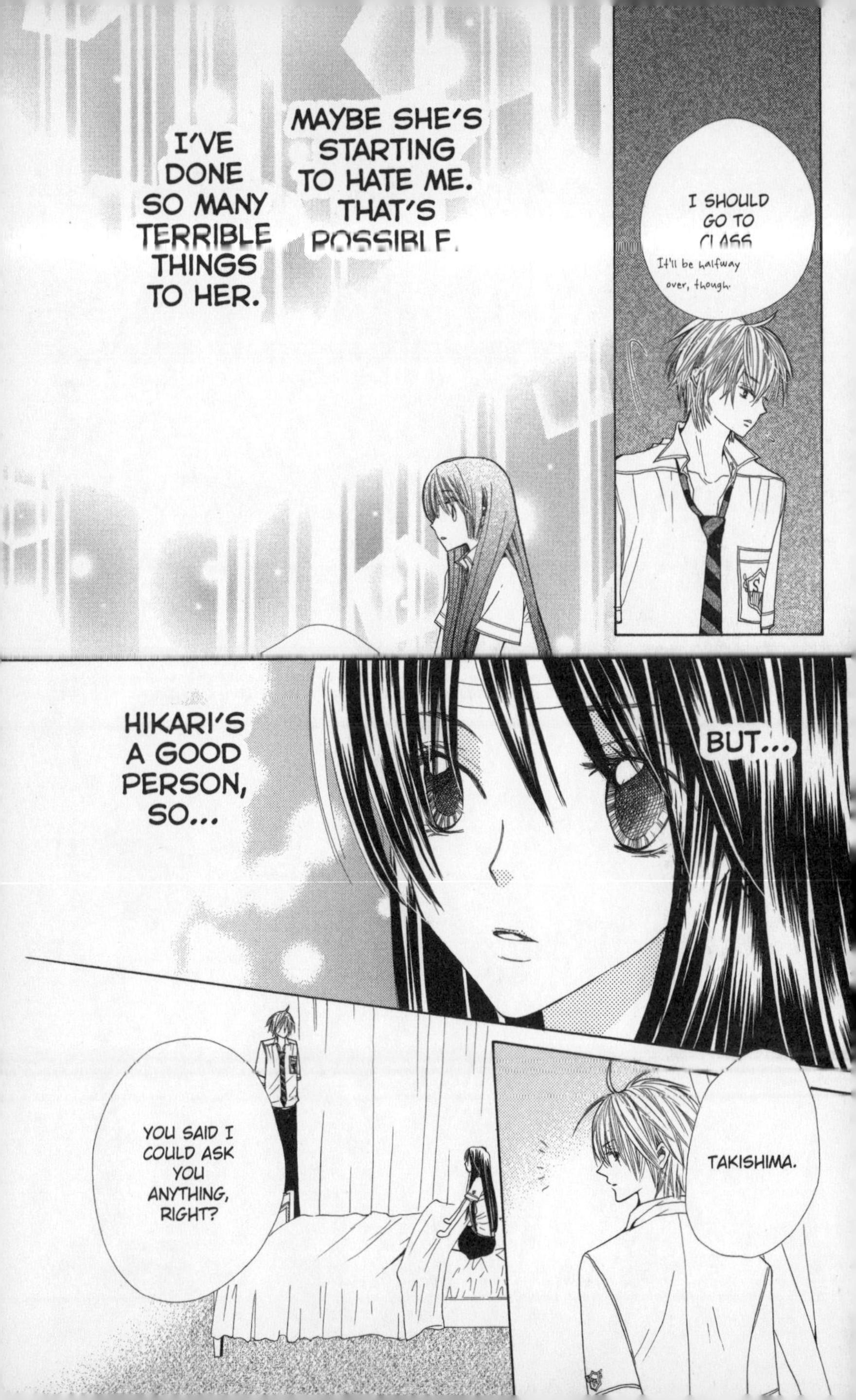
I SHOULD GO TO CLASS
It'll be halfway over, though.
MAYBE SHE'S STARTING TO HATE ME. THAT'S POSSIBLE.
I'VE DONE SO MANY TERRIBLE THINGS TO HER.
BUT...
HIKARI'S A GOOD PERSON, SO...
TAKISHIMA.
YOU SAID I COULD ASK YOU ANYTHING, RIGHT?

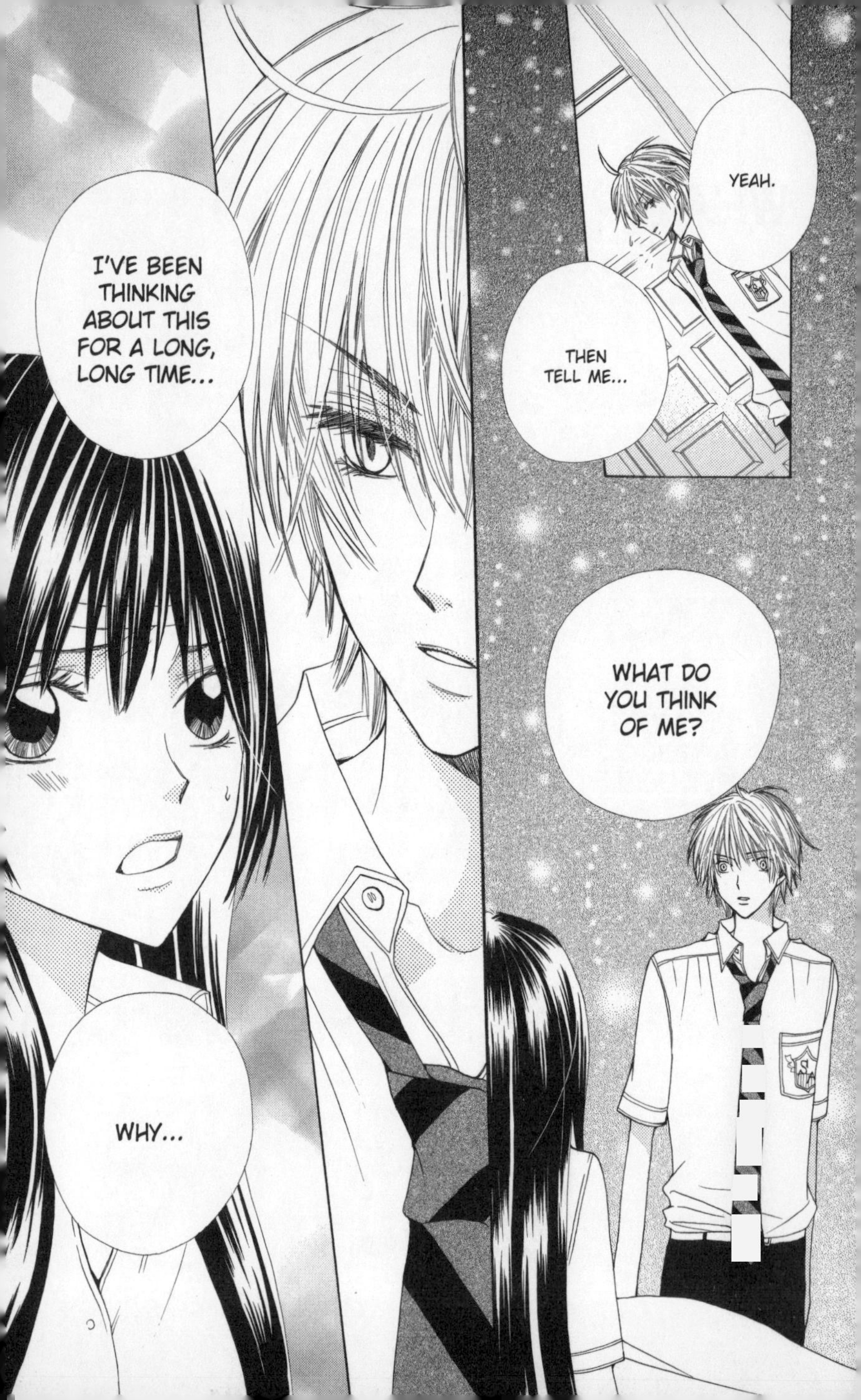

YEAH.
THEN TELL ME...
WHAT DO YOU THINK OF ME?
......
I'VE BEEN THINKING ABOUT THIS FOR A LONG, LONG TIME...
WHY...

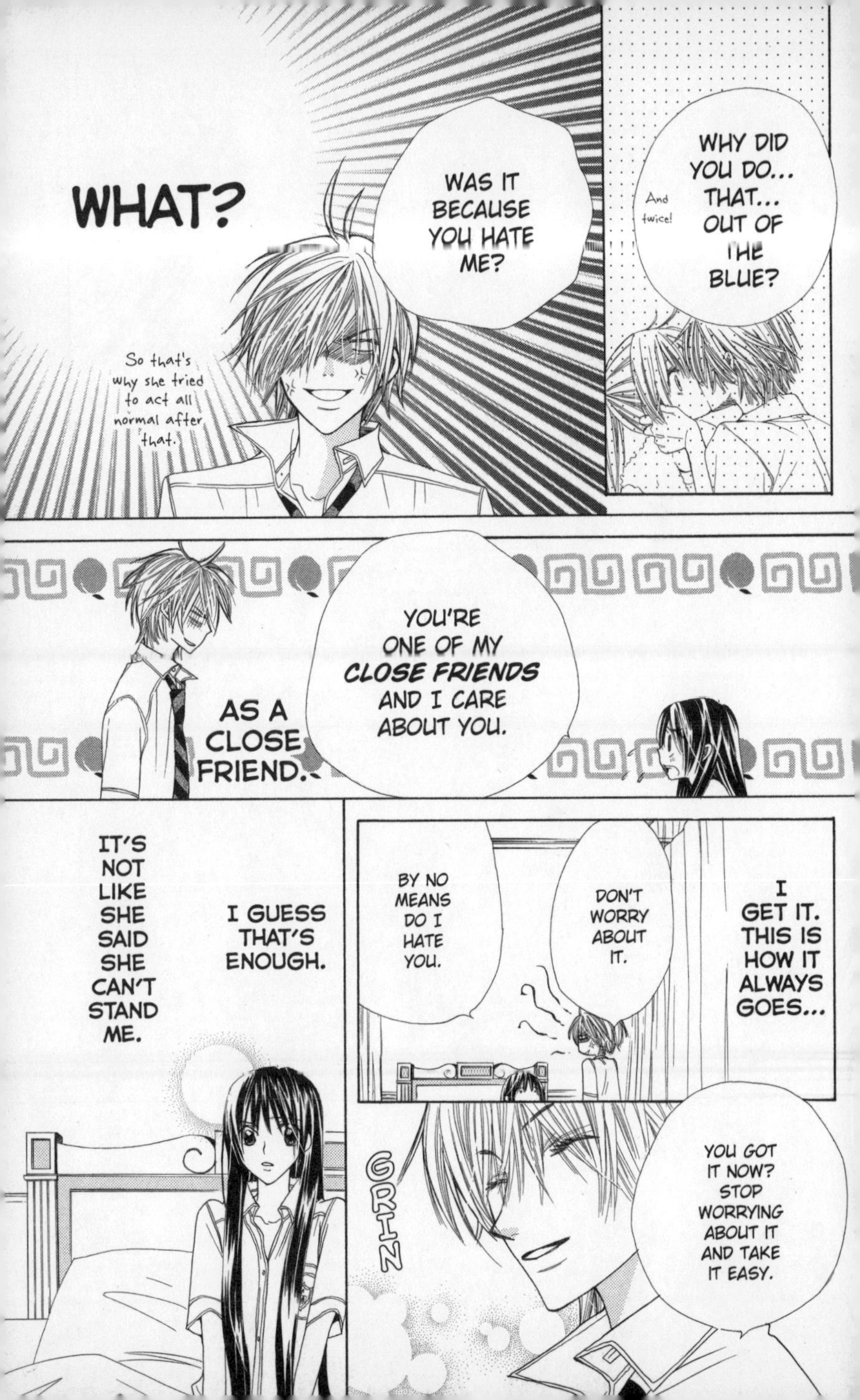
WHY DID YOU DO... THAT... OUT OF THE BLUE?
And twice!
WAS IT BECAUSE YOU HATE ME?
WHAT?
So that's why she tried to act all normal after that.
YOU'RE ONE OF MY CLOSE FRIENDS AND I CARE ABOUT YOU.
AS A CLOSE FRIEND.
I GET IT. THIS IS HOW IT ALWAYS GOES...
DON'T WORRY ABOUT IT.
BY NO MEANS DO I HATE YOU.
YOU GOT IT NOW? STOP WORRYING ABOUT IT AND TAKE IT EASY.
GRIN
I GUESS THAT'S ENOUGH.
IT'S NOT LIKE SHE SAID SHE CAN'T STAND ME.

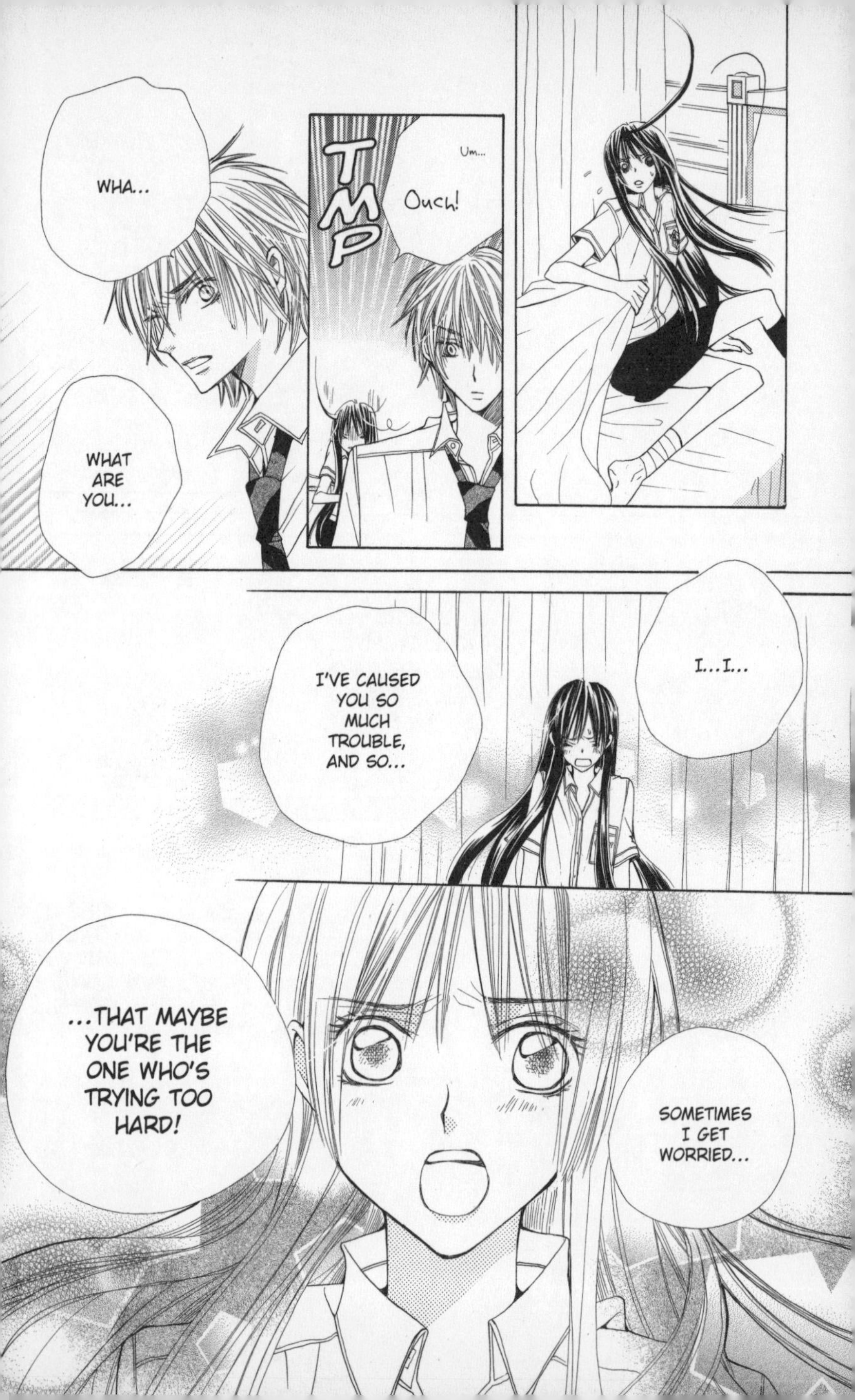

Um...
Ouch!
TMP
WHA...
WHAT ARE YOU...
I...I...
I'VE CAUSED YOU SO MUCH TROUBLE, AND SO...
SOMETIMES I GET WORRIED...
...THAT MAYBE YOU'RE THE ONE WHO'S TRYING TOO HARD!

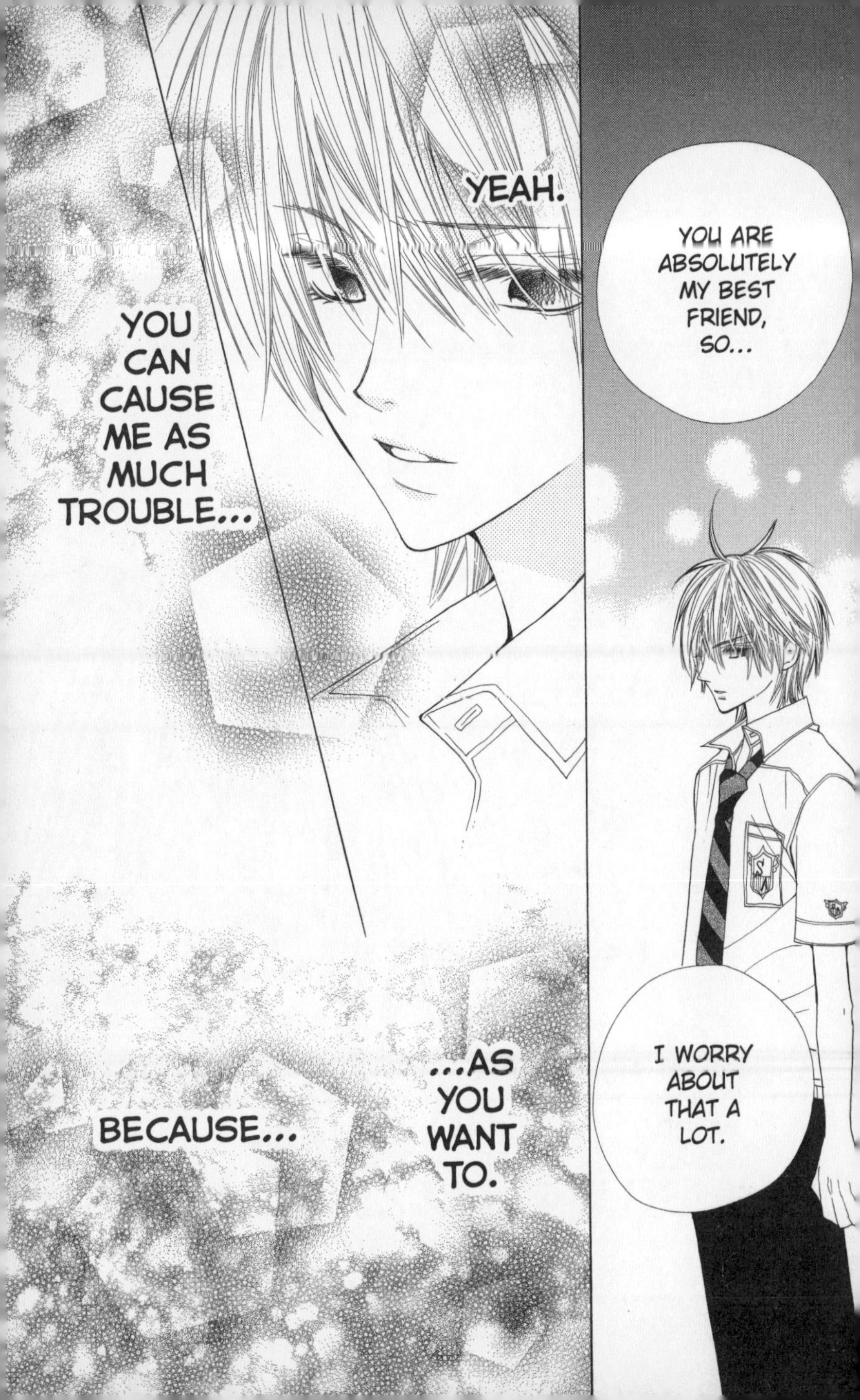
YOU ARE ABSOLUTELY MY BEST FRIEND, SO...
I WORRY ABOUT THAT A LOT.
YEAH.
YOU CAN CAUSE ME AS MUCH TROUBLE...
...AS YOU WANT TO.
BECAUSE...

I LOVE YOU.
...SILLY.
ISN'T IT A LITTLE LATE IN THE GAME FOR THIS?
WHAT?!
hmph
I LIKE YOU TOO.
YOU PROBABLY...
...CAN'T SEE WHAT THOSE WORDS REALLY MEAN YET.

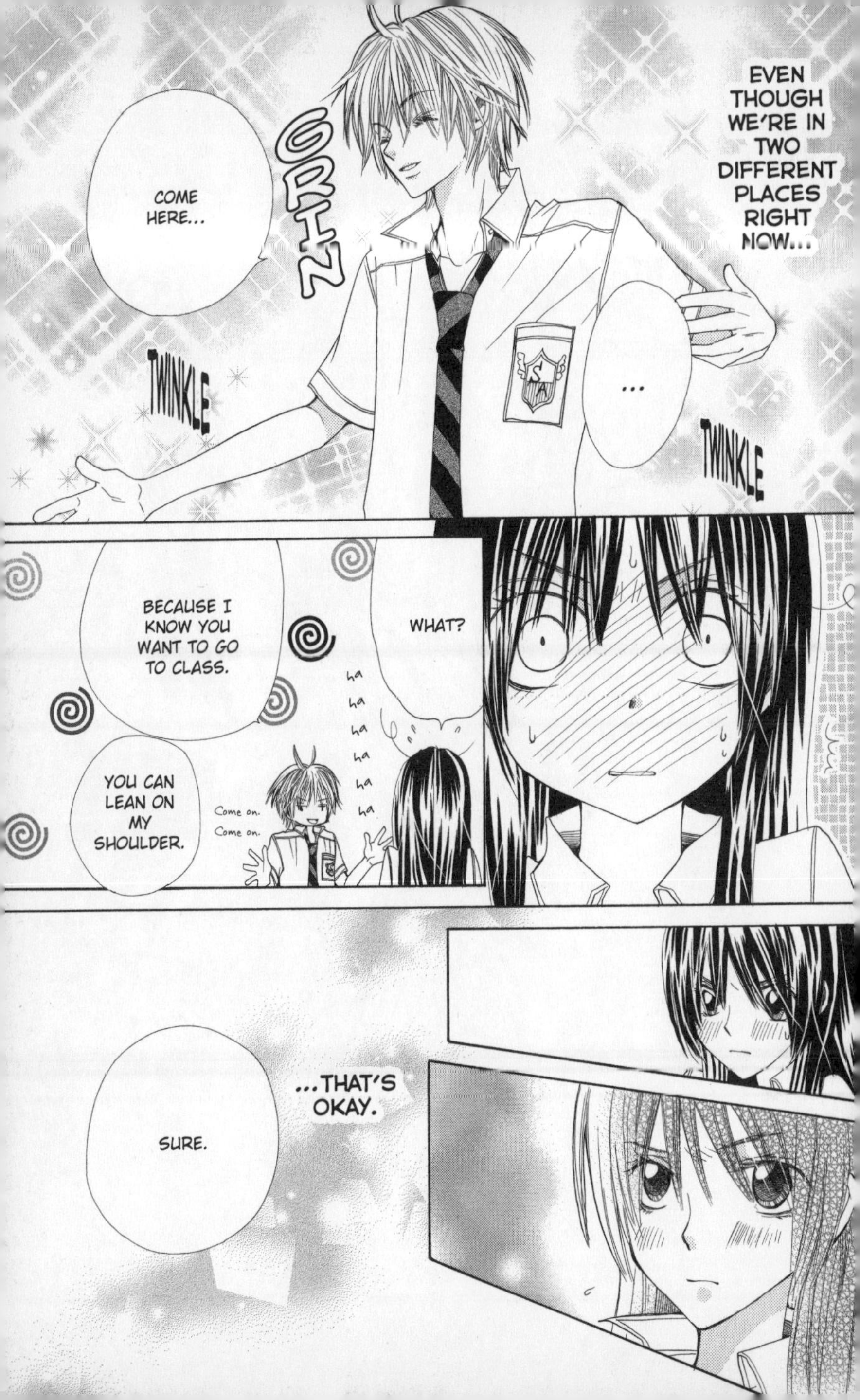
EVEN THOUGH WE'RE IN TWO DIFFERENT PLACES RIGHT NOW...
GRIN
COME HERE...
...
TWINKLE
TWINKLE
WHAT?
BECAUSE I KNOW YOU WANT TO GO TO CLASS.
ha ha ha ha ha ha
Come on. Come on.
YOU CAN LEAN ON MY SHOULDER.
...THAT'S OKAY.
SURE.

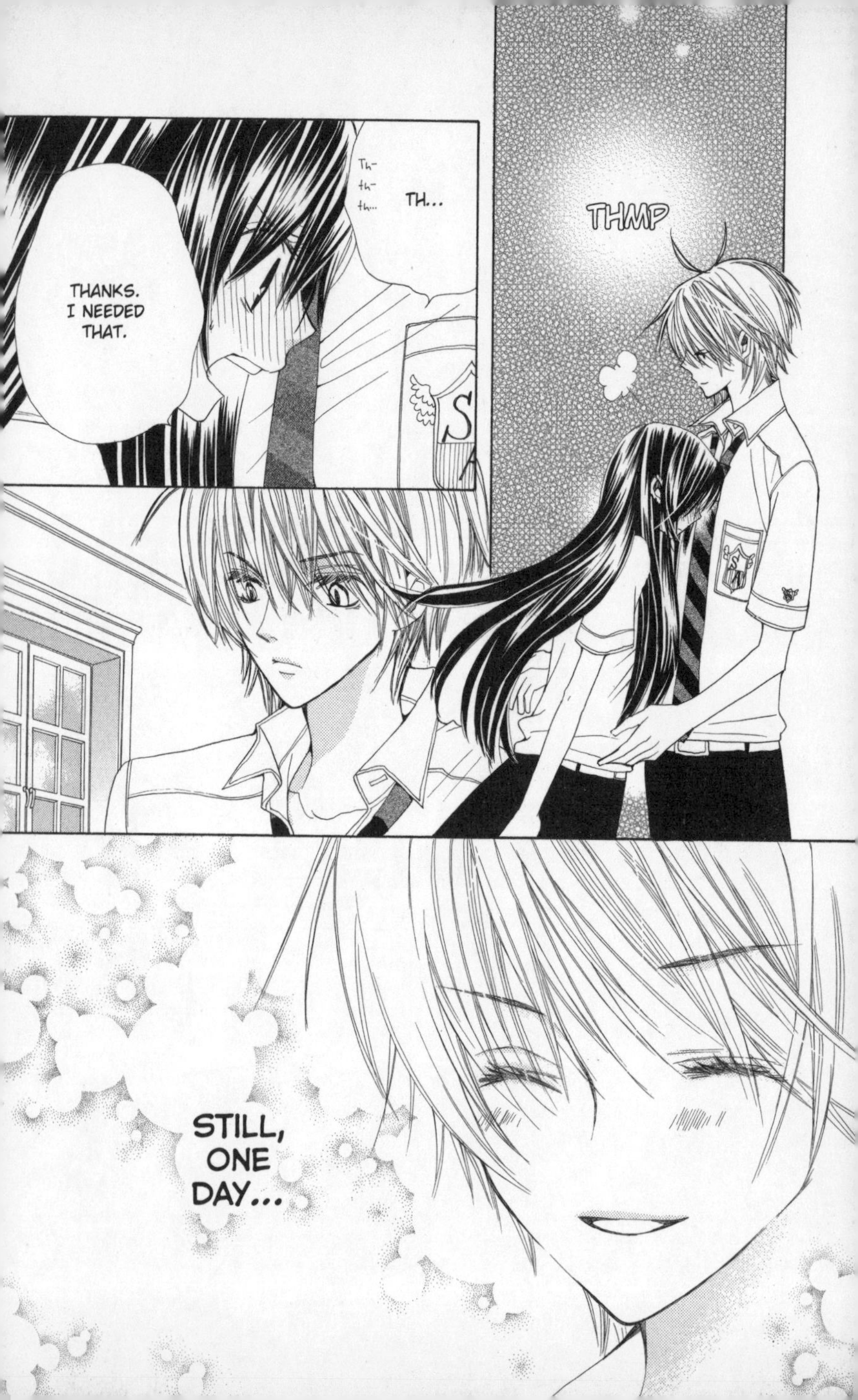
THMP
Th- th- th...
TH...
THANKS. I NEEDED THAT.
STILL, ONE DAY...

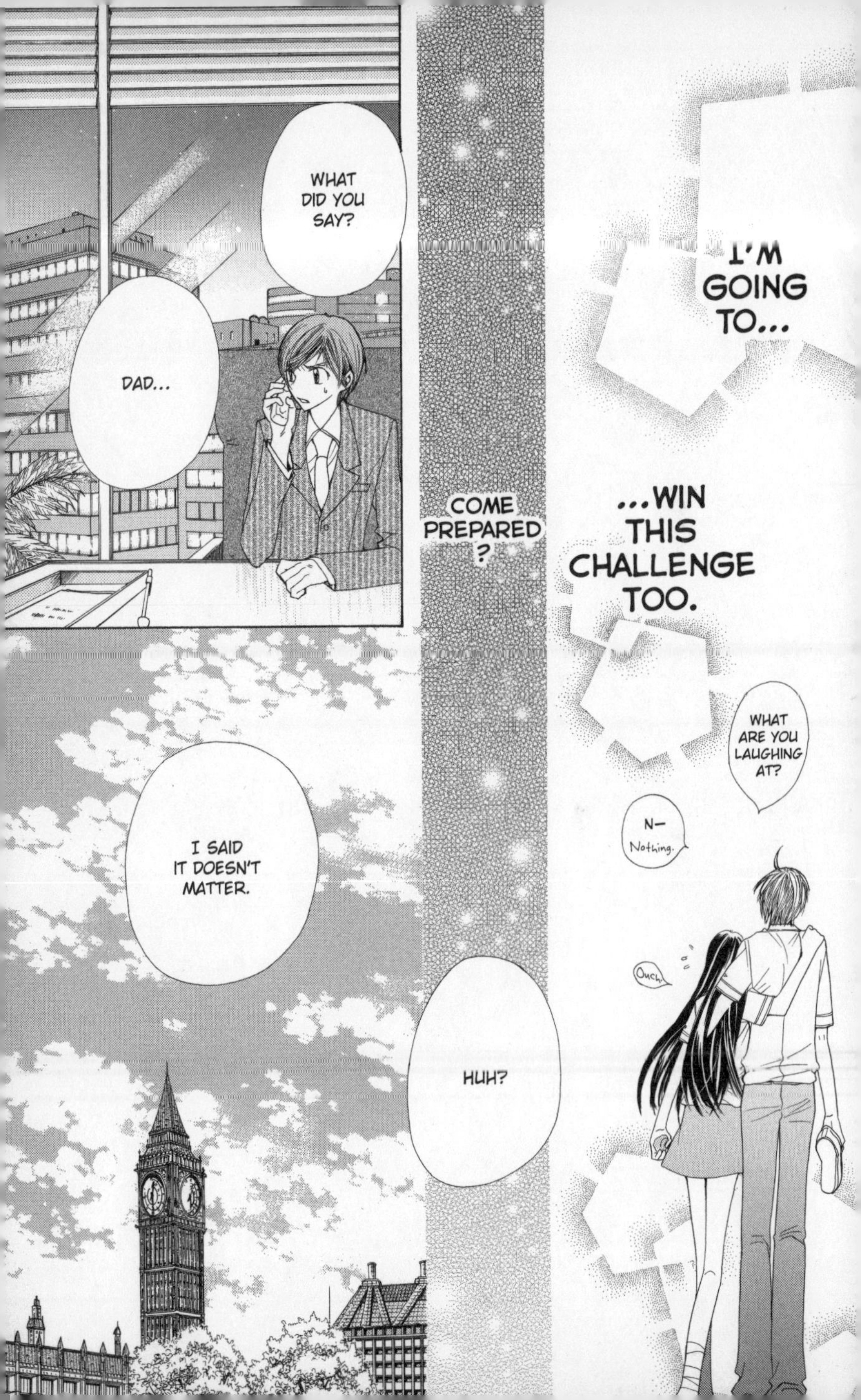
I'M GOING TO...
...WIN THIS CHALLENGE TOO.
WHAT ARE YOU LAUGHING AT?
N— Nothing.
Ouch.
COME PREPARED?
HUH?
WHAT DID YOU SAY?
DAD...
I SAID IT DOESN'T MATTER.

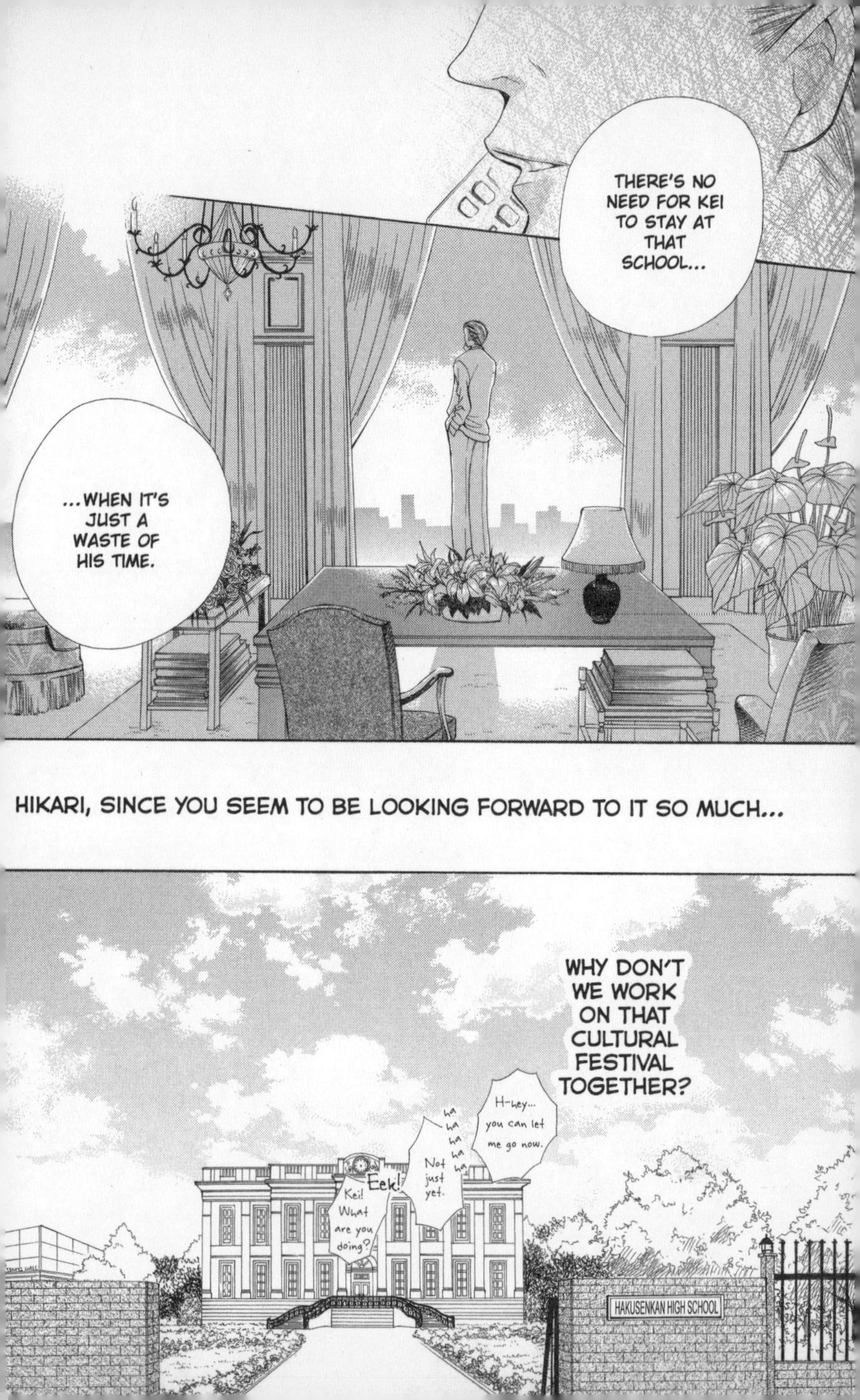
THERE'S NO NEED FOR KEI TO STAY AT THAT SCHOOL...
...WHEN IT'S JUST A WASTE OF HIS TIME.
HIKARI, SINCE YOU SEEM TO BE LOOKING FORWARD TO IT SO MUCH...
WHY DON'T WE WORK ON THAT CULTURAL FESTIVAL TOGETHER?
H-hey... you can let me go now.
ha ha ha ha ha
Not just yet.
Eek!
Kei! What are you doing?
HAKUSENKAN HIGH SCHOOL

Chapter 26

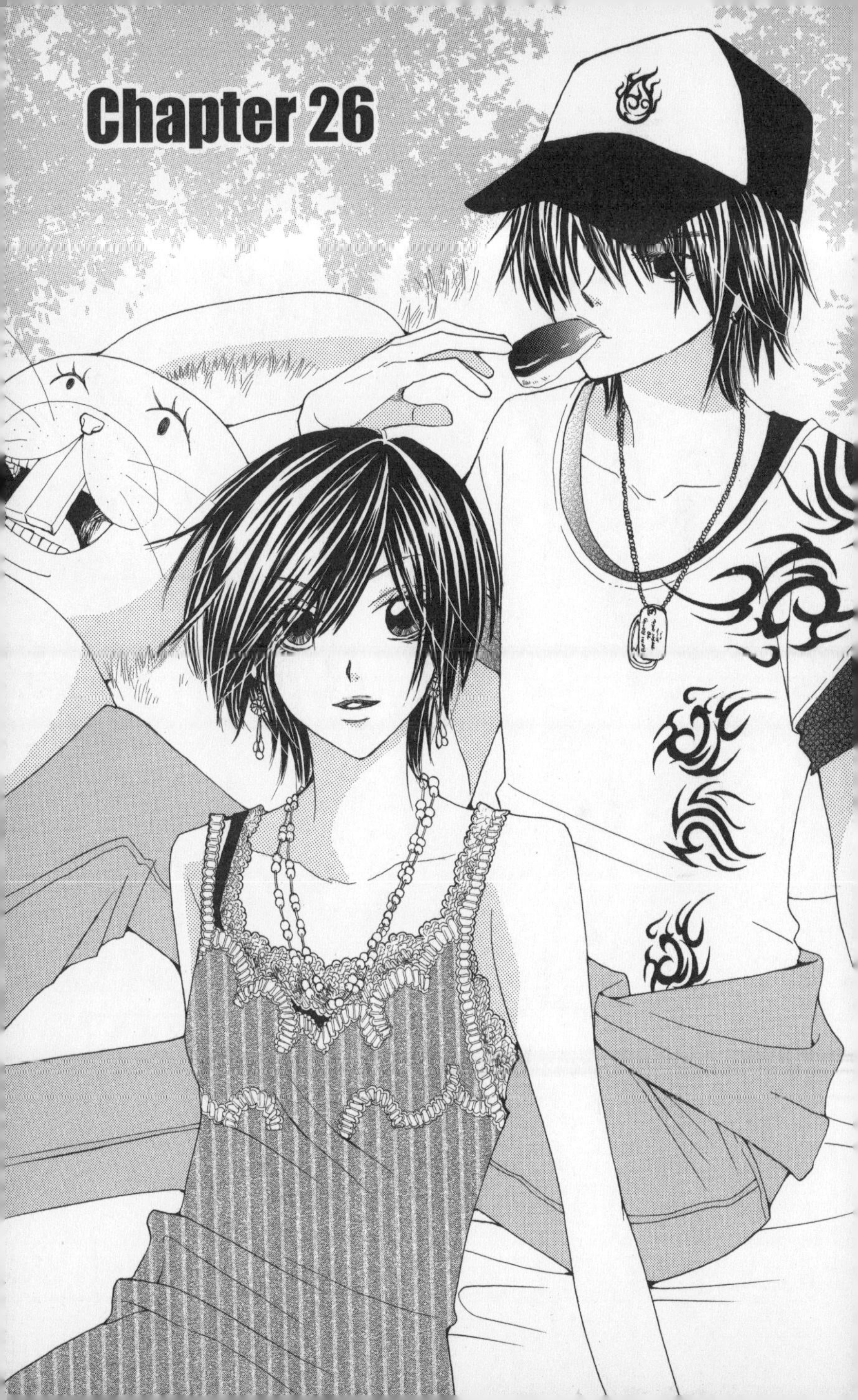

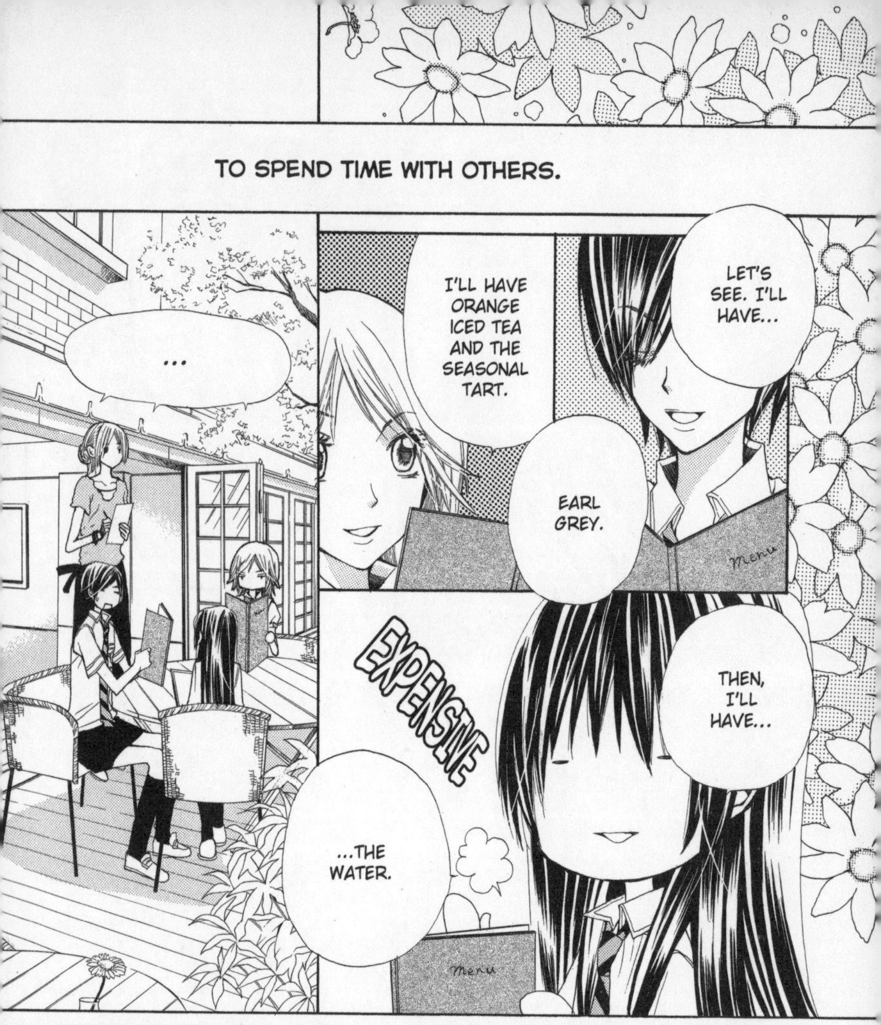
TO SPEND TIME WITH OTHERS.
LET'S SEE. I'LL HAVE...
EARL GREY.
I'LL HAVE ORANGE ICED TEA AND THE SEASONAL TART.
THEN, I'LL HAVE...
EXPENSIVE
...THE WATER.
...
Menu
Menu

• COLOR •

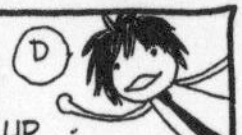

MOST OF THE TIME, I USE COLORED INKS WHEN I WANT TO DO MY DRAWINGS IN COLOR. IT MAKES ME FEEL SO HAPPY WHEN I SEE ALL THE DIFFERENT COLORED INKS, AND I END UP BUYING COLORS THAT I DON'T EVEN USE. I HAVE A RIDICULOUS AMOUNT OF INKS. AND RIGHT NOW, I'M STUDYING GRAPHICS. AND GRAPHICS SOFTWARE IS REALLY EXPENSIVE, ISN'T IT? IT COULD ALMOST MAKE YOUR EYES POP OUT! haah haah

I WISH I COULD USE "RUMA" TO COLOR PEOPLE'S SKIN... BUT THE PINK I'VE BEEN USING FOR SKIN WAS DISCONTINUED. AND NOW THEY'RE SAYING THAT SOME OF MY OTHER FAVORITE COLORS ARE BEING DISCONTINUED TOO.

THAT'S SAD.

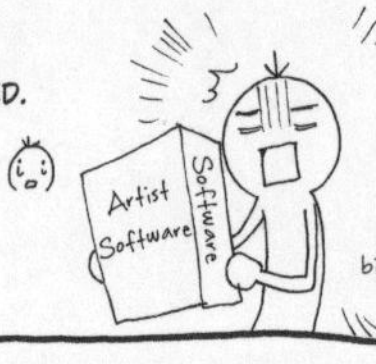
Artist Software
Software

What?! This is expensive! I could get the biggest steak on the menu for that!

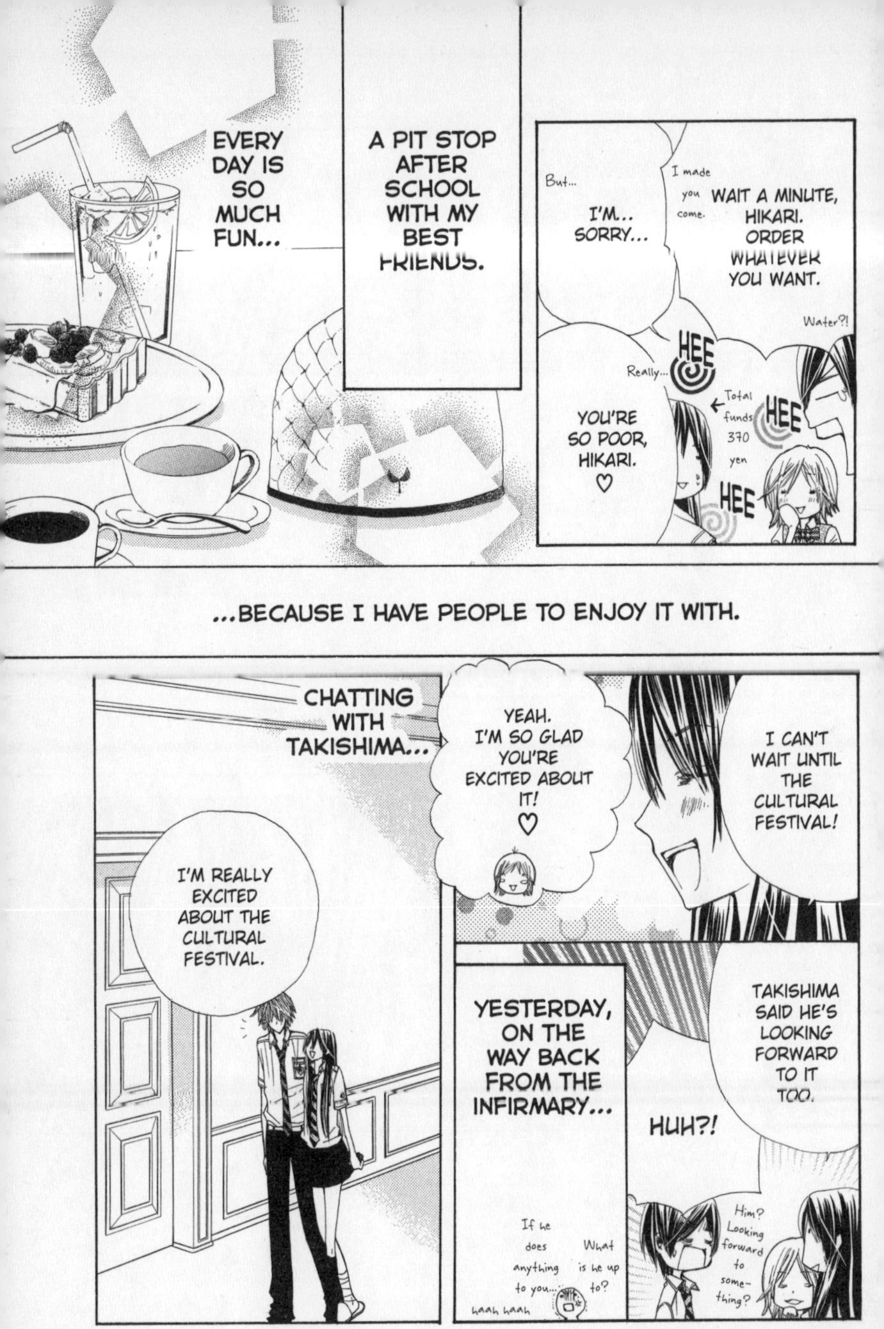

WAIT A MINUTE, HIKARI. ORDER WHATEVER YOU WANT.
I made you come.
But...
I'M... SORRY...
Water?!
HEE
Total funds 370 yen
HEE
Really...
YOU'RE SO POOR, HIKARI. ♡
HEE
A PIT STOP AFTER SCHOOL WITH MY BEST FRIENDS.
EVERY DAY IS SO MUCH FUN...
...BECAUSE I HAVE PEOPLE TO ENJOY IT WITH.
I CAN'T WAIT UNTIL THE CULTURAL FESTIVAL!
YEAH. I'M SO GLAD YOU'RE EXCITED ABOUT IT! ♡
TAKISHIMA SAID HE'S LOOKING FORWARD TO IT TOO.
HUH?!
Him? Looking forward to some-thing?
YESTERDAY, ON THE WAY BACK FROM THE INFIRMARY...
What is he up to?
If he does anything to you...
haah haah
CHATTING WITH TAKISHIMA...
I'M REALLY EXCITED ABOUT THE CULTURAL FESTIVAL.

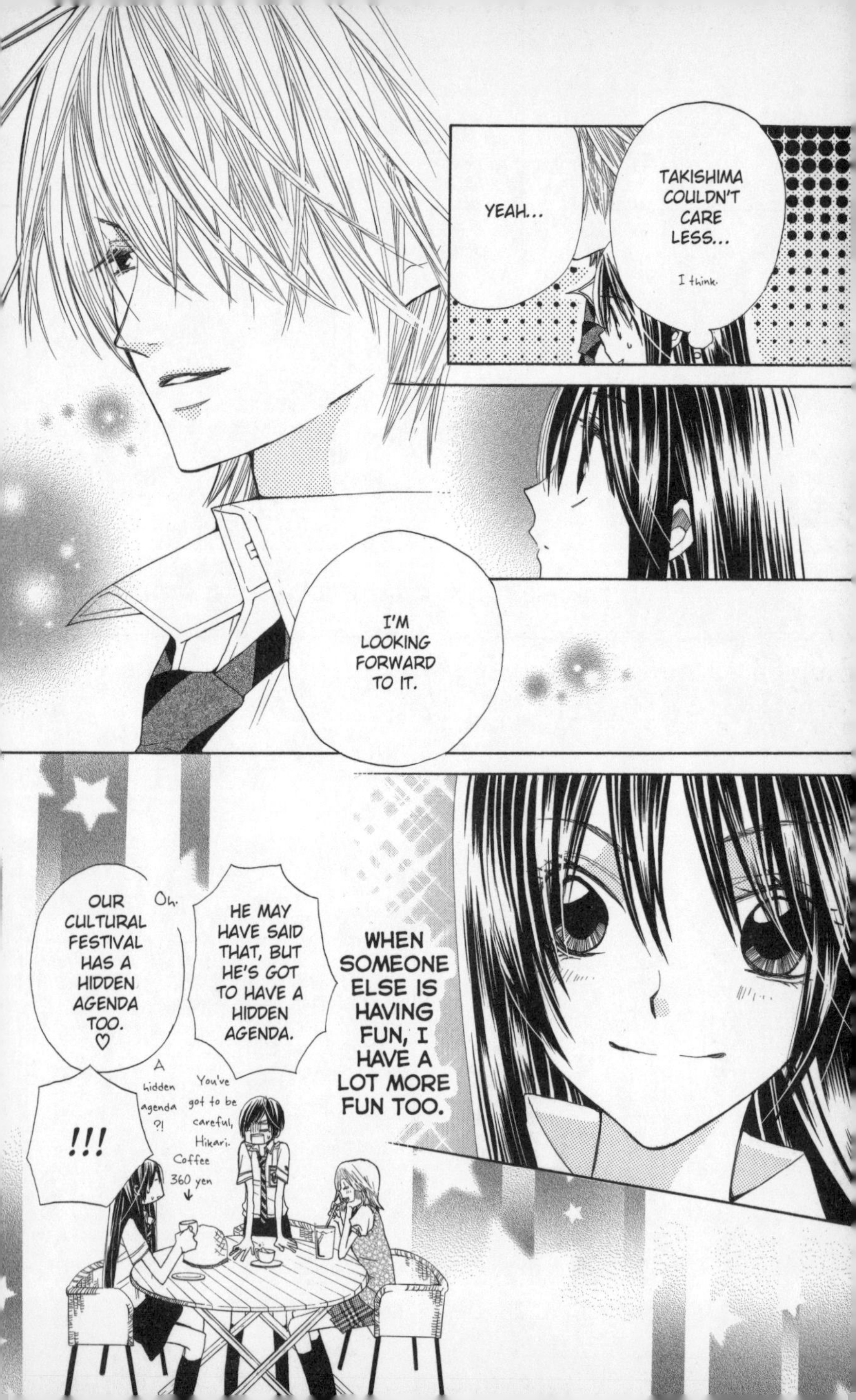

TAKISHIMA COULDN'T CARE LESS...
I think.
YEAH...
I'M LOOKING FORWARD TO IT.
WHEN SOMEONE ELSE IS HAVING FUN, I HAVE A LOT MORE FUN TOO.
HE MAY HAVE SAID THAT, BUT HE'S GOT TO HAVE A HIDDEN AGENDA.
Oh.
OUR CULTURAL FESTIVAL HAS A HIDDEN AGENDA TOO. ♡
You've got to be careful, Hikari.
A hidden agenda?!
!!!
Coffee 360 yen

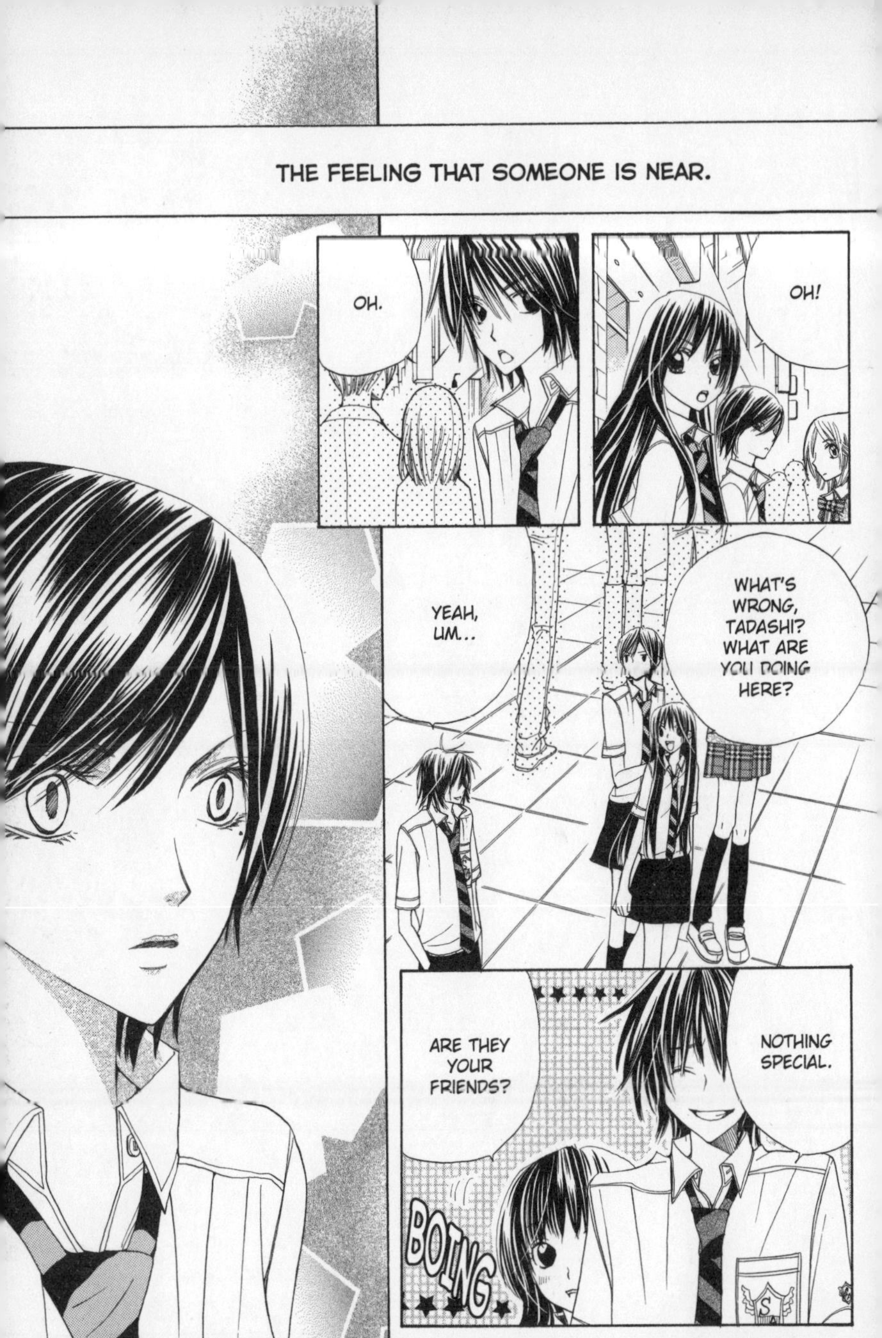
THE FEELING THAT SOMEONE IS NEAR.
OH!
OH.
WHAT'S WRONG, TADASHI? WHAT ARE YOU DOING HERE?
YEAH, UM..
NOTHING SPECIAL.
ARE THEY YOUR FRIENDS?
BOING

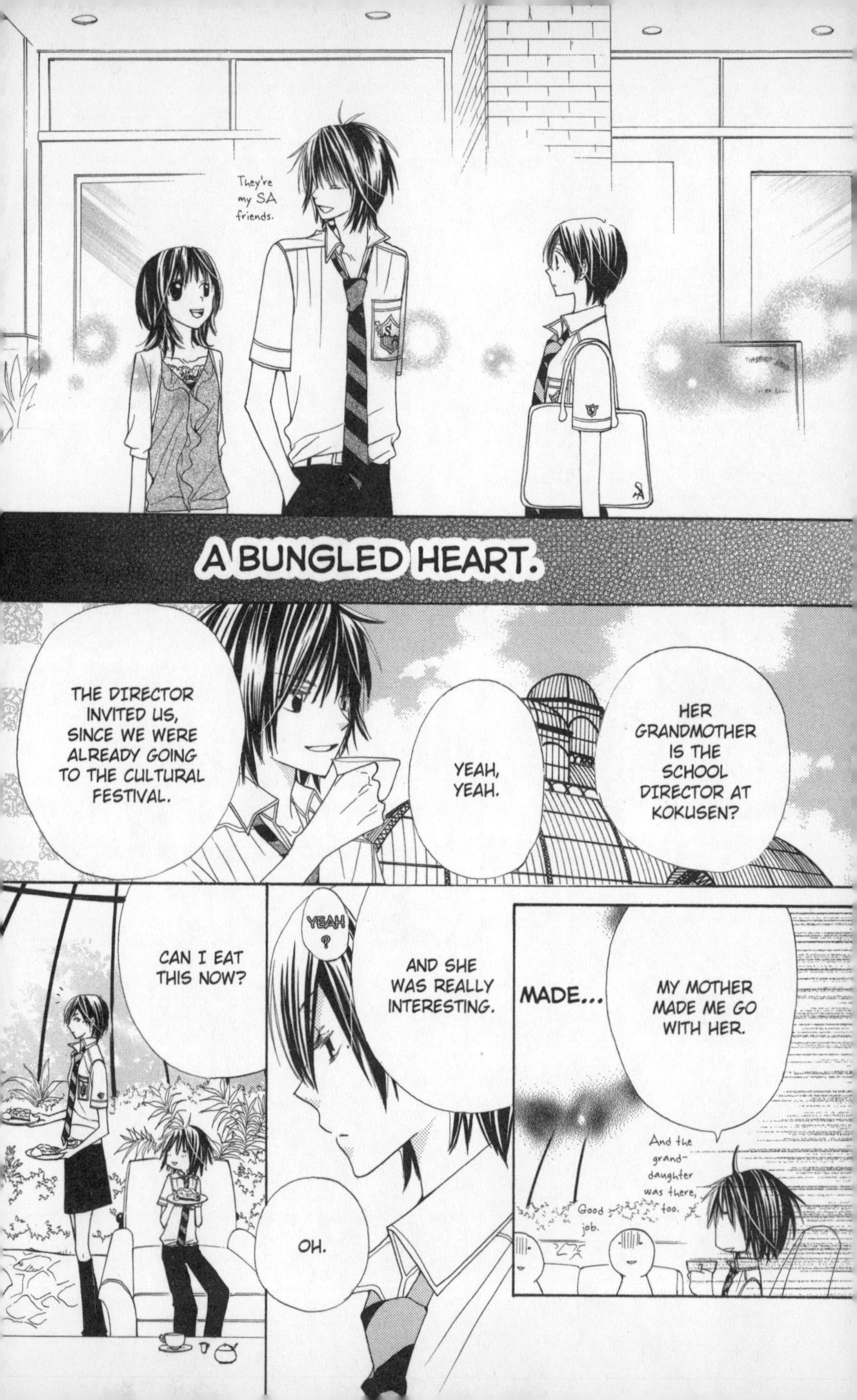
They're my SA friends.
A BUNGLED HEART.
HER GRANDMOTHER IS THE SCHOOL DIRECTOR AT KOKUSEN?
YEAH, YEAH.
THE DIRECTOR INVITED US, SINCE WE WERE ALREADY GOING TO THE CULTURAL FESTIVAL.
MY MOTHER MADE ME GO WITH HER.
MADE...
And the grand-daughter was there, too.
Good job.
YEAH?
AND SHE WAS REALLY INTERESTING.
OH.
CAN I EAT THIS NOW?

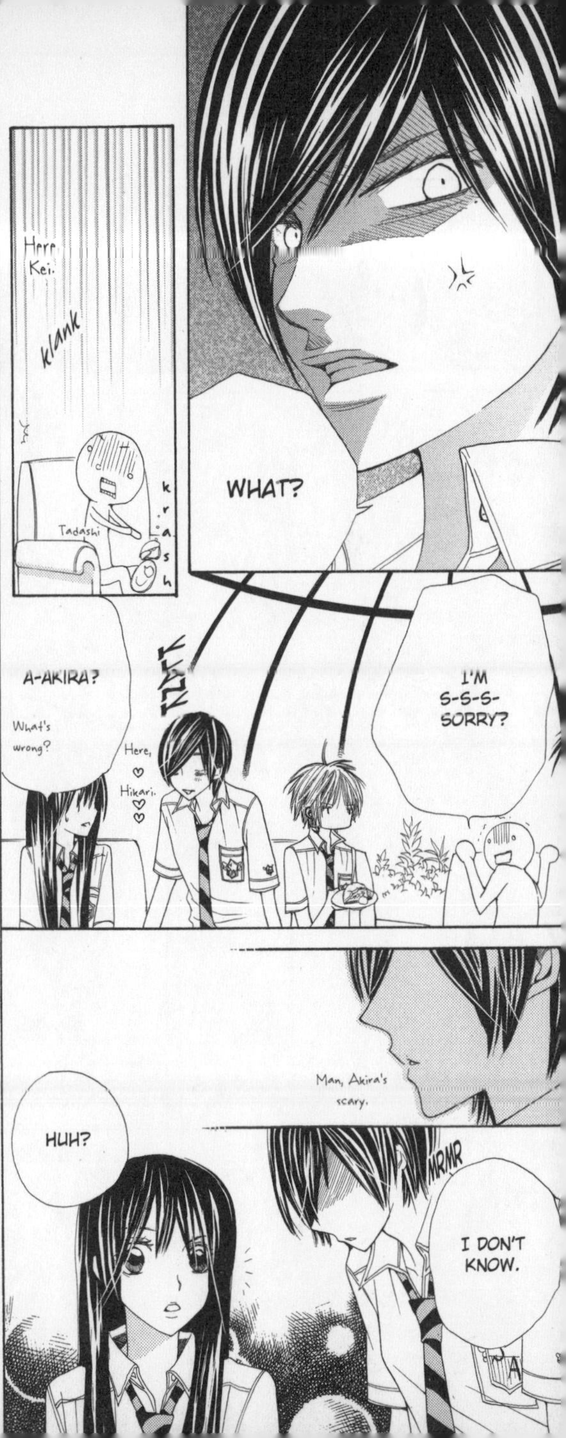
WHAT?
Here Kei.
klank
Tadashi
krash
I'M S-S-S-SORRY?
A-AKIRA?
What's wrong?
Here, Hikari.
Man, Akira's scary.
HUH?
MRMR
I DON'T KNOW.

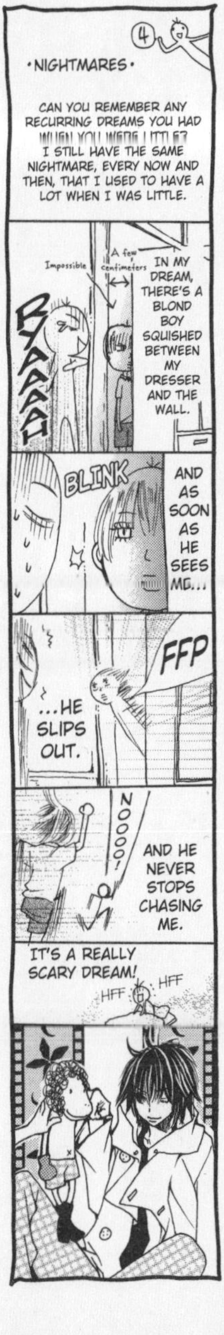
4
•NIGHTMARES•
CAN YOU REMEMBER ANY RECURRING DREAMS YOU HAD WHEN YOU WERE LITTLE?
I STILL HAVE THE SAME NIGHTMARE, EVERY NOW AND THEN, THAT I USED TO HAVE A LOT WHEN I WAS LITTLE.
IN MY DREAM, THERE'S A BLOND BOY SQUISHED BETWEEN MY DRESSER AND THE WALL.
A few centimeters
Impossible
RYAAAAH
AND AS SOON AS HE SEES ME...
BLINK
...HE SLIPS OUT.
FFP
AND HE NEVER STOPS CHASING ME.
NOOOOO!
IT'S A REALLY SCARY DREAM!
HFF HFF

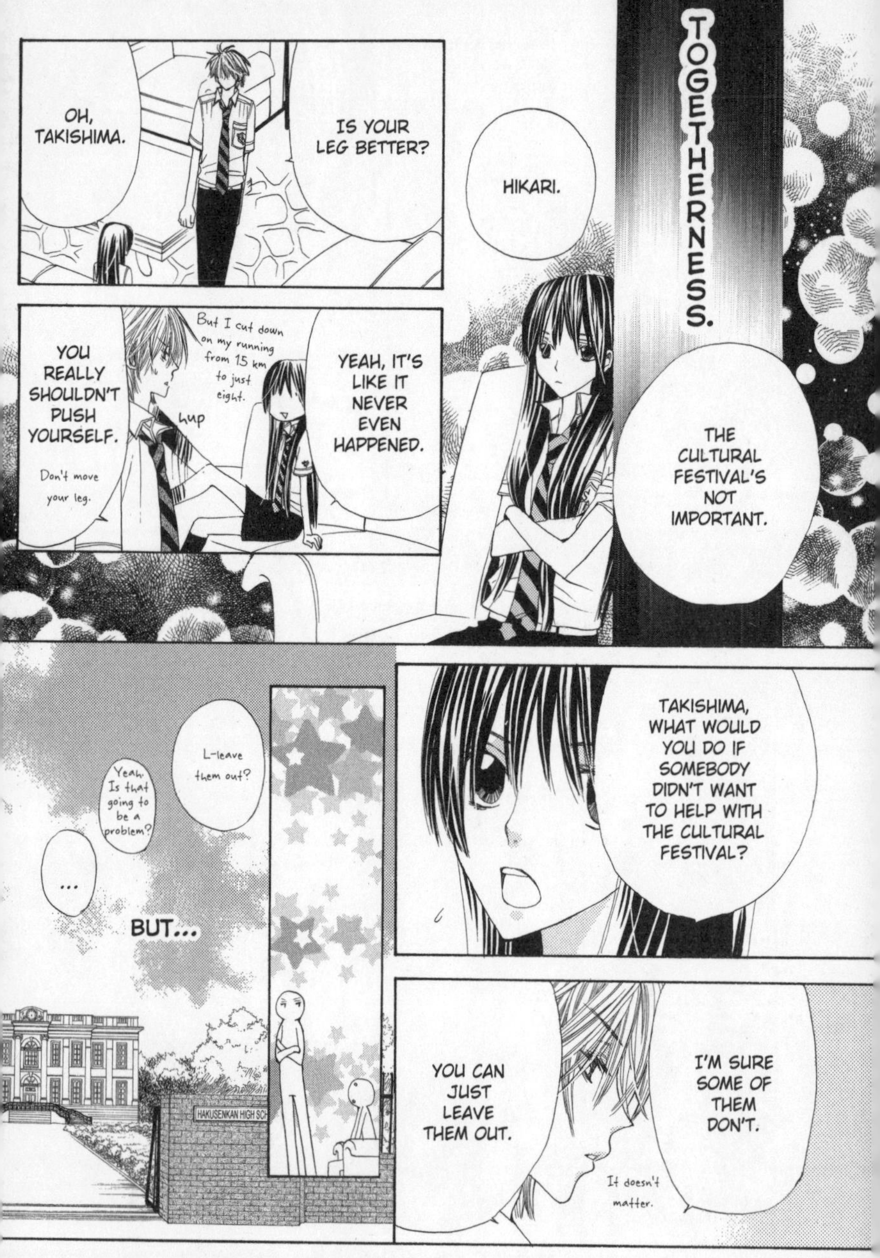
TOGETHERNESS.
HIKARI.
THE CULTURAL FESTIVAL'S NOT IMPORTANT.
IS YOUR LEG BETTER?
OH, TAKISHIMA.
YEAH, IT'S LIKE IT NEVER EVEN HAPPENED.
But I cut down on my running from 15 km to just eight.
hup
YOU REALLY SHOULDN'T PUSH YOURSELF.
Don't move your leg.
TAKISHIMA, WHAT WOULD YOU DO IF SOMEBODY DIDN'T WANT TO HELP WITH THE CULTURAL FESTIVAL?
I'M SURE SOME OF THEM DON'T.
It doesn't matter.
YOU CAN JUST LEAVE THEM OUT.
L-leave them out?
Yeah. Is that going to be a problem?
...
BUT...
HAKUSENKAN HIGH SCH

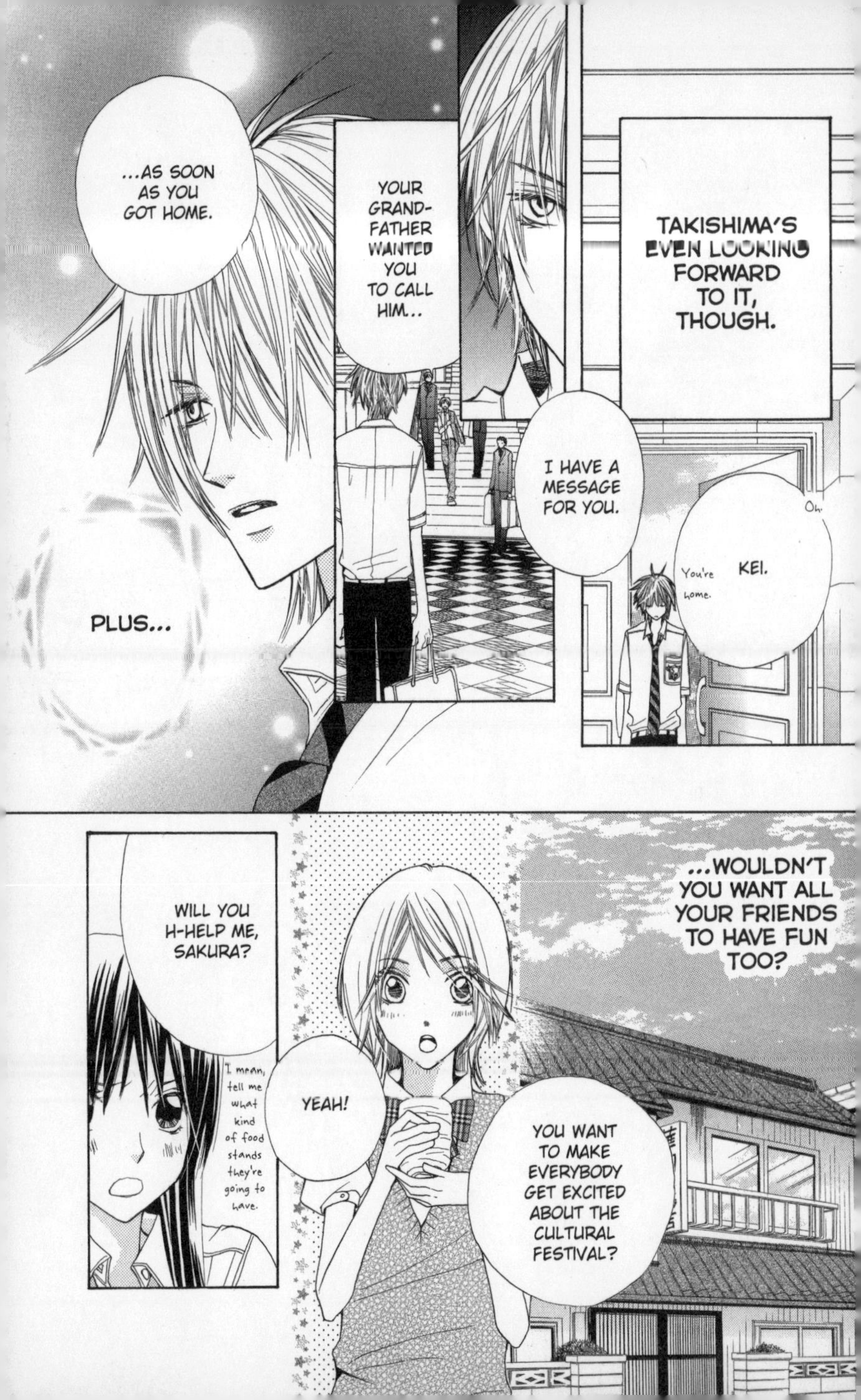
TAKISHIMA'S EVEN LOOKING FORWARD TO IT, THOUGH.
Oh. You're home.
KEI.
I HAVE A MESSAGE FOR YOU.
YOUR GRANDFATHER WANTED YOU TO CALL HIM...
...AS SOON AS YOU GOT HOME.
PLUS...
...WOULDN'T YOU WANT ALL YOUR FRIENDS TO HAVE FUN TOO?
YOU WANT TO MAKE EVERYBODY GET EXCITED ABOUT THE CULTURAL FESTIVAL?
YEAH!
WILL YOU H-HELP ME, SAKURA?
I mean, tell me what kind of food stands they're going to have.

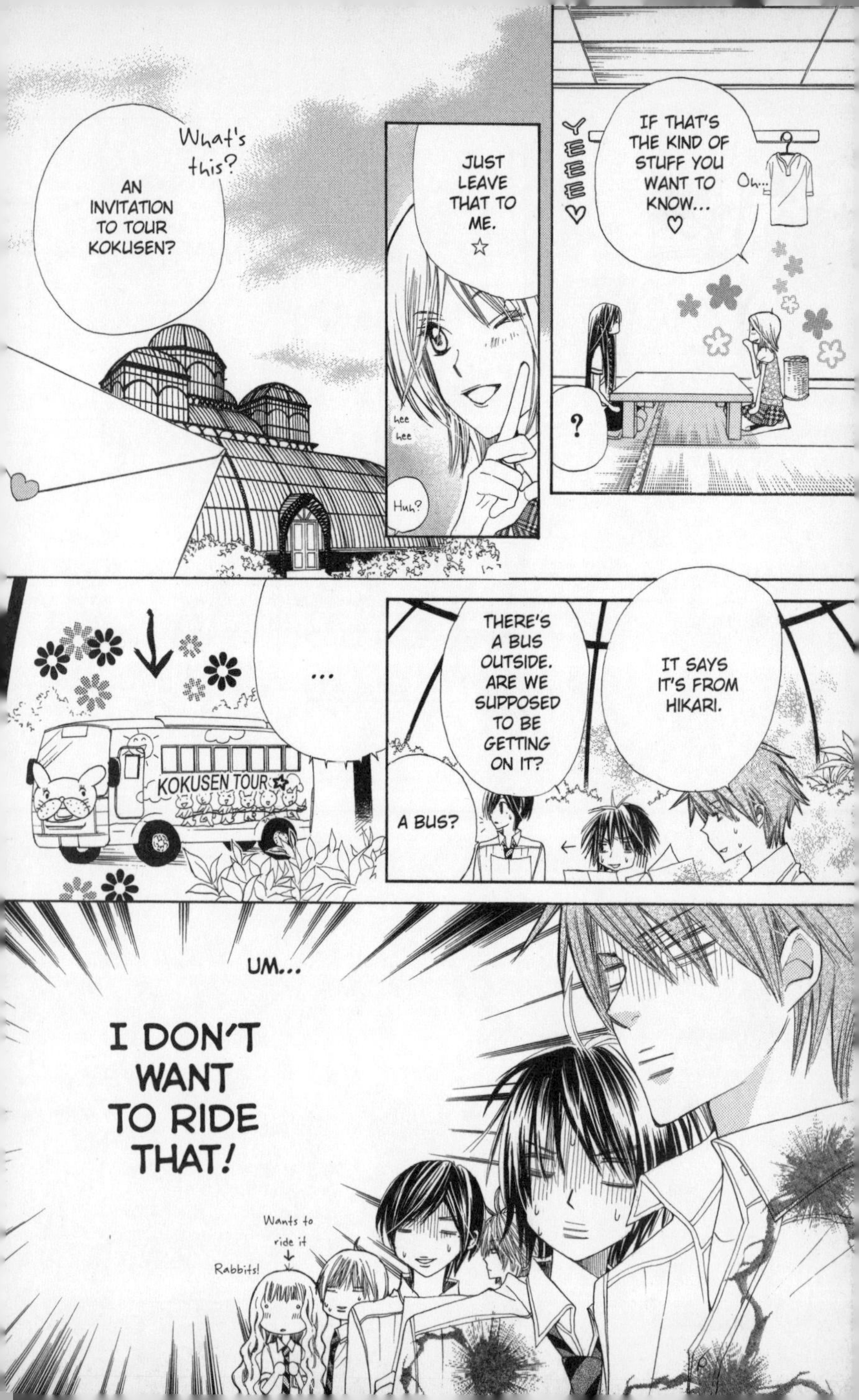
YEEE ♡
IF THAT'S THE KIND OF STUFF YOU WANT TO KNOW... ♡
Oh...
?
JUST LEAVE THAT TO ME. ☆
hee hee
Huh?
What's this?
AN INVITATION TO TOUR KOKUSEN?
IT SAYS IT'S FROM HIKARI.
THERE'S A BUS OUTSIDE. ARE WE SUPPOSED TO BE GETTING ON IT?
A BUS?
...
KOKUSEN TOUR
UM...
I DON'T WANT TO RIDE THAT!
Wants to ride it
Rabbits!

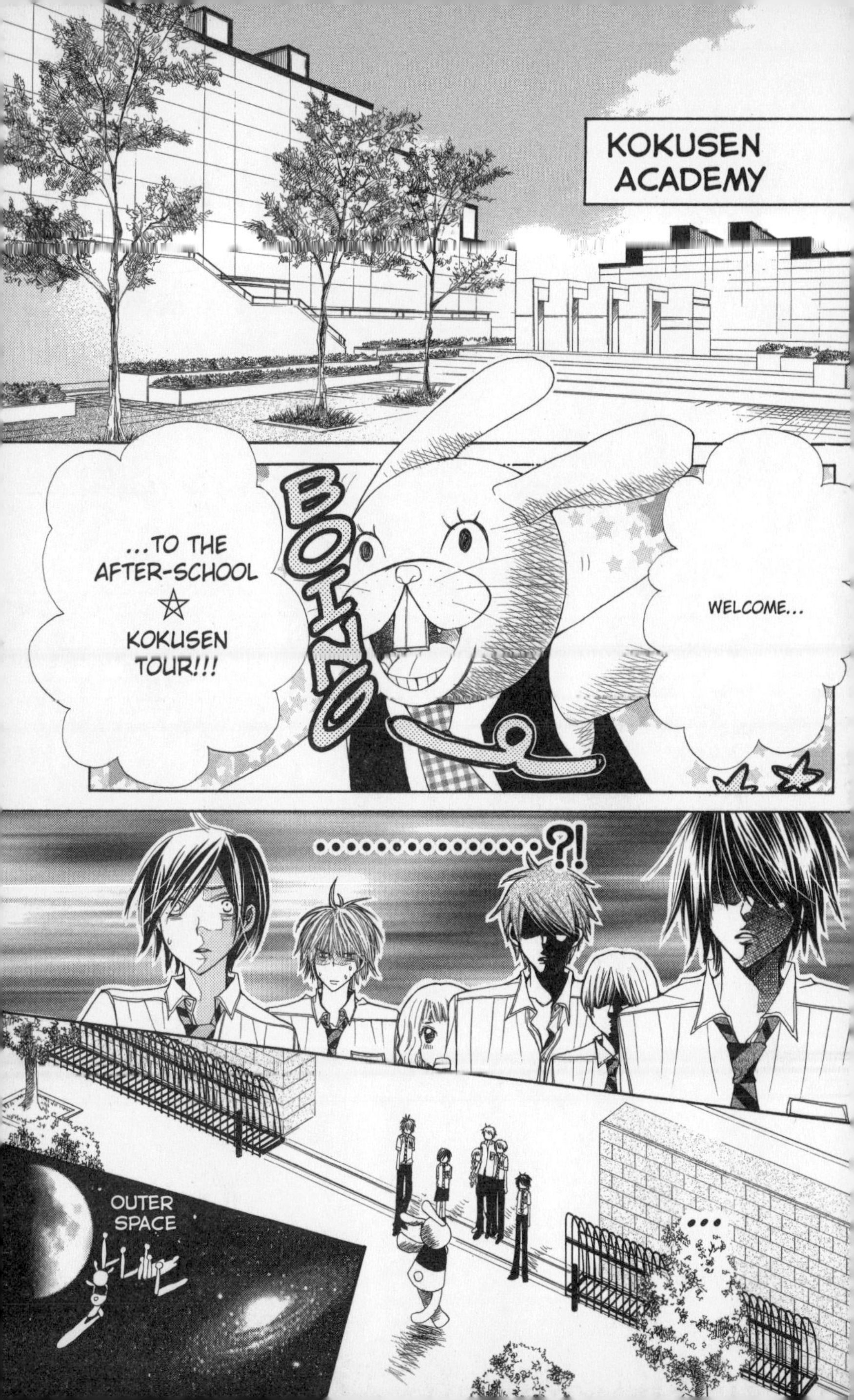
KOKUSEN ACADEMY
WELCOME...
BOING
...TO THE AFTER-SCHOOL ☆ KOKUSEN TOUR!!!
...............?!
...
OUTER SPACE

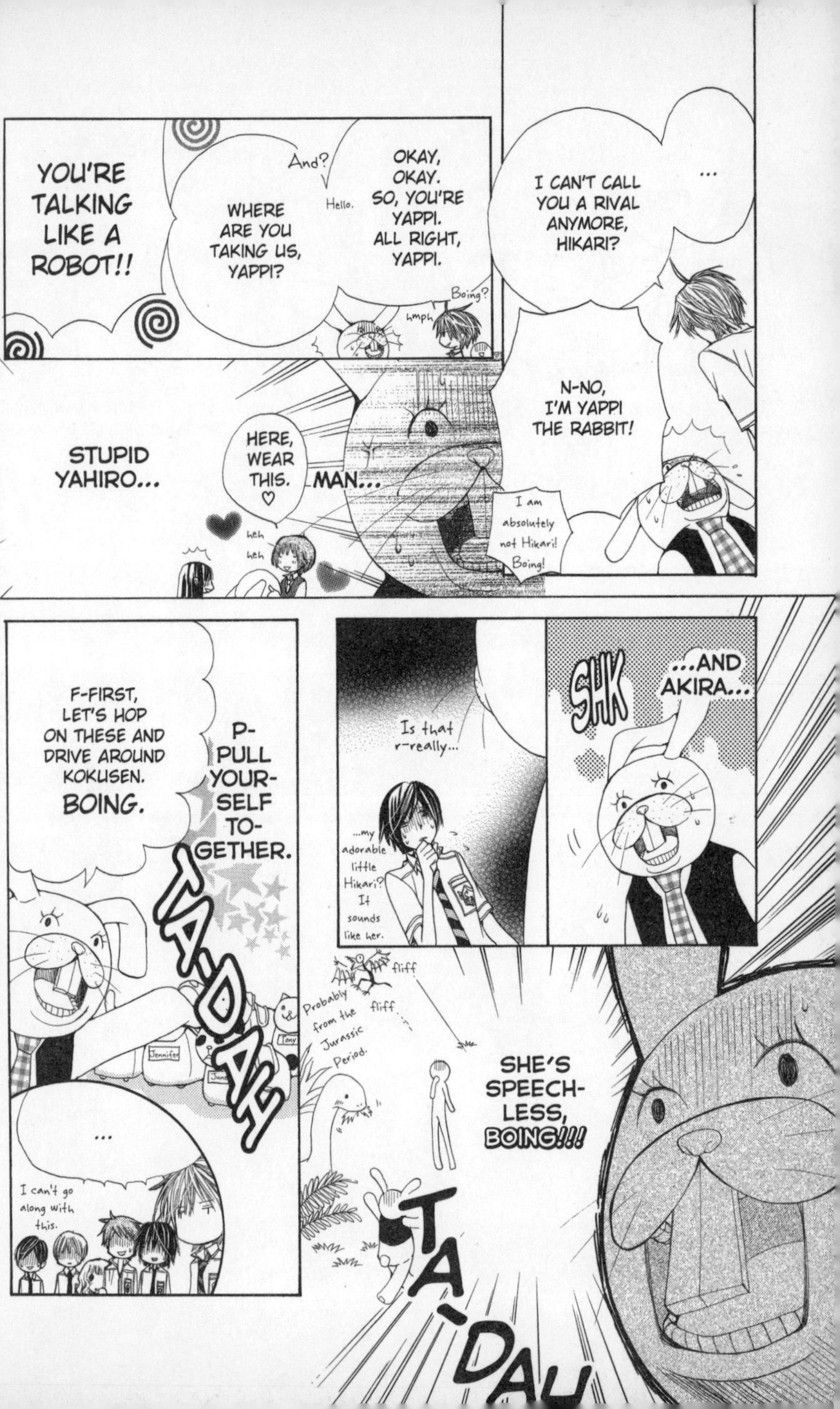
I CAN'T CALL YOU A RIVAL ANYMORE, HIKARI?
...
N-NO, I'M YAPPI THE RABBIT!
I am absolutely not Hikari! Boing!
OKAY, OKAY. SO, YOU'RE YAPPI. ALL RIGHT, YAPPI.
And?
Hello.
WHERE ARE YOU TAKING US, YAPPI?
YOU'RE TALKING LIKE A ROBOT!!
Boing?
hmph
MAN...
HERE, WEAR THIS. ♡
heh heh
STUPID YAHIRO...
...AND AKIRA...
SHK
Is that r-really...
...my adorable little Hikari? It sounds like her.
F-FIRST, LET'S HOP ON THESE AND DRIVE AROUND KOKUSEN. BOING.
P-PULL YOURSELF TOGETHER.
TA-DAH
Jennifer
June
Tony
...
I can't go along with this.
SHE'S SPEECHLESS, BOING!!!
TA-DAH
fliff
fliff
Probably from the Jurassic Period.

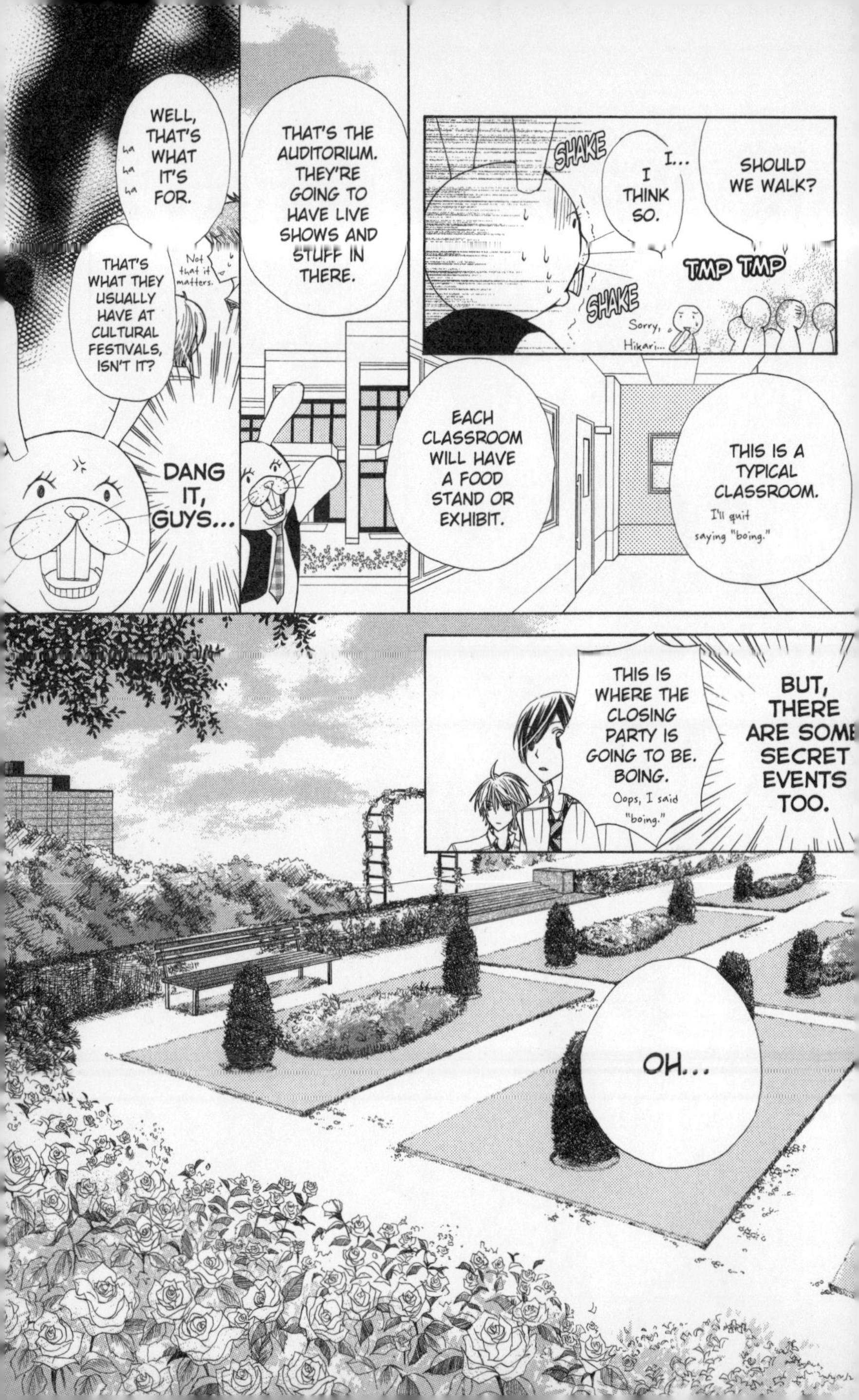

SHOULD WE WALK?
I... I THINK SO.
SHAKE
SHAKE
TMP TMP
Sorry, Hikari...
THIS IS A TYPICAL CLASSROOM.
I'll quit saying "boing."
EACH CLASSROOM WILL HAVE A FOOD STAND OR EXHIBIT.
THAT'S THE AUDITORIUM. THEY'RE GOING TO HAVE LIVE SHOWS AND STUFF IN THERE.
WELL, THAT'S WHAT IT'S FOR.
ha ha ha
Not that it matters.
THAT'S WHAT THEY USUALLY HAVE AT CULTURAL FESTIVALS, ISN'T IT?
DANG IT, GUYS...
BUT, THERE ARE SOME SECRET EVENTS TOO.
THIS IS WHERE THE CLOSING PARTY IS GOING TO BE. BOING.
Oops, I said "boing."
OH...

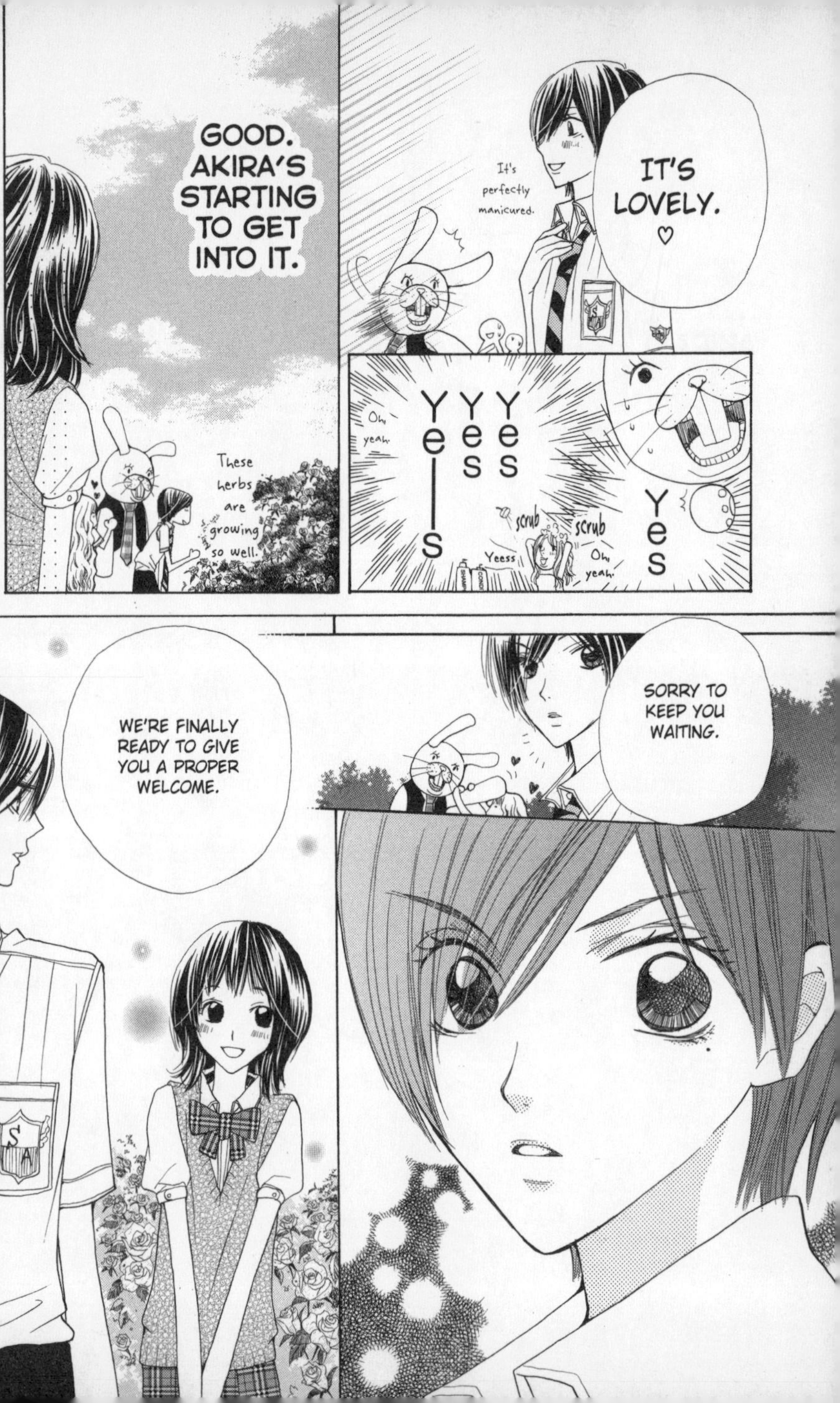
IT'S LOVELY. ♡
It's perfectly manicured.
Yes
Yes
Yes
Yes
Oh yeah.
scrub
scrub
Yeess
Oh yeah.
GOOD. AKIRA'S STARTING TO GET INTO IT.
These herbs are growing so well.
SORRY TO KEEP YOU WAITING.
WE'RE FINALLY READY TO GIVE YOU A PROPER WELCOME.

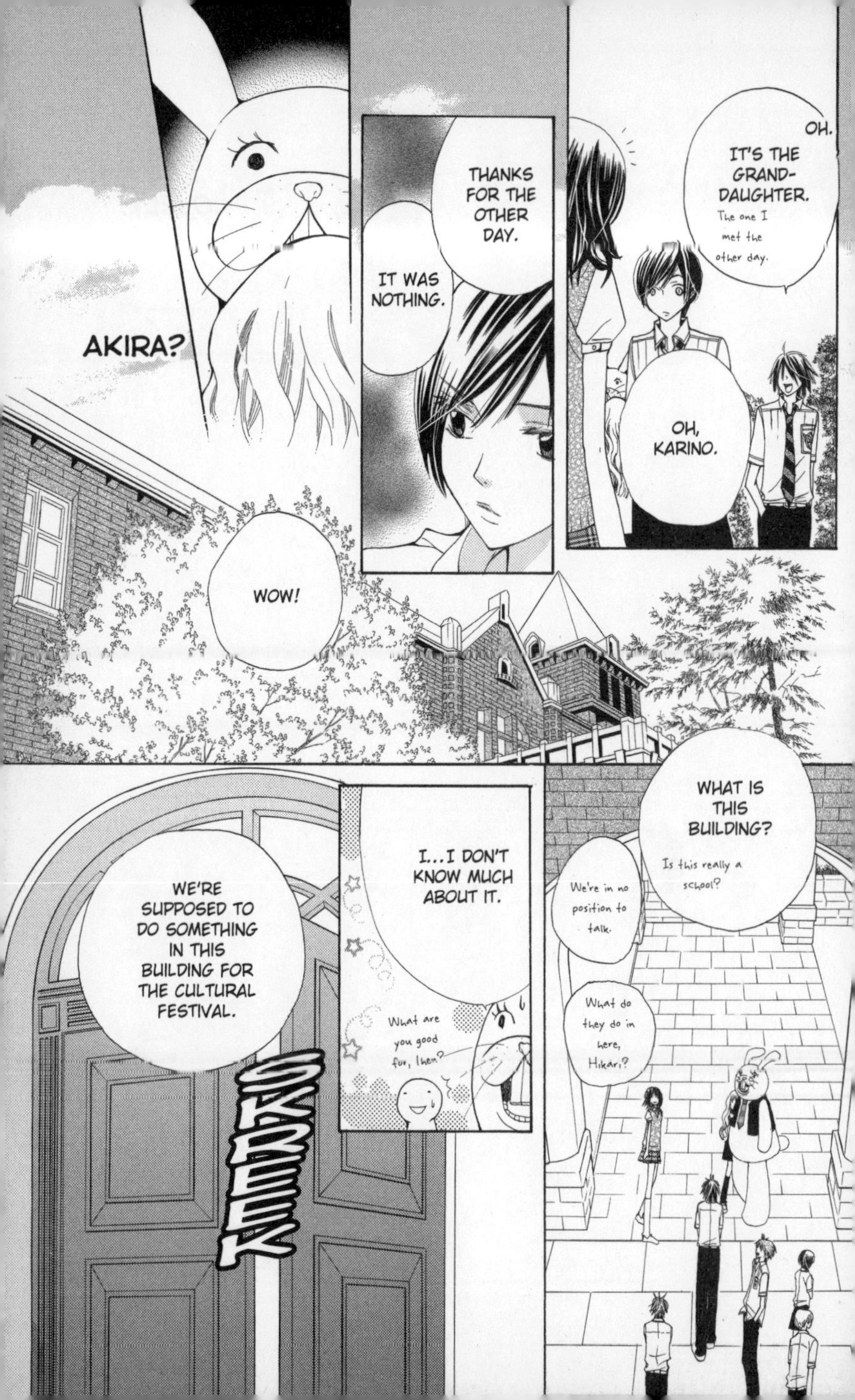
OH.
IT'S THE GRAND-DAUGHTER.
The one I met the other day.
OH, KARINO.
THANKS FOR THE OTHER DAY.
IT WAS NOTHING.
AKIRA?
WOW!
WHAT IS THIS BUILDING?
Is this really a school?
We're in no position to talk.
What do they do in here, Hikari?
I...I DON'T KNOW MUCH ABOUT IT.
What are you good for, then?
WE'RE SUPPOSED TO DO SOMETHING IN THIS BUILDING FOR THE CULTURAL FESTIVAL.
SKREEK

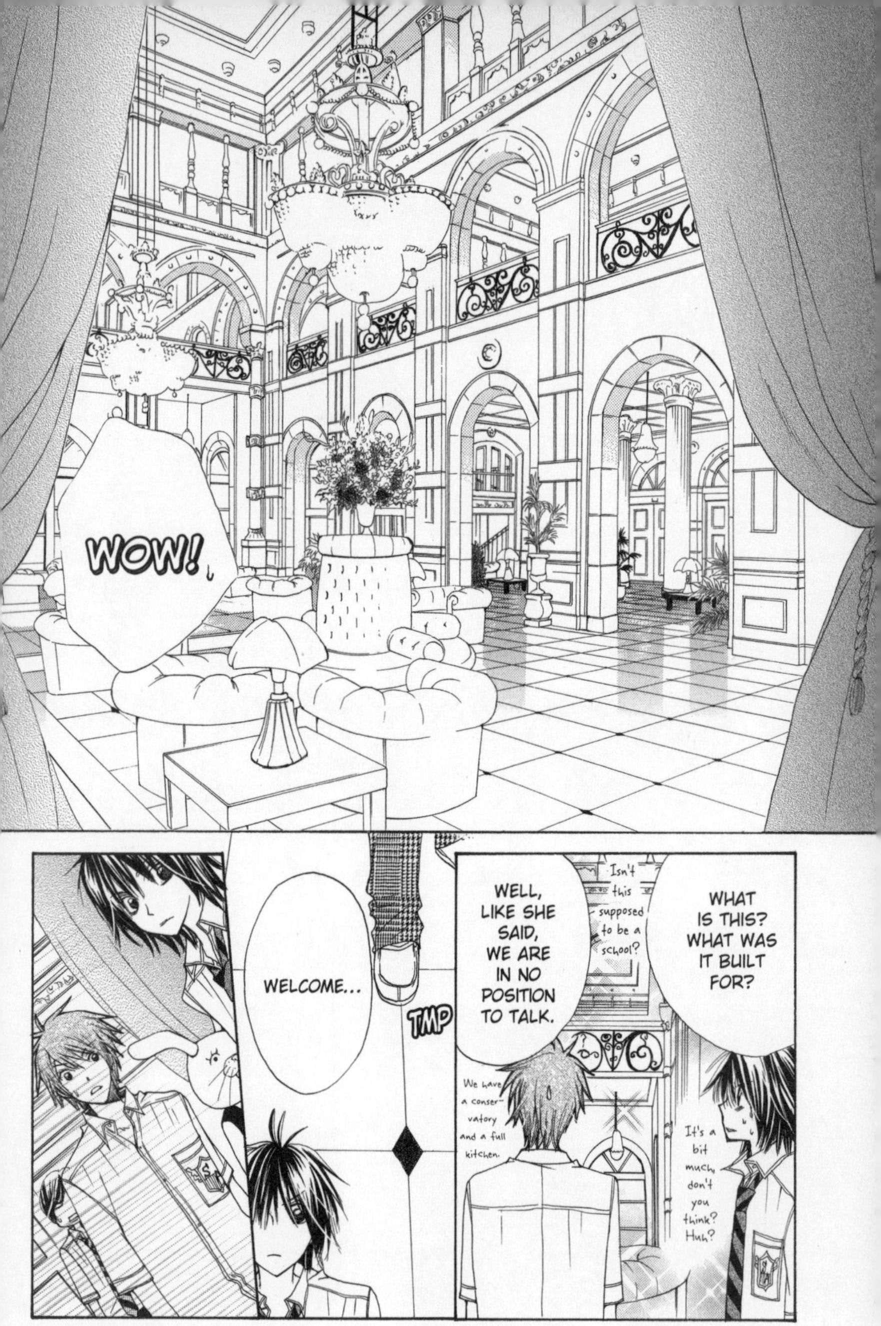
WOW!
WHAT IS THIS? WHAT WAS IT BUILT FOR?
Isn't this supposed to be a school?
WELL, LIKE SHE SAID, WE ARE IN NO POSITION TO TALK.
It's a bit much don't you think? Huh?
We have a conser-vatory and a full kitchen.
WELCOME...
TMP

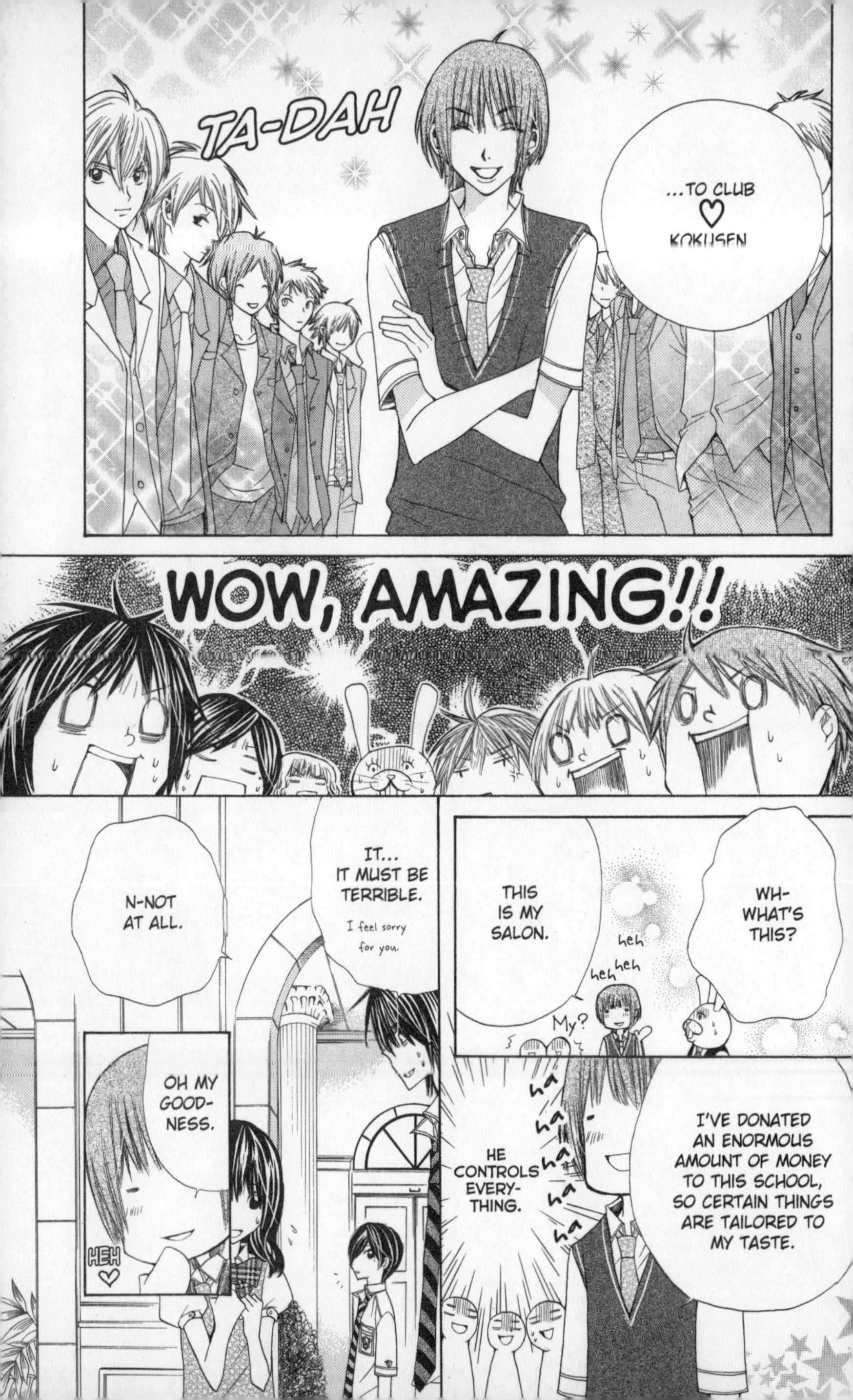
...TO CLUB ♡ KOKUSEN
TA-DAH
WOW, AMAZING!!
WH- WHAT'S THIS?
THIS IS MY SALON.
heh heh heh
My?
I'VE DONATED AN ENORMOUS AMOUNT OF MONEY TO THIS SCHOOL, SO CERTAIN THINGS ARE TAILORED TO MY TASTE.
ha ha ha ha ha
HE CONTROLS EVERY-THING.
IT... IT MUST BE TERRIBLE.
I feel sorry for you.
N-NOT AT ALL.
OH MY GOOD-NESS.
HEH ♡

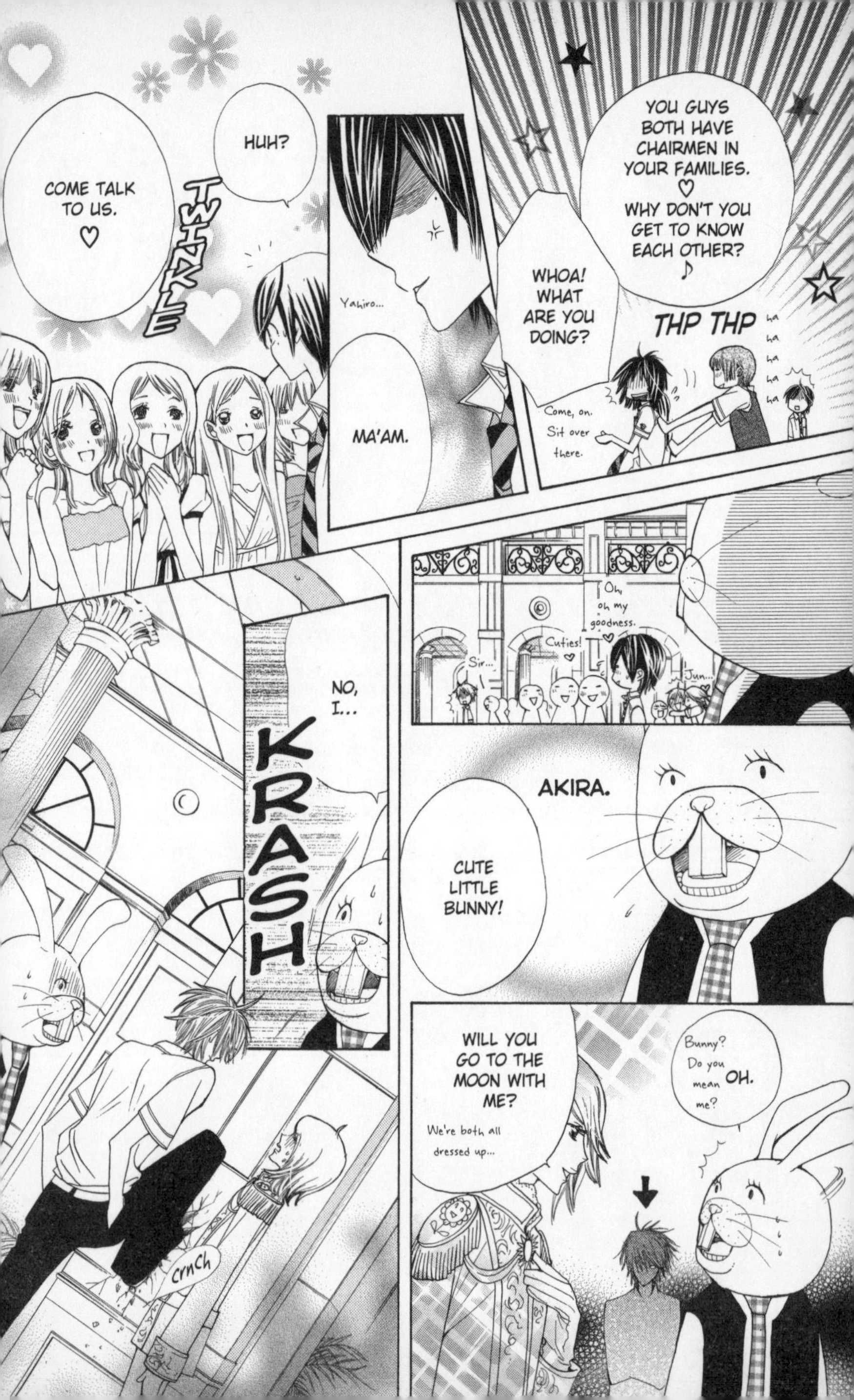
YOU GUYS BOTH HAVE CHAIRMEN IN YOUR FAMILIES. ♡ WHY DON'T YOU GET TO KNOW EACH OTHER? ♪
WHOA! WHAT ARE YOU DOING?
THP THP
ha ha ha ha ha
Come, on. Sit over there.
Yahiro...
MA'AM.
HUH?
COME TALK TO US. ♡
TWINKLE
Oh, oh my goodness. ♡
Cuties! ♡
Sir...
Jun...
AKIRA.
CUTE LITTLE BUNNY!
WILL YOU GO TO THE MOON WITH ME?
We're both all dressed up...
Bunny? Do you mean me?
OH.
NO, I...
KRASH
crnch

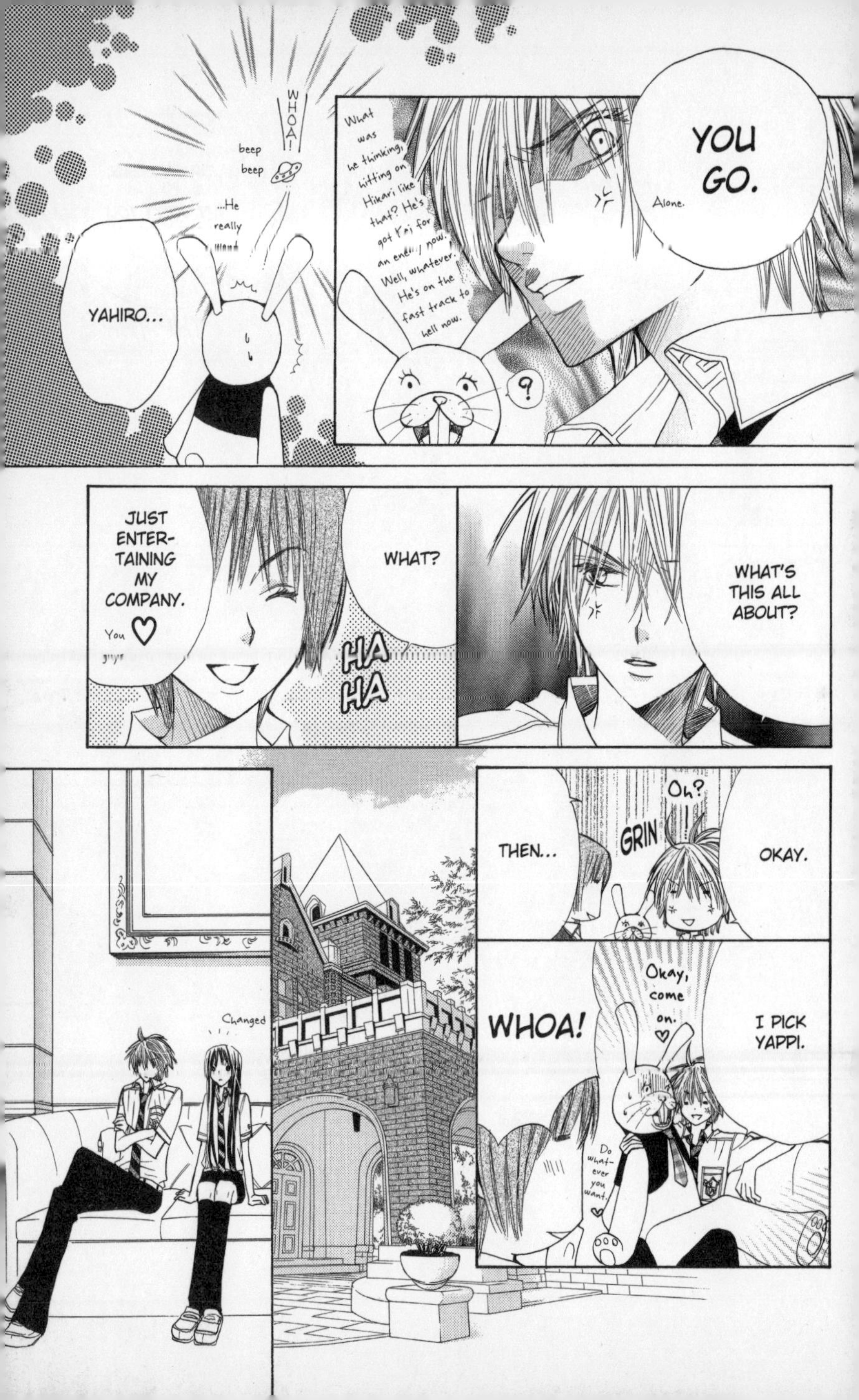
YOU GO.
Alone.
What was he thinking, hitting on Hikari like that? He's got Kei for an enemy now. Well, whatever. He's on the fast track to hell now.
?
WHOA!
beep beep
...He really
YAHIRO...
WHAT'S THIS ALL ABOUT?
WHAT?
HA HA
JUST ENTERTAINING MY COMPANY.
You guys ♡
Oh?
OKAY.
GRIN
THEN...
I PICK YAPPI.
Okay, come on. ♡
WHOA!
Do whatever you want. ♡
Changed

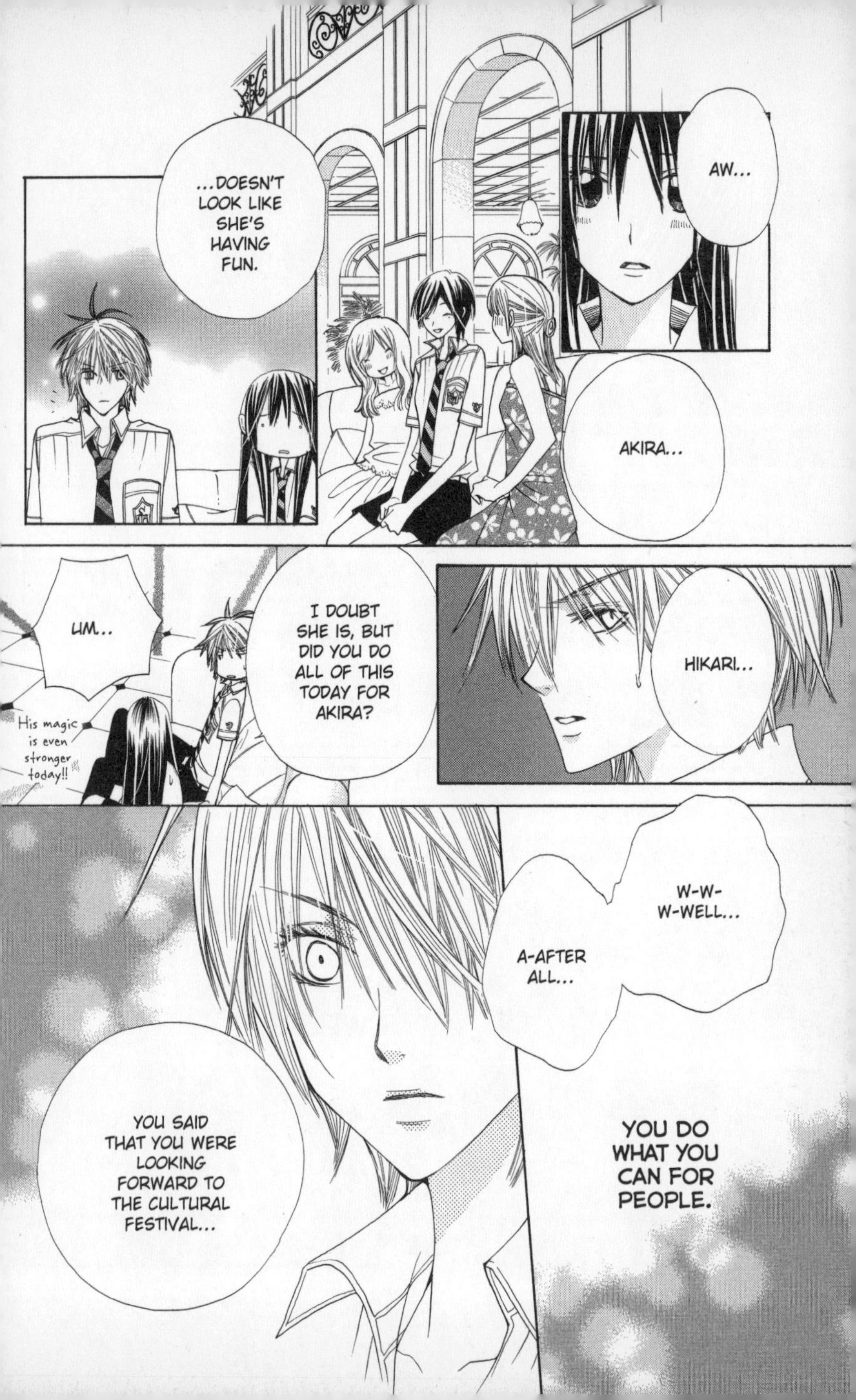
AW...
AKIRA...
...DOESN'T LOOK LIKE SHE'S HAVING FUN.
HIKARI...
I DOUBT SHE IS, BUT DID YOU DO ALL OF THIS TODAY FOR AKIRA?
UM...
His magic is even stronger today!!
W-W-W-WELL...
A-AFTER ALL...
YOU DO WHAT YOU CAN FOR PEOPLE.
YOU SAID THAT YOU WERE LOOKING FORWARD TO THE CULTURAL FESTIVAL...

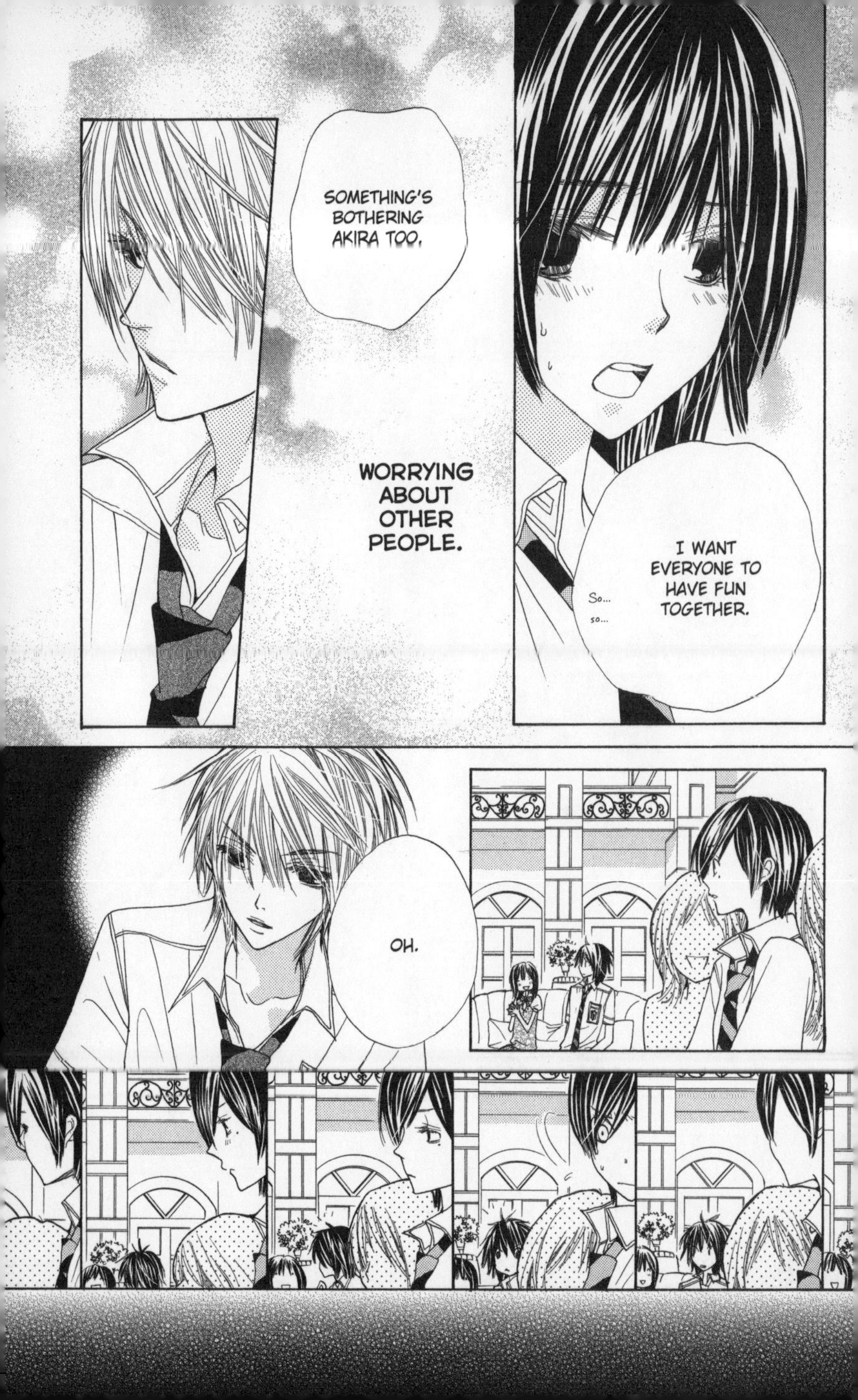
So... so...
I WANT EVERYONE TO HAVE FUN TOGETHER.
SOMETHING'S BOTHERING AKIRA TOO.
WORRYING ABOUT OTHER PEOPLE.
OH.

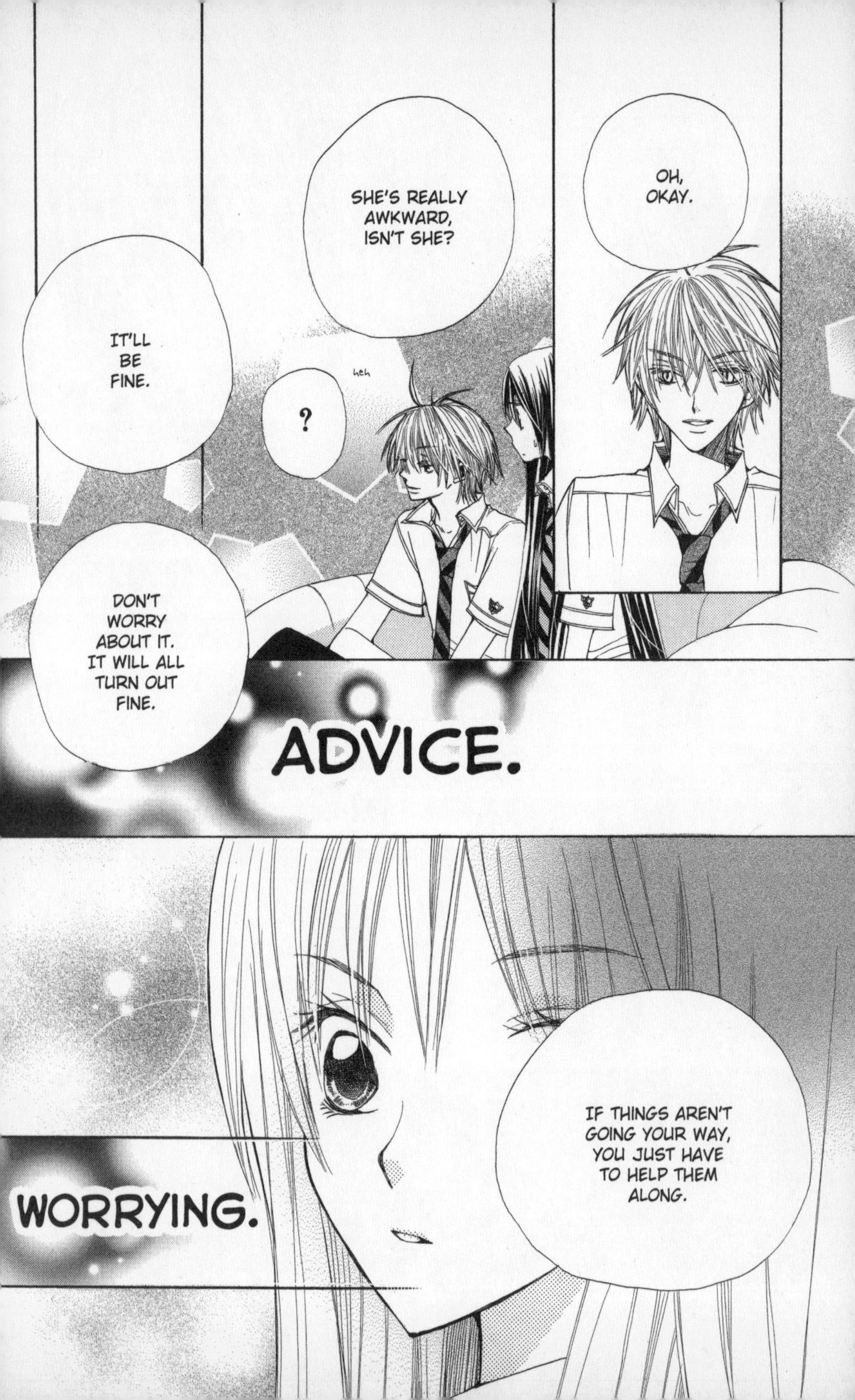
OH, OKAY.
SHE'S REALLY AWKWARD, ISN'T SHE?
heh
?
IT'LL BE FINE.
DON'T WORRY ABOUT IT. IT WILL ALL TURN OUT FINE.
ADVICE.
IF THINGS AREN'T GOING YOUR WAY, YOU JUST HAVE TO HELP THEM ALONG.
WORRYING.

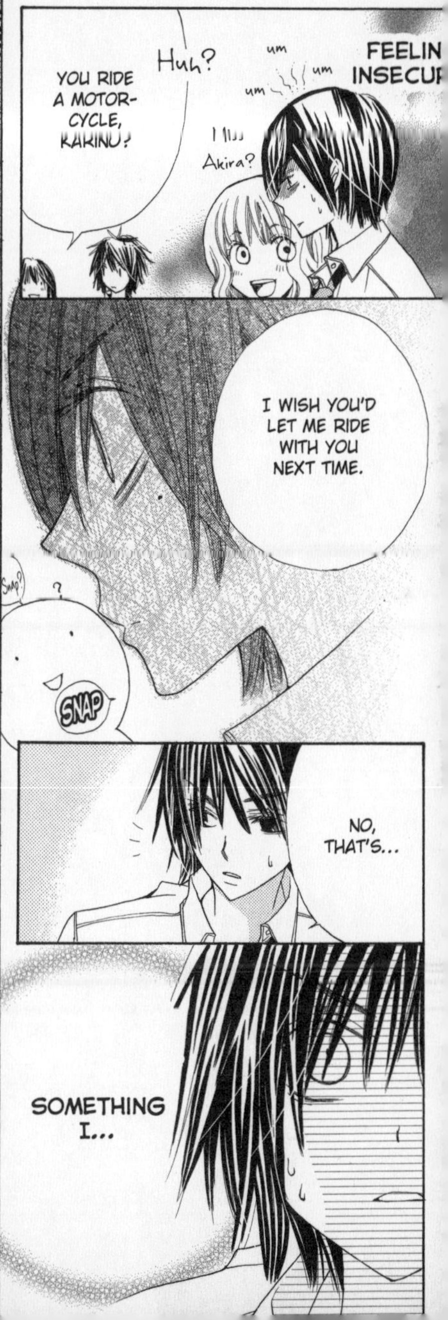
FEELIN
INSECUR
um
um
um
Akira?
Huh?
YOU RIDE A MOTOR-CYCLE, KAKINO?
I WISH YOU'D LET ME RIDE WITH YOU NEXT TIME.
Snap?
SNAP
NO, THAT'S...
SOMETHING I...
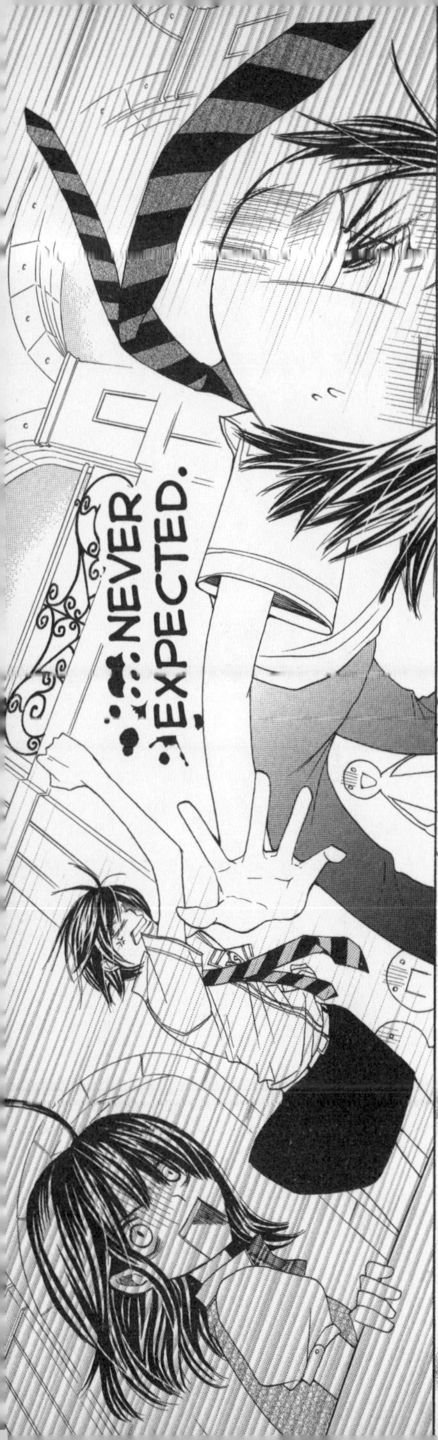
...NEVER EXPECTED.

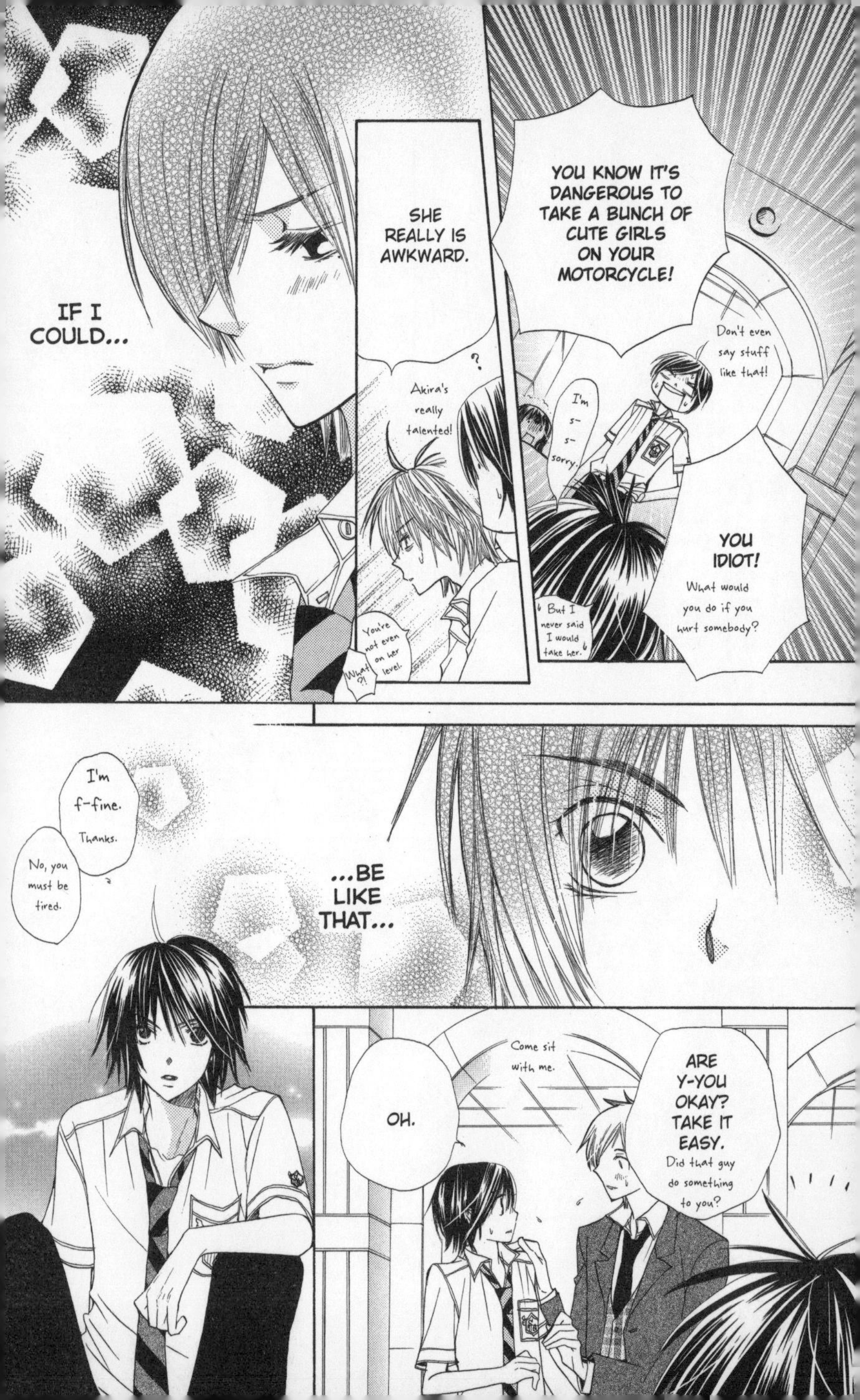
YOU KNOW IT'S DANGEROUS TO TAKE A BUNCH OF CUTE GIRLS ON YOUR MOTORCYCLE!
Don't even say stuff like that!
I'm s-s-sorry.
YOU IDIOT!
What would you do if you hurt somebody?
But I never said I would take her.
SHE REALLY IS AWKWARD.
?
Akira's really talented!
You're not even on her level.
What?!
IF I COULD...
...BE LIKE THAT...
ARE Y-YOU OKAY? TAKE IT EASY.
Did that guy do something to you?
Come sit with me.
OH.
I'm f-fine.
Thanks.
No, you must be tired.

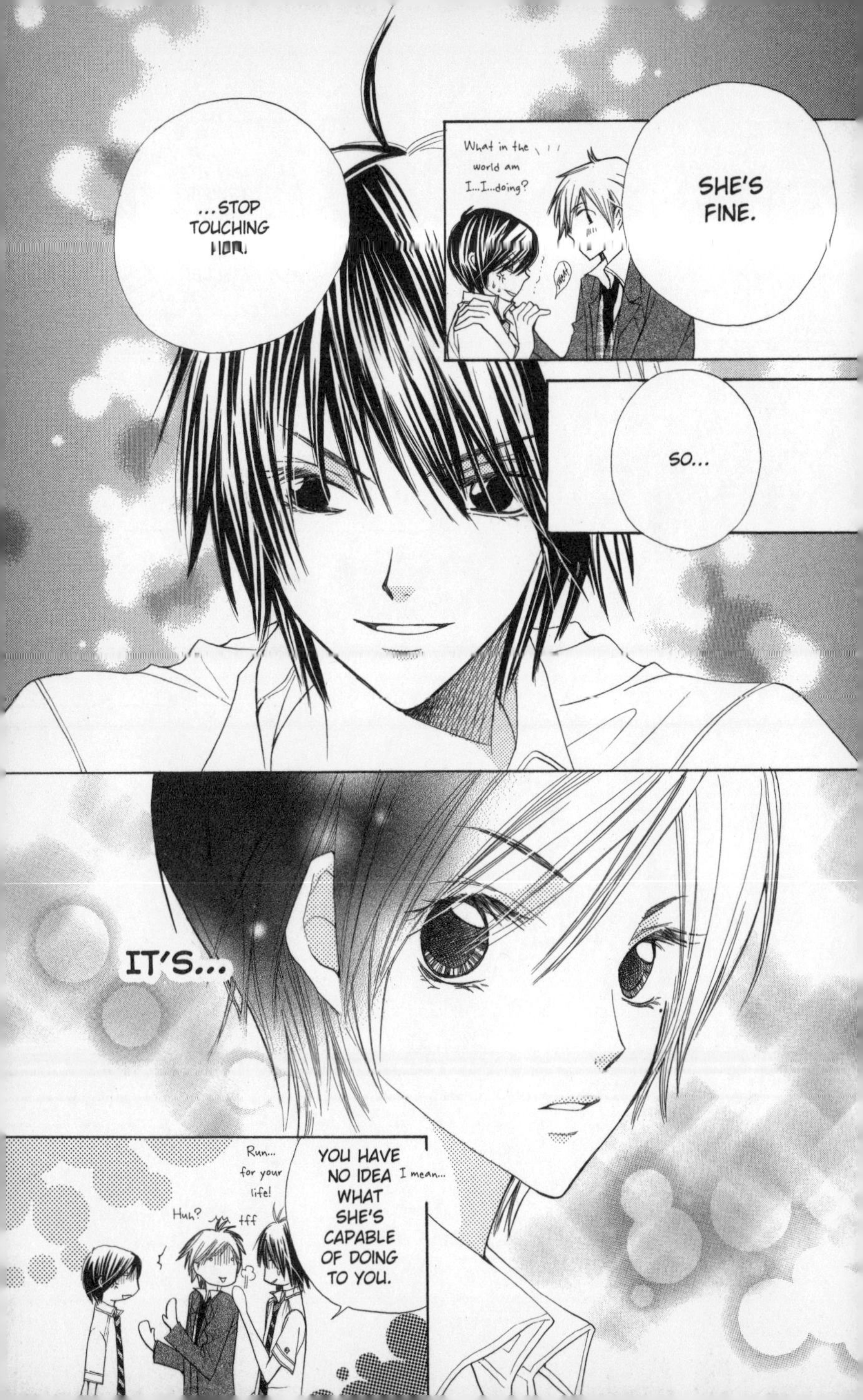
What in the world am I...I...doing?
SHE'S FINE.
SO...
...STOP TOUCHING HER.
IT'S...
YOU HAVE NO IDEA WHAT SHE'S CAPABLE OF DOING TO YOU.
I mean...
Run... for your life!
Huh?
fff

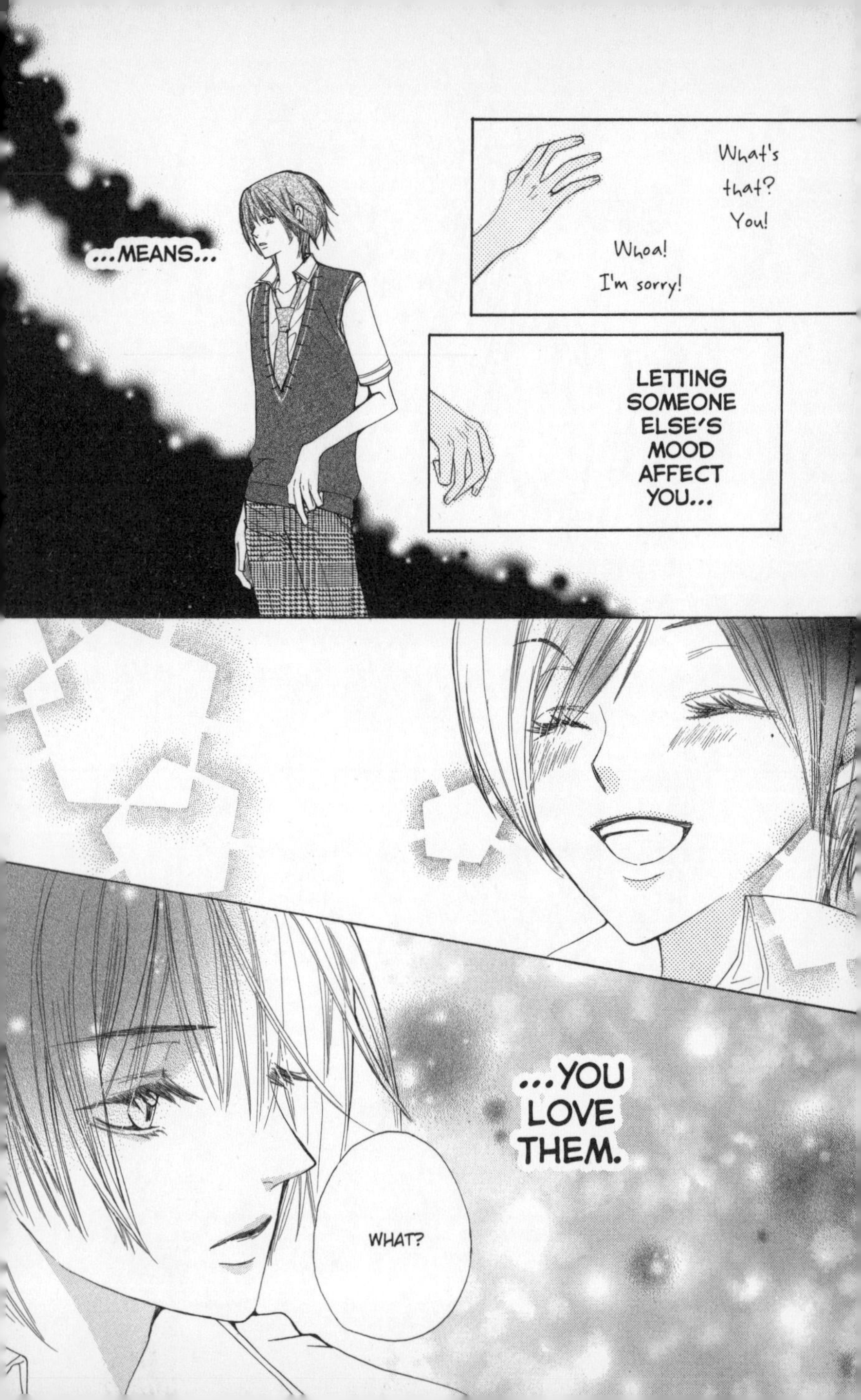
What's that? You!
Whoa! I'm sorry!
LETTING SOMEONE ELSE'S MOOD AFFECT YOU...
...MEANS...
...YOU LOVE THEM.
WHAT?

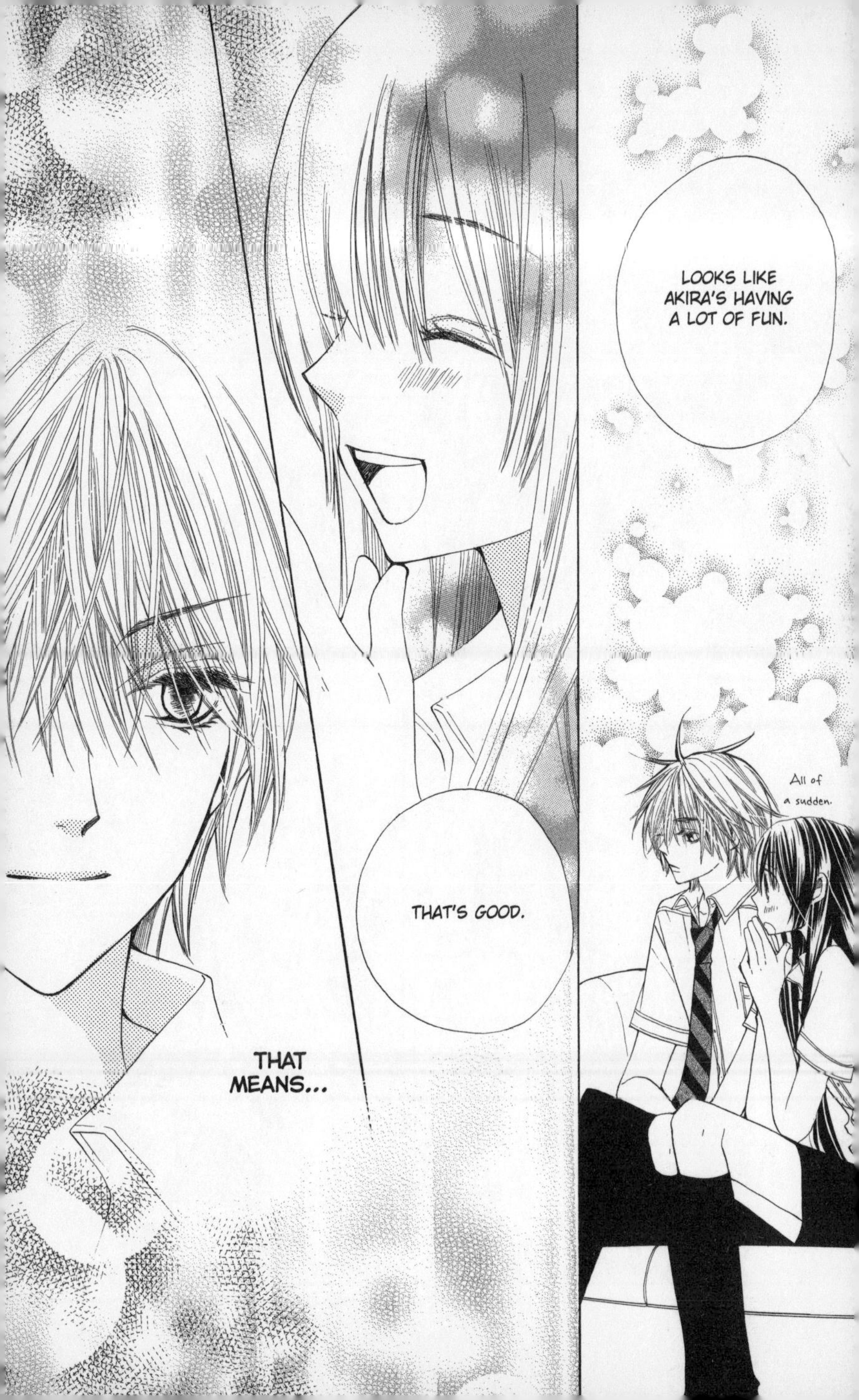
LOOKS LIKE AKIRA'S HAVING A LOT OF FUN.
All of a sudden.
THAT'S GOOD.
THAT MEANS...

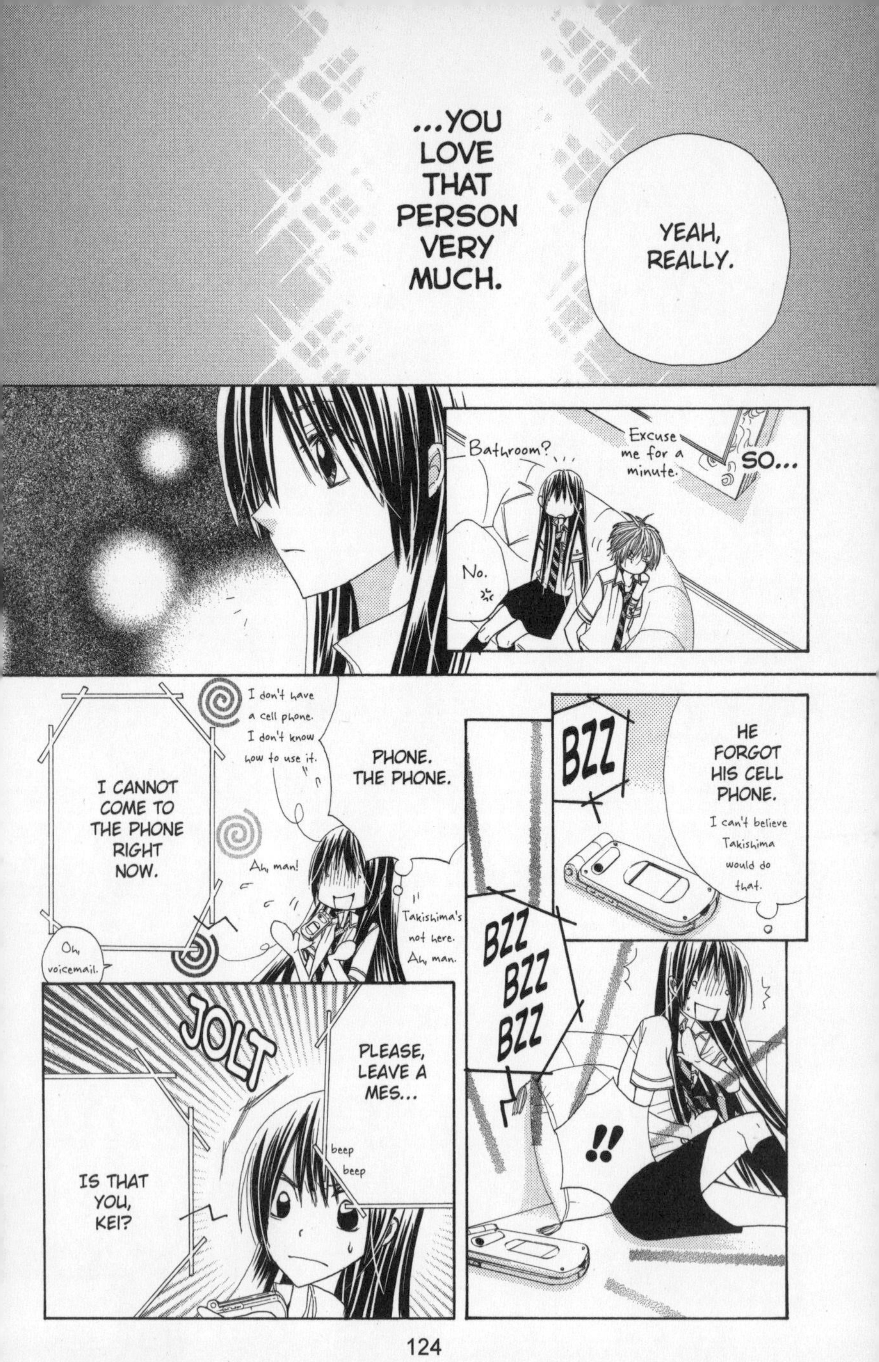
...YOU LOVE THAT PERSON VERY MUCH.
YEAH, REALLY.
SO...
Excuse me for a minute.
Bathroom?
No.
BZZ
HE FORGOT HIS CELL PHONE.
I can't believe Takishima would do that.
BZZ BZZ BZZ
!!
PHONE. THE PHONE.
I don't have a cell phone. I don't know how to use it.
Ah, man!
Takishima's not here. Ah, man.
I CANNOT COME TO THE PHONE RIGHT NOW.
Oh, voicemail.
PLEASE, LEAVE A MES...
beep
beep
JOLT
IS THAT YOU, KEI?

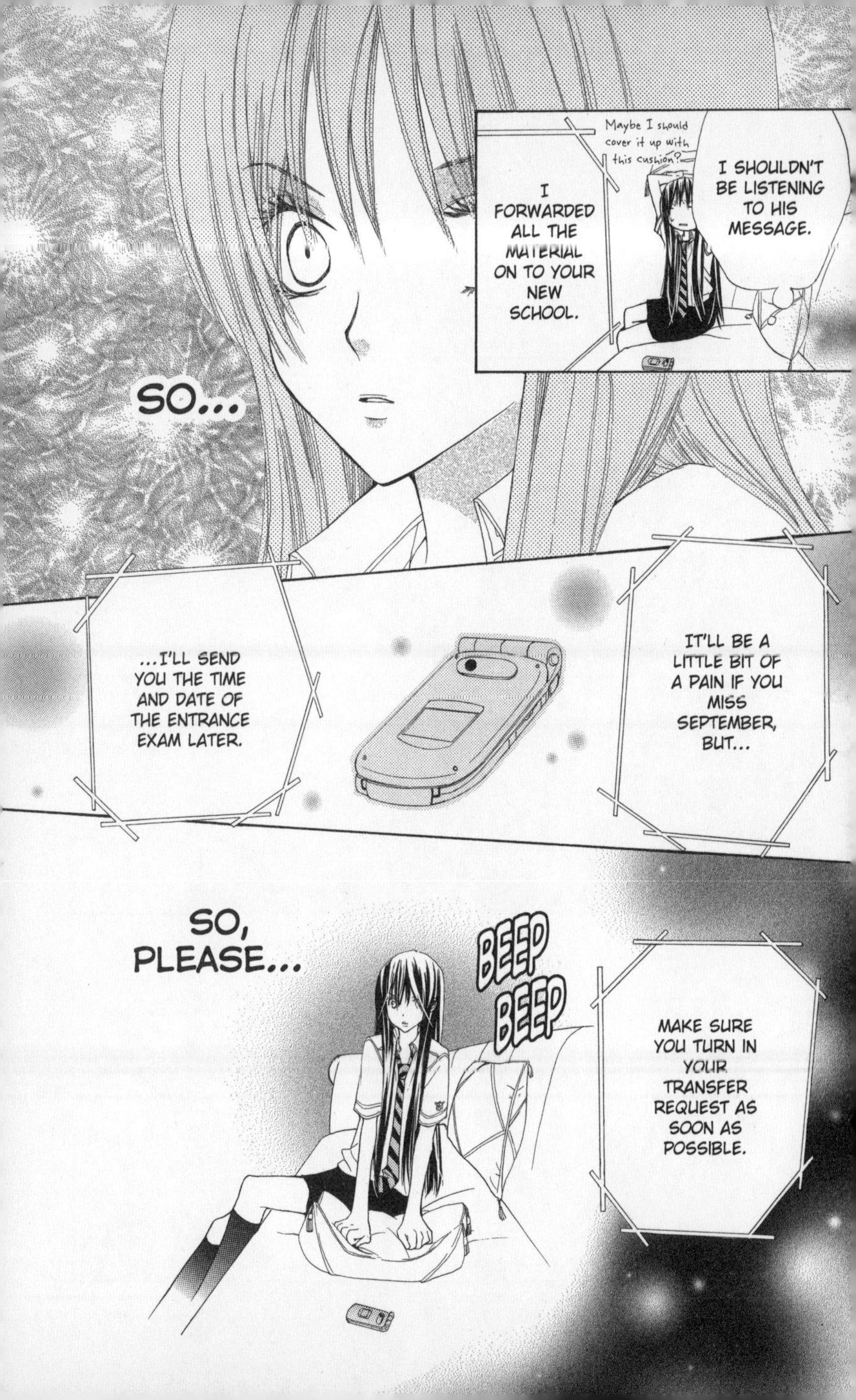
I SHOULDN'T BE LISTENING TO HIS MESSAGE.
Maybe I should cover it up with this cushion?
I FORWARDED ALL THE MATERIAL ON TO YOUR NEW SCHOOL.
SO...
IT'LL BE A LITTLE BIT OF A PAIN IF YOU MISS SEPTEMBER, BUT...
...I'LL SEND YOU THE TIME AND DATE OF THE ENTRANCE EXAM LATER.
SO, PLEASE...
BEEP BEEP
MAKE SURE YOU TURN IN YOUR TRANSFER REQUEST AS SOON AS POSSIBLE.

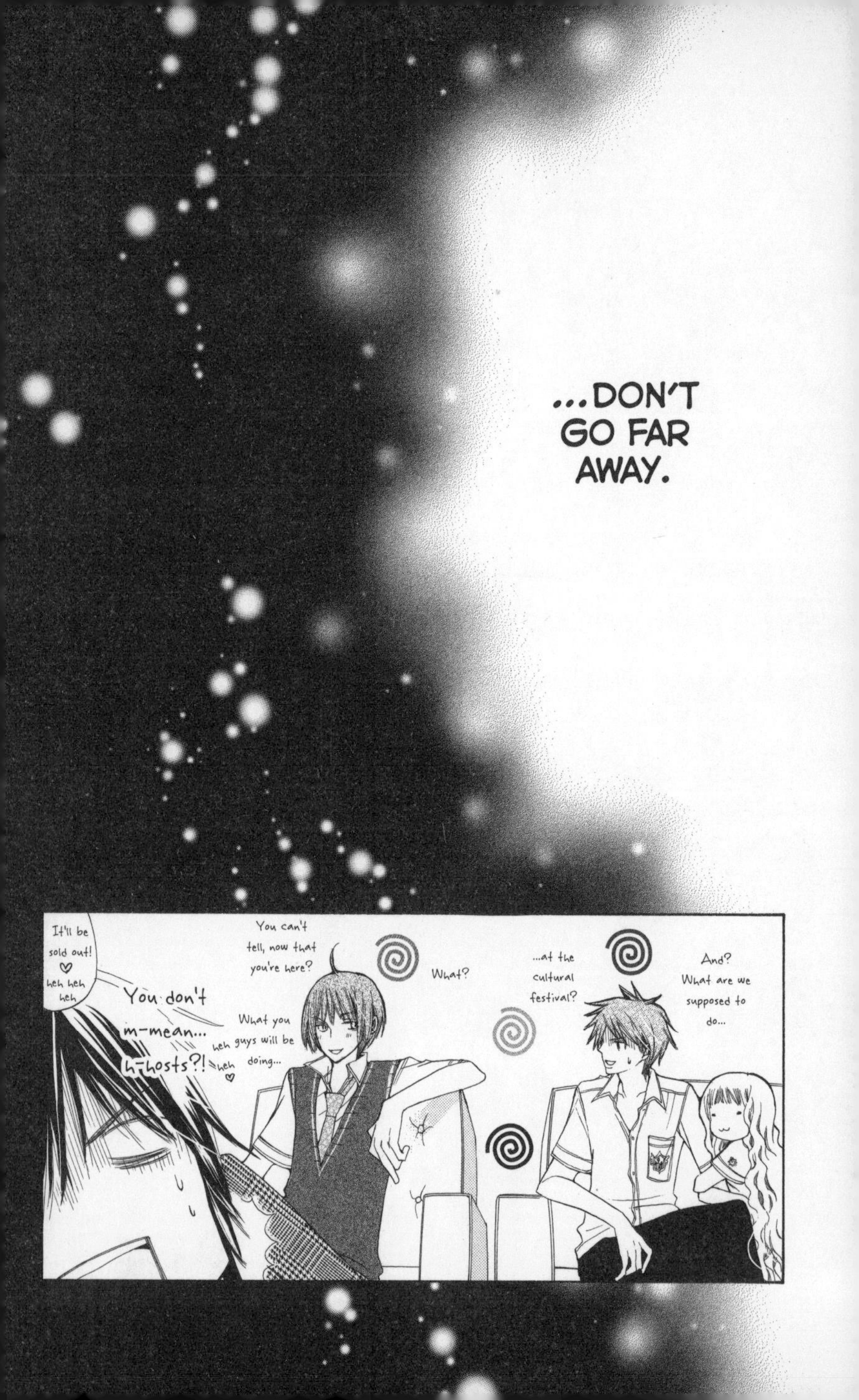
...DON'T GO FAR AWAY.
And? What are we supposed to do...
...at the cultural festival?
What?
You can't tell, now that you're here?
What you guys will be doing...
heh heh ♥
You don't m-mean... h-hosts?!
It'll be sold out! ♥ heh heh heh

Chapter 27

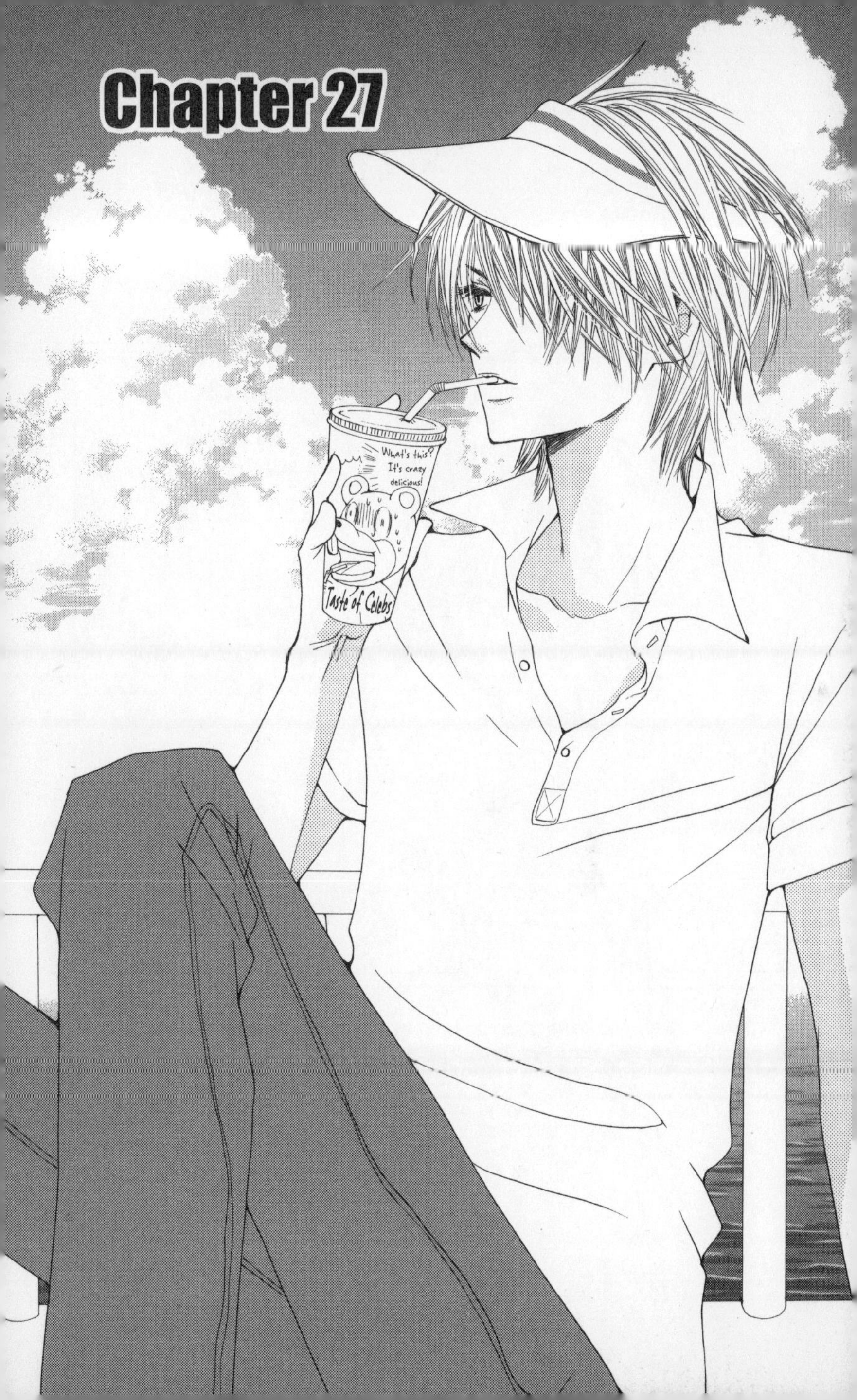
What's this? It's crazy delicious!
Taste of Celebs

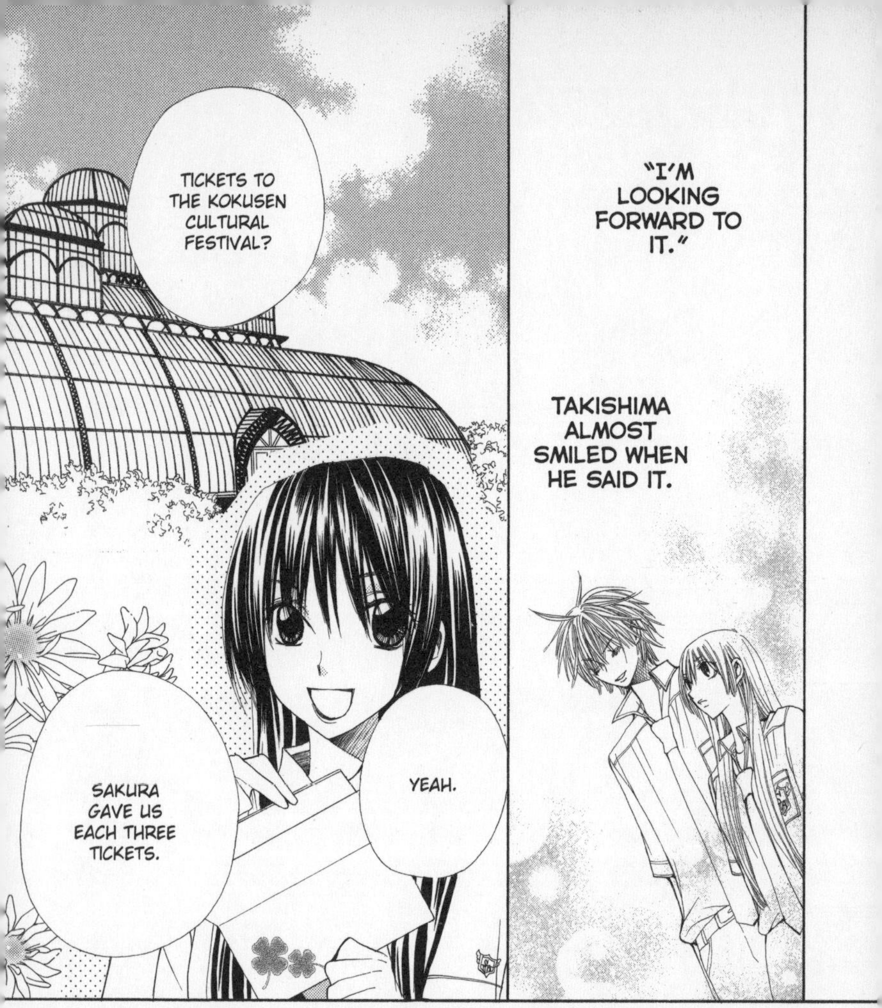
"I'M LOOKING FORWARD TO IT."
TAKISHIMA ALMOST SMILED WHEN HE SAID IT.
TICKETS TO THE KOKUSEN CULTURAL FESTIVAL?
YEAH.
SAKURA GAVE US EACH THREE TICKETS.

• WORK SUPPLIES •

ARE THERE CERTAIN THINGS THAT YOU NEED WHEN YOU'RE STUDYING, WORKING, OR MAKING SOMETHING? FOR ME, IT HELPS ME WORK IF I HAVE MUSIC AND SOMETHING TO DRINK. IF I HAVE SOMETHING TO EAT, I CAN WORK FOR HOURS. HA HA! NOW THAT I THINK ABOUT IT, ARE THERE ANY SONGS THAT MAKE THE TIME GO BY FASTER WHEN YOU'RE WORKING? AND THEN, ARE THERE ANY SONGS THAT MAKE IT IMPOSSIBLE FOR YOU TO CONCENTRATE? I GUESS SOME SONGS WORK FOR YOU AND SOME DON'T.

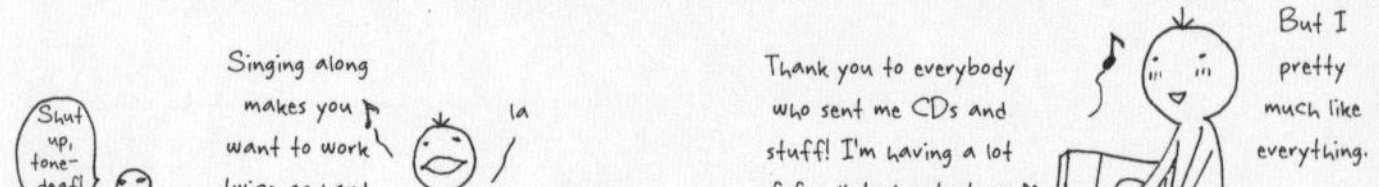
ha ha ha
But I pretty much like everything.
Thank you to everybody who sent me CDs and stuff! I'm having a lot of fun listening to them.♡
la
Singing along makes you want to work twice as hard.
Shut up, tone-deaf!

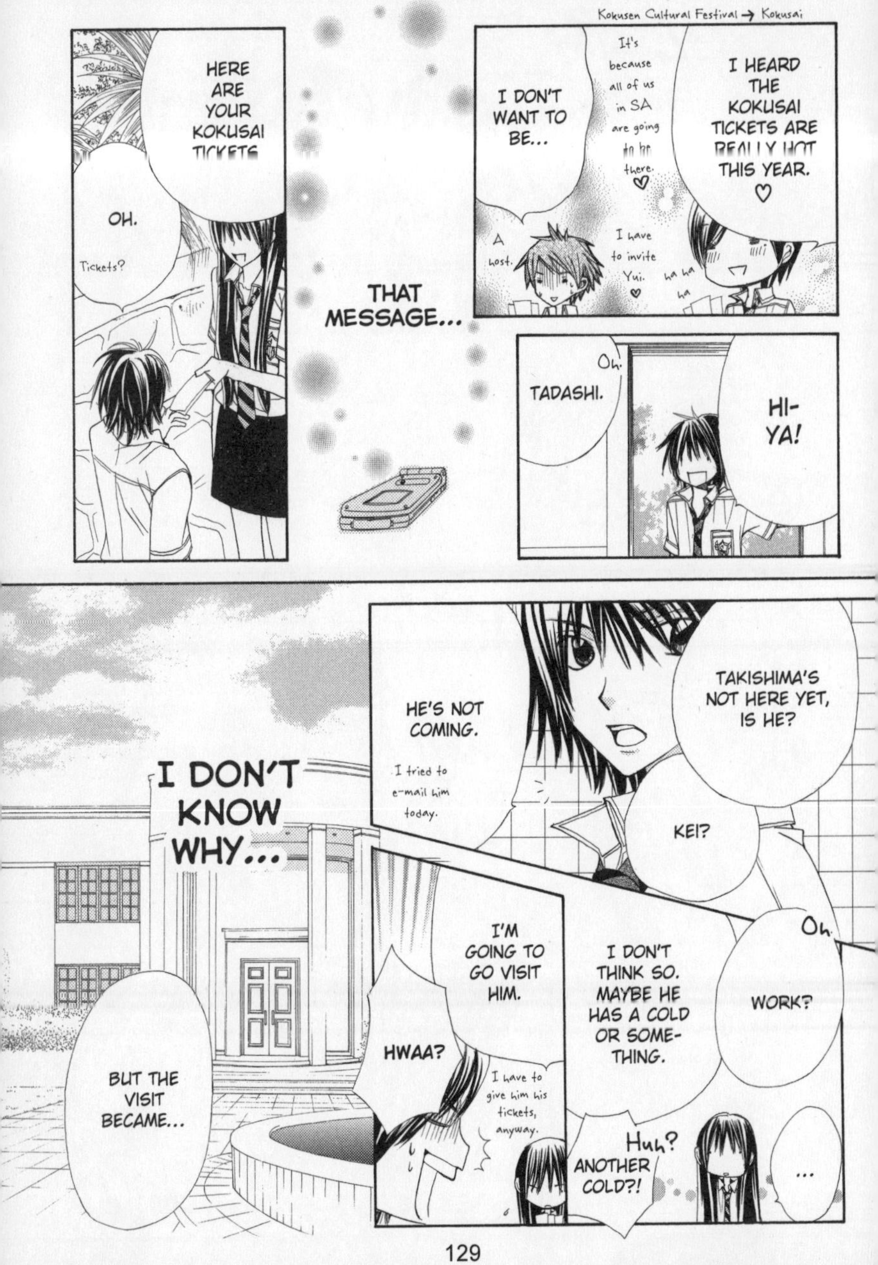
Kokusen Cultural Festival → Kokusai
I HEARD THE KOKUSAI TICKETS ARE REALLY HOT THIS YEAR. ♡
ha ha ha
It's because all of us in SA are going to be there. ♡
I have to invite Yui. ♡
I DON'T WANT TO BE...
A host.
HI-YA!
Oh.
TADASHI.
THAT MESSAGE...
HERE ARE YOUR KOKUSAI TICKETS
OH.
Tickets?
TAKISHIMA'S NOT HERE YET, IS HE?
HE'S NOT COMING.
I tried to e-mail him today.
KEI?
Oh.
WORK?
I DON'T THINK SO. MAYBE HE HAS A COLD OR SOME-THING.
...
Huh?
ANOTHER COLD?!
I'M GOING TO GO VISIT HIM.
I have to give him his tickets, anyway.
HWAA?
I DON'T KNOW WHY...
BUT THE VISIT BECAME...

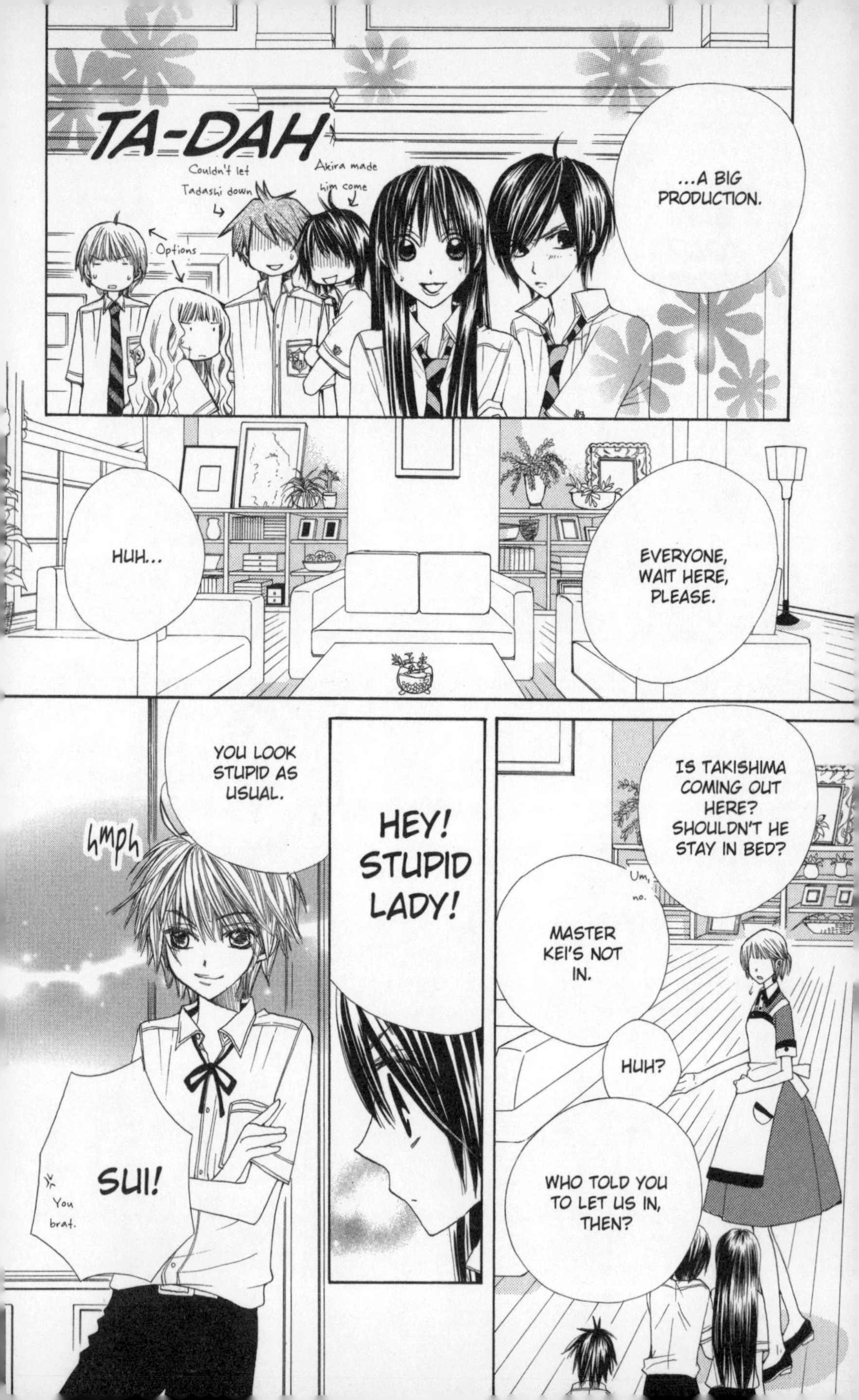
...A BIG PRODUCTION.
TA-DAH
Akira made him come
Couldn't let Tadashi down
Options
EVERYONE, WAIT HERE, PLEASE.
HUH...
IS TAKISHIMA COMING OUT HERE? SHOULDN'T HE STAY IN BED?
Um, no.
MASTER KEI'S NOT IN.
HUH?
WHO TOLD YOU TO LET US IN, THEN?
HEY! STUPID LADY!
YOU LOOK STUPID AS USUAL.
hmph
SUI!
You brat.

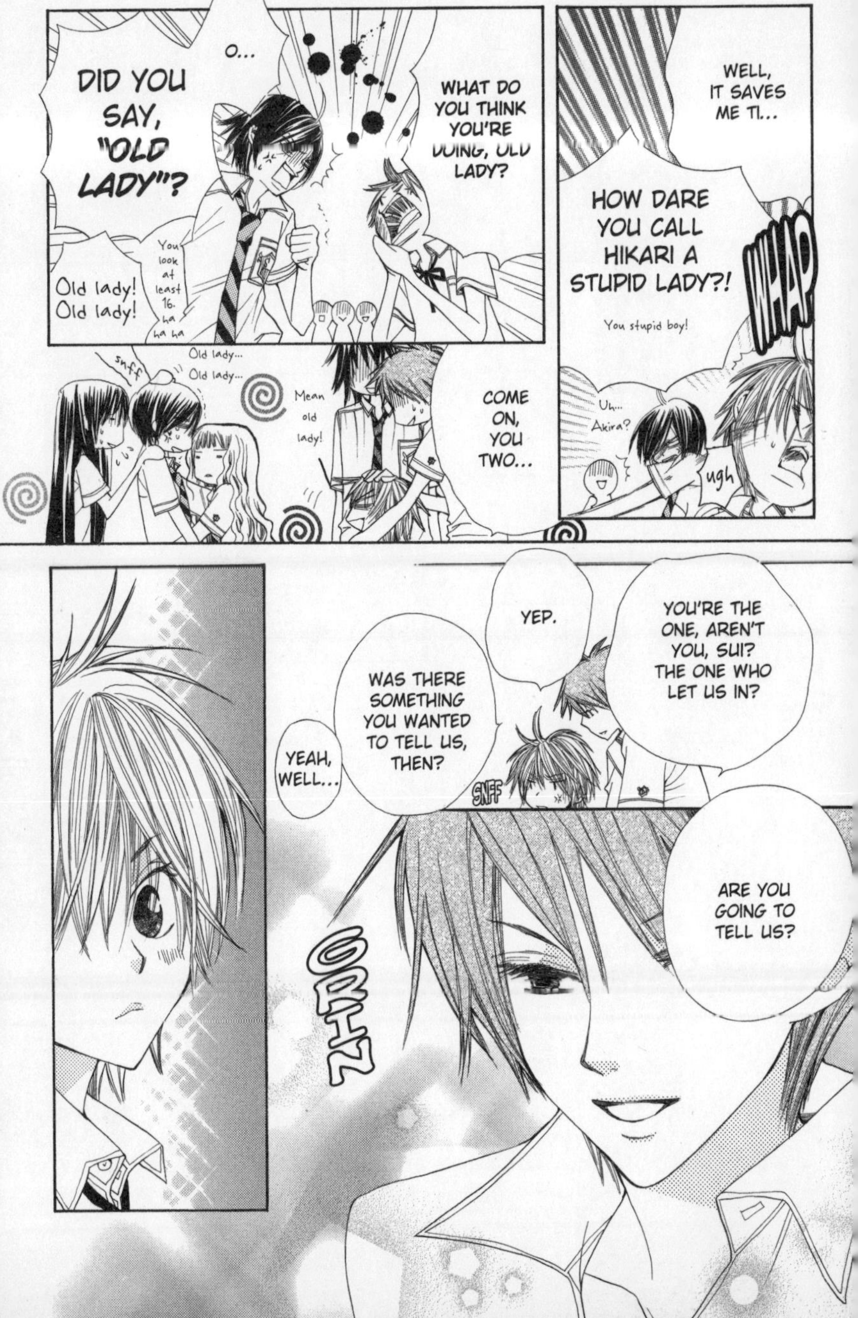

WELL, IT SAVES ME TI...
HOW DARE YOU CALL HIKARI A STUPID LADY?!
WHAP
You stupid boy!
Uh... Akira?
ugh
WHAT DO YOU THINK YOU'RE DOING, OLD LADY?
O...
DID YOU SAY, "OLD LADY"?
You look at least 16. ha ha ha
Old lady! Old lady!
COME ON, YOU TWO...
Mean old lady!
Old lady... Old lady...
snff
YOU'RE THE ONE, AREN'T YOU, SUI? THE ONE WHO LET US IN?
YEP.
WAS THERE SOMETHING YOU WANTED TO TELL US, THEN?
YEAH, WELL...
SNFF
ARE YOU GOING TO TELL US?
GRIN

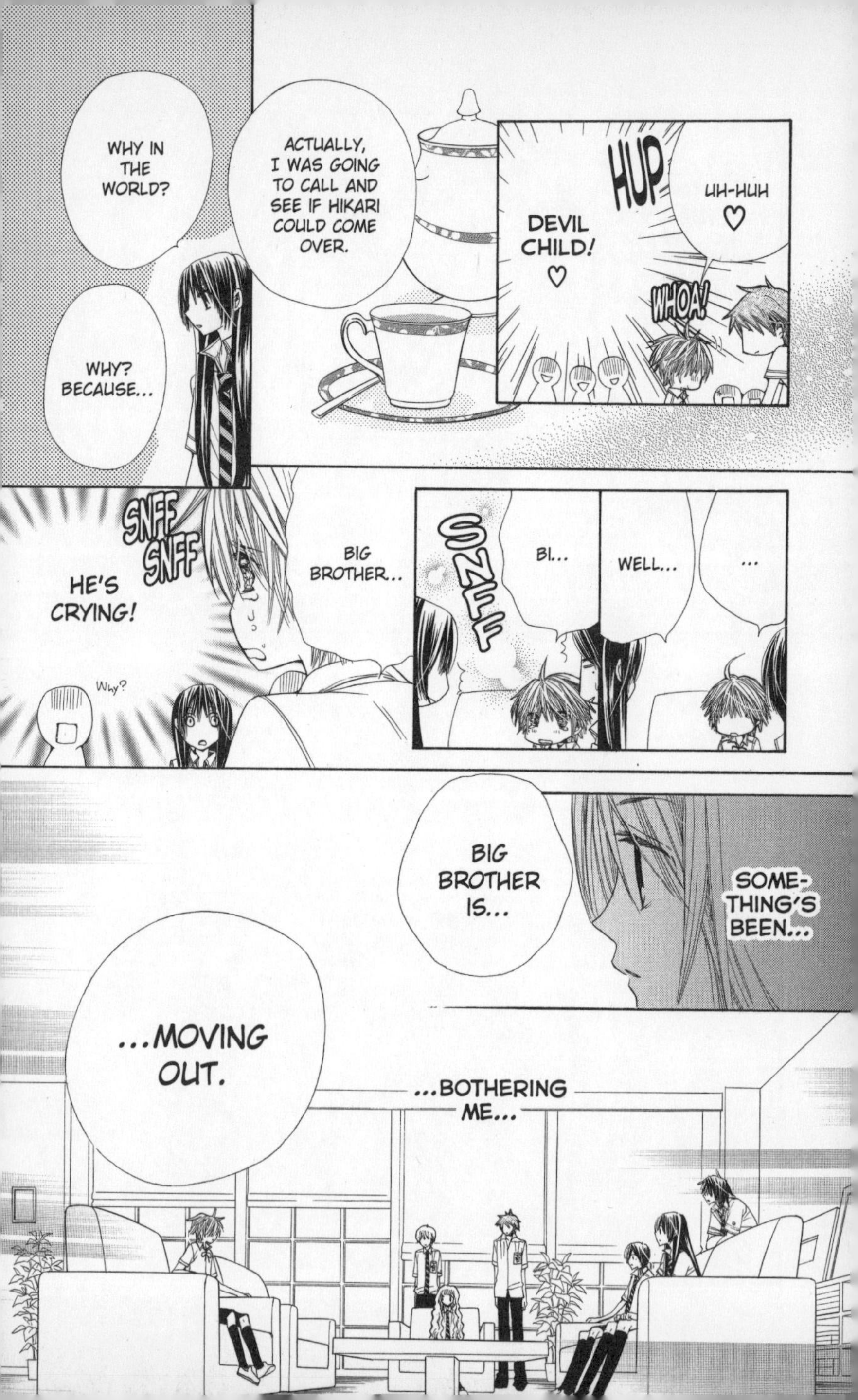
UH-HUH ♡
HUP
DEVIL CHILD! ♡
WHOA!
ACTUALLY, I WAS GOING TO CALL AND SEE IF HIKARI COULD COME OVER.
WHY IN THE WORLD?
WHY? BECAUSE...
...
WELL...
BI...
SNFF
BIG BROTHER...
SNFF SNFF
HE'S CRYING!
Why?
SOME-THING'S BEEN...
BIG BROTHER IS...
...BOTHERING ME...
...MOVING OUT.

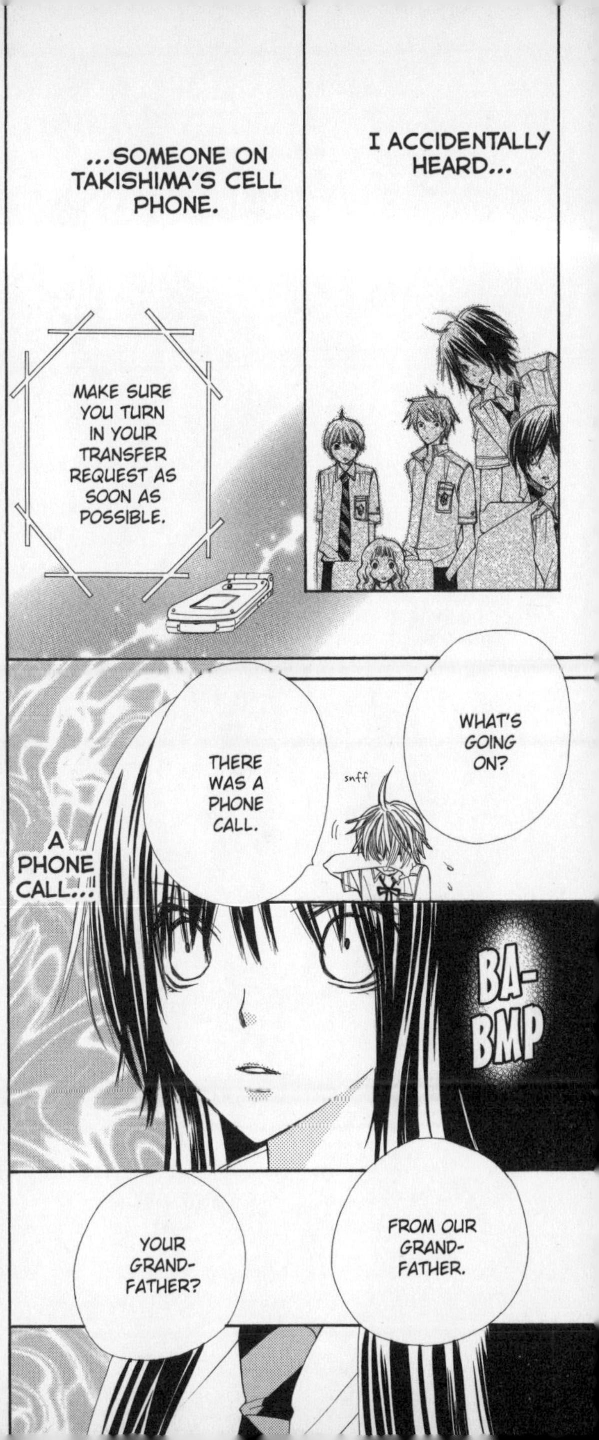
I ACCIDENTALLY HEARD...
...SOMEONE ON TAKISHIMA'S CELL PHONE.
MAKE SURE YOU TURN IN YOUR TRANSFER REQUEST AS SOON AS POSSIBLE.
WHAT'S GOING ON?
snff
THERE WAS A PHONE CALL.
A PHONE CALL...!
BA-BMP
FROM OUR GRAND-FATHER.
YOUR GRAND-FATHER?

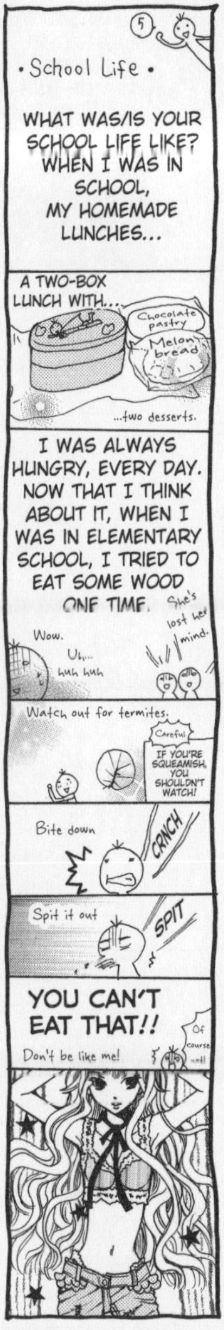
5
• School Life •
WHAT WAS/IS YOUR SCHOOL LIFE LIKE? WHEN I WAS IN SCHOOL, MY HOMEMADE LUNCHES...
A TWO-BOX LUNCH WITH...
Chocolate pastry
Melon bread
...two desserts.
I WAS ALWAYS HUNGRY, EVERY DAY. NOW THAT I THINK ABOUT IT, WHEN I WAS IN ELEMENTARY SCHOOL, I TRIED TO EAT SOME WOOD ONE TIME.
She's lost her mind.
Wow.
Uh... huh huh
Watch out for termites.
Careful
IF YOU'RE SQUEAMISH, YOU SHOULDN'T WATCH!
Bite down
CRNCH
Spit it out
SPIT
YOU CAN'T EAT THAT!!
Of course not!
Don't be like me!

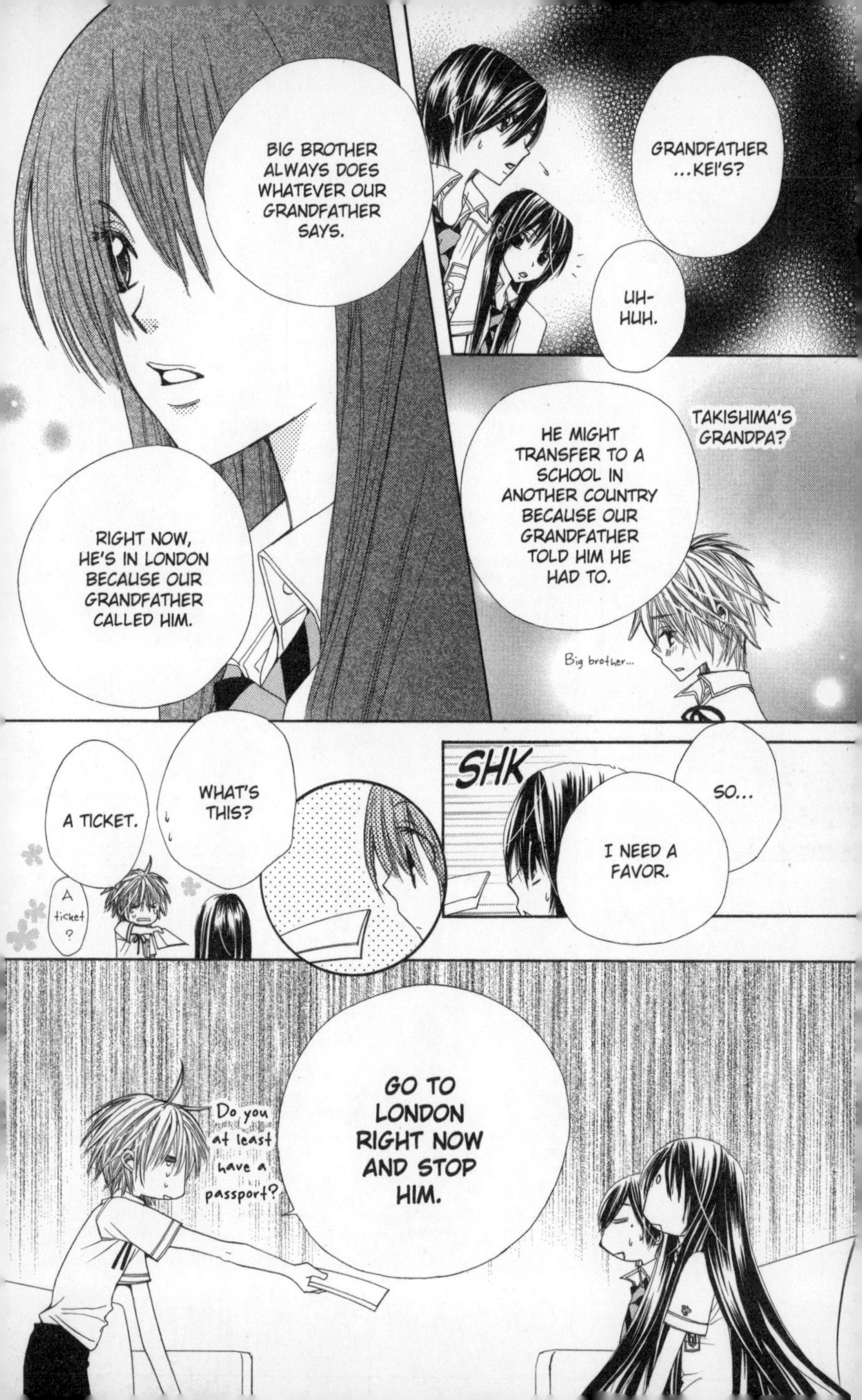
BIG BROTHER ALWAYS DOES WHATEVER OUR GRANDFATHER SAYS.
GRANDFATHER ...KEI'S?
UH-HUH.
HE MIGHT TRANSFER TO A SCHOOL IN ANOTHER COUNTRY BECAUSE OUR GRANDFATHER TOLD HIM HE HAD TO.
TAKISHIMA'S GRANDPA?
Big brother...
RIGHT NOW, HE'S IN LONDON BECAUSE OUR GRANDFATHER CALLED HIM.
SHK
SO...
I NEED A FAVOR.
WHAT'S THIS?
A TICKET.
A ticket?
GO TO LONDON RIGHT NOW AND STOP HIM.
Do you at least have a passport?

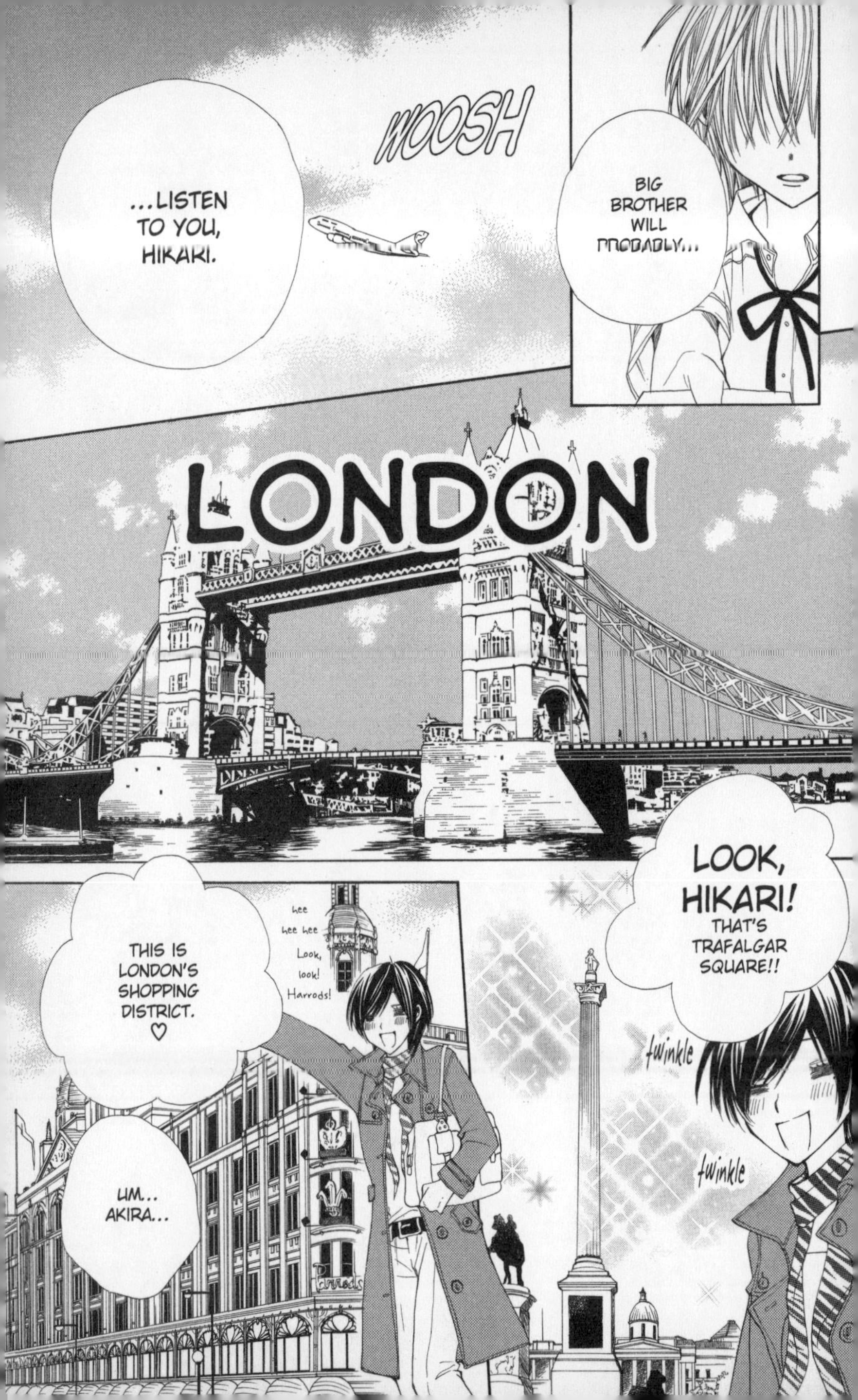
BIG BROTHER WILL PROBABLY...
WOOSH
...LISTEN TO YOU, HIKARI.
LONDON
LOOK, HIKARI! THAT'S TRAFALGAR SQUARE!!
twinkle
twinkle
THIS IS LONDON'S SHOPPING DISTRICT. ♡
hee hee hee
Look, look! Harrods!
UM... AKIRA...

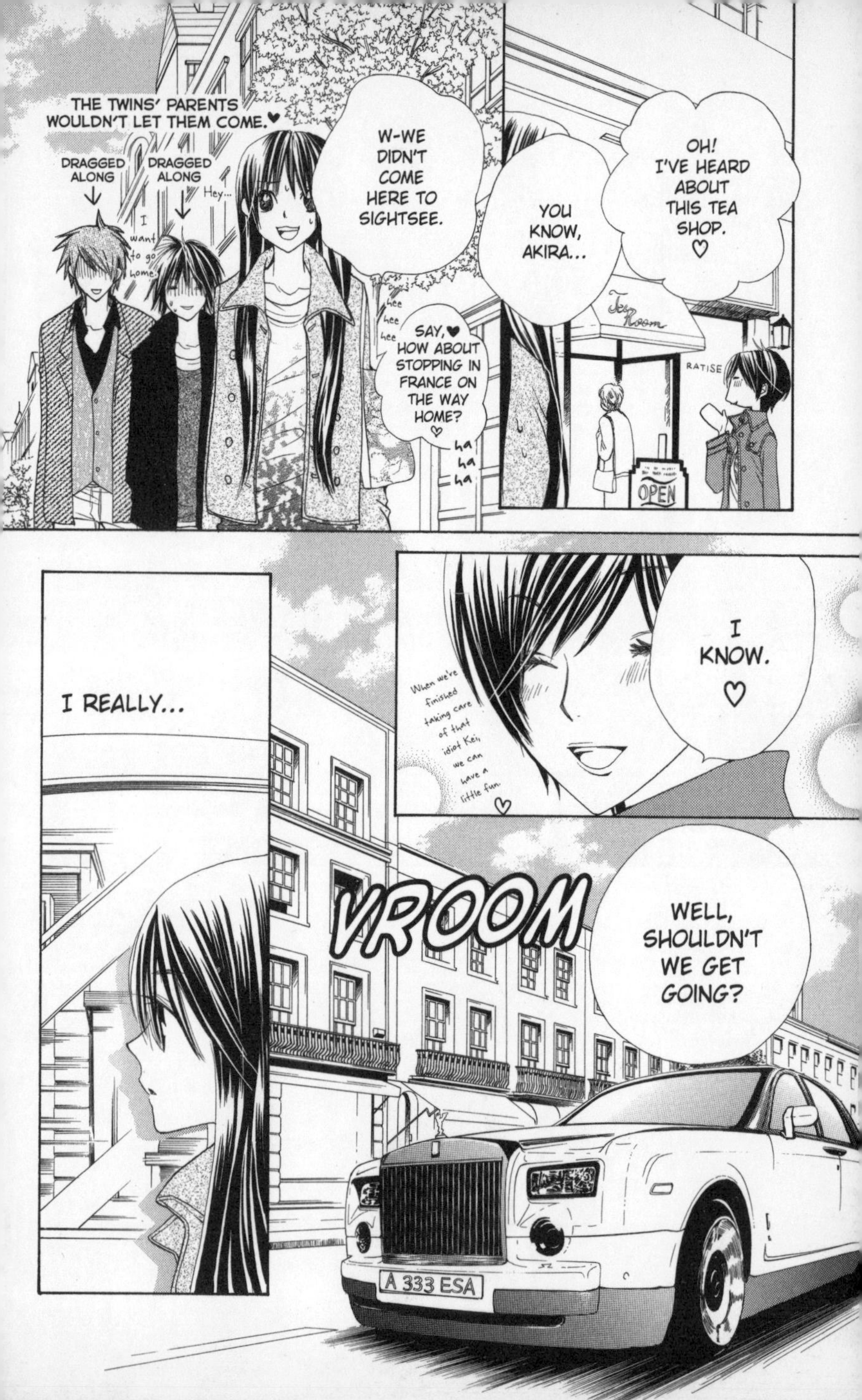
OH! I'VE HEARD ABOUT THIS TEA SHOP. ♡
YOU KNOW, AKIRA...
Tea Room
RATISE
OPEN
W-WE DIDN'T COME HERE TO SIGHTSEE.
hee hee hee
SAY, ♥ HOW ABOUT STOPPING IN FRANCE ON THE WAY HOME? ♡
ha ha ha
Hey...
I want to go home.
DRAGGED ALONG
DRAGGED ALONG
THE TWINS' PARENTS WOULDN'T LET THEM COME. ♥
I KNOW. ♡
When we're finished taking care of that idiot Kei, we can have a little fun. ♡
WELL, SHOULDN'T WE GET GOING?
VROOM
A 333 ESA
I REALLY...

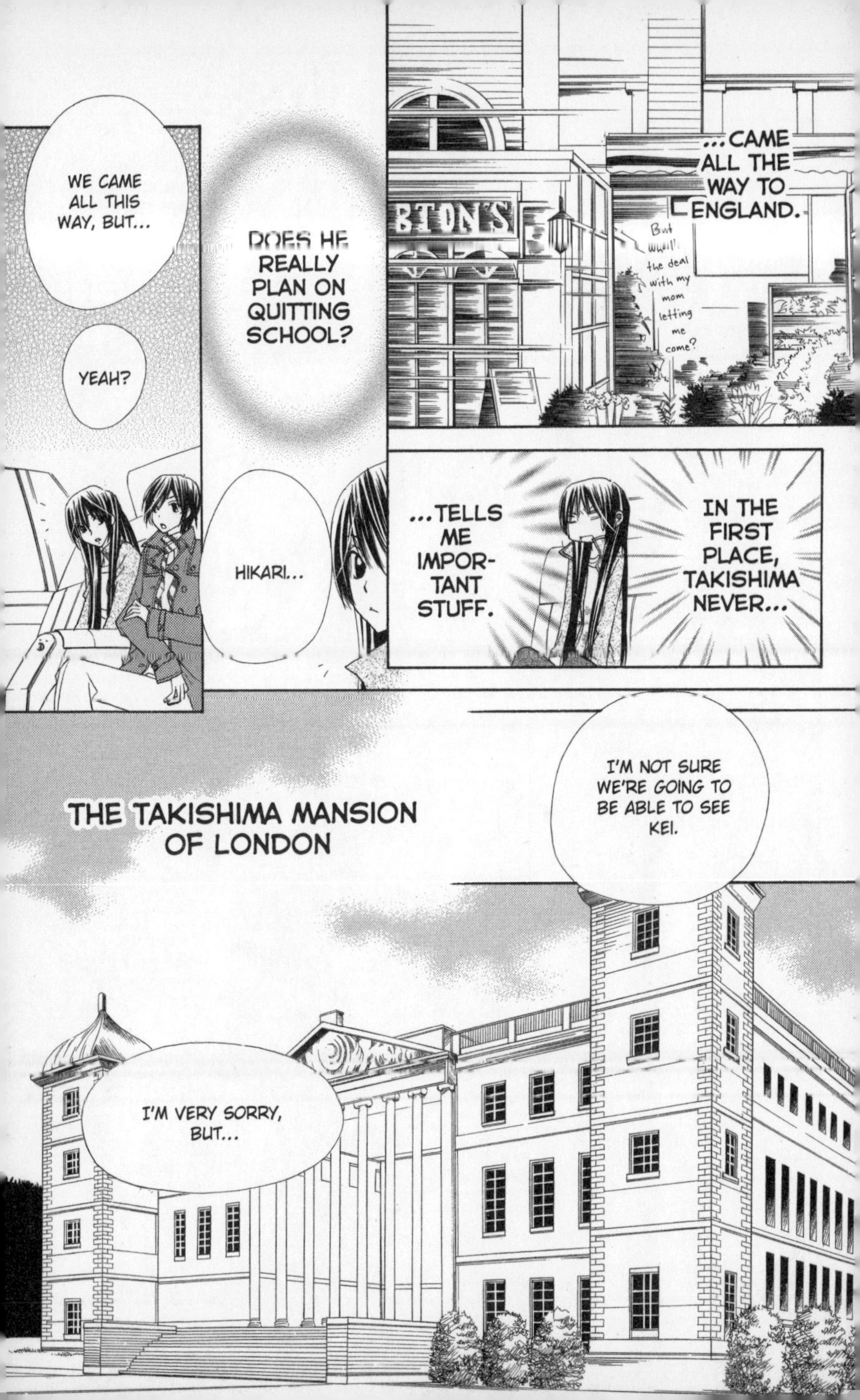
BTONS
...CAME ALL THE WAY TO ENGLAND.
But what'll the deal with my mom letting me come?
IN THE FIRST PLACE, TAKISHIMA NEVER...
...TELLS ME IMPORTANT STUFF.
WE CAME ALL THIS WAY, BUT...
YEAH?
DOES HE REALLY PLAN ON QUITTING SCHOOL?
HIKARI...
I'M NOT SURE WE'RE GOING TO BE ABLE TO SEE KEI.
THE TAKISHIMA MANSION OF LONDON
I'M VERY SORRY, BUT...

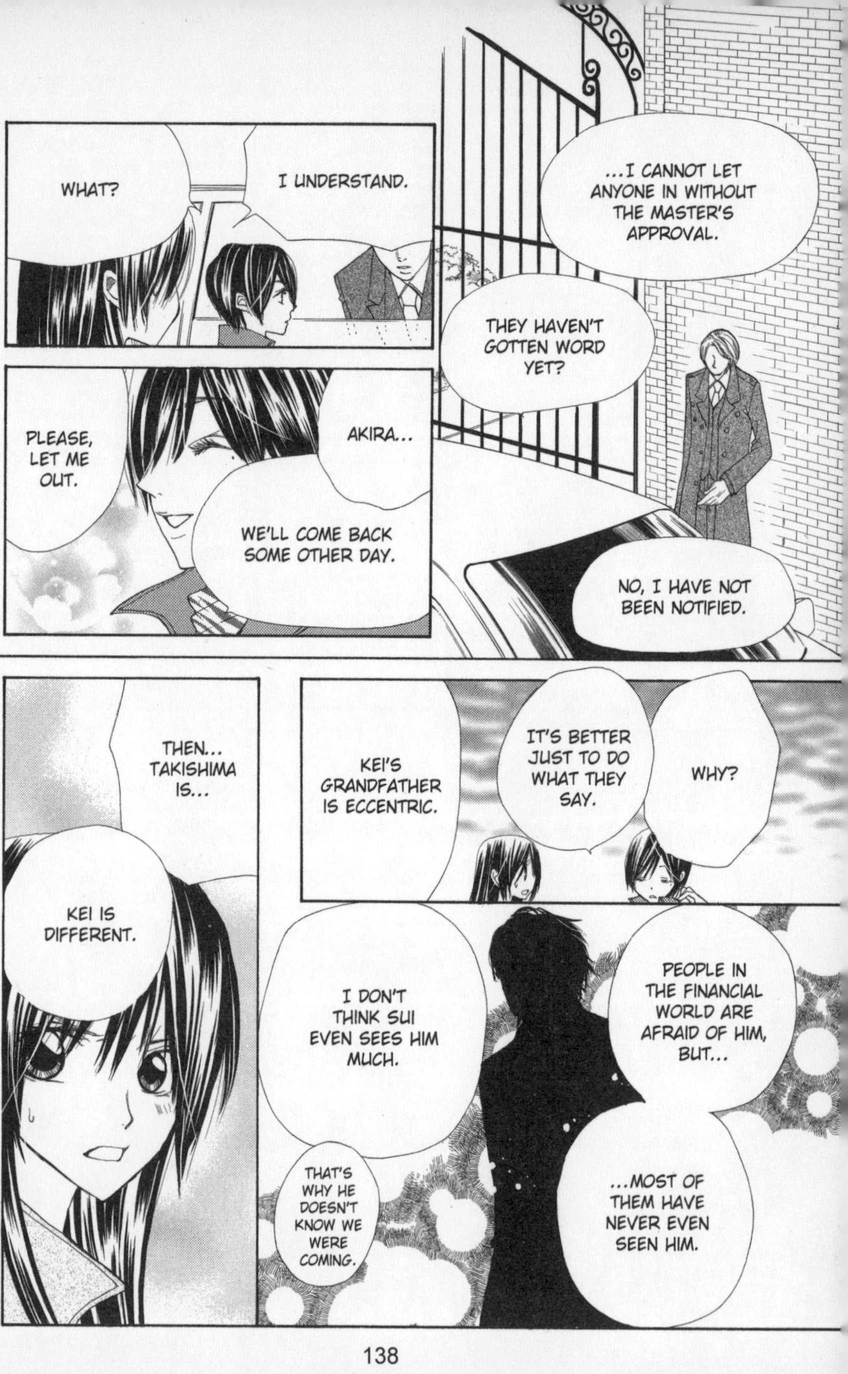
...I CANNOT LET ANYONE IN WITHOUT THE MASTER'S APPROVAL.
THEY HAVEN'T GOTTEN WORD YET?
NO, I HAVE NOT BEEN NOTIFIED.
I UNDERSTAND.
WHAT?
AKIRA...
PLEASE, LET ME OUT.
WE'LL COME BACK SOME OTHER DAY.
WHY?
IT'S BETTER JUST TO DO WHAT THEY SAY.
KEI'S GRANDFATHER IS ECCENTRIC.
PEOPLE IN THE FINANCIAL WORLD ARE AFRAID OF HIM, BUT...
...MOST OF THEM HAVE NEVER EVEN SEEN HIM.
I DON'T THINK SUI EVEN SEES HIM MUCH.
THAT'S WHY HE DOESN'T KNOW WE WERE COMING.
THEN... TAKISHIMA IS...
KEI IS DIFFERENT.

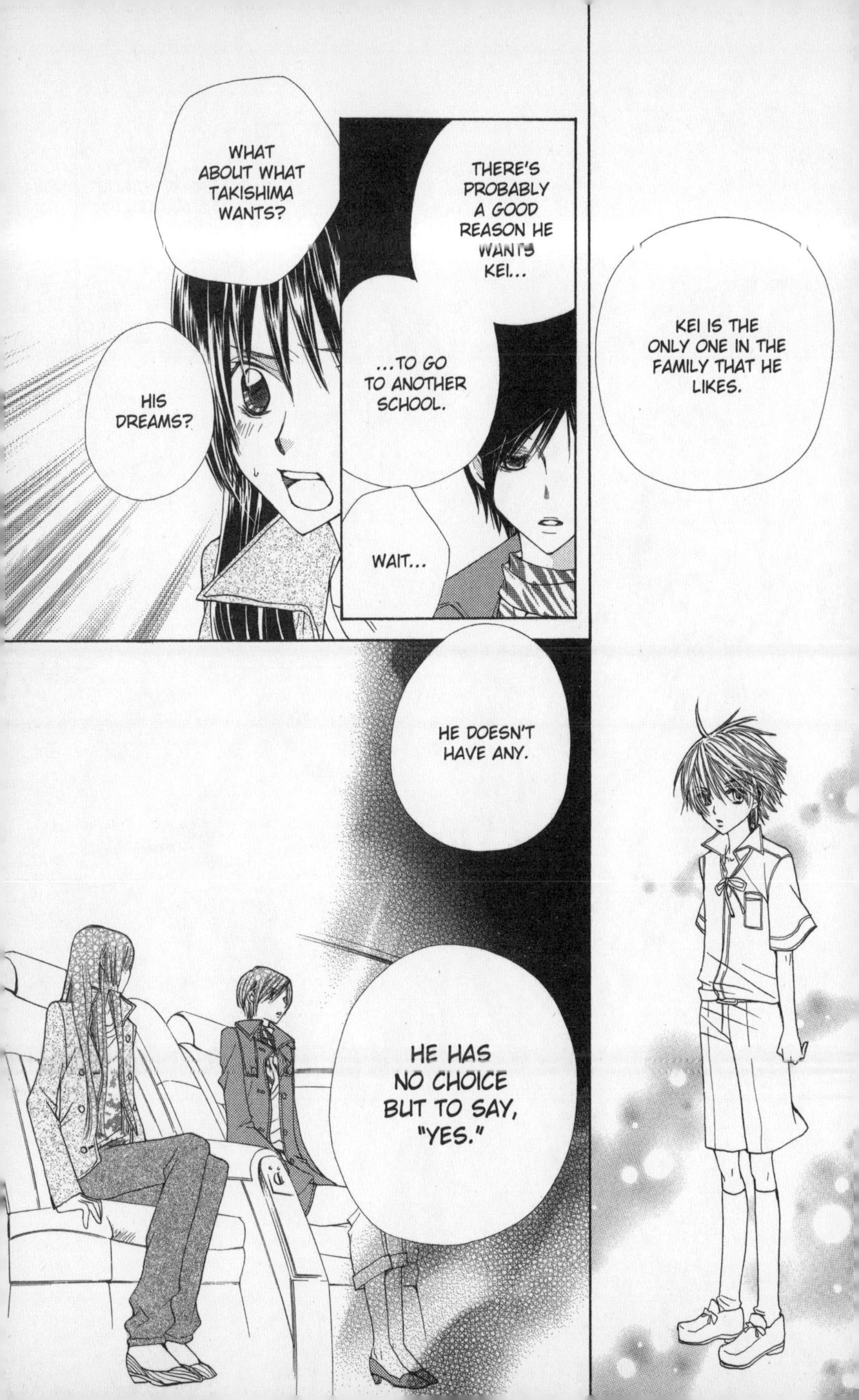
KEI IS THE ONLY ONE IN THE FAMILY THAT HE LIKES.
THERE'S PROBABLY A GOOD REASON HE WANTS KEI...
...TO GO TO ANOTHER SCHOOL.
WAIT...
WHAT ABOUT WHAT TAKISHIMA WANTS?
HIS DREAMS?
HE DOESN'T HAVE ANY.
HE HAS NO CHOICE BUT TO SAY, "YES."

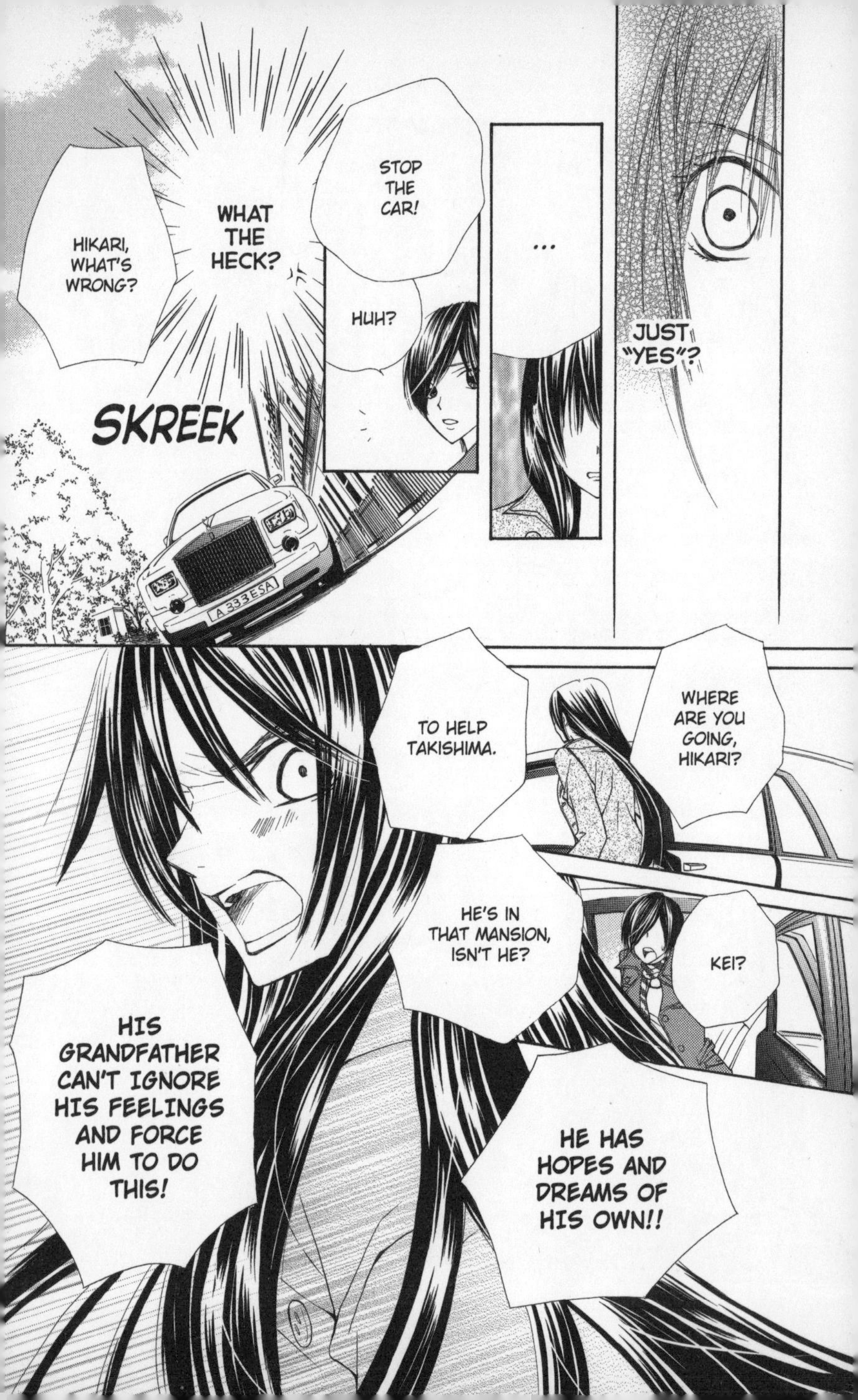
JUST "YES"?
...
STOP THE CAR!
HUH?
WHAT THE HECK?
HIKARI, WHAT'S WRONG?
SKREEK
A 333 ESA
WHERE ARE YOU GOING, HIKARI?
TO HELP TAKISHIMA.
KEI?
HE'S IN THAT MANSION, ISN'T HE?
HIS GRANDFATHER CAN'T IGNORE HIS FEELINGS AND FORCE HIM TO DO THIS!
HE HAS HOPES AND DREAMS OF HIS OWN!!

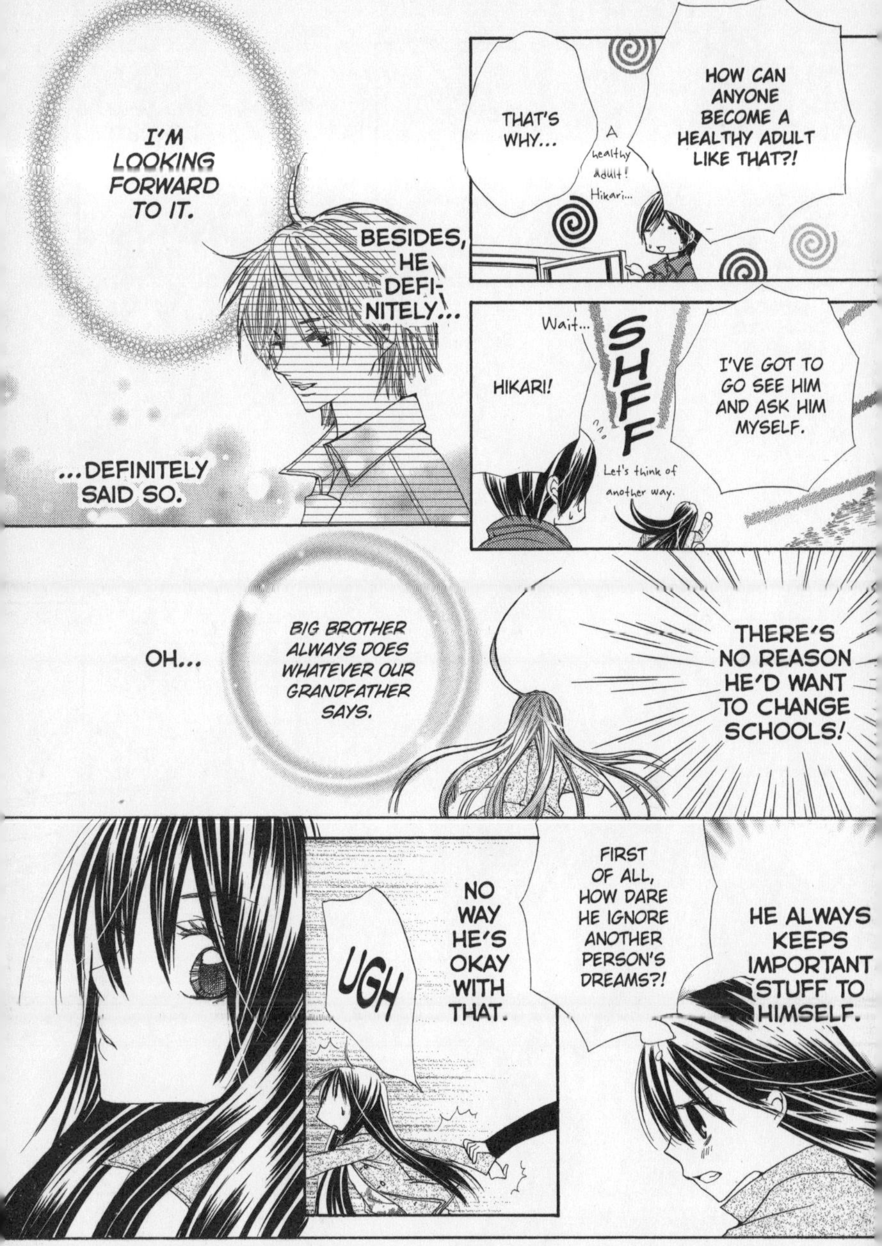
HOW CAN ANYONE BECOME A HEALTHY ADULT LIKE THAT?!
A healthy adult! Hikari...
THAT'S WHY...
I'VE GOT TO GO SEE HIM AND ASK HIM MYSELF.
SHFF
Wait...
HIKARI!
Let's think of another way.
I'M LOOKING FORWARD TO IT.
BESIDES, HE DEFI-NITELY...
...DEFINITELY SAID SO.
THERE'S NO REASON HE'D WANT TO CHANGE SCHOOLS!
BIG BROTHER ALWAYS DOES WHATEVER OUR GRANDFATHER SAYS.
OH...
HE ALWAYS KEEPS IMPORTANT STUFF TO HIMSELF.
FIRST OF ALL, HOW DARE HE IGNORE ANOTHER PERSON'S DREAMS?!
NO WAY HE'S OKAY WITH THAT.
UGH

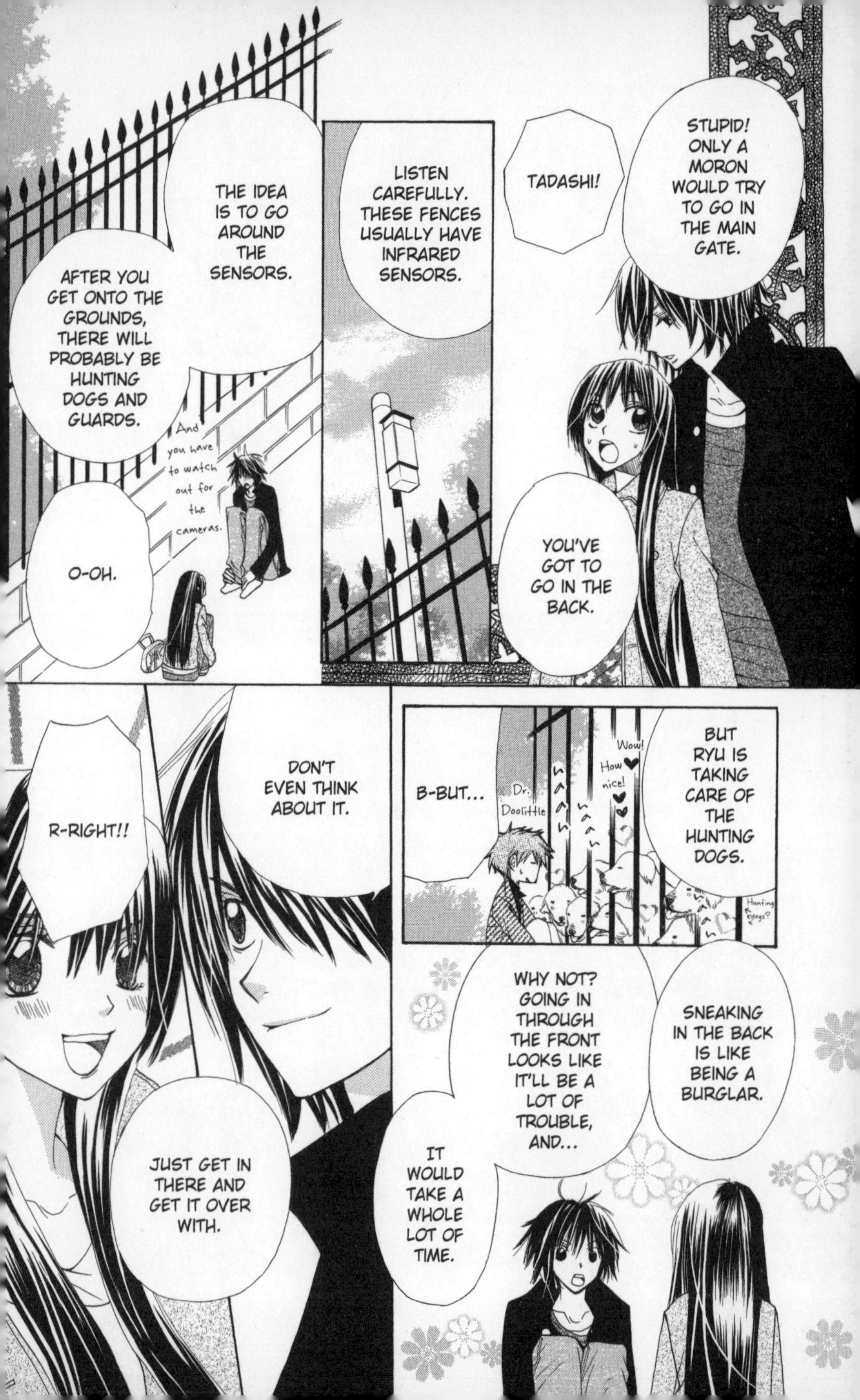
STUPID! ONLY A MORON WOULD TRY TO GO IN THE MAIN GATE.
TADASHI!
YOU'VE GOT TO GO IN THE BACK.
LISTEN CAREFULLY. THESE FENCES USUALLY HAVE INFRARED SENSORS.
THE IDEA IS TO GO AROUND THE SENSORS.
AFTER YOU GET ONTO THE GROUNDS, THERE WILL PROBABLY BE HUNTING DOGS AND GUARDS.
And you have to watch out for the cameras.
O-OH.
BUT RYU IS TAKING CARE OF THE HUNTING DOGS.
Wow! How nice!
B-BUT...
Dr. Doolittle
Hunting dogs?
SNEAKING IN THE BACK IS LIKE BEING A BURGLAR.
WHY NOT? GOING IN THROUGH THE FRONT LOOKS LIKE IT'LL BE A LOT OF TROUBLE, AND...
IT WOULD TAKE A WHOLE LOT OF TIME.
DON'T EVEN THINK ABOUT IT.
R-RIGHT!!
JUST GET IN THERE AND GET IT OVER WITH.

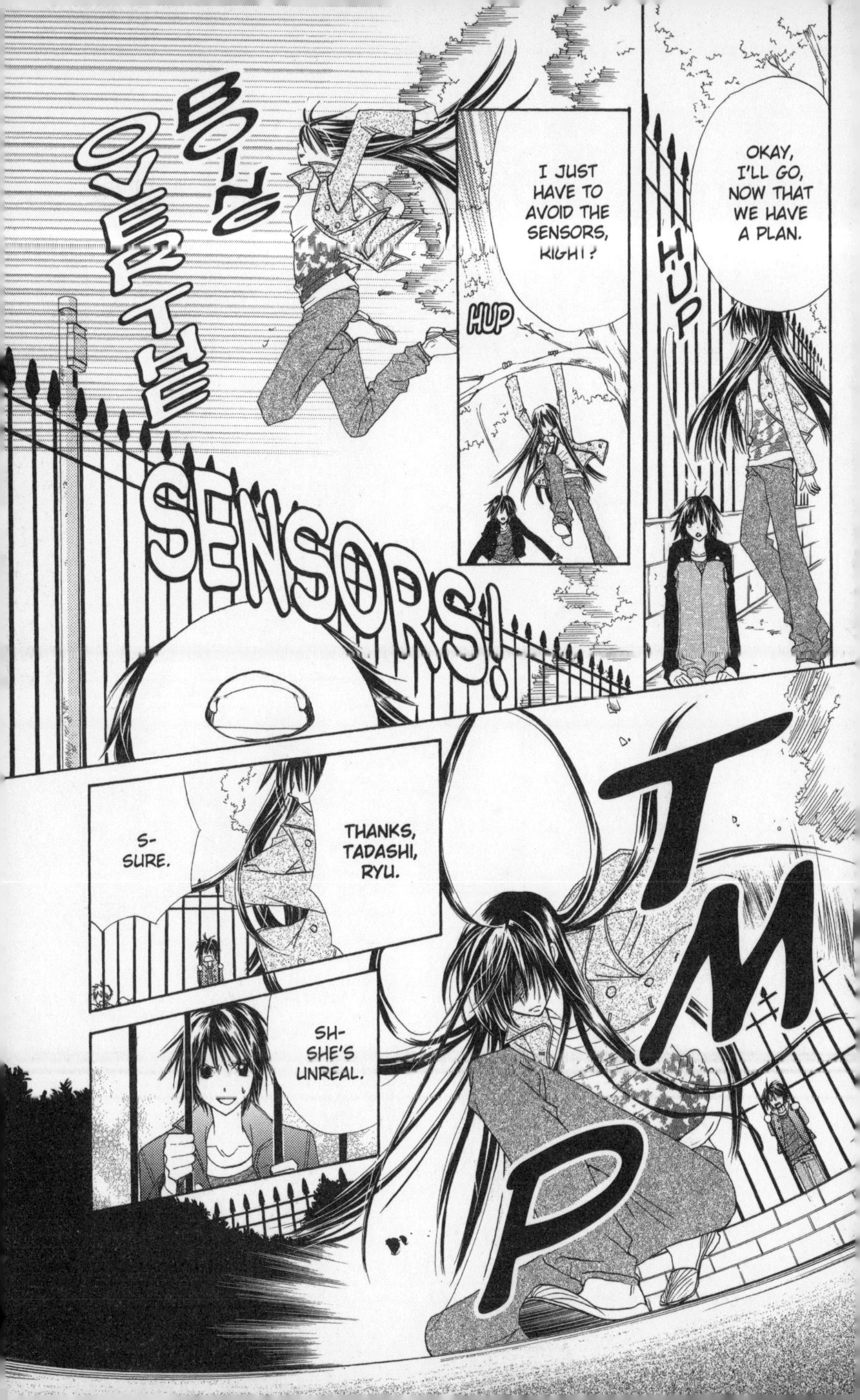
OKAY, I'LL GO, NOW THAT WE HAVE A PLAN.
HUP
I JUST HAVE TO AVOID THE SENSORS, RIGHT?
HUP
BOING
OVER THE
SENSORS!
TMP
THANKS, TADASHI, RYU.
S-SURE.
SH-SHE'S UNREAL.

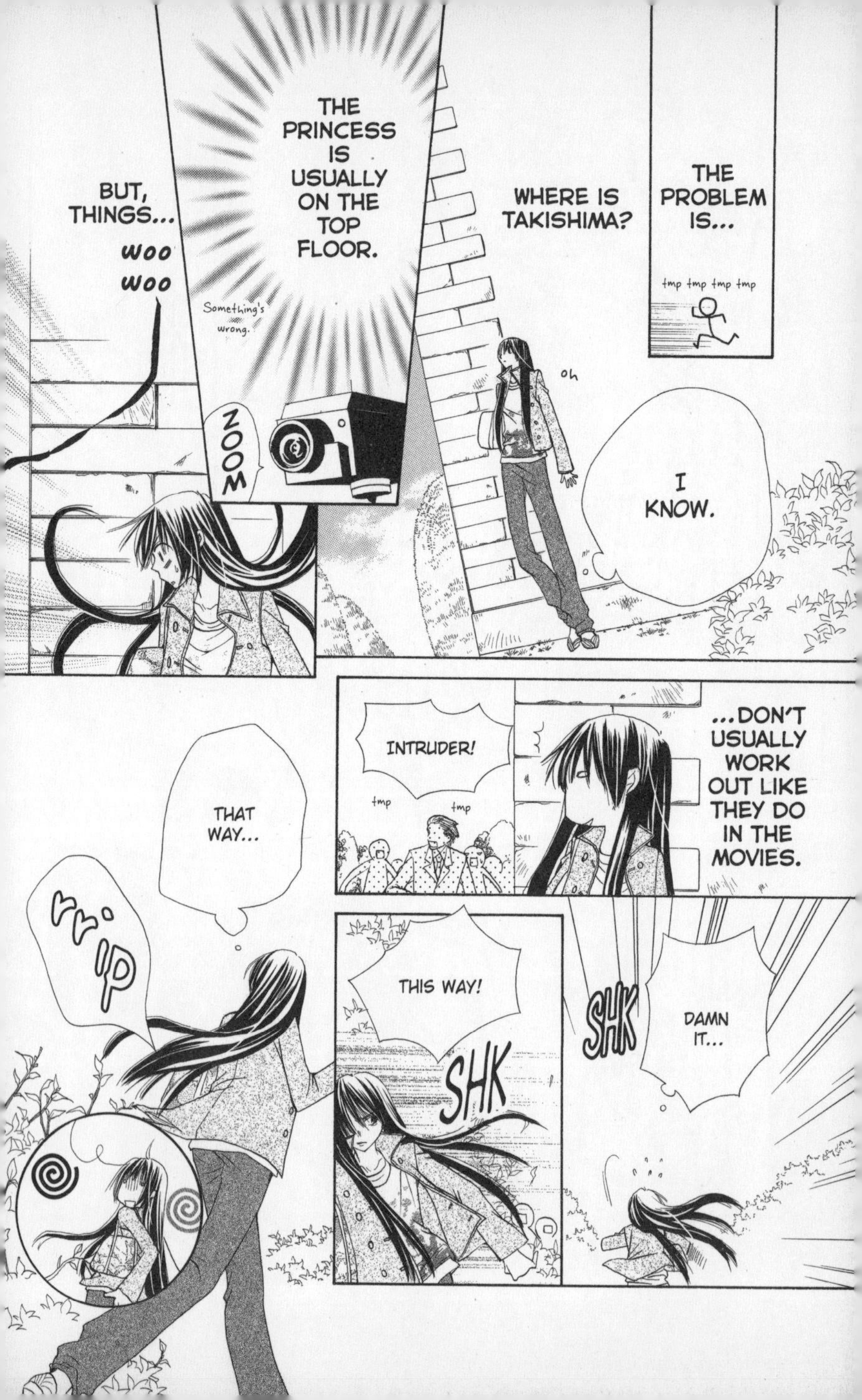
THE PROBLEM IS...
tmp tmp tmp tmp
WHERE IS TAKISHIMA?
oh
I KNOW.
THE PRINCESS IS USUALLY ON THE TOP FLOOR.
ZOOM
Something's wrong.
BUT, THINGS...
woo woo
...DON'T USUALLY WORK OUT LIKE THEY DO IN THE MOVIES.
INTRUDER!
tmp
tmp
THAT WAY...
rrip
SHK
DAMN IT...
THIS WAY!
SHK

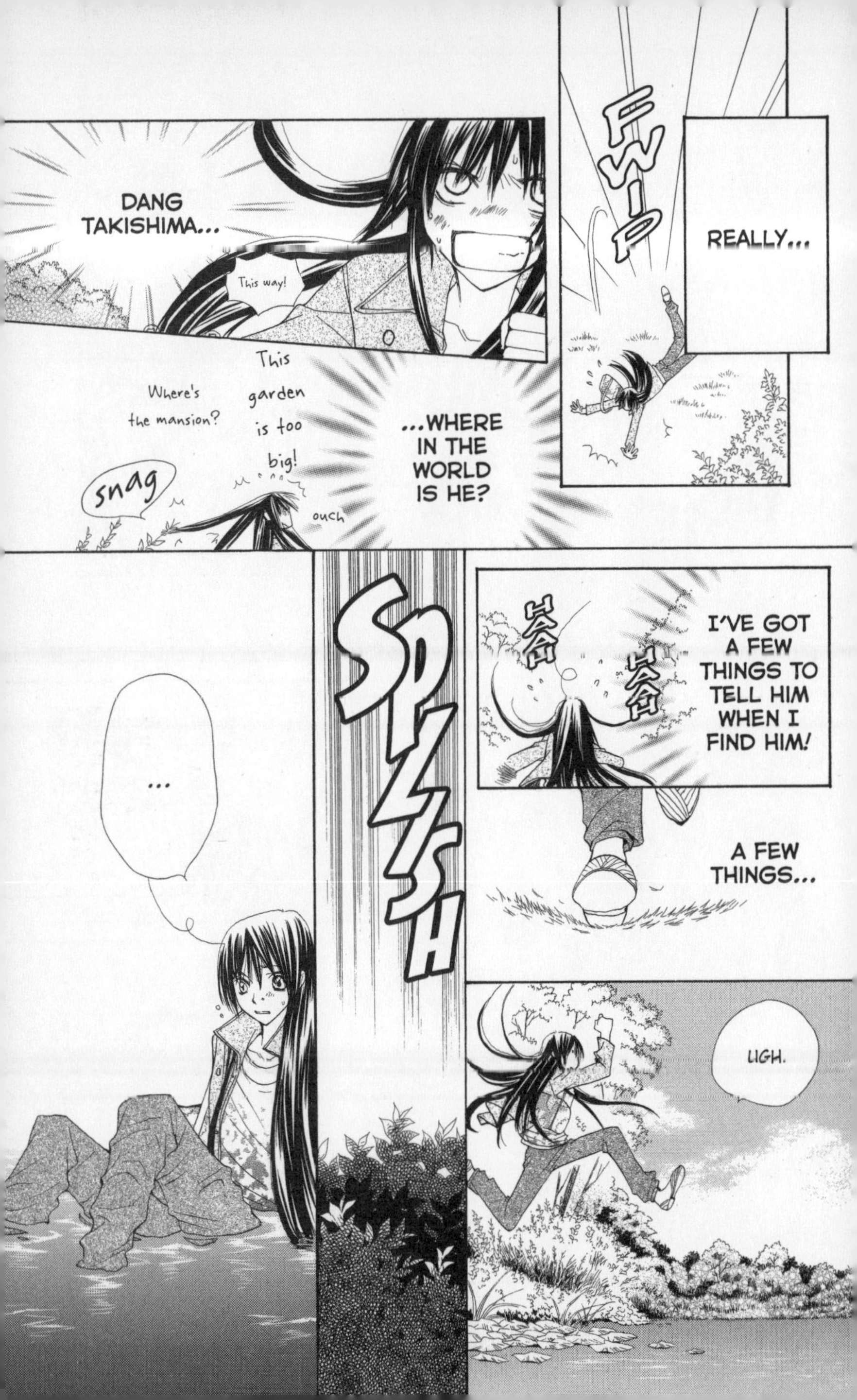
FWIP
REALLY...
DANG TAKISHIMA...
This way!
...WHERE IN THE WORLD IS HE?
This garden is too big!
Where's the mansion?
snag
ouch
I'VE GOT A FEW THINGS TO TELL HIM WHEN I FIND HIM!
A FEW THINGS...
UGH.
SPLSH
...

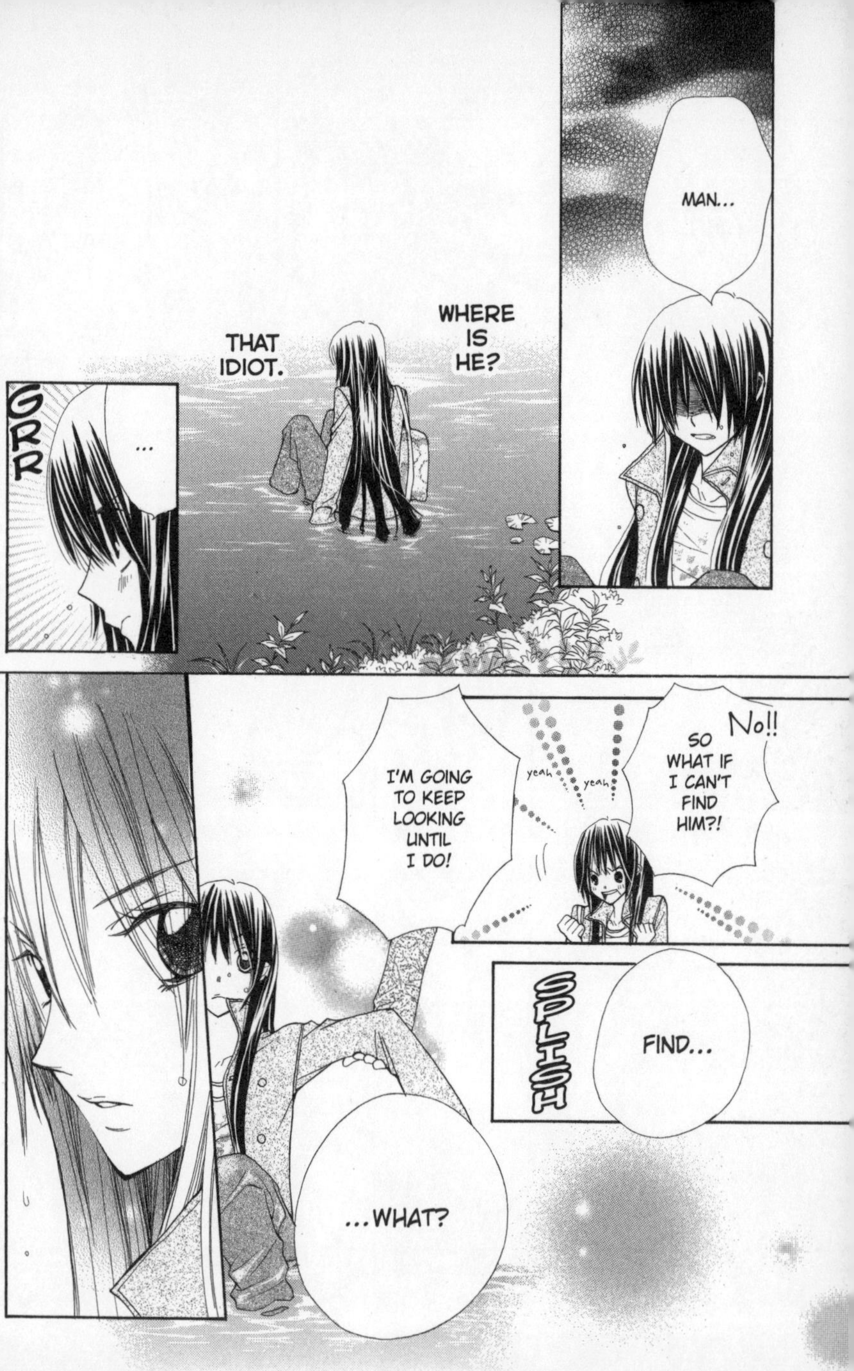
MAN...
WHERE IS HE?
THAT IDIOT.
GRR
...
No!!
SO WHAT IF I CAN'T FIND HIM?!
yeah
yeah
I'M GOING TO KEEP LOOKING UNTIL I DO!
SPLISH
FIND...
...WHAT?

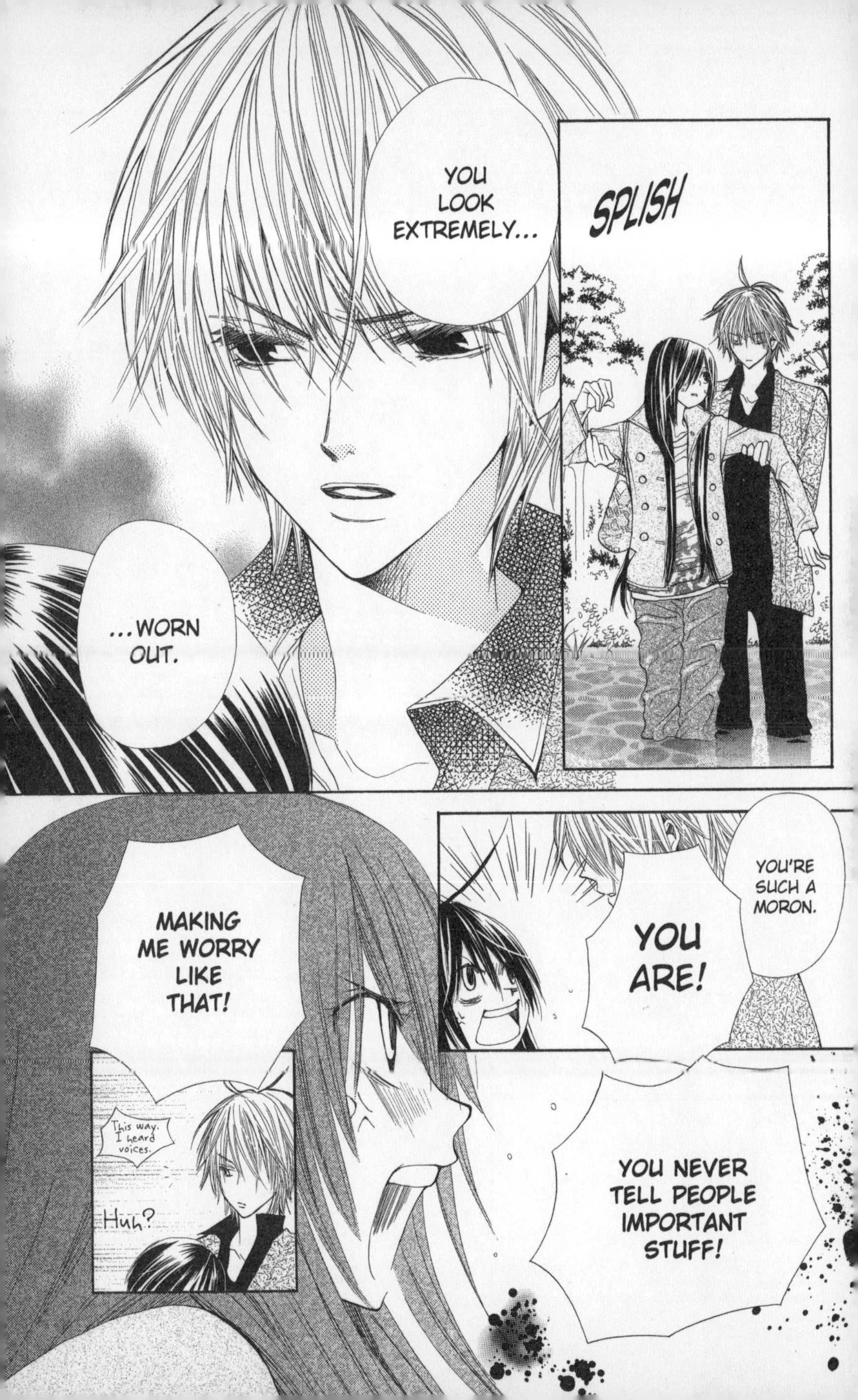
SPLISH
YOU LOOK EXTREMELY...
...WORN OUT.
YOU'RE SUCH A MORON.
YOU ARE!
MAKING ME WORRY LIKE THAT!
YOU NEVER TELL PEOPLE IMPORTANT STUFF!
This way. I heard voices.
Huh?

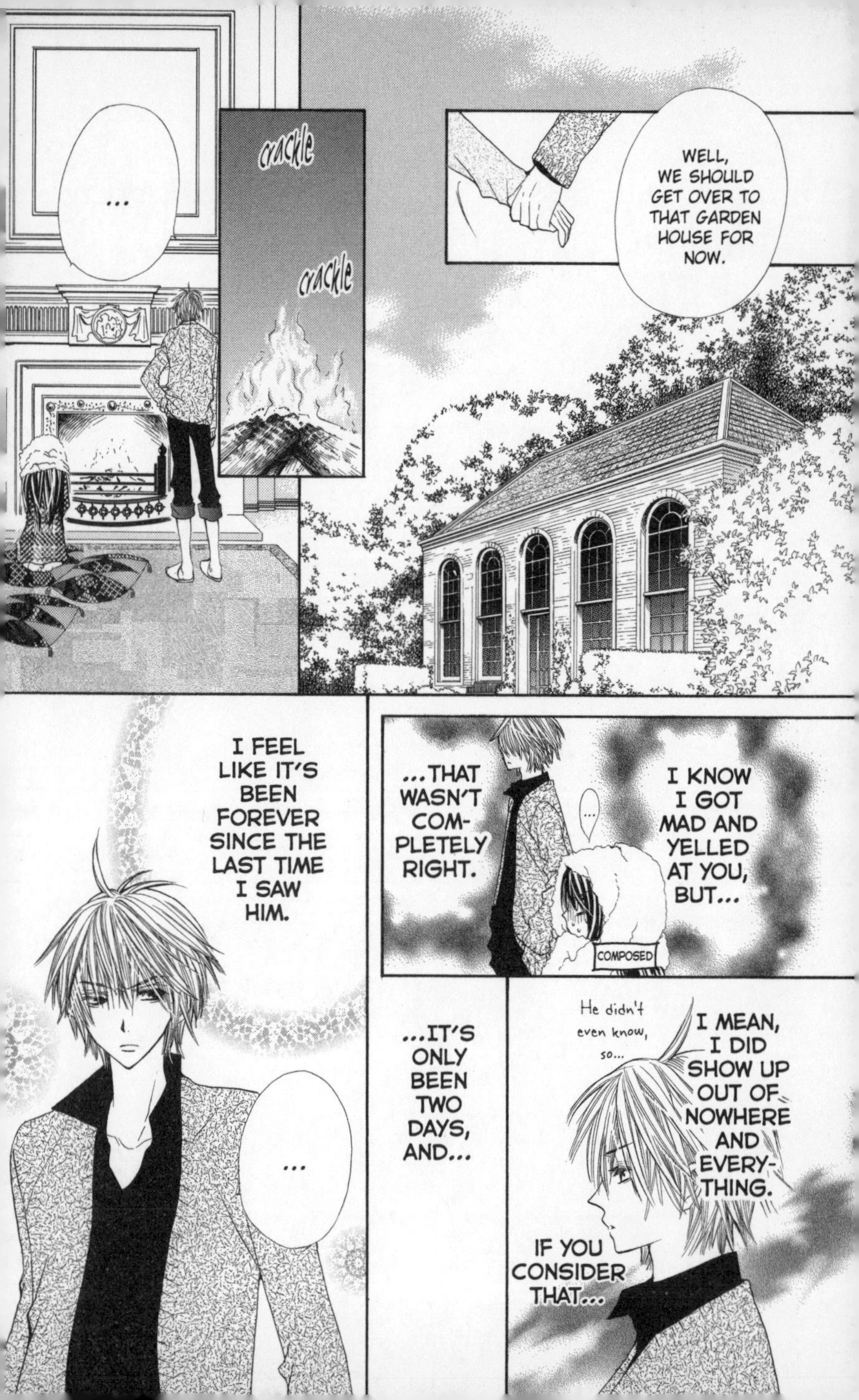
WELL, WE SHOULD GET OVER TO THAT GARDEN HOUSE FOR NOW.
crackle
crackle
...
I KNOW I GOT MAD AND YELLED AT YOU, BUT...
...THAT WASN'T COM-PLETELY RIGHT.
...
COMPOSED
I MEAN, I DID SHOW UP OUT OF NOWHERE AND EVERY-THING.
He didn't even know, so...
IF YOU CONSIDER THAT...
...IT'S ONLY BEEN TWO DAYS, AND...
I FEEL LIKE IT'S BEEN FOREVER SINCE THE LAST TIME I SAW HIM.
...

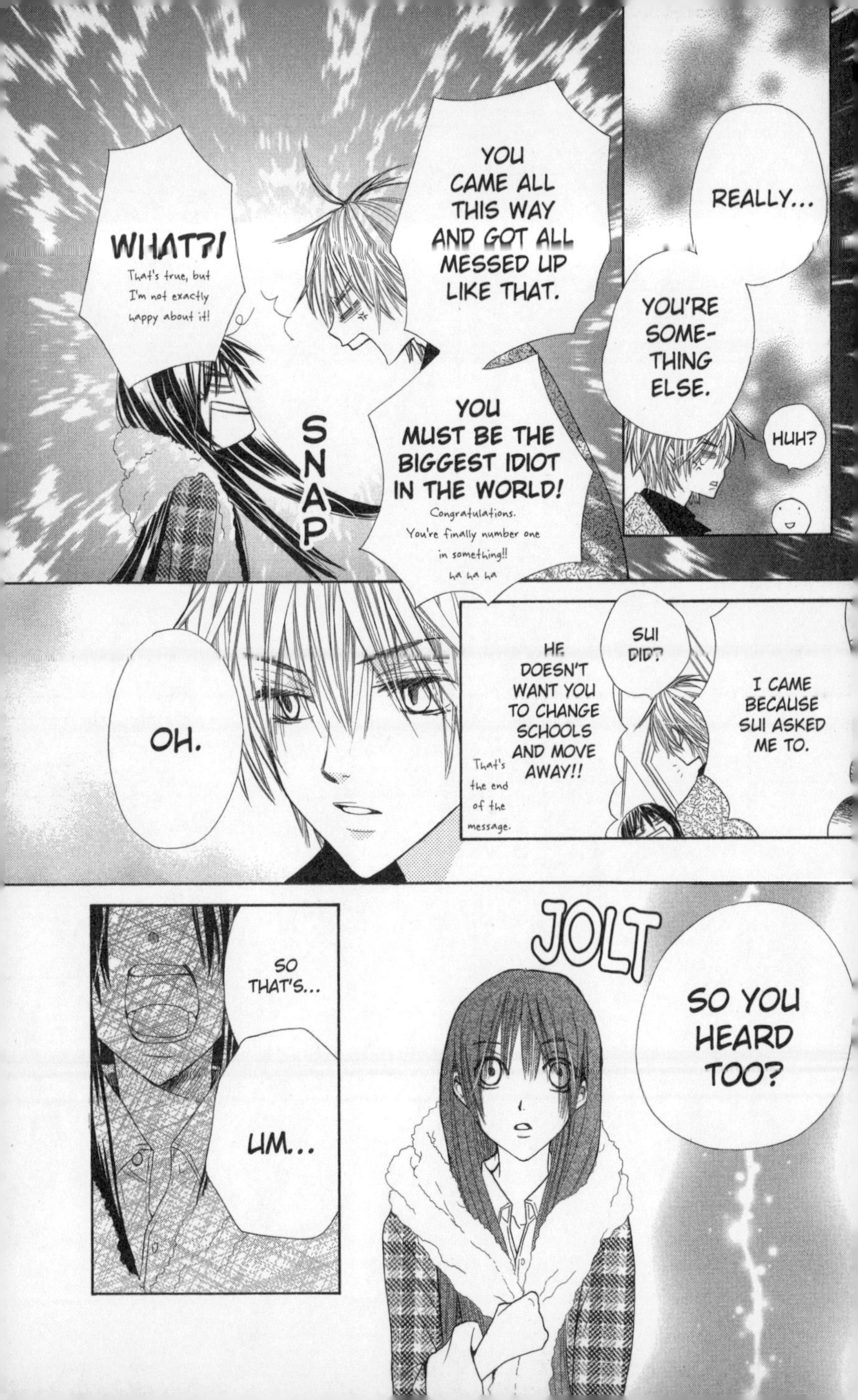
REALLY...
YOU'RE SOMETHING ELSE.
HUH?
YOU CAME ALL THIS WAY AND GOT ALL MESSED UP LIKE THAT.
YOU MUST BE THE BIGGEST IDIOT IN THE WORLD!
Congratulations. You're finally number one in something!! ha ha ha
SNAP
WHAT?!
That's true, but I'm not exactly happy about it!
I CAME BECAUSE SUI ASKED ME TO.
SUI DID?
HE DOESN'T WANT YOU TO CHANGE SCHOOLS AND MOVE AWAY!!
That's the end of the message.
OH.
JOLT
SO YOU HEARD TOO?
SO THAT'S...
UM...

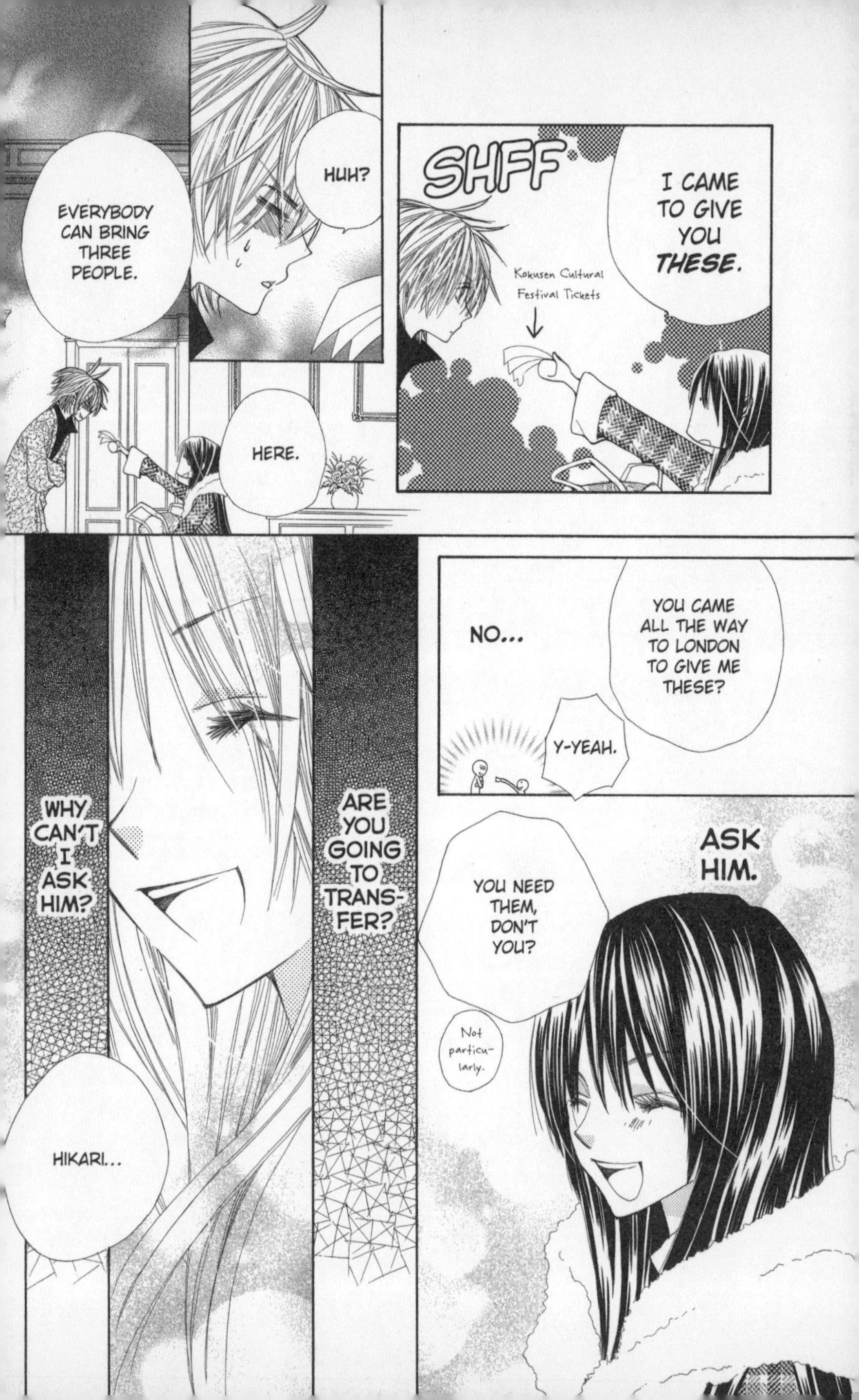
SHFF
I CAME TO GIVE YOU *THESE*.
Kokusen Cultural Festival Tickets
HUH?
EVERYBODY CAN BRING THREE PEOPLE.
HERE.
YOU CAME ALL THE WAY TO LONDON TO GIVE ME THESE?
NO...
Y-YEAH.
ASK HIM.
YOU NEED THEM, DON'T YOU?
Not particu-larly.
ARE YOU GOING TO TRANS-FER?
WHY CAN'T I ASK HIM?
HIKARI...

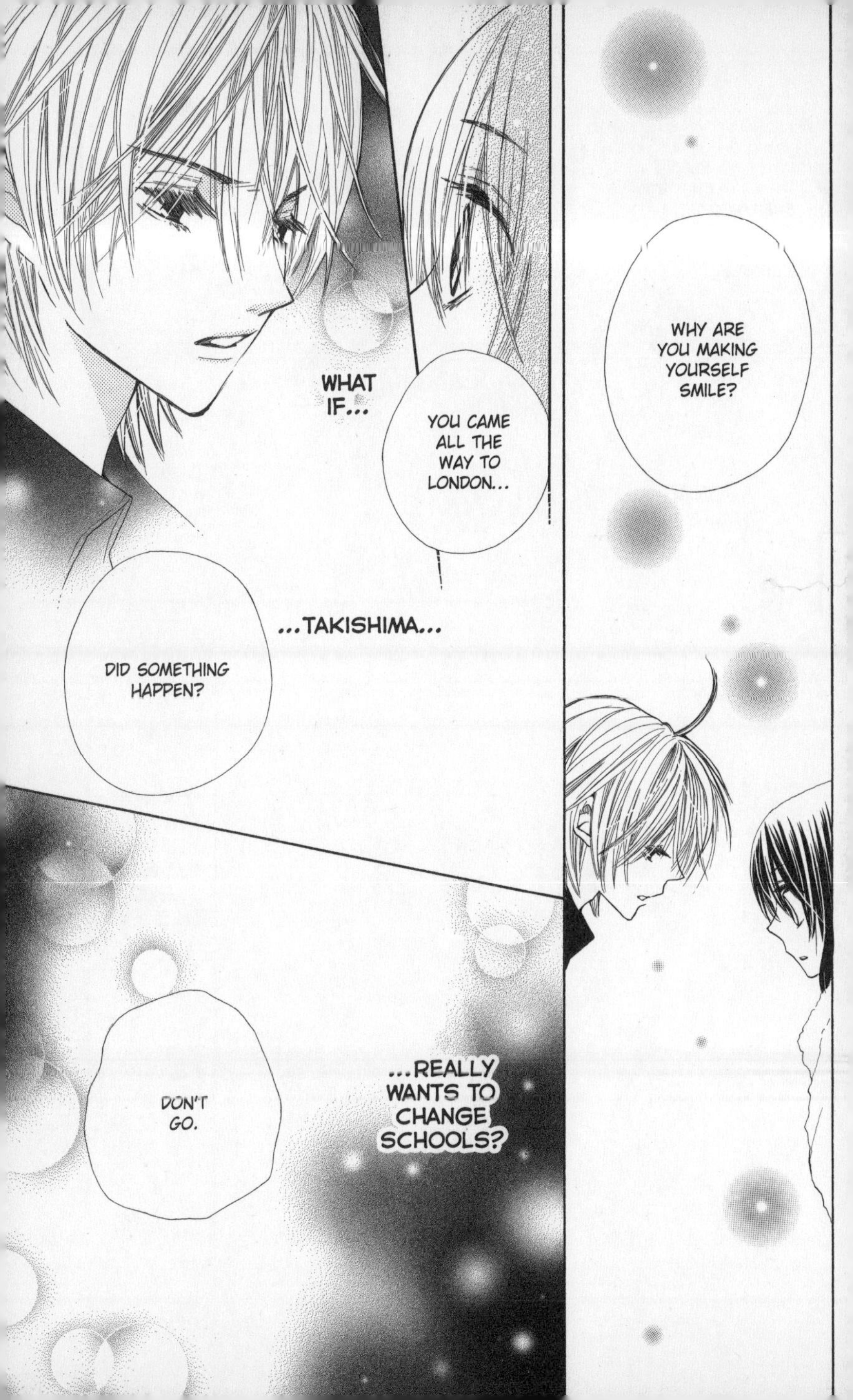
WHY ARE YOU MAKING YOURSELF SMILE?
YOU CAME ALL THE WAY TO LONDON...
WHAT IF...
...TAKISHIMA...
DID SOMETHING HAPPEN?
...REALLY WANTS TO CHANGE SCHOOLS?
DON'T GO.

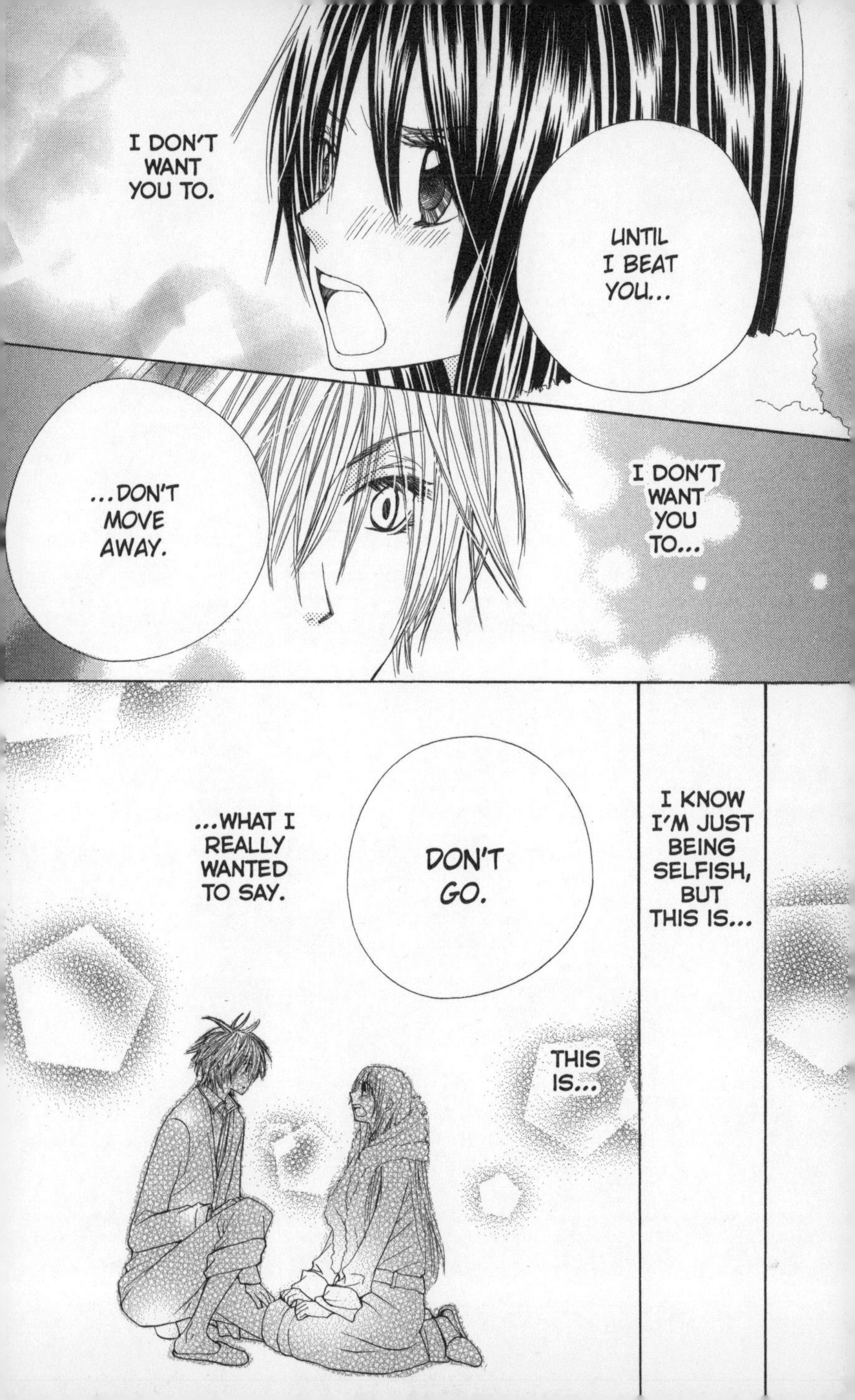
UNTIL I BEAT YOU...
I DON'T WANT YOU TO.
I DON'T WANT YOU TO...
...DON'T MOVE AWAY.
I KNOW I'M JUST BEING SELFISH, BUT THIS IS...
THIS IS...
DON'T GO.
...WHAT I REALLY WANTED TO SAY.

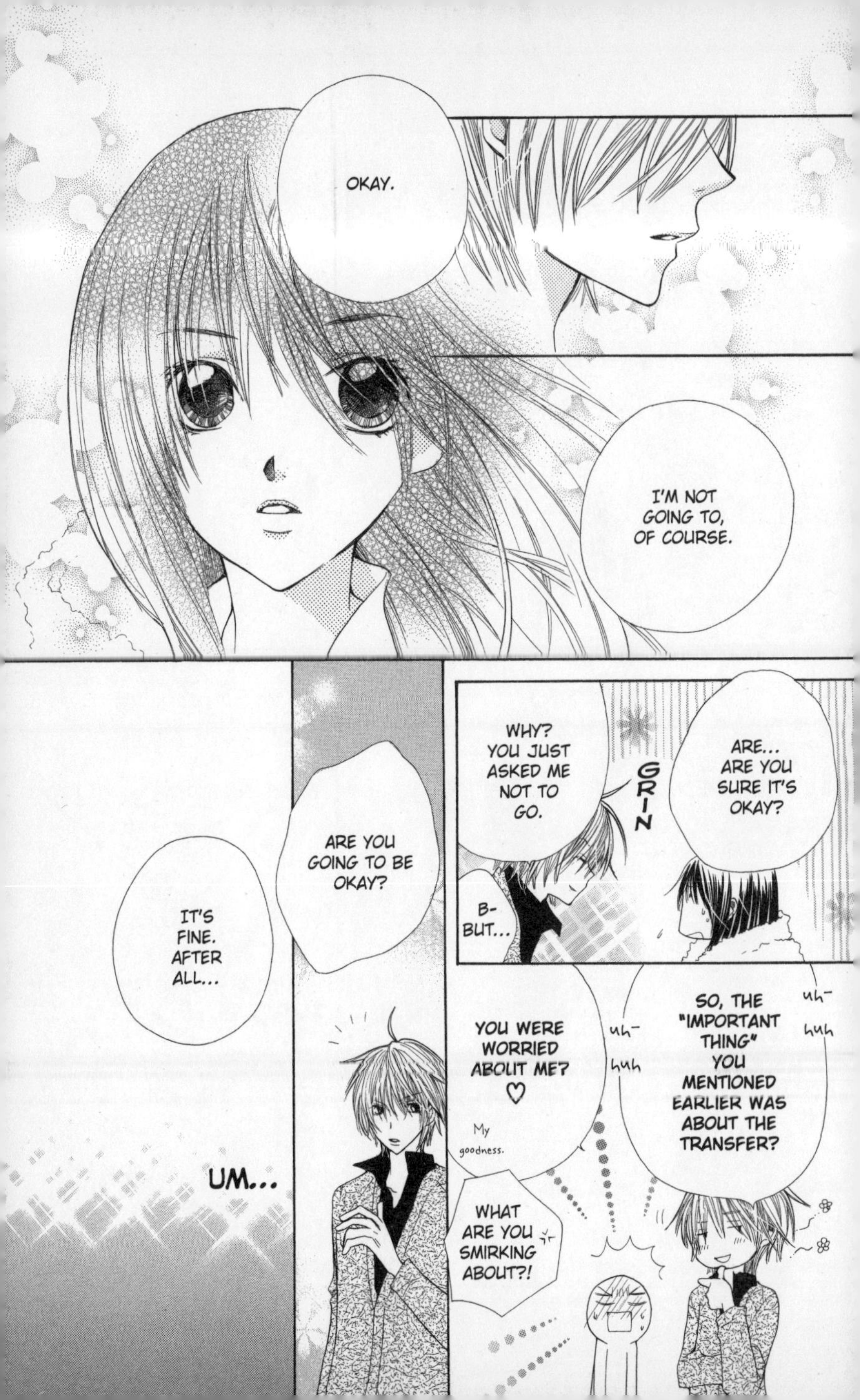

OKAY.
I'M NOT GOING TO, OF COURSE.
ARE... ARE YOU SURE IT'S OKAY?
WHY? YOU JUST ASKED ME NOT TO GO.
GRIN
B-BUT...
SO, THE "IMPORTANT THING" YOU MENTIONED EARLIER WAS ABOUT THE TRANSFER?
uh-huh
YOU WERE WORRIED ABOUT ME? ♡
uh-huh
My goodness.
WHAT ARE YOU SMIRKING ABOUT?!
ARE YOU GOING TO BE OKAY?
IT'S FINE. AFTER ALL...
UM...

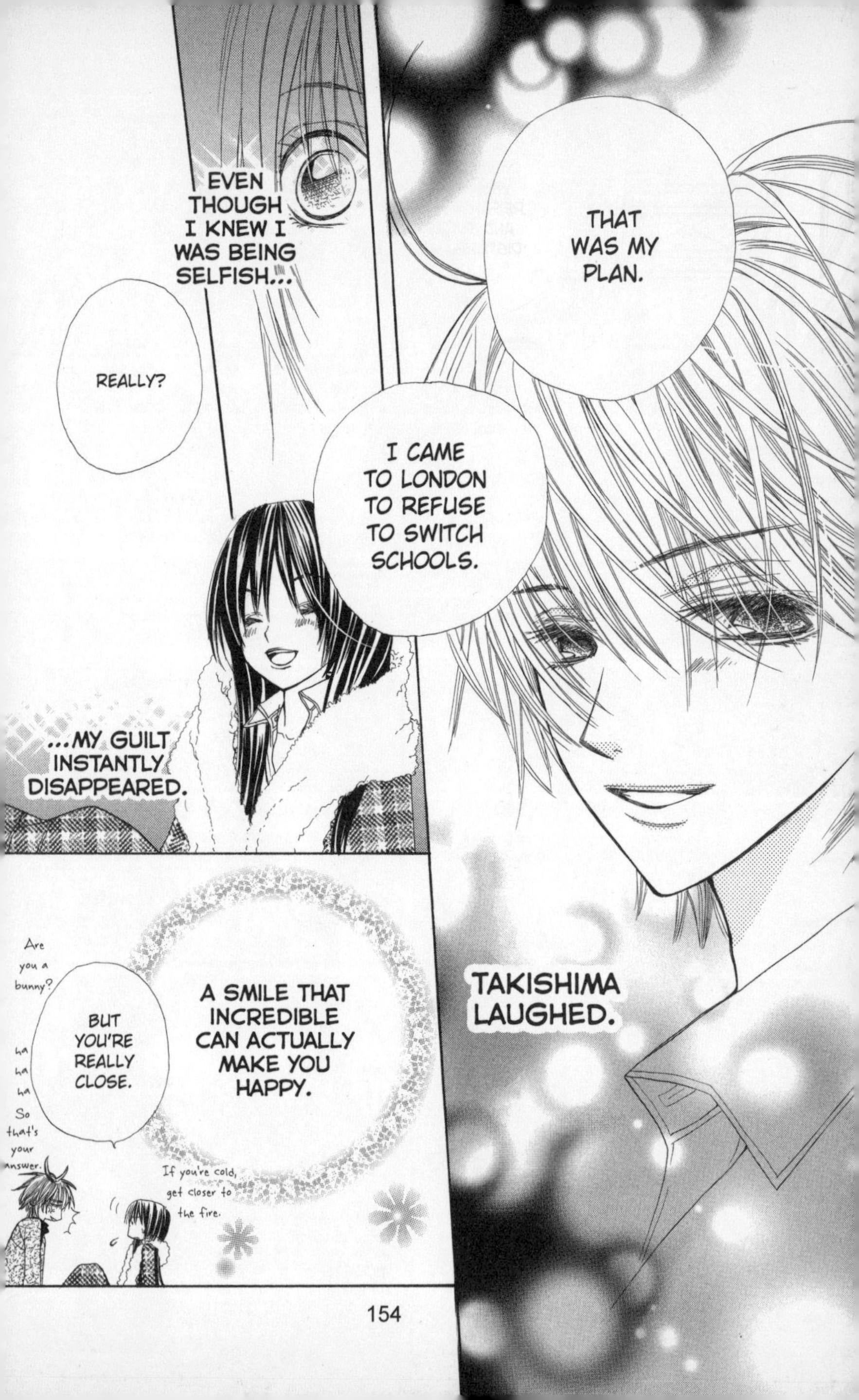
THAT WAS MY PLAN.
I CAME TO LONDON TO REFUSE TO SWITCH SCHOOLS.
TAKISHIMA LAUGHED.
EVEN THOUGH I KNEW I WAS BEING SELFISH...
REALLY?
...MY GUILT INSTANTLY DISAPPEARED.
A SMILE THAT INCREDIBLE CAN ACTUALLY MAKE YOU HAPPY.
If you're cold, get closer to the fire.
BUT YOU'RE REALLY CLOSE.
Are you a bunny?
ha ha ha
So that's your answer.

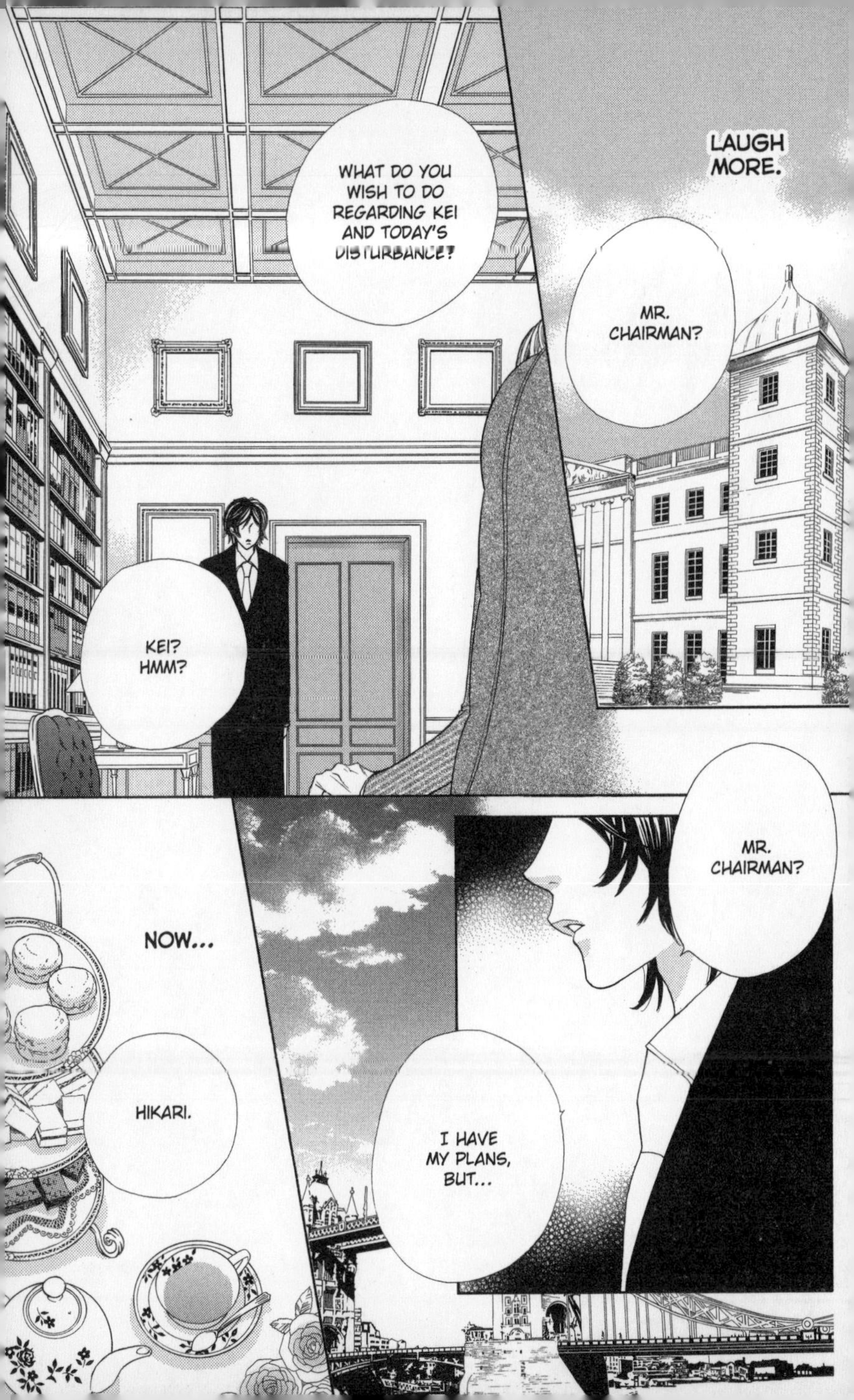
LAUGH MORE.
MR. CHAIRMAN?
WHAT DO YOU WISH TO DO REGARDING KEI AND TODAY'S DISTURBANCE?
KEI? HMM?
MR. CHAIRMAN?
I HAVE MY PLANS, BUT...
NOW...
HIKARI.

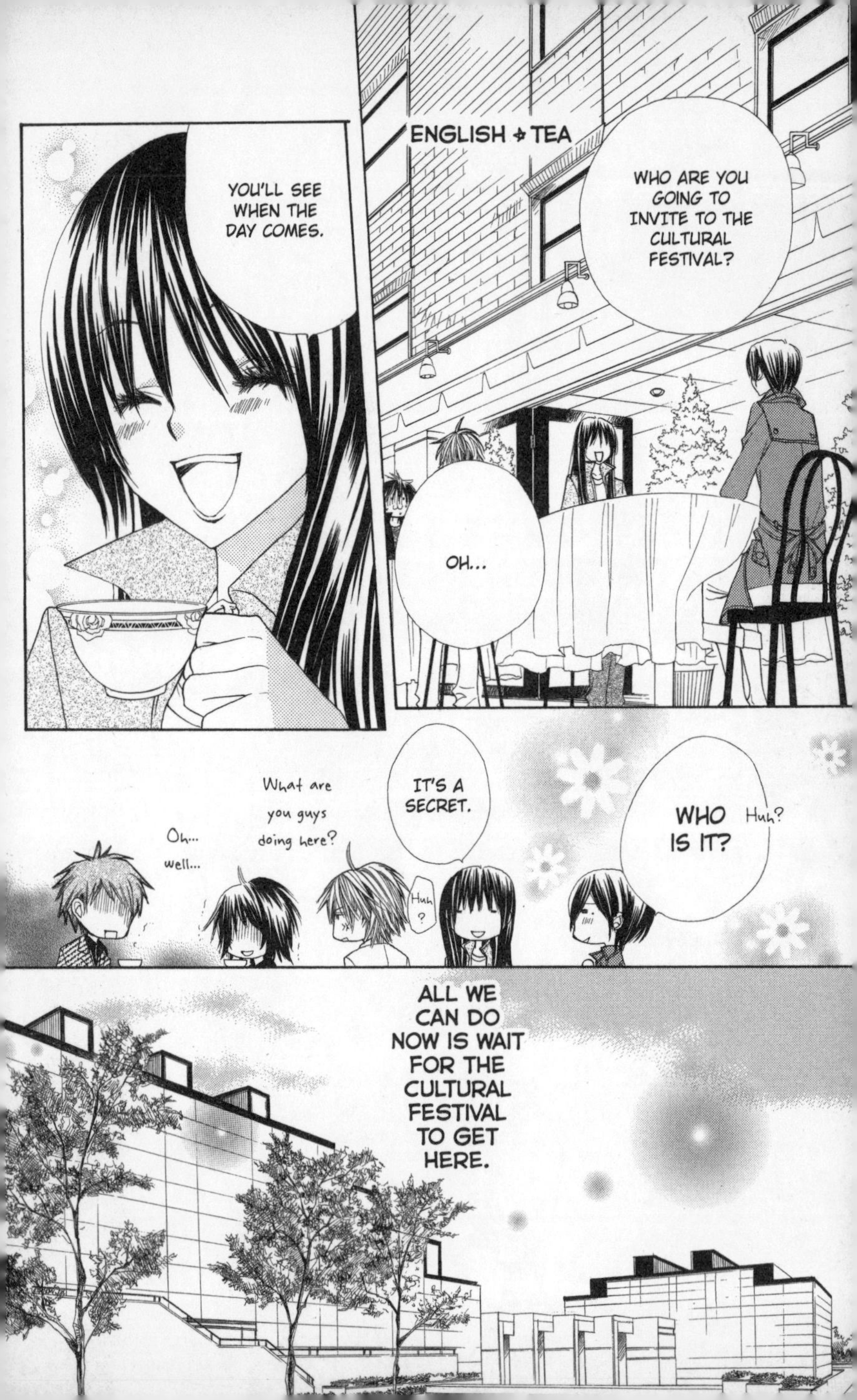
ENGLISH & TEA
WHO ARE YOU GOING TO INVITE TO THE CULTURAL FESTIVAL?
OH...
YOU'LL SEE WHEN THE DAY COMES.
WHO IS IT?
Huh?
IT'S A SECRET.
Huh ?
What are you guys doing here?
Oh... well...
ALL WE CAN DO NOW IS WAIT FOR THE CULTURAL FESTIVAL TO GET HERE.

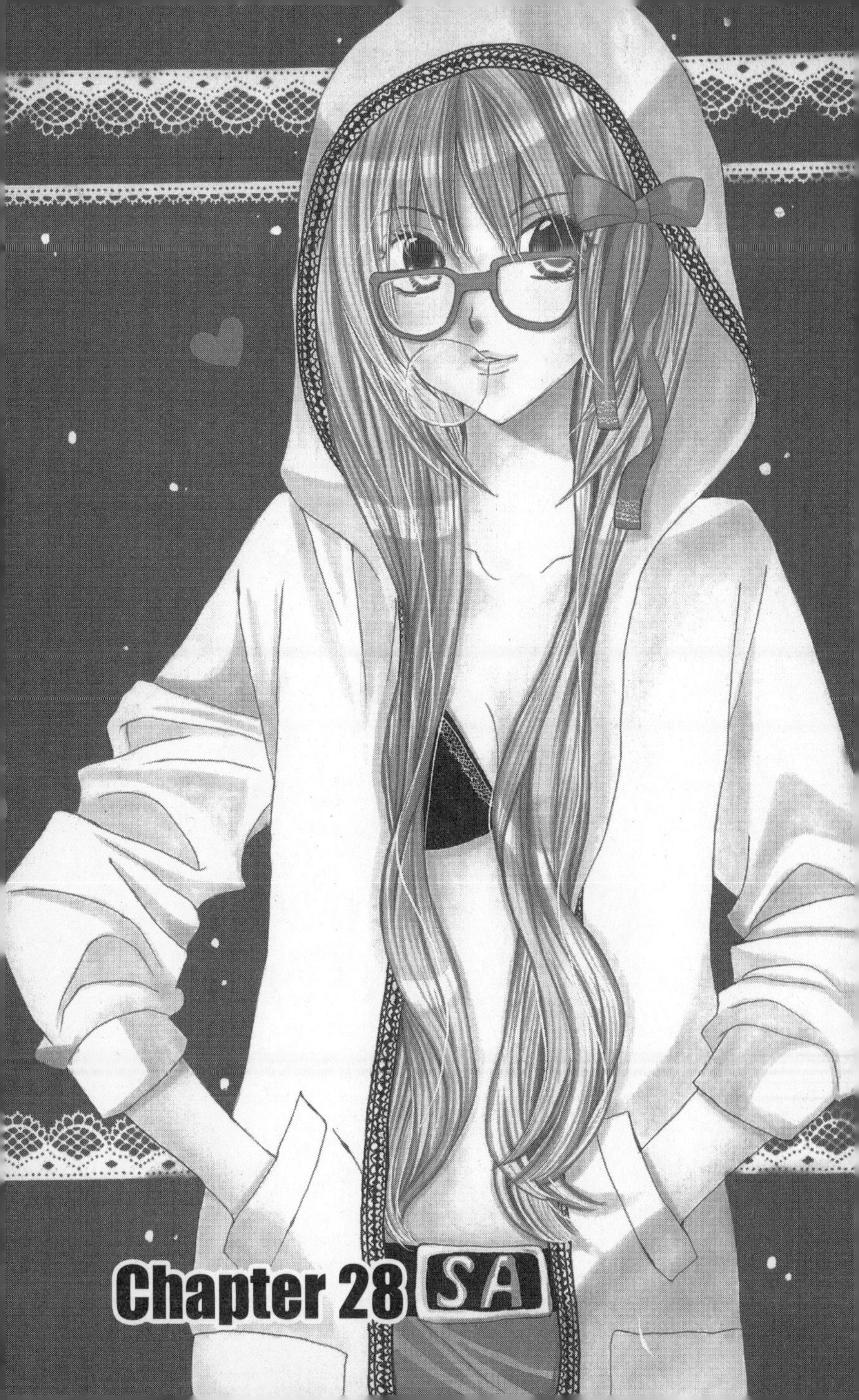
Chapter 28 SA

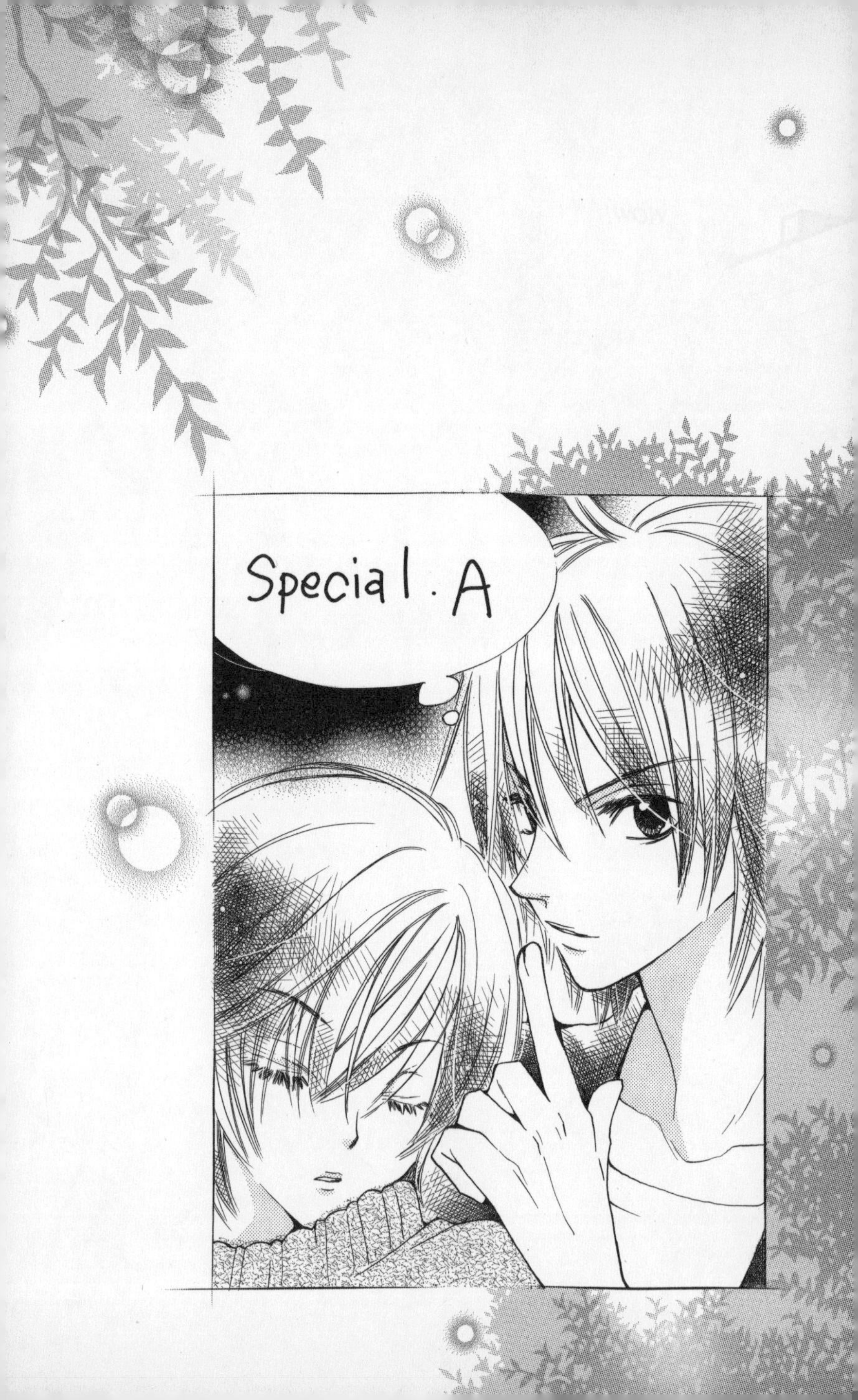
Special . A

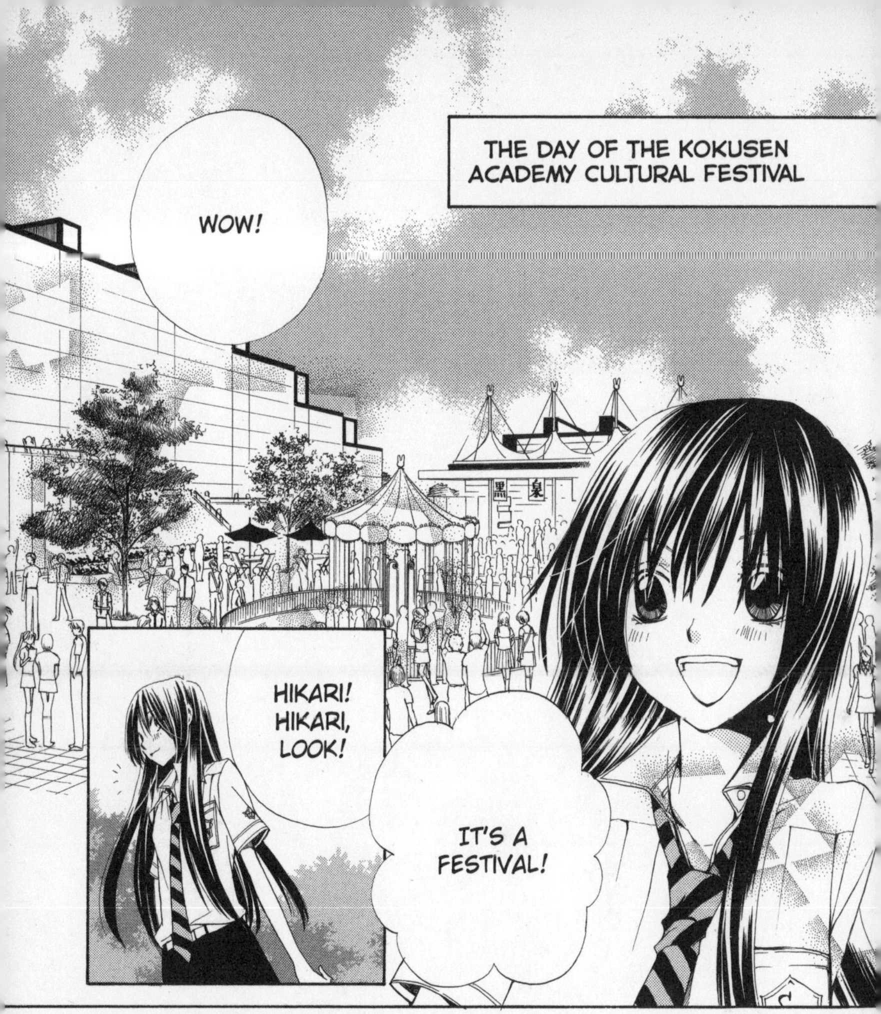
THE DAY OF THE KOKUSEN ACADEMY CULTURAL FESTIVAL
WOW!
HIKARI! HIKARI, LOOK!
IT'S A FESTIVAL!

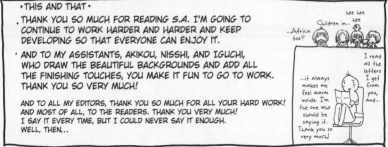

•THIS AND THAT•

- THANK YOU SO MUCH FOR READING *S.A.* I'M GOING TO CONTINUE TO WORK HARDER AND HARDER AND KEEP DEVELOPING SO THAT EVERYONE CAN ENJOY IT.
- AND TO MY ASSISTANTS, AKIKOU, NISSHI, AND IGUCHI, WHO DRAW THE BEAUTIFUL BACKGROUNDS AND ADD ALL THE FINISHING TOUCHES, YOU MAKE IT FUN TO GO TO WORK. THANK YOU SO VERY MUCH!

AND TO ALL MY EDITORS, THANK YOU SO MUCH FOR ALL YOUR HARD WORK! AND MOST OF ALL, TO THE READERS. THANK YOU VERY MUCH! I SAY IT EVERY TIME, BUT I COULD NEVER SAY IT ENOUGH. WELL, THEN...

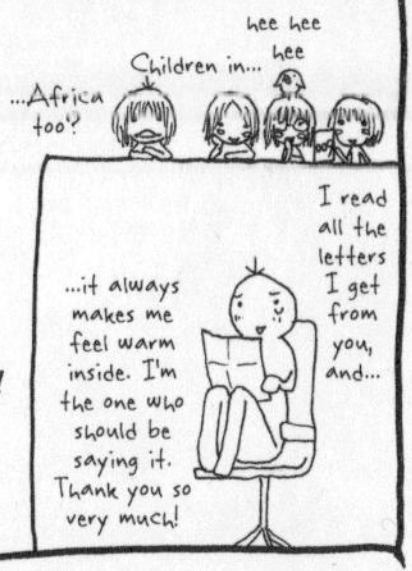
hee hee hee
Children in...
...Africa too?
I read all the letters I get from you, and...
...it always makes me feel warm inside. I'm the one who should be saying it. Thank you so very much!

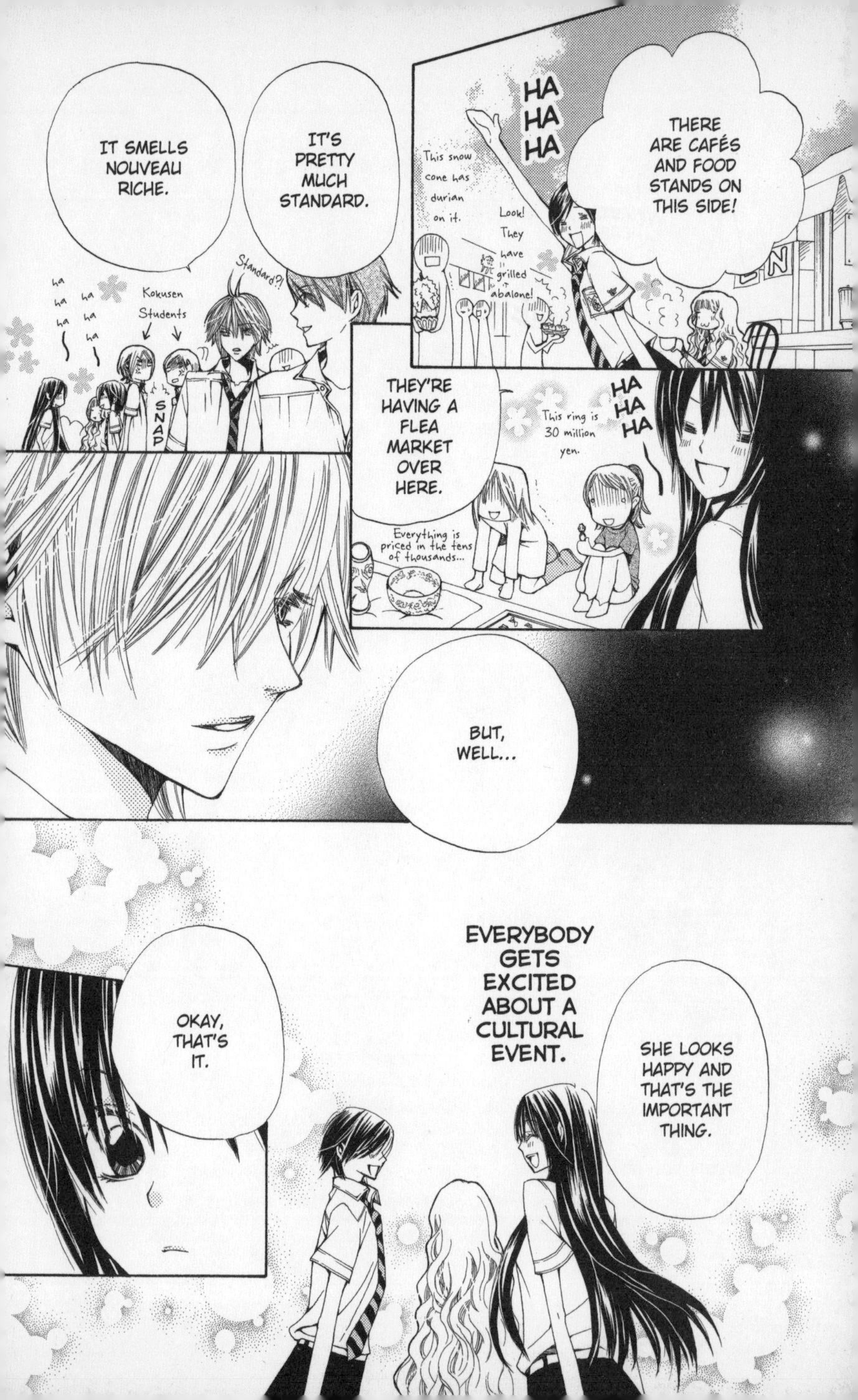
HA
HA
HA
THERE ARE CAFÉS AND FOOD STANDS ON THIS SIDE!
This snow cone has durian on it.
Look! They have grilled abalone!
THEY'RE HAVING A FLEA MARKET OVER HERE.
HA
HA
HA
This ring is 30 million yen.
Everything is priced in the tens of thousands...
IT'S PRETTY MUCH STANDARD.
IT SMELLS NOUVEAU RICHE.
Standard?!
Kokusen Students
SNAP
ha ha ha
ha ha ha
BUT, WELL...
EVERYBODY GETS EXCITED ABOUT A CULTURAL EVENT.
SHE LOOKS HAPPY AND THAT'S THE IMPORTANT THING.
OKAY, THAT'S IT.

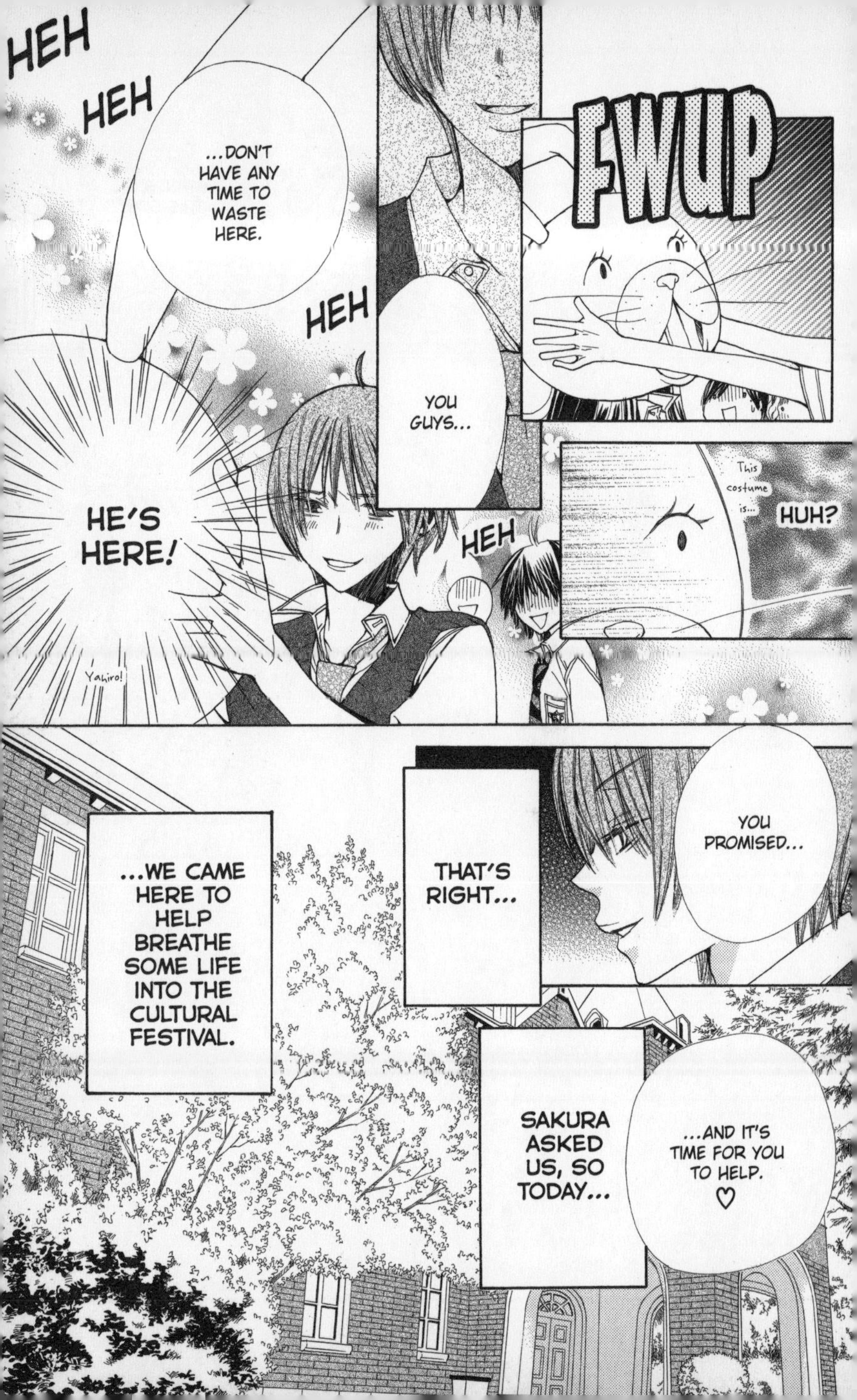

FWUP
This costume is...
HUH?
YOU GUYS...
...DON'T HAVE ANY TIME TO WASTE HERE.
HEH
HEH
HEH
HE'S HERE!
Yahiro!
HEH
YOU PROMISED...
...AND IT'S TIME FOR YOU TO HELP. ♡
SAKURA ASKED US, SO TODAY...
THAT'S RIGHT...
...WE CAME HERE TO HELP BREATHE SOME LIFE INTO THE CULTURAL FESTIVAL.

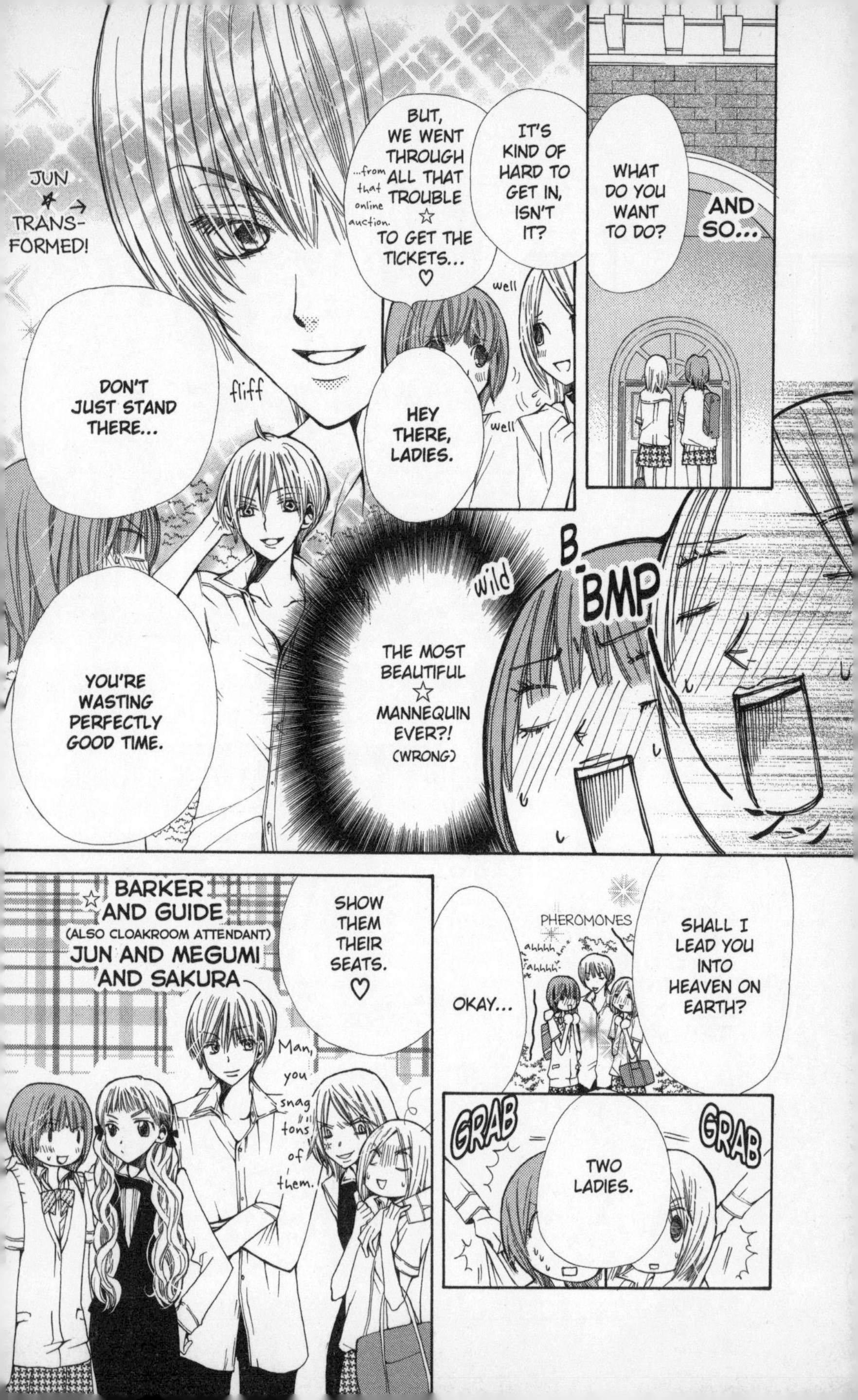
AND SO...
WHAT DO YOU WANT TO DO?
IT'S KIND OF HARD TO GET IN, ISN'T IT?
BUT, WE WENT THROUGH ALL THAT TROUBLE ☆ TO GET THE TICKETS... ♡
...from that online auction.
well
well
HEY THERE, LADIES.
B-BMP
wild
THE MOST BEAUTIFUL ☆ MANNEQUIN EVER?! (WRONG)
JUN ☆ TRANSFORMED!
fliff
DON'T JUST STAND THERE...
YOU'RE WASTING PERFECTLY GOOD TIME.
SHALL I LEAD YOU INTO HEAVEN ON EARTH?
PHEROMONES
ahhhh
ahhhh
OKAY...
GRAB
GRAB
TWO LADIES.
SHOW THEM THEIR SEATS. ♡
☆ BARKER AND GUIDE (ALSO CLOAKROOM ATTENDANT) JUN AND MEGUMI AND SAKURA
Man, you snag tons of them.

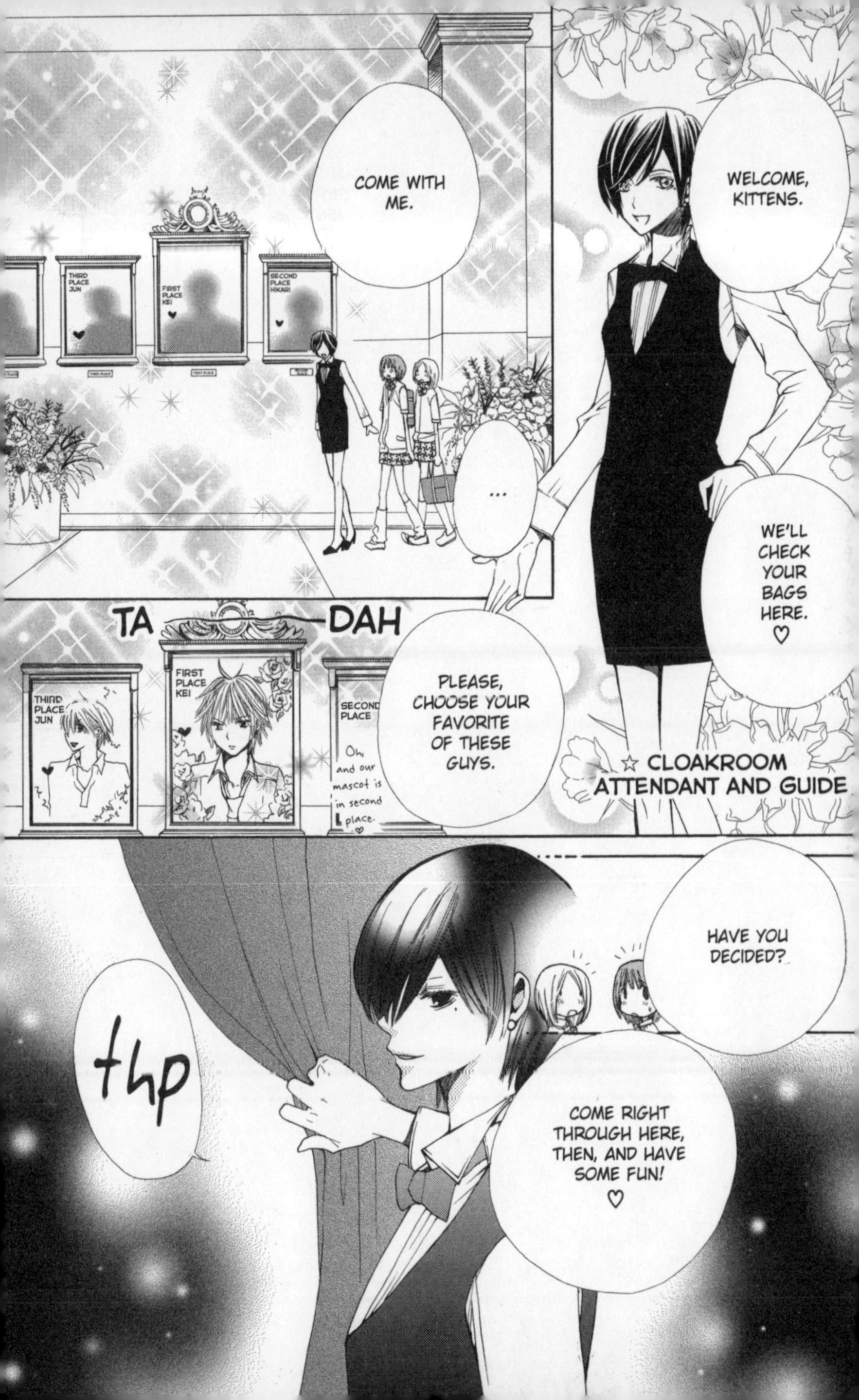
WELCOME, KITTENS.
WE'LL CHECK YOUR BAGS HERE. ♡
☆ CLOAKROOM ATTENDANT AND GUIDE
COME WITH ME.
...
SECOND PLACE HIKARI
FIRST PLACE KEI
THIRD PLACE JUN
TA—DAH
PLEASE, CHOOSE YOUR FAVORITE OF THESE GUYS.
SECOND PLACE
Oh, and our mascot is in second place. ♡
FIRST PLACE KEI
THIRD PLACE JUN
HAVE YOU DECIDED?
COME RIGHT THROUGH HERE, THEN, AND HAVE SOME FUN! ♡
thp

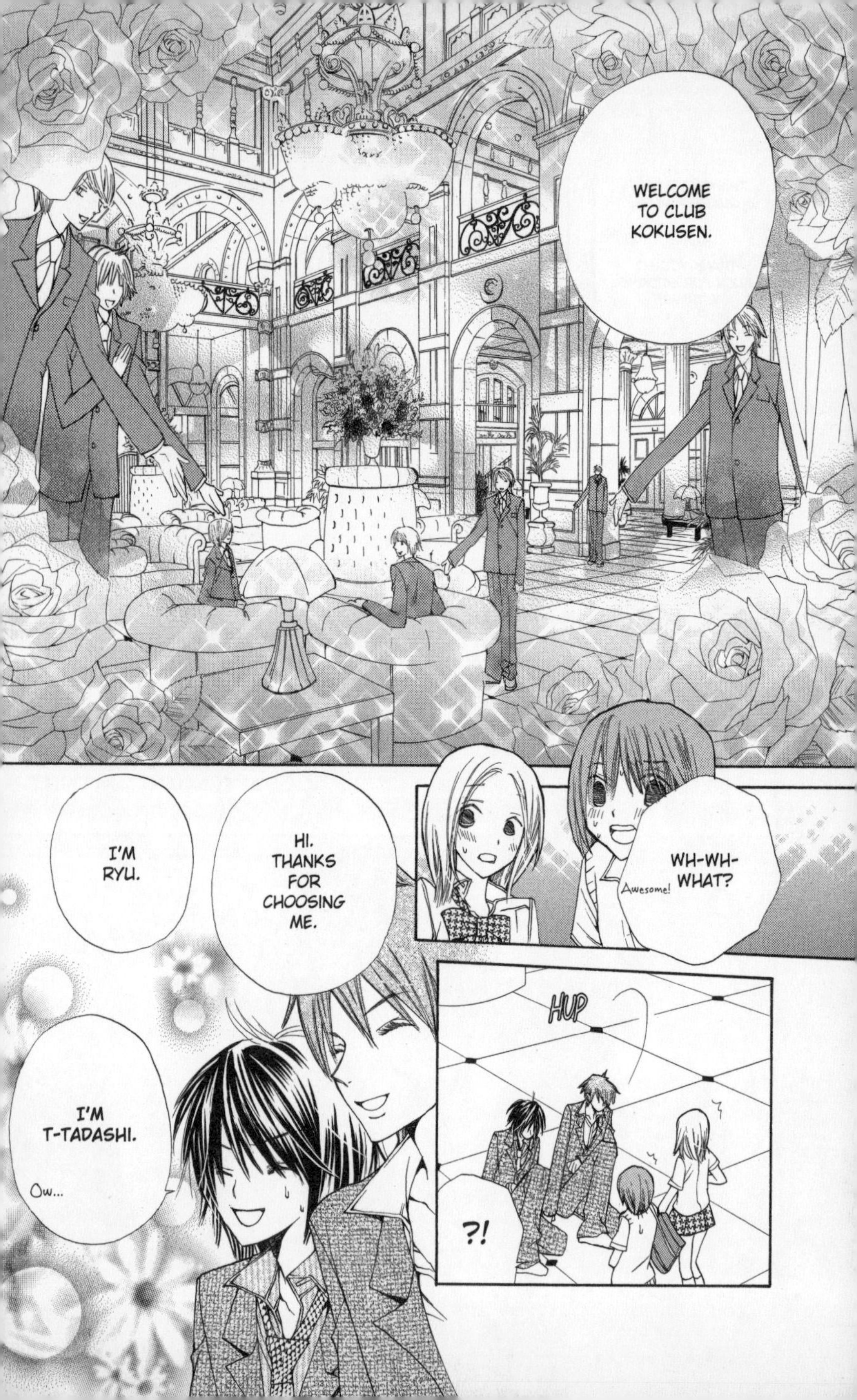
WELCOME TO CLUB KOKUSEN.
WH-WH-WHAT?
Awesome!
HI. THANKS FOR CHOOSING ME.
I'M RYU.
HUP
?!
I'M T-TADASHI.
Ow...

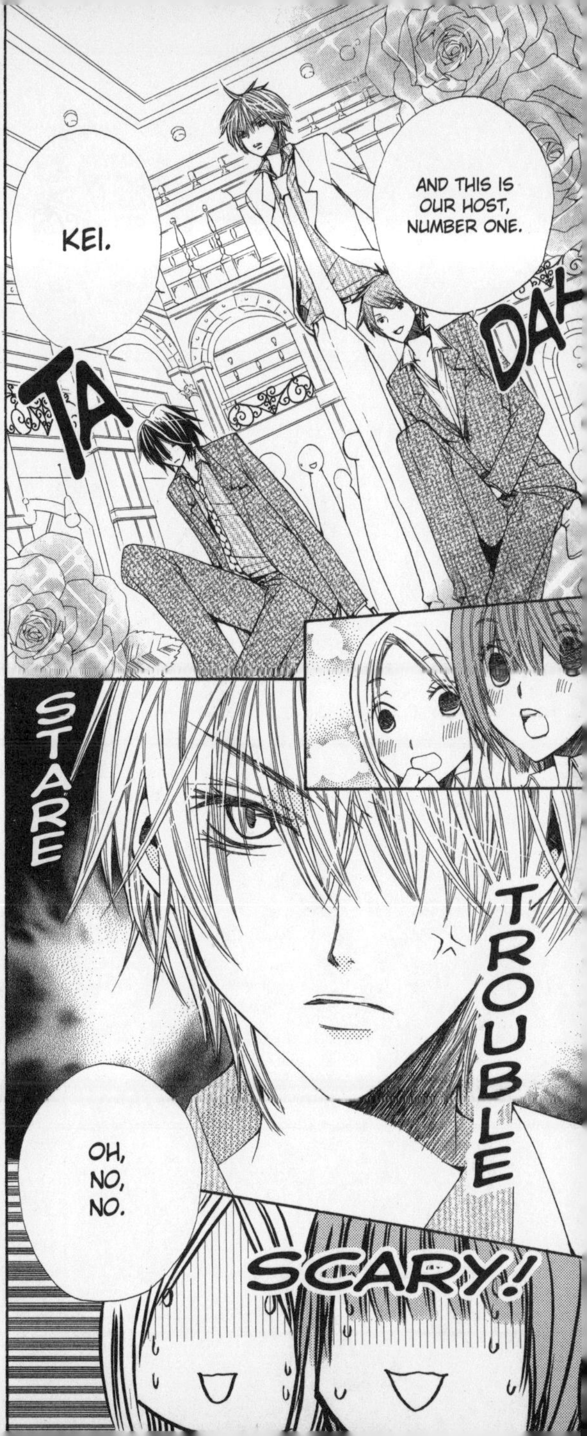
AND THIS IS OUR HOST, NUMBER ONE.
KEI.
DA
TA
STARE
TROUBLE
OH, NO, NO.
SCARY!

• THIS AND THAT •

• THIS IS THE LAST QUARTER PAGE.

THANK YOU SO MUCH FOR STICKING WITH ME!!

• THIS TIME, I WROTE ANOTHER BONUS STORY BASED ON THE REQUESTS YOU'VE SENT! THANK YOU VERY MUCH!

• I REALLY AM SORRY THAT I HAVEN'T BEEN ABLE TO RESPOND TO YOUR LETTERS... I WILL DEFINITELY WRITE BACK, SO IF YOU COULD PLEASE JUST BE PATIENT AND WAIT, IT WOULD MAKE MY DAY. (THE JAPANESE IS STRANGE.) I'm sorry!

IF YOU'D LIKE, PLEASE TELL ME WHAT YOU THINK.

• ADDRESS •

MAKI MINAMI
C/O SA EDITOR
P.O. BOX 77010
SAN FRANCISCO, CA 94107

WELL, I HOPE TO SEE YOU AGAIN IN THE NEXT VOLUME!!

From the bottom of my heart.

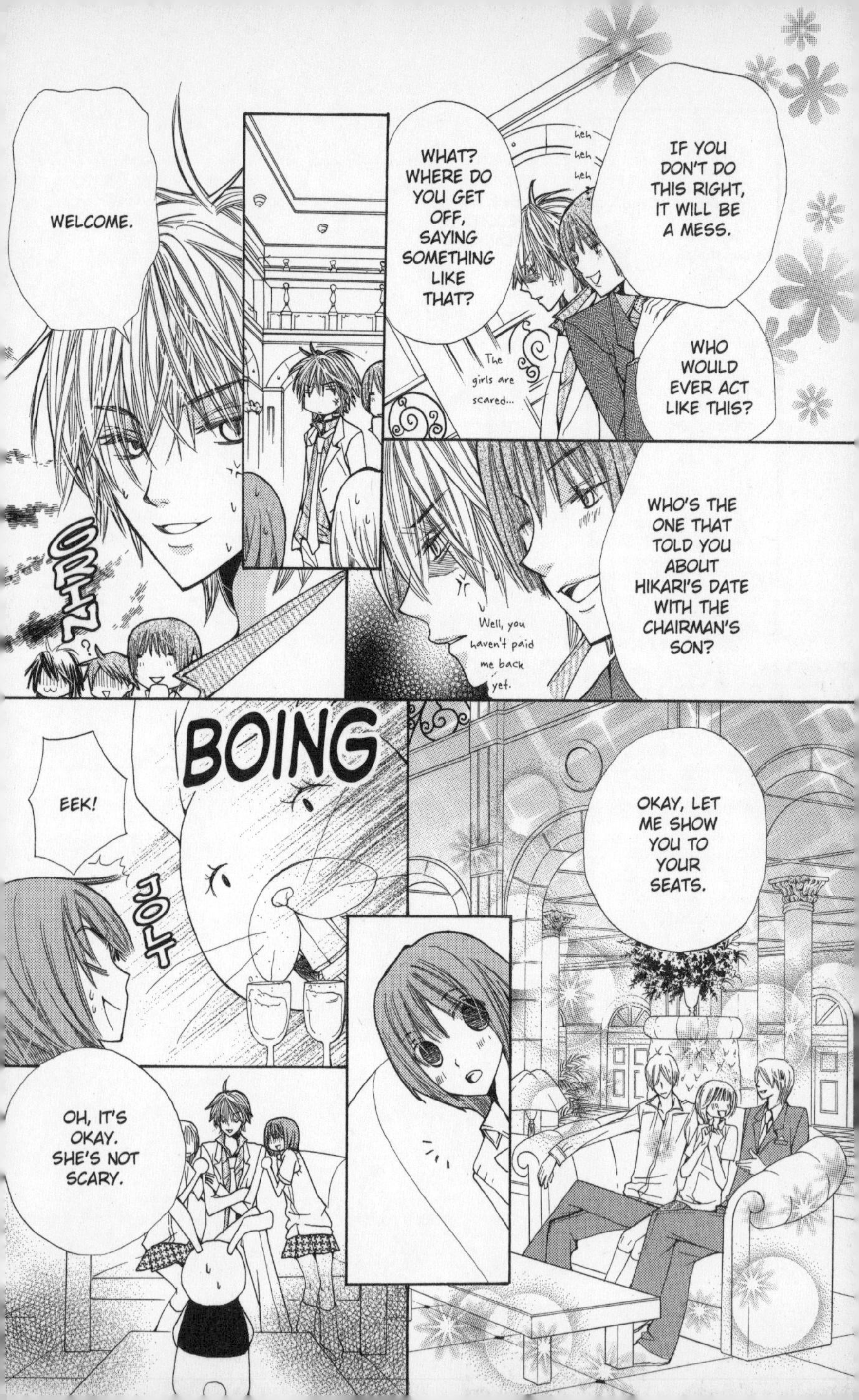
IF YOU DON'T DO THIS RIGHT, IT WILL BE A MESS.
WHO WOULD EVER ACT LIKE THIS?
heh heh heh
WHAT? WHERE DO YOU GET OFF, SAYING SOMETHING LIKE THAT?
The girls are scared...
WHO'S THE ONE THAT TOLD YOU ABOUT HIKARI'S DATE WITH THE CHAIRMAN'S SON?
Well, you haven't paid me back yet.
WELCOME.
GRIN
OKAY, LET ME SHOW YOU TO YOUR SEATS.
BOING
EEK!
JOLT
OH, IT'S OKAY. SHE'S NOT SCARY.

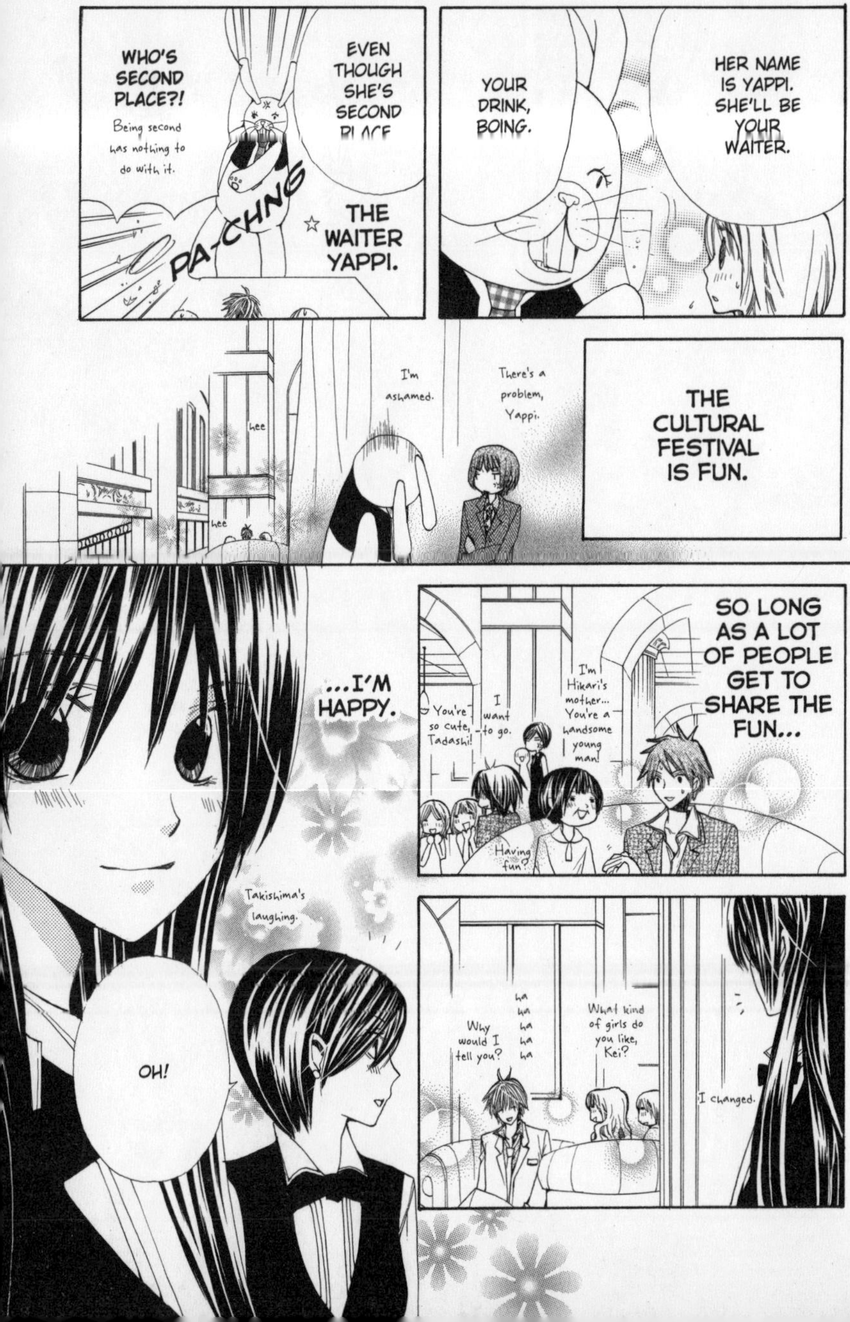
HER NAME IS YAPPI. SHE'LL BE YOUR WAITER.
YOUR DRINK, BOING.
EVEN THOUGH SHE'S SECOND PLACE
THE WAITER YAPPI.
WHO'S SECOND PLACE?!
Being second has nothing to do with it.
PA-CHNG
THE CULTURAL FESTIVAL IS FUN.
There's a problem, Yappi.
I'm ashamed.
hee
hee
SO LONG AS A LOT OF PEOPLE GET TO SHARE THE FUN...
I'm Hikari's mother... You're a handsome young man!
I want to go.
You're so cute, Tadashi!
Having fun?
I changed.
What kind of girls do you like, Kei?
ha ha ha ha ha
Why would I tell you?
...I'M HAPPY.
Takishima's laughing.
OH!

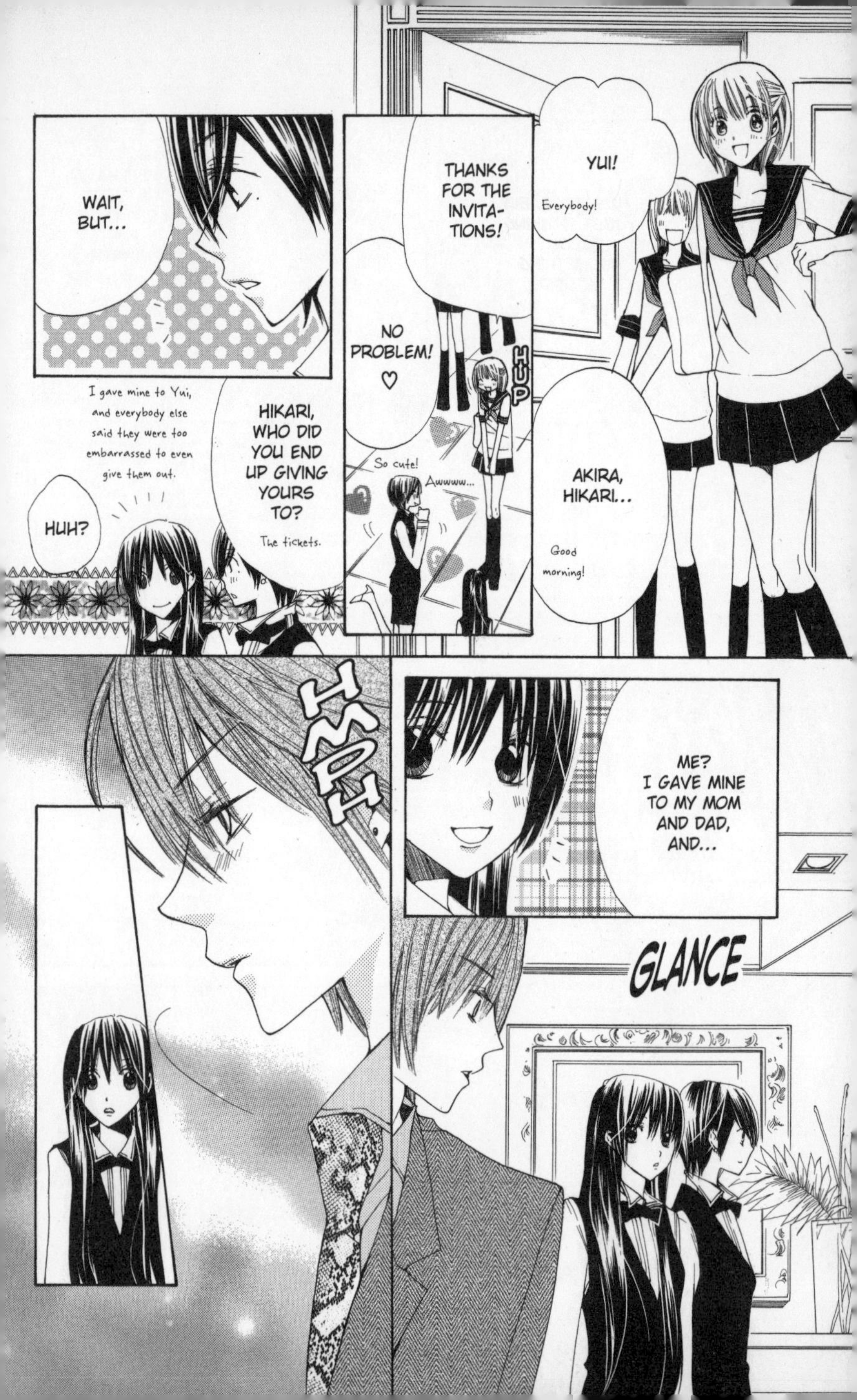
YUI!
Everybody!
AKIRA, HIKARI...
Good morning!
THANKS FOR THE INVITATIONS!
NO PROBLEM! ♡
HUP
So cute!
Awwww...
WAIT, BUT...
HIKARI, WHO DID YOU END UP GIVING YOURS TO?
The tickets.
I gave mine to Yui, and everybody else said they were too embarrassed to even give them out.
HUH?
ME? I GAVE MINE TO MY MOM AND DAD, AND...
GLANCE
HMPH

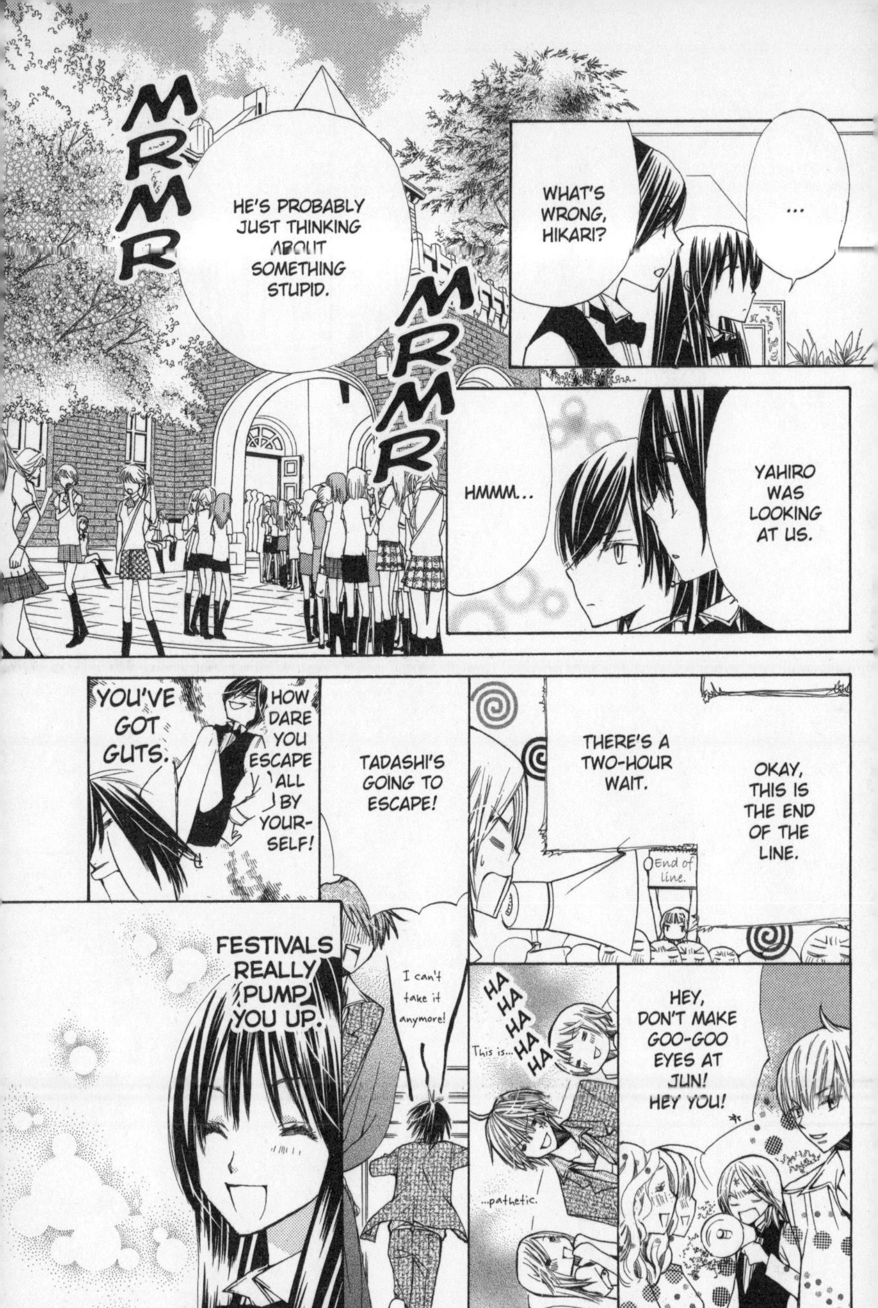
...
WHAT'S WRONG, HIKARI?
YAHIRO WAS LOOKING AT US.
HMMM...
MRMR
HE'S PROBABLY JUST THINKING ABOUT SOMETHING STUPID.
MRMR
OKAY, THIS IS THE END OF THE LINE.
THERE'S A TWO-HOUR WAIT.
End of line.
TADASHI'S GOING TO ESCAPE!
HOW DARE YOU ESCAPE ALL BY YOURSELF!
YOU'VE GOT GUTS.
HEY, DON'T MAKE GOO-GOO EYES AT JUN! HEY YOU!
HA HA HA HA HA
This is...
...pathetic.
I can't take it anymore!
FESTIVALS REALLY PUMP YOU UP.

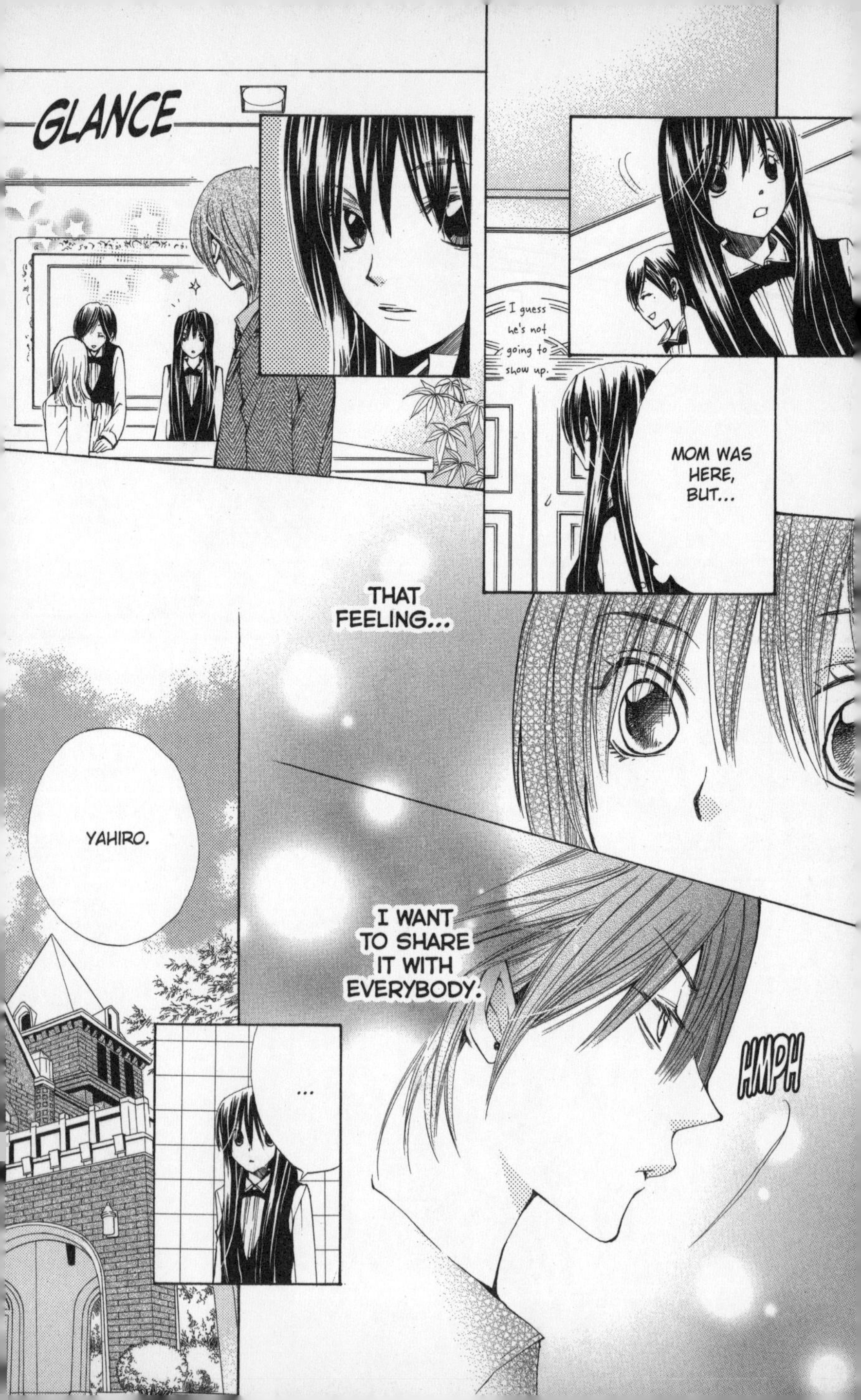

I guess he's not going to show up.
MOM WAS HERE, BUT...
GLANCE
THAT FEELING...
I WANT TO SHARE IT WITH EVERYBODY.
HMPH
YAHIRO.
...

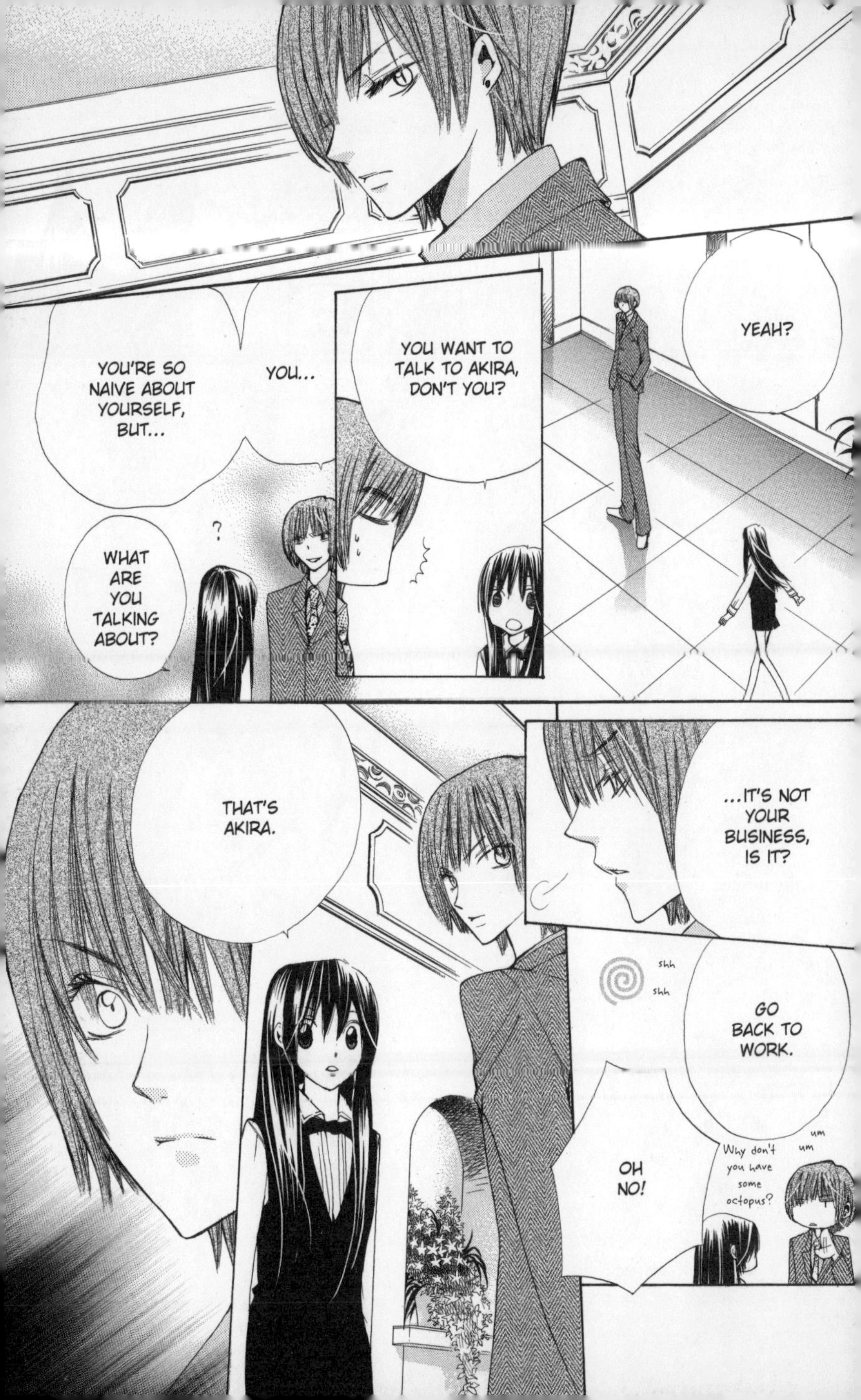
YEAH?
YOU WANT TO TALK TO AKIRA, DON'T YOU?
YOU...
YOU'RE SO NAIVE ABOUT YOURSELF, BUT...
?
WHAT ARE YOU TALKING ABOUT?
...IT'S NOT YOUR BUSINESS, IS IT?
GO BACK TO WORK.
shh
shh
um
um
Why don't you have some octopus?
OH NO!
THAT'S AKIRA.

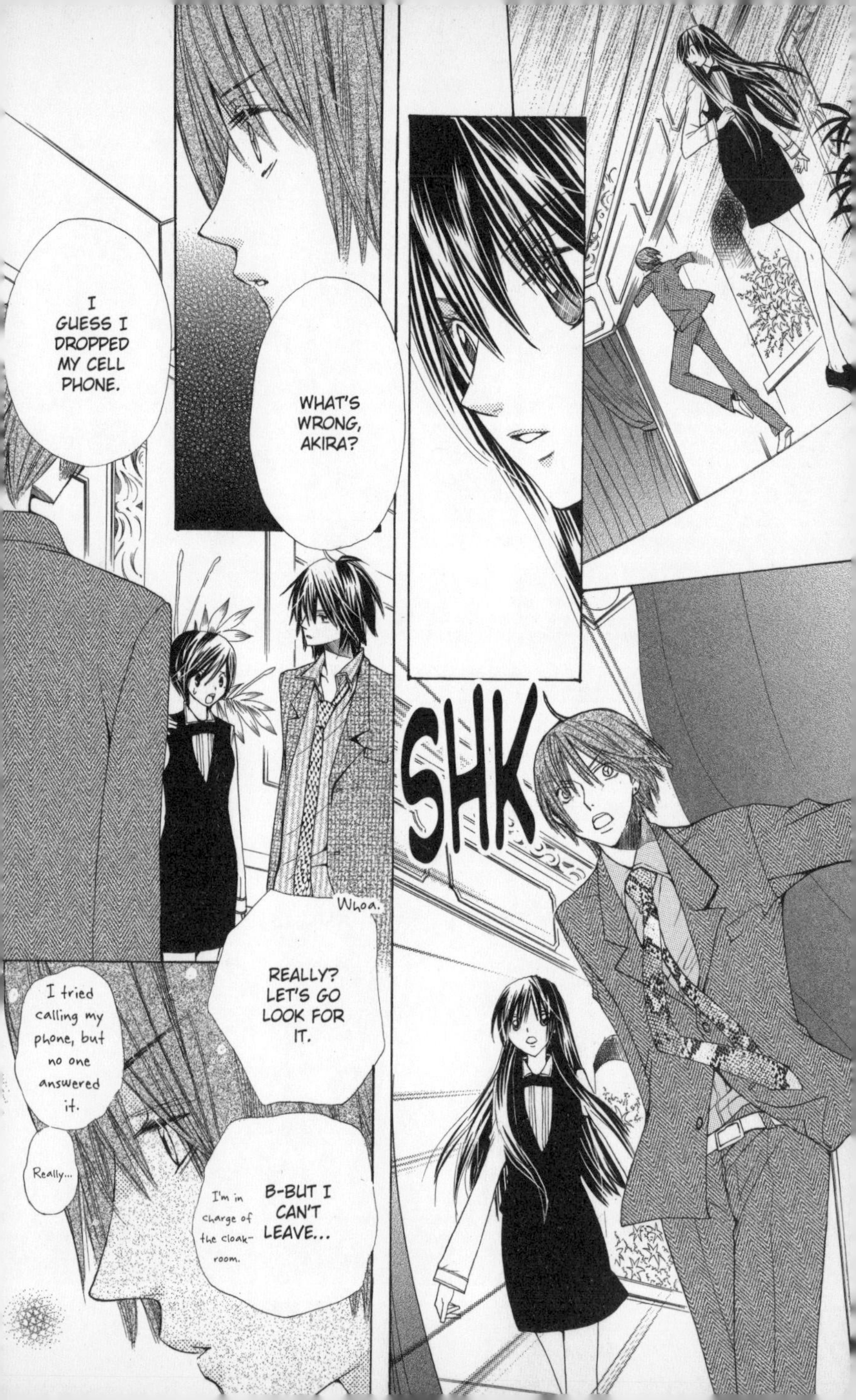
SHK
WHAT'S WRONG, AKIRA?
I GUESS I DROPPED MY CELL PHONE.
Whoa.
REALLY? LET'S GO LOOK FOR IT.
B-BUT I CAN'T LEAVE...
I'm in charge of the cloak-room.
I tried calling my phone, but no one answered it.
Really...

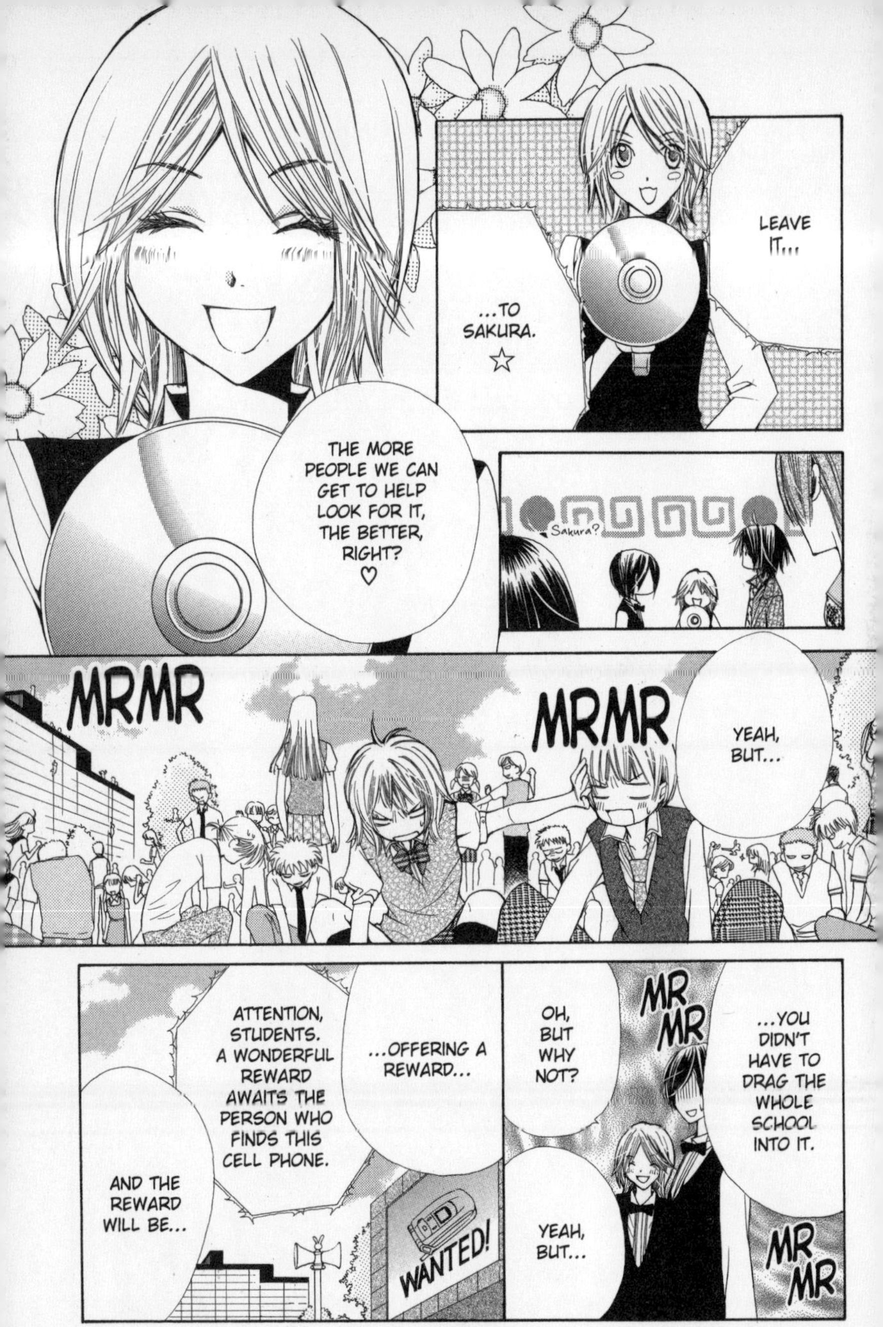
LEAVE IT...
...TO SAKURA. ☆
Sakura?
THE MORE PEOPLE WE CAN GET TO HELP LOOK FOR IT, THE BETTER, RIGHT? ♡
YEAH, BUT...
MRMR
MRMR
...YOU DIDN'T HAVE TO DRAG THE WHOLE SCHOOL INTO IT.
MR MR
OH, BUT WHY NOT?
YEAH, BUT...
MR MR
...OFFERING A REWARD...
ATTENTION, STUDENTS. A WONDERFUL REWARD AWAITS THE PERSON WHO FINDS THIS CELL PHONE.
AND THE REWARD WILL BE...
WANTED!

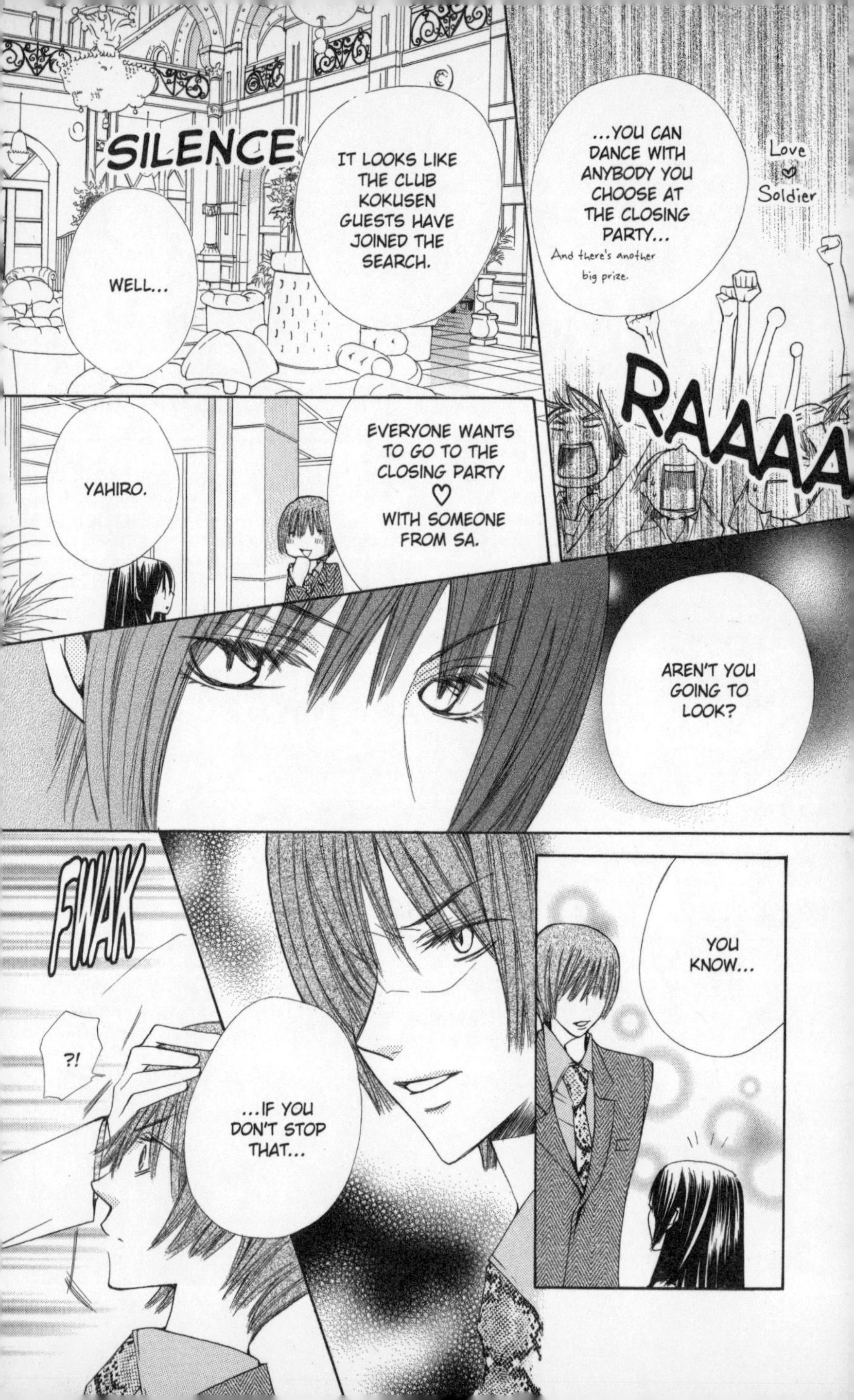

...YOU CAN DANCE WITH ANYBODY YOU CHOOSE AT THE CLOSING PARTY...
And there's another big prize.
Love ♥ Soldier
RAAAA
IT LOOKS LIKE THE CLUB KOKUSEN GUESTS HAVE JOINED THE SEARCH.
SILENCE
WELL...
EVERYONE WANTS TO GO TO THE CLOSING PARTY ♡ WITH SOMEONE FROM SA.
YAHIRO.
AREN'T YOU GOING TO LOOK?
YOU KNOW...
...IF YOU DON'T STOP THAT...
?!
FWAK

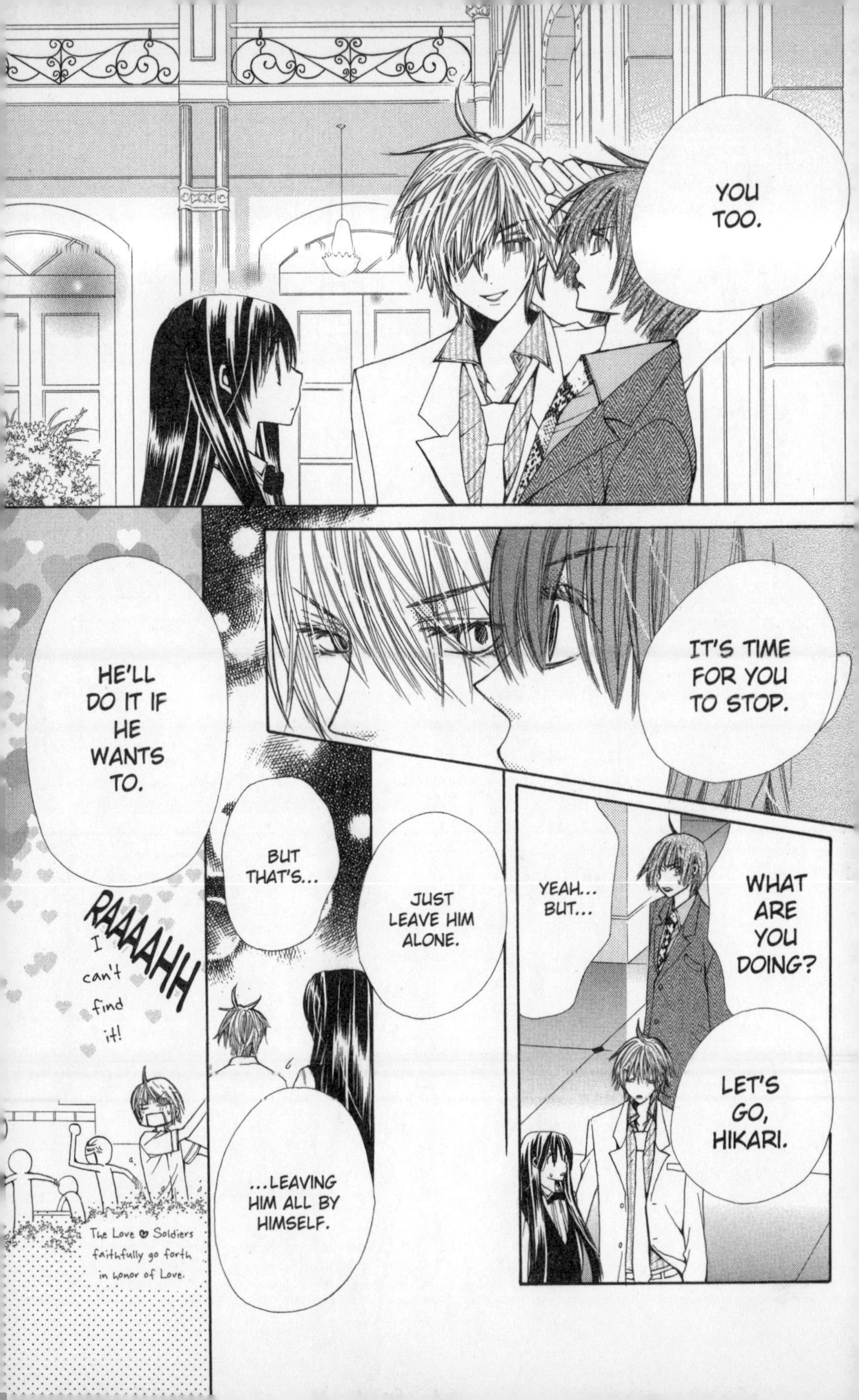
YOU TOO.
IT'S TIME FOR YOU TO STOP.
WHAT ARE YOU DOING?
YEAH... BUT...
LET'S GO, HIKARI.
JUST LEAVE HIM ALONE.
BUT THAT'S...
...LEAVING HIM ALL BY HIMSELF.
HE'LL DO IT IF HE WANTS TO.
RAAAAHH
I can't find it!
The Love ♥ Soldiers faithfully go forth in honor of Love.

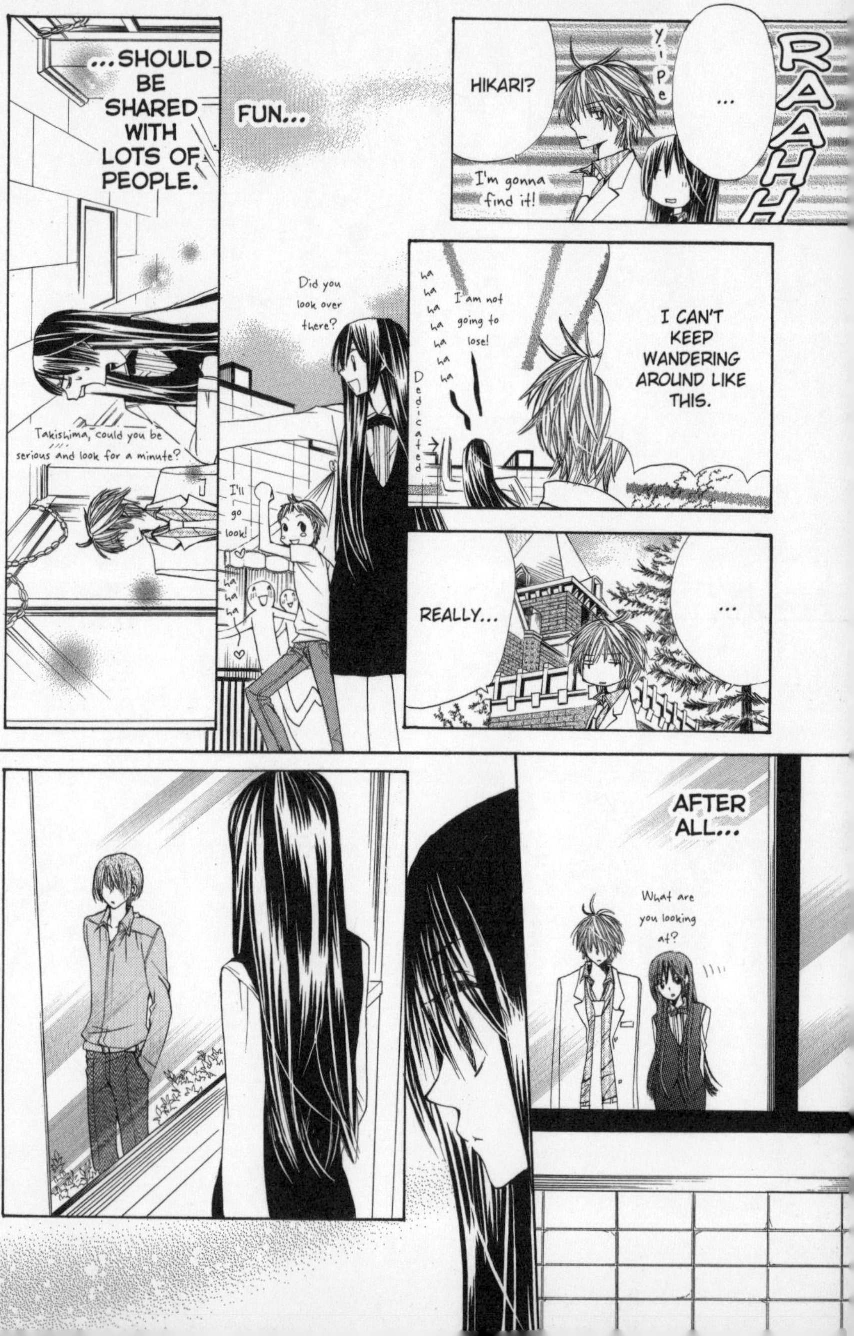
RAAHH
...
Yipe
HIKARI?
I'm gonna find it!
I CAN'T KEEP WANDERING AROUND LIKE THIS.
ha ha ha ha ha ha ha
I am not going to lose!
Dedicated
...
REALLY...
FUN...
Did you look over there?
I'll go look!
ha ha ha
...SHOULD BE SHARED WITH LOTS OF PEOPLE.
Takishima, could you be serious and look for a minute?
AFTER ALL...
What are you looking at?

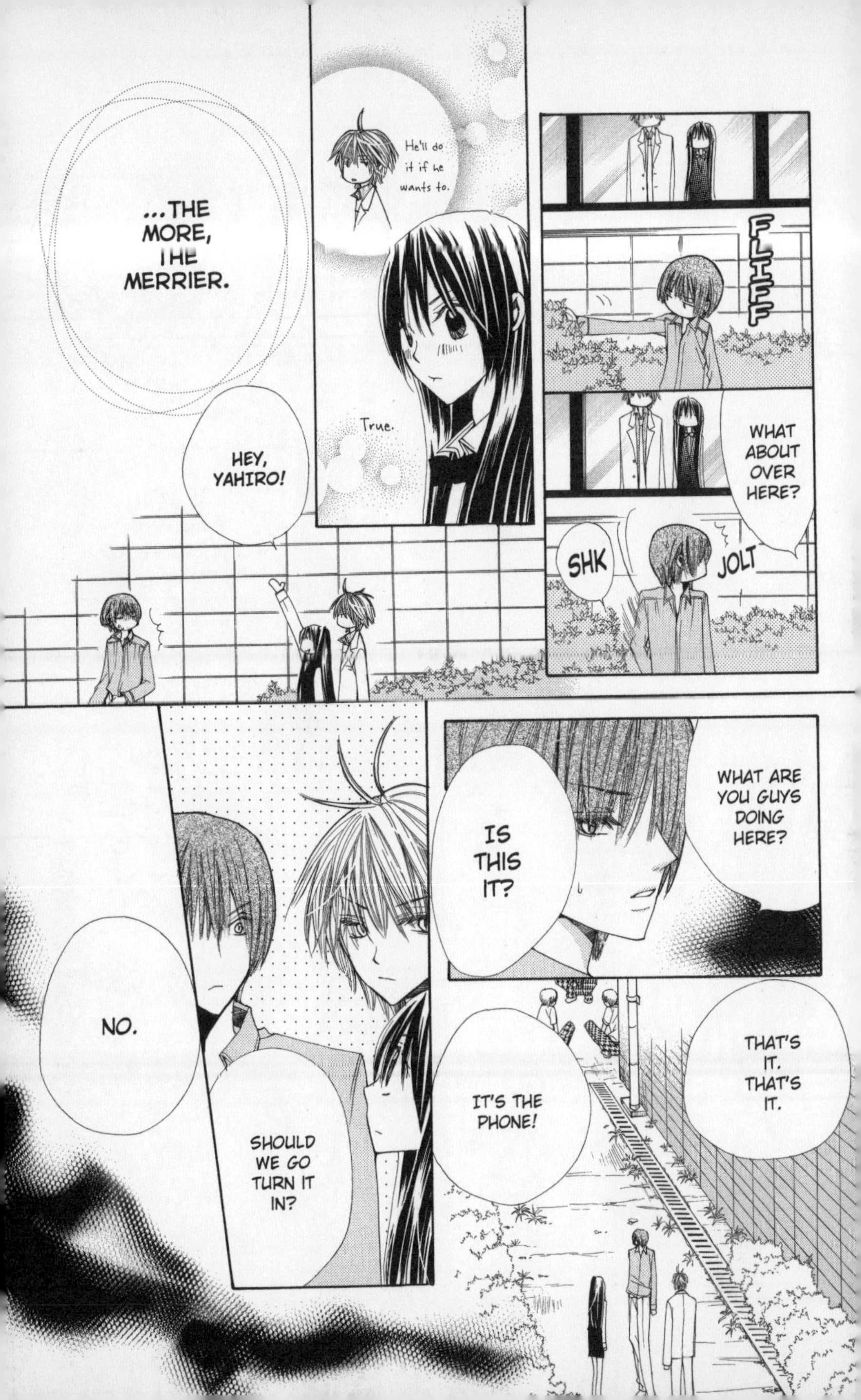
FLIFF
WHAT ABOUT OVER HERE?
SHK
JOLT
He'll do it if he wants to.
True.
...THE MORE, THE MERRIER.
HEY, YAHIRO!
WHAT ARE YOU GUYS DOING HERE?
IS THIS IT?
THAT'S IT. THAT'S IT.
IT'S THE PHONE!
SHOULD WE GO TURN IT IN?
NO.

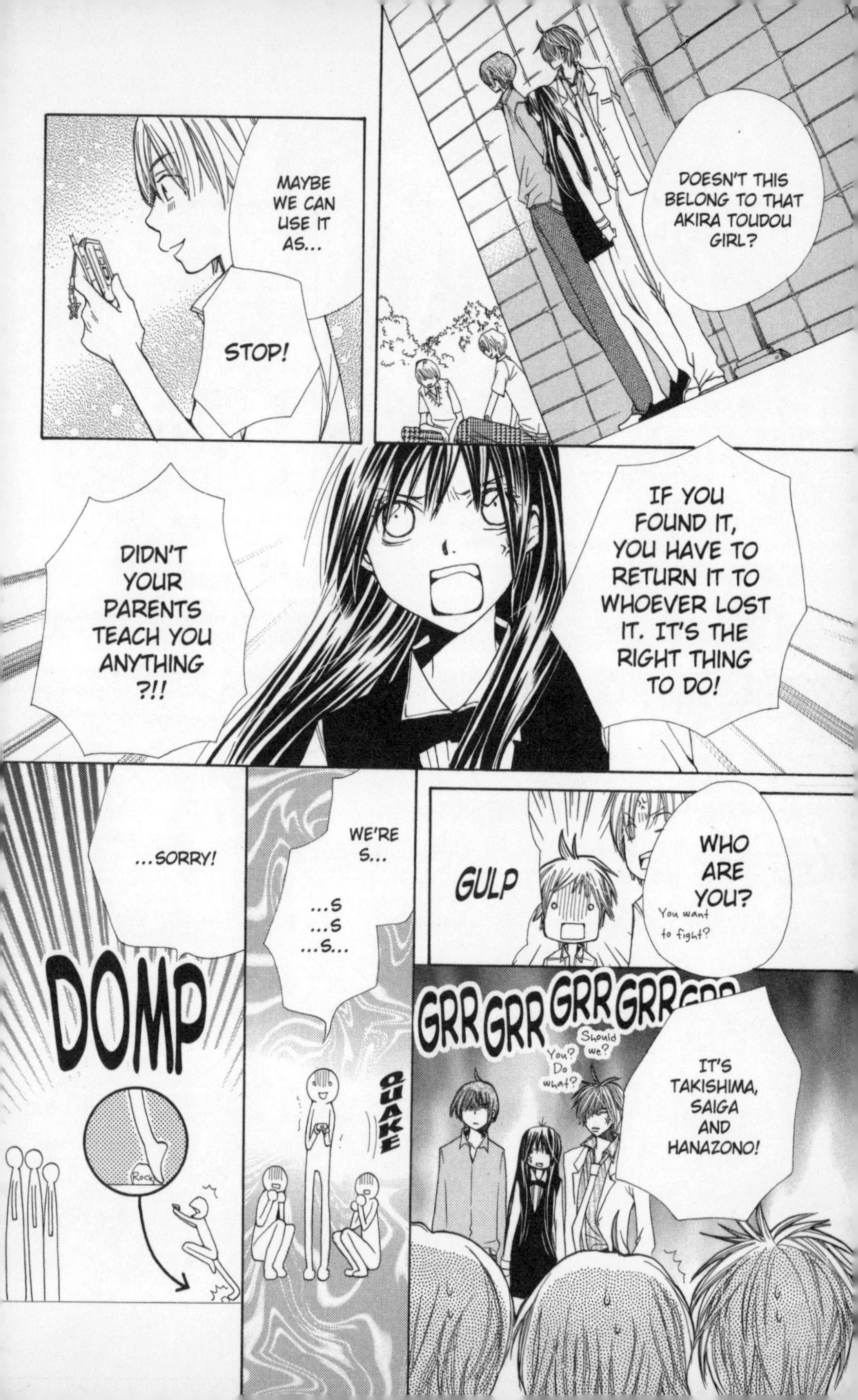
DOESN'T THIS BELONG TO THAT AKIRA TOUDOU GIRL?
MAYBE WE CAN USE IT AS...
STOP!
IF YOU FOUND IT, YOU HAVE TO RETURN IT TO WHOEVER LOST IT. IT'S THE RIGHT THING TO DO!
DIDN'T YOUR PARENTS TEACH YOU ANYTHING ?!!
WHO ARE YOU?
You want to fight?
GULP
GRR GRR GRR GRR
Should we?
You? Do what?
IT'S TAKISHIMA, SAIGA AND HANAZONO!
WE'RE S...
...S ...S ...S...
QUAKE
...SORRY!
DOMP
Rock

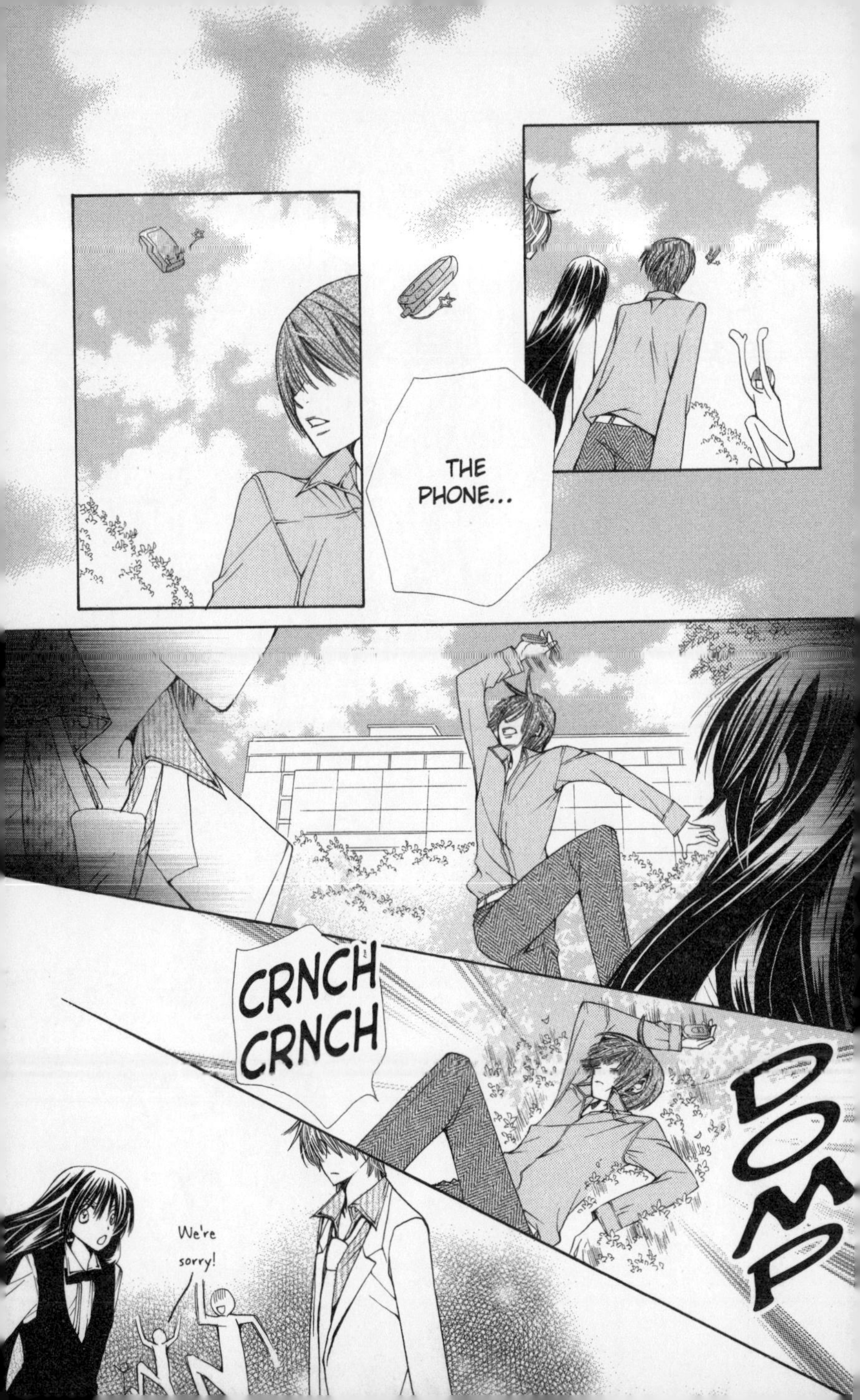
THE PHONE...
CRNCH CRNCH
DOMP
We're sorry!

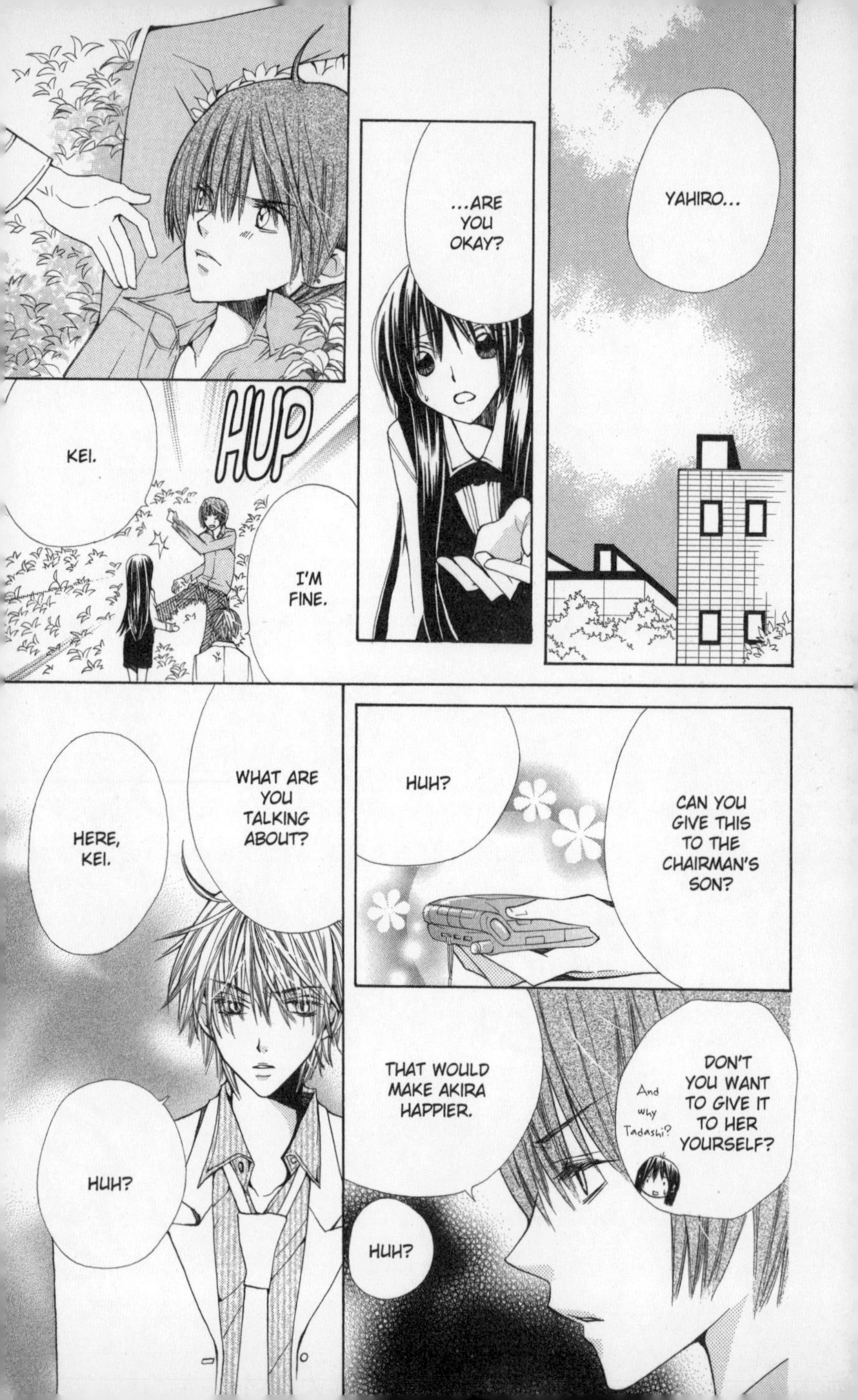
YAHIRO...
...ARE YOU OKAY?
KEI.
HUP
I'M FINE.
CAN YOU GIVE THIS TO THE CHAIRMAN'S SON?
HUH?
DON'T YOU WANT TO GIVE IT TO HER YOURSELF?
And why Tadashi?
THAT WOULD MAKE AKIRA HAPPIER.
HUH?
WHAT ARE YOU TALKING ABOUT?
HERE, KEI.
HUH?

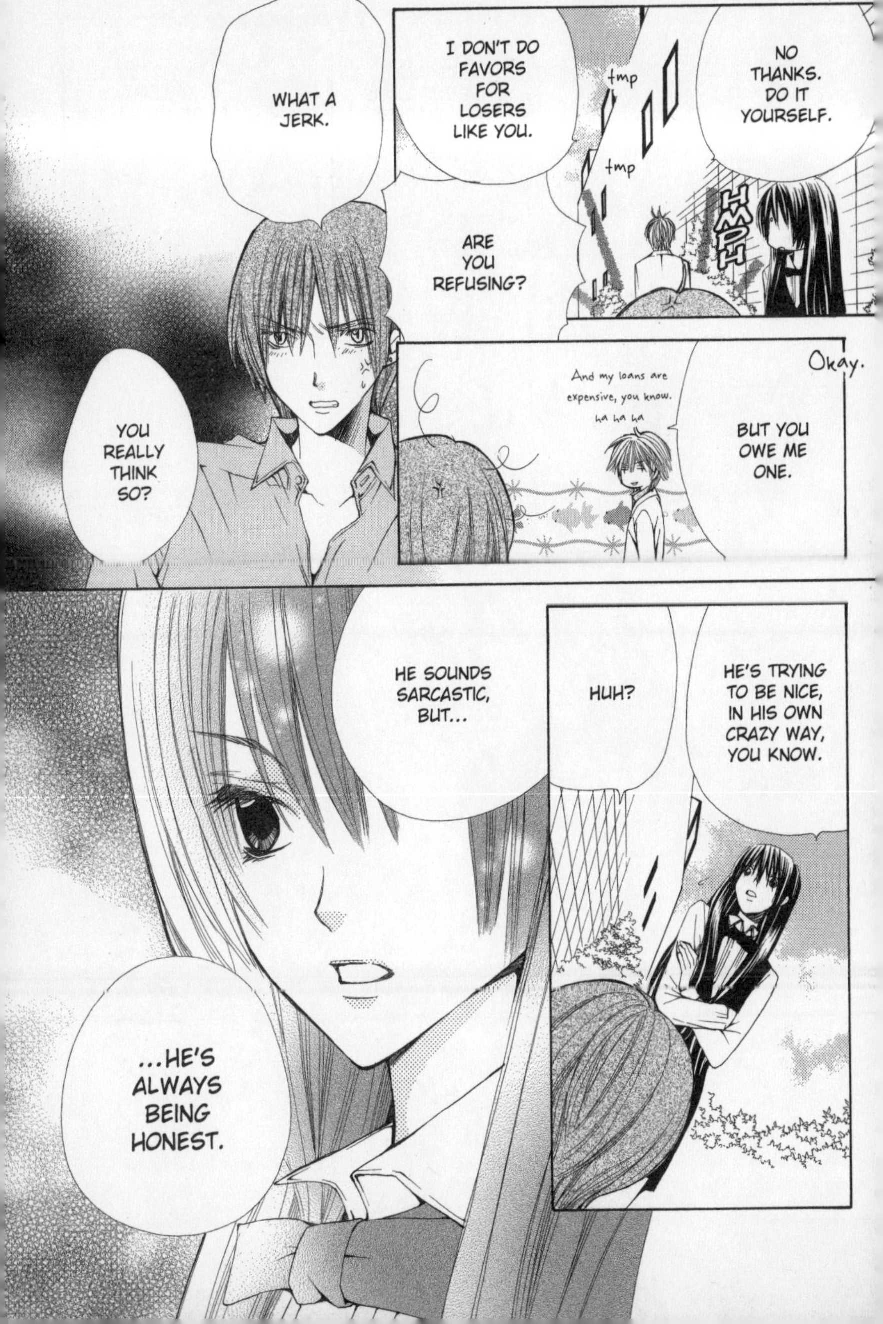
NO THANKS. DO IT YOURSELF.
tmp
tmp
HMPH
I DON'T DO FAVORS FOR LOSERS LIKE YOU.
ARE YOU REFUSING?
Okay.
BUT YOU OWE ME ONE.
And my loans are expensive, you know.
ha ha ha
WHAT A JERK.
YOU REALLY THINK SO?
HE'S TRYING TO BE NICE, IN HIS OWN CRAZY WAY, YOU KNOW.
HUH?
HE SOUNDS SARCASTIC, BUT...
...HE'S ALWAYS BEING HONEST.

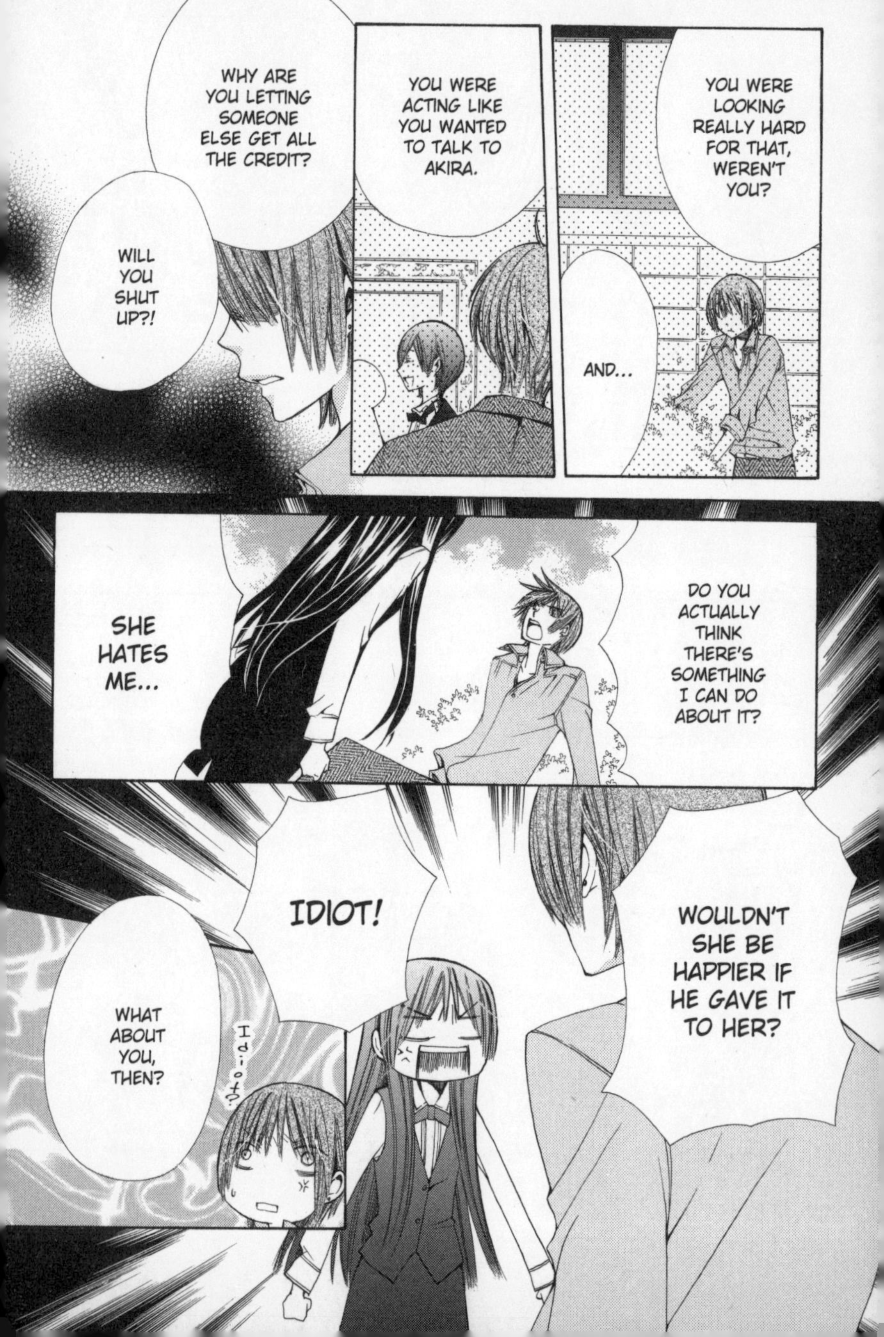
YOU WERE LOOKING REALLY HARD FOR THAT, WEREN'T YOU?
AND...
YOU WERE ACTING LIKE YOU WANTED TO TALK TO AKIRA.
WHY ARE YOU LETTING SOMEONE ELSE GET ALL THE CREDIT?
WILL YOU SHUT UP?!
DO YOU ACTUALLY THINK THERE'S SOMETHING I CAN DO ABOUT IT?
SHE HATES ME...
WOULDN'T SHE BE HAPPIER IF HE GAVE IT TO HER?
IDIOT!
Idiot?
WHAT ABOUT YOU, THEN?

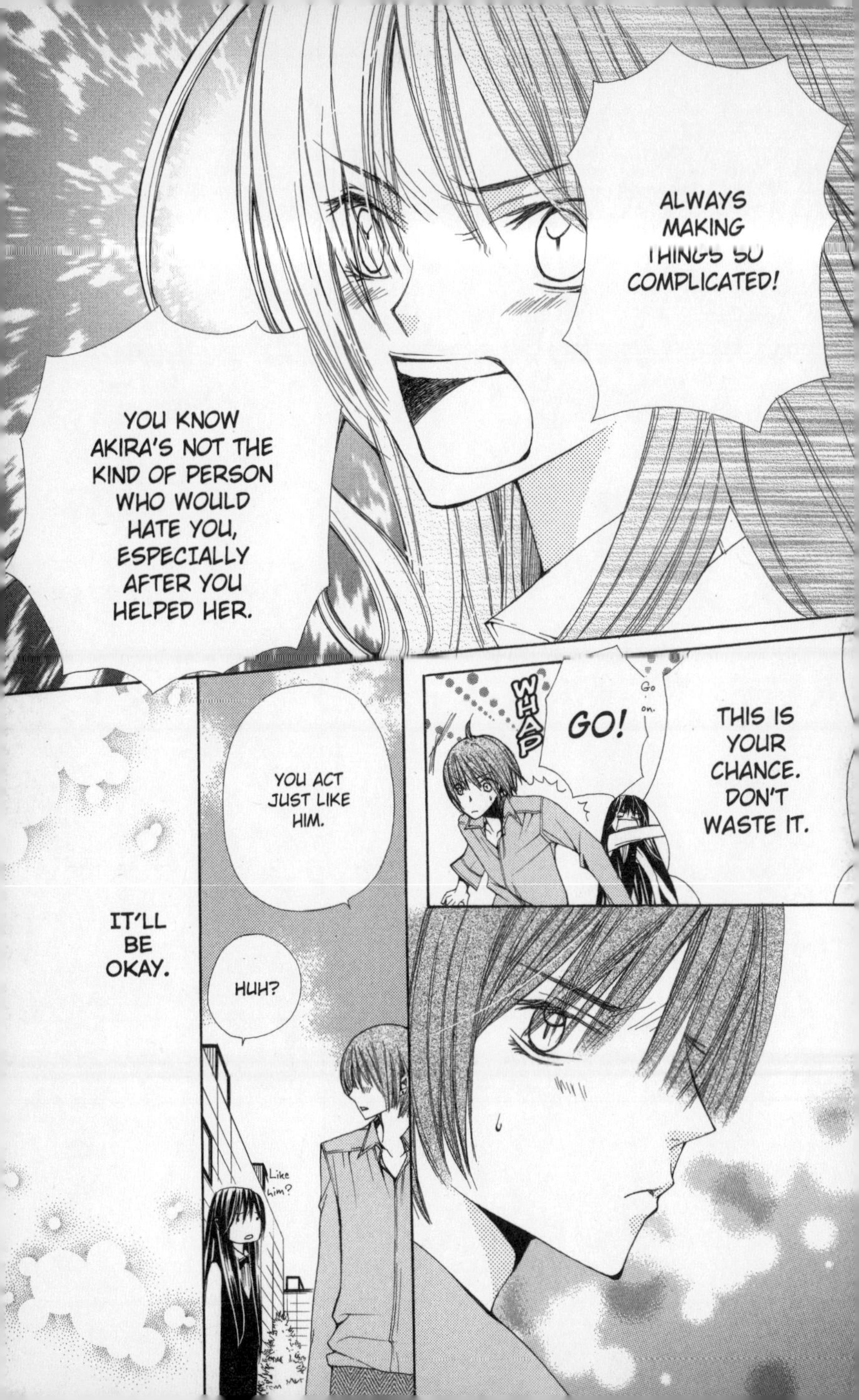
ALWAYS MAKING THINGS SO COMPLICATED!
YOU KNOW AKIRA'S NOT THE KIND OF PERSON WHO WOULD HATE YOU, ESPECIALLY AFTER YOU HELPED HER.
THIS IS YOUR CHANCE. DON'T WASTE IT.
Go on.
GO!
WHAP
YOU ACT JUST LIKE HIM.
HUH?
Like him?
IT'LL BE OKAY.

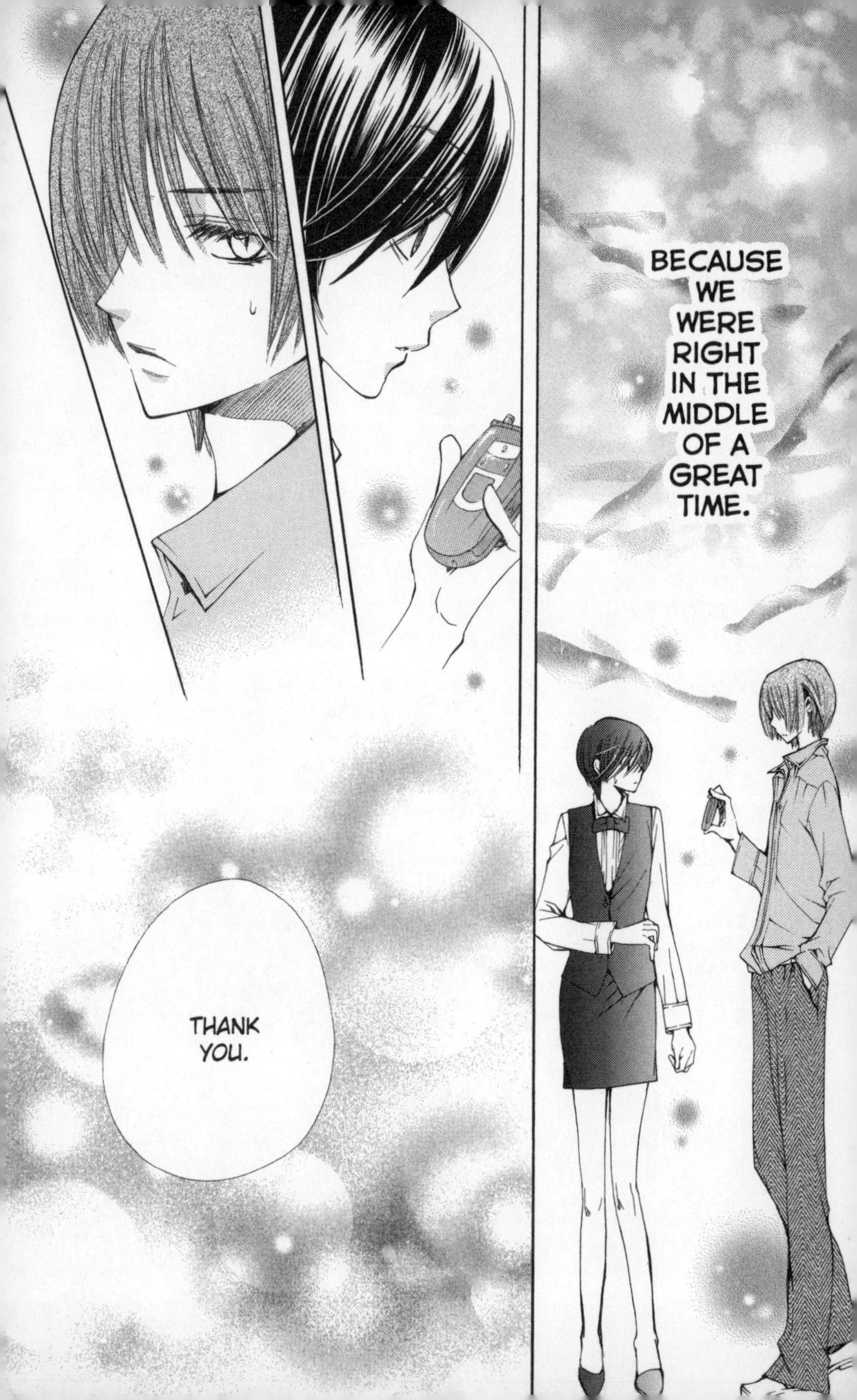
BECAUSE WE WERE RIGHT IN THE MIDDLE OF A GREAT TIME.
THANK YOU.

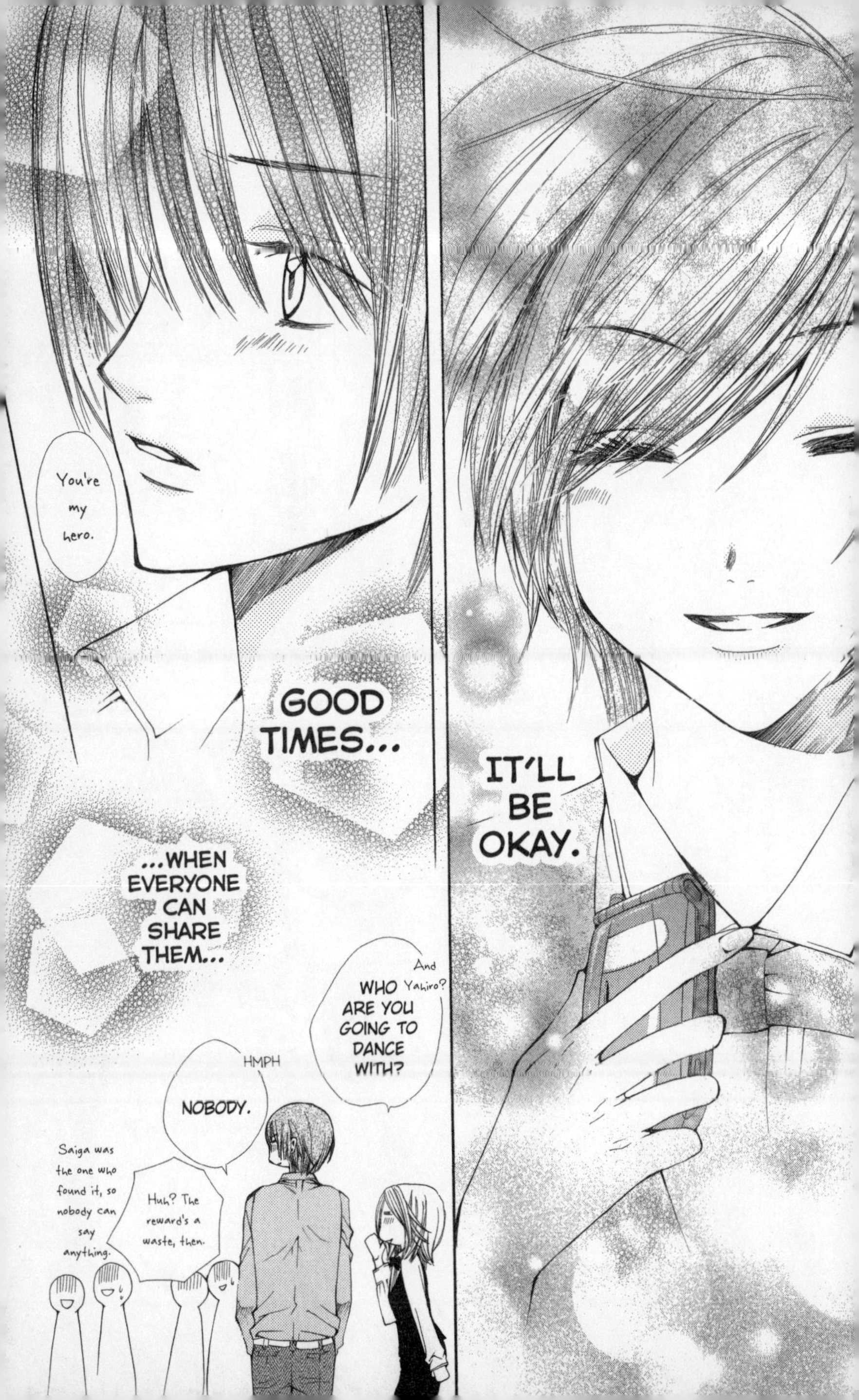
IT'LL BE OKAY.
You're my hero.
GOOD TIMES...
...WHEN EVERYONE CAN SHARE THEM...
And Yahiro?
WHO ARE YOU GOING TO DANCE WITH?
HMPH
NOBODY.
Huh? The reward's a waste, then.
Saiga was the one who found it, so nobody can say anything.

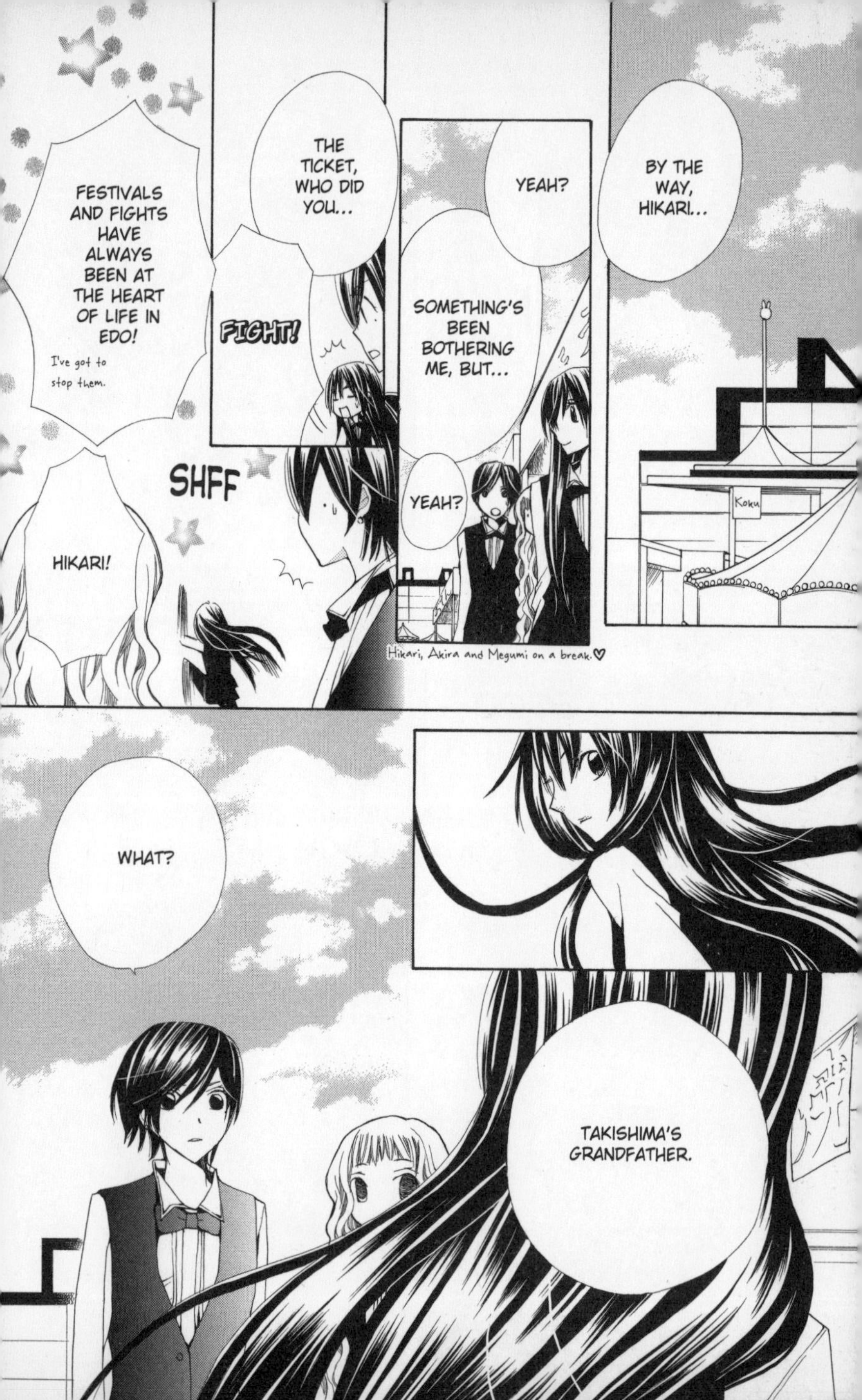
BY THE WAY, HIKARI...
Koku
YEAH?
SOMETHING'S BEEN BOTHERING ME, BUT...
YEAH?
Hikari, Akira and Megumi on a break.♡
THE TICKET, WHO DID YOU...
FIGHT!
FESTIVALS AND FIGHTS HAVE ALWAYS BEEN AT THE HEART OF LIFE IN EDO!
I've got to stop them.
SHFF
HIKARI!
WHAT?
TAKISHIMA'S GRANDFATHER.

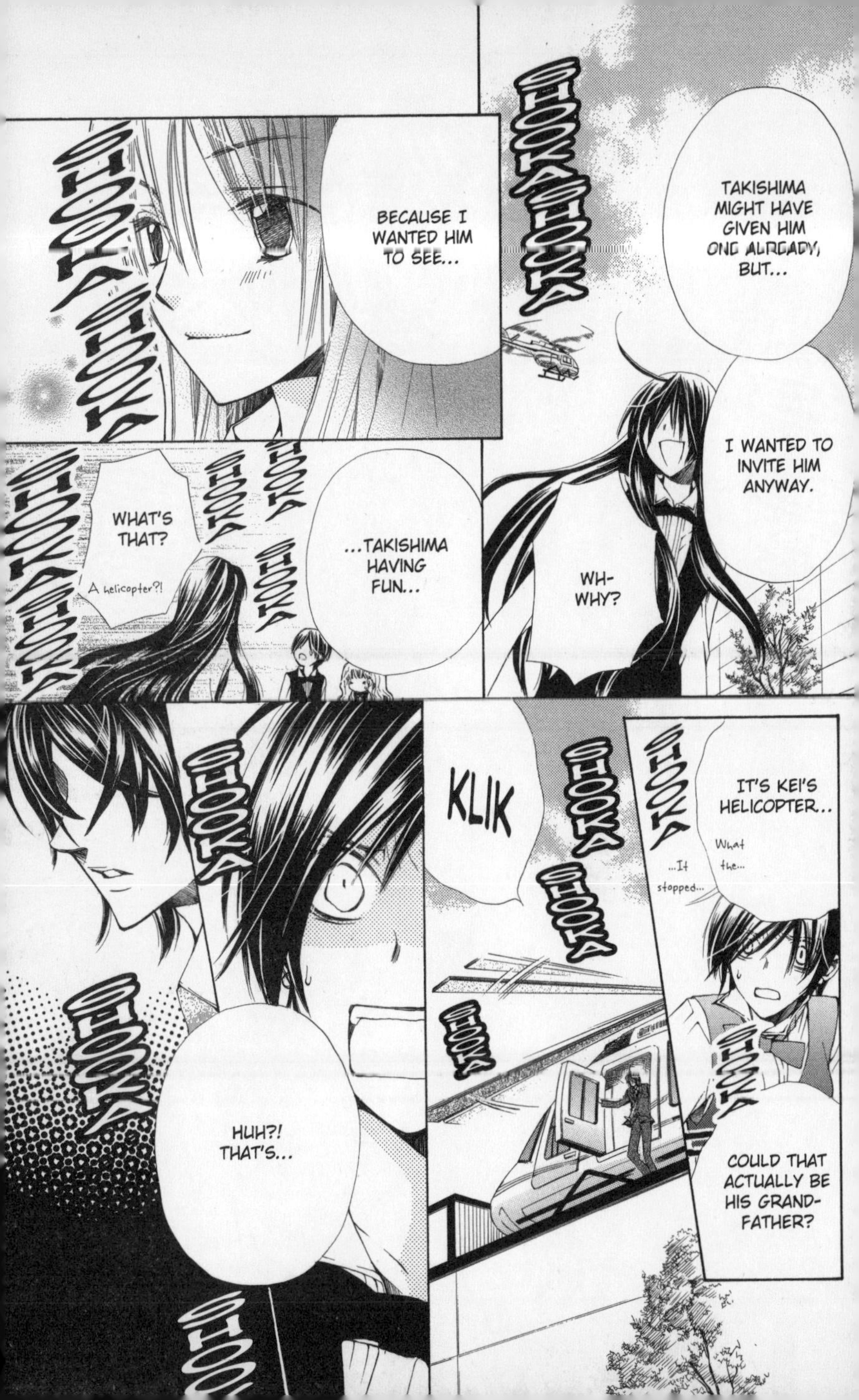
SHOOKASHOOKA
TAKISHIMA MIGHT HAVE GIVEN HIM ONE ALREADY, BUT...
I WANTED TO INVITE HIM ANYWAY.
WH-WHY?
SHOOKASHOOKA
BECAUSE I WANTED HIM TO SEE...
SHOOKA SHOOKA
...TAKISHIMA HAVING FUN...
SHOOKASHOOKA
WHAT'S THAT?
A helicopter?!
SHOOKA
IT'S KEI'S HELICOPTER...
What the...
...It stopped...
SHOOKA
COULD THAT ACTUALLY BE HIS GRANDFATHER?
KLIK
SHOOKA SHOOKA
SHOOKA
SHOOKA
SHOOKA
HUH?! THAT'S...
SHOO

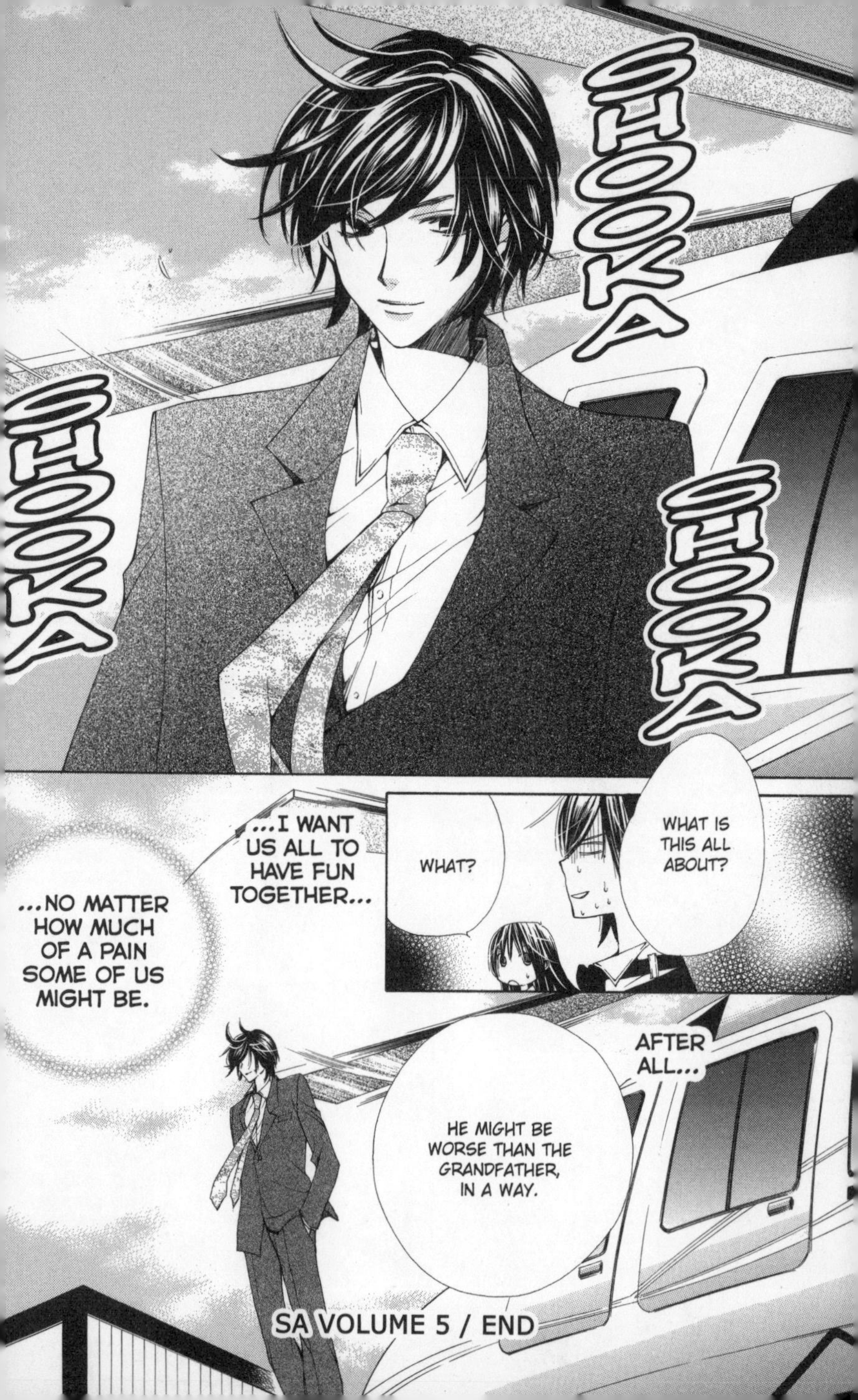
SHOOKA
SHOOKA
SHOOKA
WHAT IS THIS ALL ABOUT?
WHAT?
...I WANT US ALL TO HAVE FUN TOGETHER...
...NO MATTER HOW MUCH OF A PAIN SOME OF US MIGHT BE.
AFTER ALL...
HE MIGHT BE WORSE THAN THE GRANDFATHER, IN A WAY.
SA VOLUME 5 / END

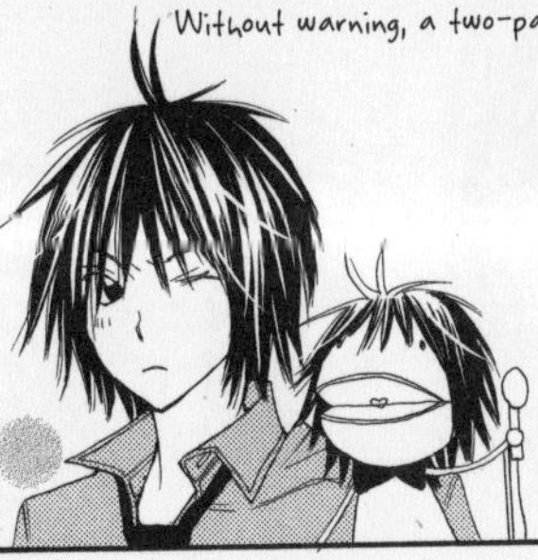

Without warning, a two-page manga!

BONUS PAGES

GO TADASHI! PART 5!

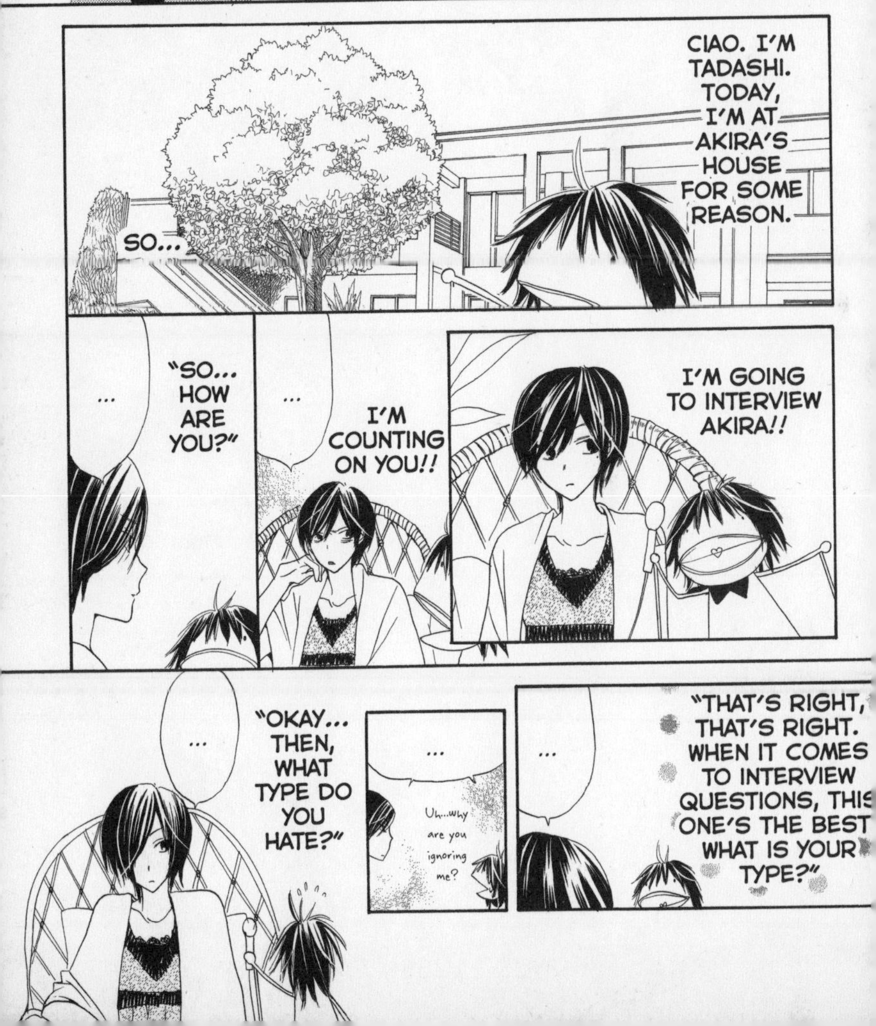

CIAO. I'M TADASHI. TODAY, I'M AT AKIRA'S HOUSE FOR SOME REASON.
SO...
I'M GOING TO INTERVIEW AKIRA!!
I'M COUNTING ON YOU!!
...
"SO... HOW ARE YOU?"
...
"THAT'S RIGHT, THAT'S RIGHT. WHEN IT COMES TO INTERVIEW QUESTIONS, THIS ONE'S THE BEST. WHAT IS YOUR TYPE?"
...
...
Uh...why are you ignoring me?
"OKAY... THEN, WHAT TYPE DO YOU HATE?"
...

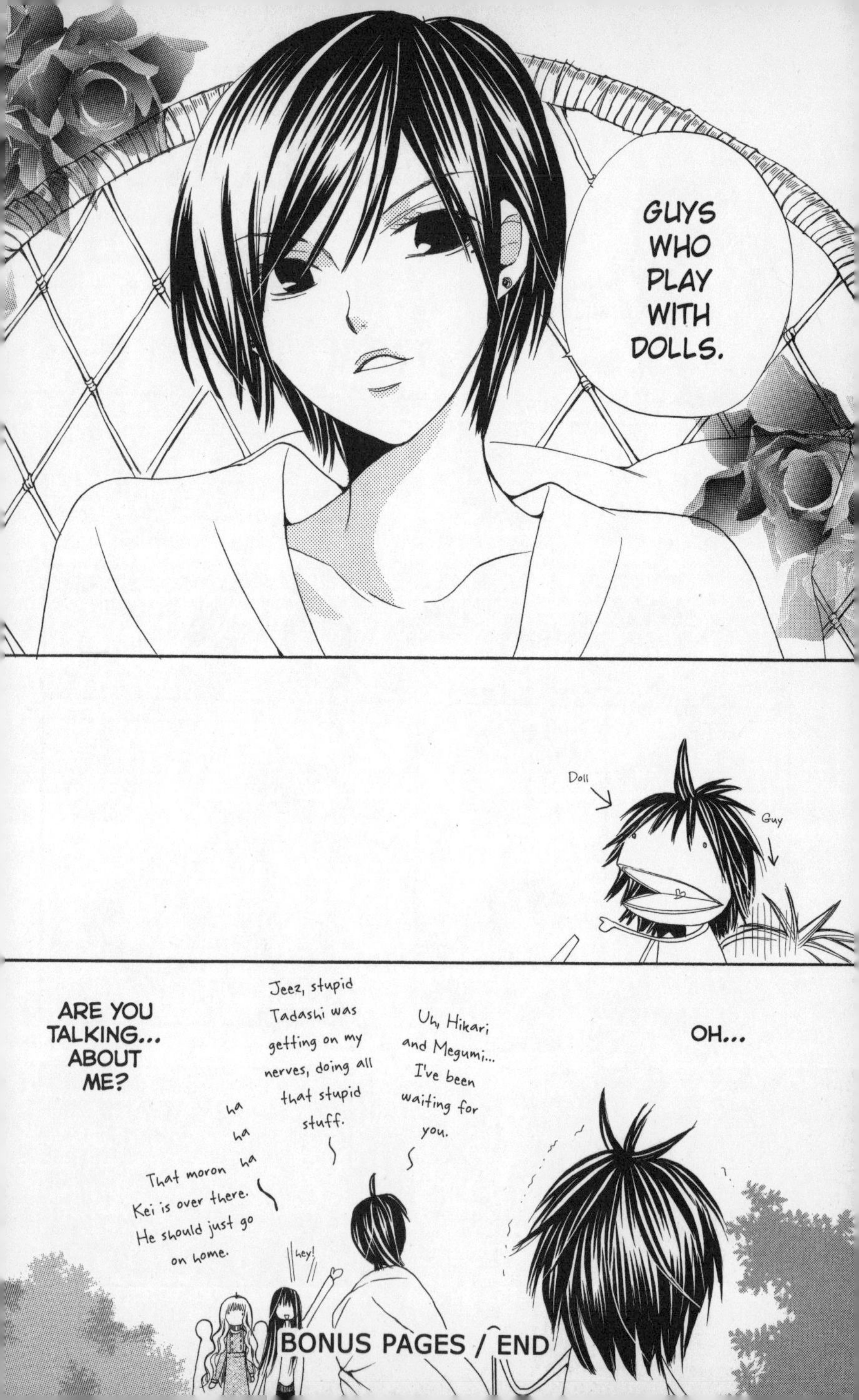
GUYS WHO PLAY WITH DOLLS.
Guy
Doll
OH...
Uh, Hikari and Megumi... I've been waiting for you.
Jeez, stupid Tadashi was getting on my nerves, doing all that stupid stuff.
ha ha ha
That moron Kei is over there. He should just go on home.
hey!
ARE YOU TALKING... ABOUT ME?
BONUS PAGES / END

Maki Minami is from Saitama prefecture in Japan. She debuted in 2001 with *Kanata no Ao* (Faraway Blue). Her other works include *Kimi wa Girlfriend* (You're My Girlfriend), *Mainichi ga Takaramono* (Every Day Is a Treasure) and *Yuki Atataka* (Warm Winter). *S•A* is her current series in Japan's *Hana to Yume* magazine.

S•A

Vol. 5
The Shojo Beat Manga Edition

STORY & ART BY
MAKI MINAMI

English Adaptation/Amanda Hubbard
Translation/JN Productions
Touch-up Art & Lettering/Sean McCoy
Design/Izumi Hirayama
Editor/Carol Fox

Editor in Chief, Books/Alvin Lu
Editor in Chief, Magazines/Marc Weidenbaum
VP of Publishing Licensing/Rika Inouye
VP of Sales/Gonzalo Ferreyra
Sr. VP of Marketing/Liza Coppola
Publisher/Hyoe Narita

Printed in Canada

Published by VIZ Media, LLC
P.O. Box 77010
San Francisco, CA 94107

Shojo Beat Manga Edition
10 9 8 7 6 5 4 3 2 1
First printing, July 2008

www.viz.com   store.viz.com

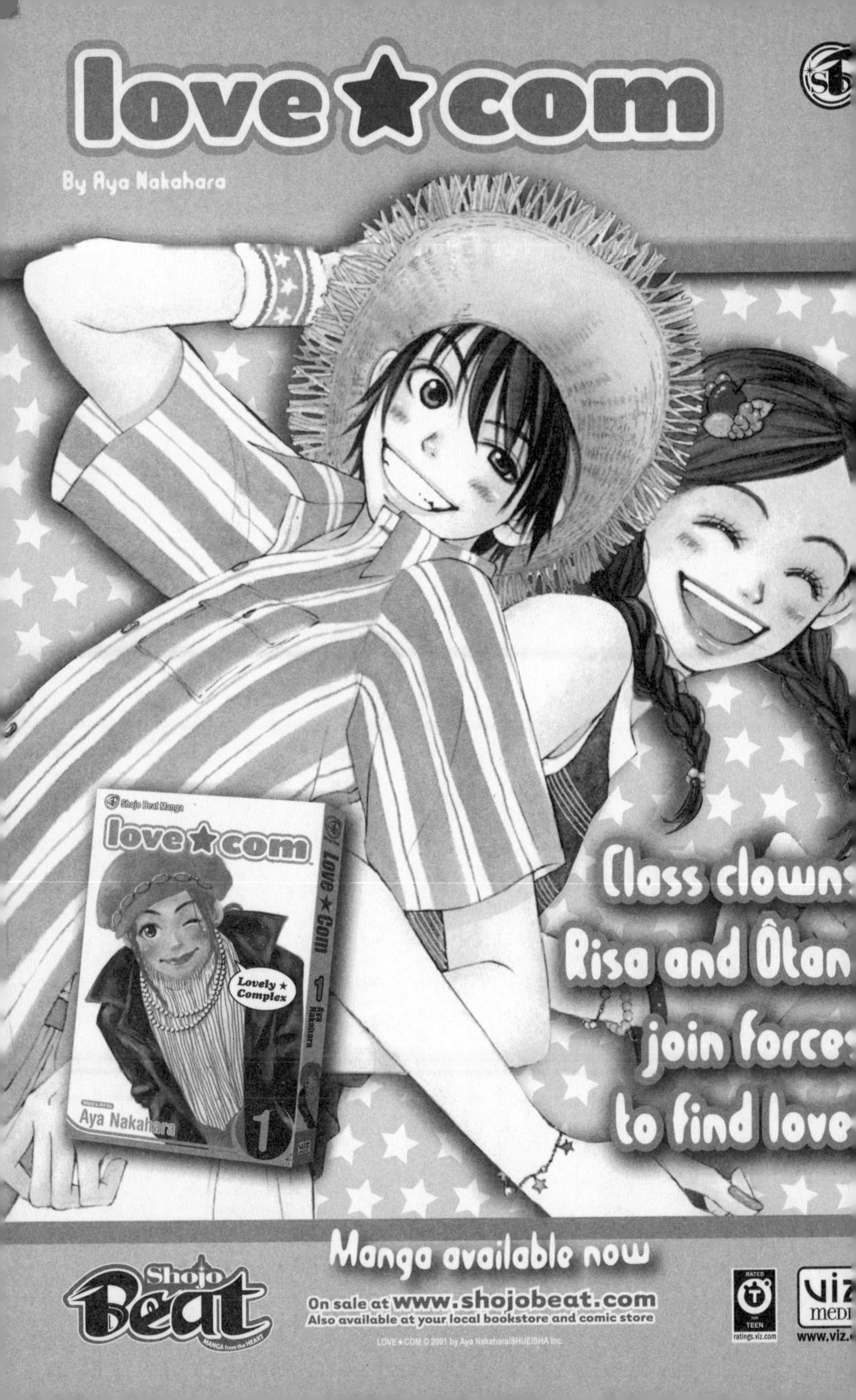
love★com
By Aya Nakahara
Shojo Beat Manga
love★com
Lovely★Complex
Love★Com
1
Aya Nakahara
Story & Art by
Aya Nakahara
Class clowns
Risa and Ôtan
join forces
to find love
Manga available now
Shojo Beat
MANGA from the HEART
On sale at www.shojobeat.com
Also available at your local bookstore and comic store
LOVE★COM © 2001 by Aya Nakahara/SHUEISHA Inc.
RATED T FOR TEEN
ratings.viz.com

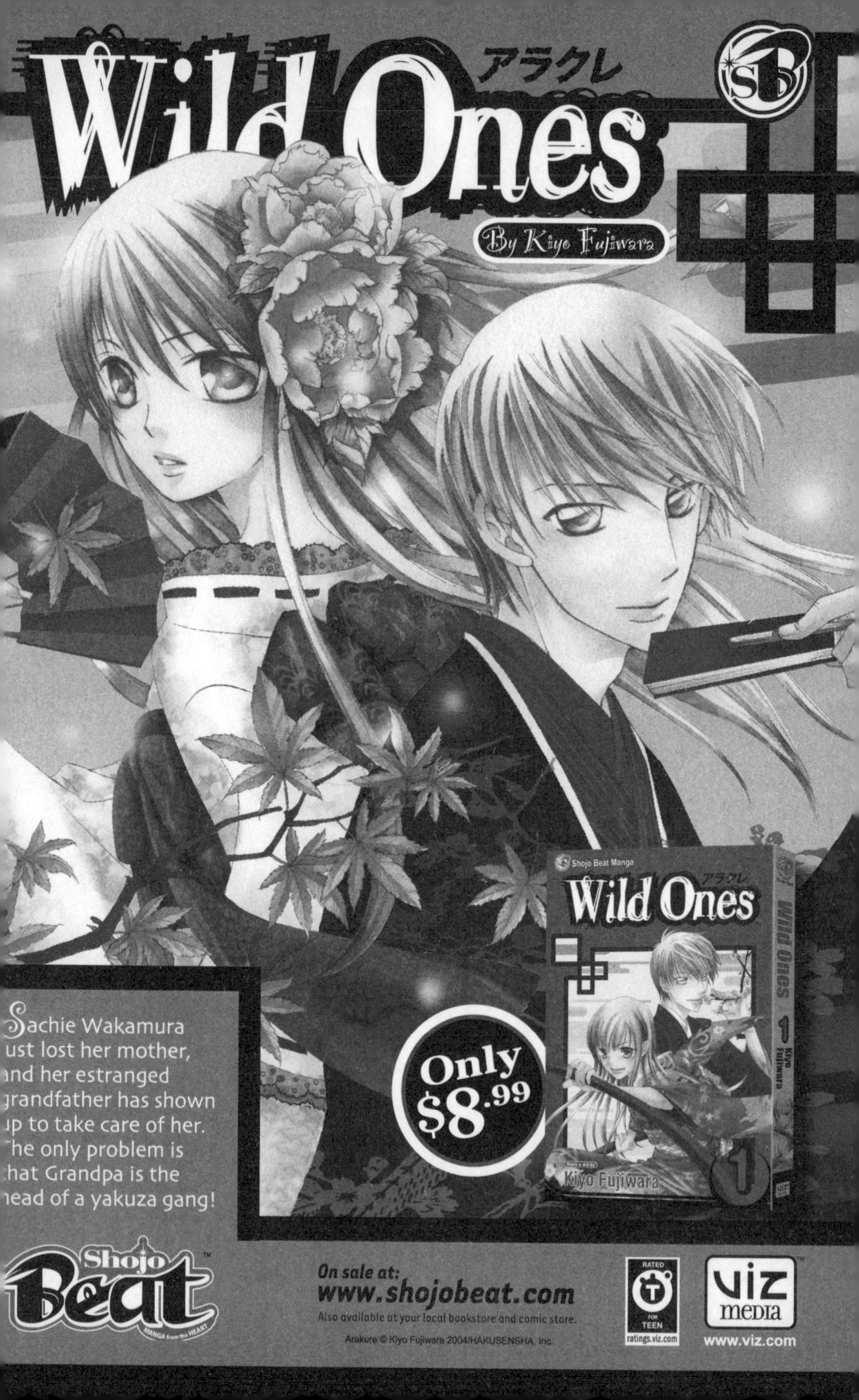

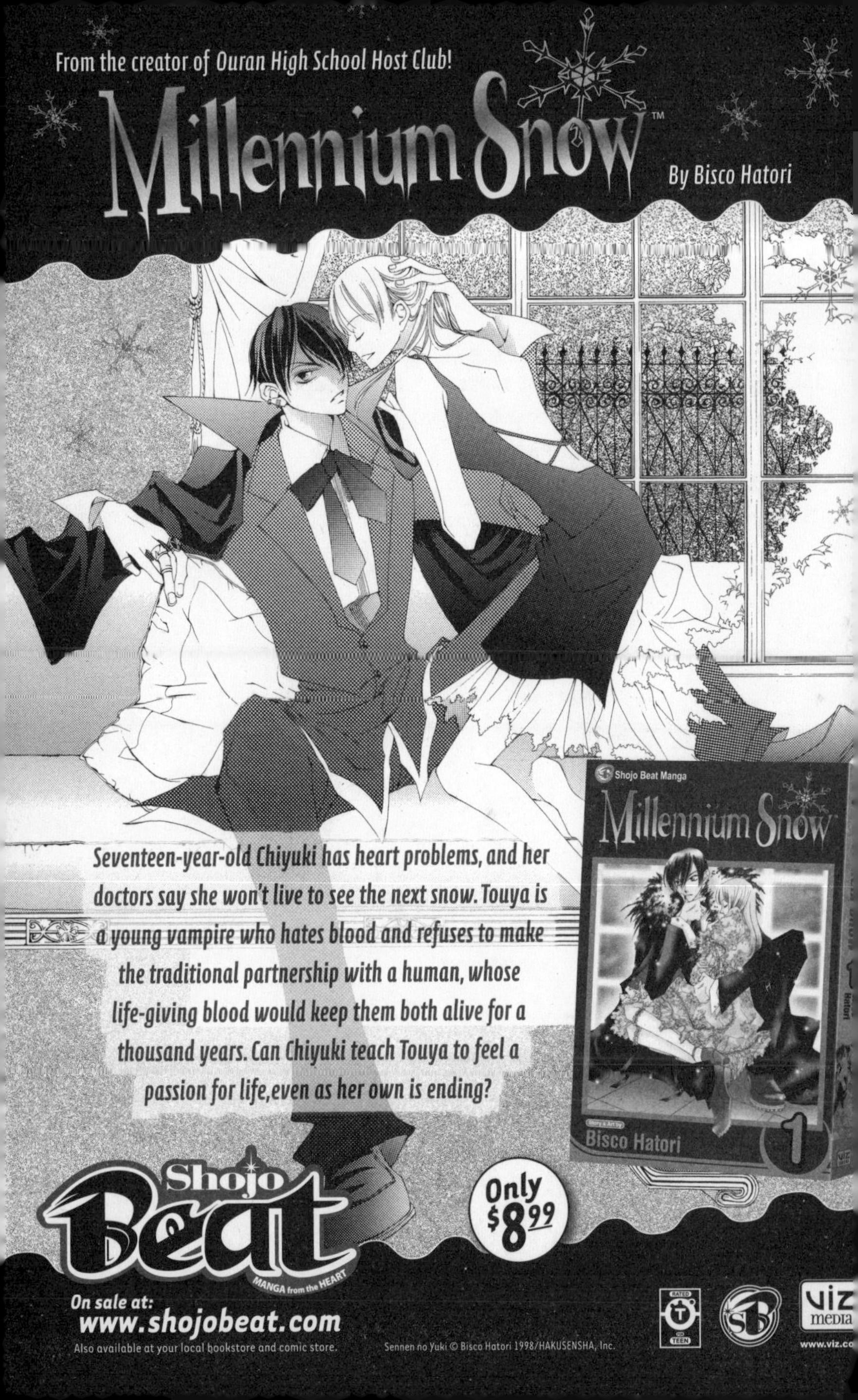
From the creator of Ouran High School Host Club!
Millennium Snow™
By Bisco Hatori
Shojo Beat Manga
Millennium Snow
Bisco Hatori
1
Seventeen-year-old Chiyuki has heart problems, and her doctors say she won't live to see the next snow. Touya is a young vampire who hates blood and refuses to make the traditional partnership with a human, whose life-giving blood would keep them both alive for a thousand years. Can Chiyuki teach Touya to feel a passion for life,even as her own is ending?
Shojo Beat
MANGA from the HEART
Only $8.99
On sale at:
www.shojobeat.com
Also available at your local bookstore and comic store.
Sennen no Yuki © Bisco Hatori 1998/HAKUSENSHA, Inc.
RATED T TEEN
viz media
www.viz.co

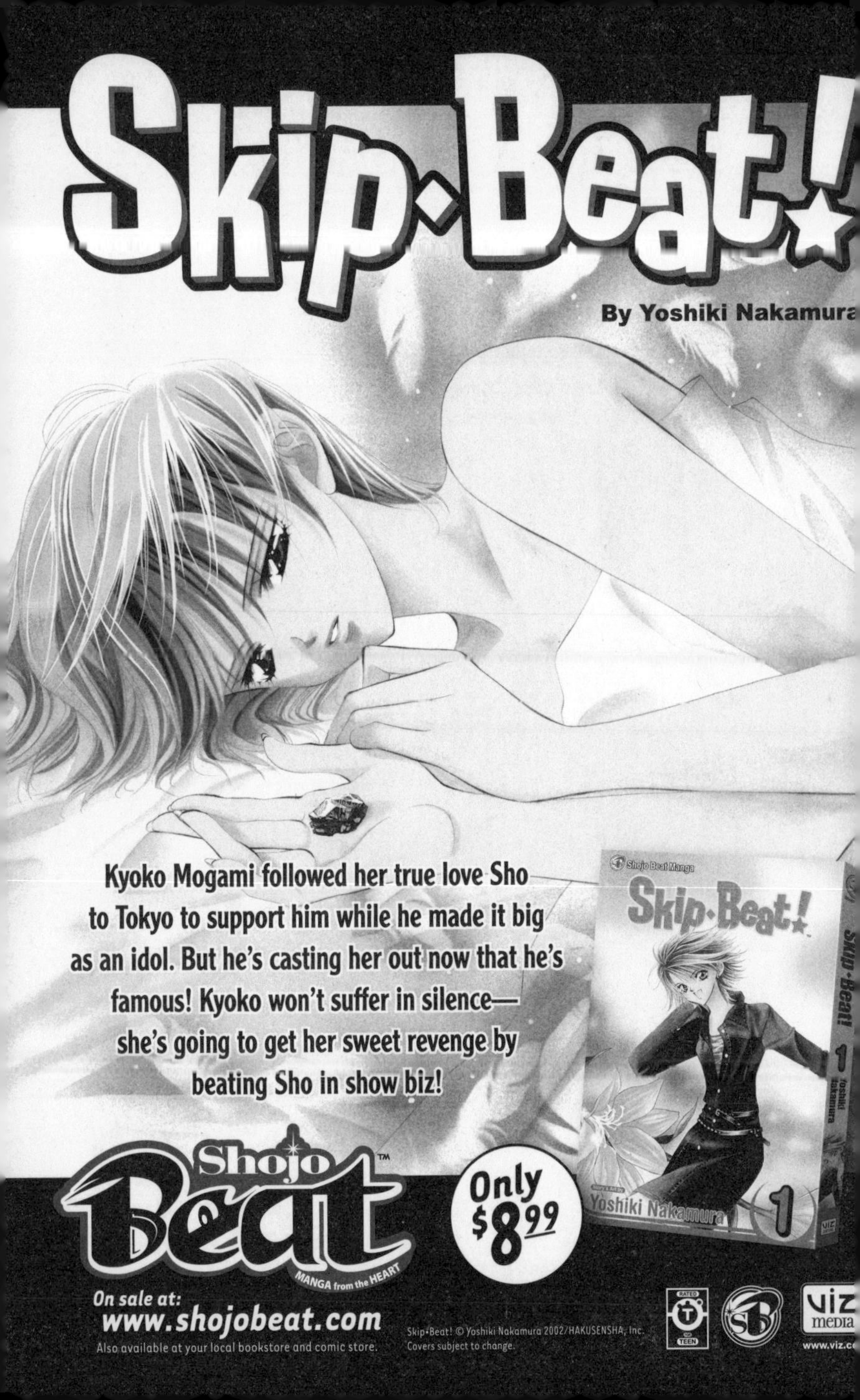
Skip·Beat!
By Yoshiki Nakamura
Kyoko Mogami followed her true love Sho to Tokyo to support him while he made it big as an idol. But he's casting her out now that he's famous! Kyoko won't suffer in silence— she's going to get her sweet revenge by beating Sho in show biz!
Shojo Beat Manga
Skip·Beat!
Yoshiki Nakamura
1
Shojo Beat™
MANGA from the HEART
Only $8.99
On sale at:
www.shojobeat.com
Also available at your local bookstore and comic store.
Skip•Beat! © Yoshiki Nakamura 2002/HAKUSENSHA, Inc.
Covers subject to change.
RATED T TEEN
VIZ media
www.viz.c